GW00871569

In Search of Living Water

The Fiery Arrow Collection

Editors: Hein Blommestijn and Jos Huls of Titus Brandsma Institute

Advisory Board:

The *Fiery Arrow series* aims at the publication of books which connect their readers with the legacy of great teachers of spirituality from the distant and more recent past. Readers are offered a language and conceptual framework which can lead them to a deepened understanding of the spiritual life. The treasures of the spiritual tradition form a veritable "school of love", which is accessible to all who in contemplation desire to be touched by the fire of divine love. In 1270 A.D. Nicholas of France, former prior general of the Carmelites, wrote a letter bearing the title *Fiery Arrow* to his fellow brothers to urge them to call to mind again the fire of the beginning in which, in silence and solitude, they were consumed by the inescapable claim of the One. Based on the Carmelite tradition, this series seeks to share this spiritual legacy – which presents itself in a multiplicity of cultures and traditions – with all those who in a great variety of ways are in search of interior life and the fire of love. The series, which is grounded in scientific research, is aimed at a broad public interested in spirituality.

The Titus Brandsma Institute is an academic center of research in spirituality founded in 1968 by the Catholic University of Nijmegen and the Carmelite Order. Titus Brandsma, who from 1923 on was a professor of philosophy and the history of mysticism, especially that of the Low Countries, died in 1942 as a martyr in the Nazi death camp of Dachau and was beatified in 1985. The Institute continues his research in spirituality and mysticism with a staff of assistants and in collaboration with other researchers. In addition to this and other series, the Institute publishes the international periodical *Studies in Spirituality* and the series *Studies in Spirituality Supplement* (Peeters, Louvain).

Already published in this series:

IN SEARCH OF LIVING WATER

ESSAYS ON THE MYSTICAL HERITAGE OF THE NETHERLANDS

by
Titus BRANDSMA

Introduction by Fernando MILLAN o.carm

Translation by Joachim SMET o.carm †

Edition and annotation by Jos HULS o.carm

PEETERS

EDIZIONI CARMELITANE

LEUVEN – PARIS – WALPOLE, MA
2013

A catalogue record for this book is available from the Library of Congress.

ISBN 978-90-429-2976-0
D/2013/0602/143

©2013 – Peeters, Bondgenotenlaan 153, B-3000 Leuven

Table of Contents

Introduction

It is an honor for me and a source of great joy to write an introduction to this collection of writings by Blessed Titus Brandsma on a variety of themes in the history of spirituality, now translated into English. It is a long awaited work that will allow us, without a doubt, to get a better grasp of the thinking of this illustrious Carmelite, and will make his work accessible to large sectors of the Carmelite family worldwide and to students of mysticism and spirituality.

After more than three years of traveling and getting to know the Order of Carmel in five continents, meeting many groups of laity, parishes, schools, study groups, cultural associations of Carmelite inspiration and Carmelite youth, etc., I can state that Blessed Titus Brandsma is one of the most popular and well-loved figures of Carmel in the 21st century. In fact, his spiritual testimony, his martyrdom and his message, continue to inspire and give rise to many different types of initiative, from popular libraries to university chairs, from prayer groups to social action in the United Nations, from ecumenical groups to schools of spirituality.

These, no doubt, are an indication of how multifaceted Titus Brandsma is: Carmelite, priest, journalist and theorist of journalism, professor of philosophy and the history of mysticism, *Rector magnificus* of the University of Nijmegen, ecclesiastical advisor for the catholic press, man of prayer with an intense spiritual life, ecumenical man interested in the "apostolate of reunification", heroic witness of faith and humanity in the fires of the concentration camps and especially in the *Lager* (camp) of Dachau...

He was beatified on November 3, 1985 in St Peter's Basilica, in Rome, by Pope John Paul II, who in his homily emphasised that Brandsma had preached and proclaimed a culture of love and pardon, in the midst of the philosophy of Nazism that culminated in the concentration camps, *organized in line with a program of scorn and hatred for mankind*[1].

Blessed Titus has a fascinating biography, which continues to be examined and published from many points of view. It shows us the attitude of a Carmelite who, immersed totally in the modern world, possessed a profound spirituality, an honest and sincere piety, a loving closeness to men and women in the time in which he lived.

*

* *

Europe in the 1930's was a hotbed of ideologies, radicalism, intense nationalism, fervent cultural and political activity, international tensions, etc. In this context the spiritual and intellectual activity of Father Titus stands out (if in his case any separation can be made between the two). That is why, in order to understand better the thinking of Titus Brandsma, this work that we now present is very necessary, for, in making contact with his writings on spirituality (some of them of high academic quality), we also find his thought, his biography, his attitudes, as well as a spiritual and human profile of the author.

An old scholastic adage says that "quidquid recipitur, ad modum recipientis recipitur", (whatever is received is received in accordance with the one who receives); so, in what Professor Brandsma received from the history of mysticism (especially of Dutch mysticism) and in what is seen in his writings, we encounter a lot of his personality (ad modum recipientis...). A phrase, an insight, a brief commentary, an emphasis, a feature of the spiritual profile of the authors under study, can be a wonderful instrument in knowing the author who writes the commentary.

Therefore, in this introduction I want to highlight some of the features and aspects of these articles on spirituality by Professor

---

[1] Translated directly from the Italian Edition of L'Osservatore Romano (November, 1985).

Brandsma that, as I believe, throw light on his own spiritual journey. The historian and scholar will encounter in the same works many other elements of great interest for debate and study. It might also be useful to know the *status questionis* of some of these themes in the study of spirituality that emerged in the 1930's. For our purposes, we will focus on the glimpses of his personality that are reflected in these works that may appear to be only academic and theoretical, but are of great value in understanding the author.

First of all, in the course of these writings an idea that is very dear to Titus frequently appears: holiness, the spiritual life, or the mystical experience are not limited to a specific group of people (nuns, clergy, religious professionals) but are a basic part of all Christian life. In other words, all are called to mystical experience, all are called to feel and experience the loving presence of God in their lives. In some way, I believe we could say that Father Titus anticipated the universal call to holiness that Vatican II stressed so much.

So, in his comparative study of Ruusbroec and St. Teresa of Avila, our author stressed in various ways that every human being is essentially capable of the experience of God. That experience is not something reserved to a determined group of people or to a spiritual or intellectual elite. Brandsma shows that the human soul has a natural inclination towards mystical experience, since God himself has given this capacity, opening, or tendency. This does not mean (neither in Teresa nor in Ruusbroec) that the human soul can arrive at a mystical experience by itself, by its own efforts, since to say this would negate the gratuitousness of such an experience and the supreme initiative and grace filled action of God. That would mean falling into a kind of spiritual pelagianism that does not concord with the nature and grace relationship (the controversial issue of the "supernatural"). We don't want to get into that debate, the source of much reflection and controversy in the theology of the 20th century. Our interest is only to highlight how for Father Titus the human being is constitutively open to the experience of God and, therefore, that this experience is not something exclusive to a determined category of people, but something essential in the life of the all believers.[2] In his conference about Geert Grote (which we will come back to later) he will insist on this theme. Brandsma emphasizes how for this 14th century author neither holiness nor a mystical experience are reserved to a particular group of people and he calls our attention to how Grote already defended the idea that a mystical experience is not something exclusive to nuns or priests.

Secondly, I would like to emphasize his profound knowledge of and admiration for Teresa of Avila. It is well known that for much of his life, Titus Brandsma had a deep devotion to this Carmelite Saint.[3] His first academic work of any significance was a 300 page translation from French of an anthology about the life of St Teresa by Arnauld d'Andilly, published in 1901. His final work also was a *Life of St Teresa*, written while he was in the prison of Scheveningen. It seems to be that before the war he had pre-arranged for it to be published in *Spectrum*, even though he had to delay the work a number of times because of his many activities. Thus, in the solitude of the prison cell and with a lot of "free time", he decided to write his biography of the Saint of Avila. All he had was the work of Kwakman, *Het Leven van de heilige Theresia*[4] (The Life of saint Teresa, one of the two books that they permitted him to bring with him and one that he really did not like according to some of the comments in his letters) and all the stored learning from years of study. He would write more than 300 pages. The

---

[2] It would be difficult not to recall here the famous saying of Karl Rahner, so often quoted: ... der Fromme von morgen wird ein 'Mystiker' sein, einer, der etwas 'erfahren' hat, oder wird nicht mehr sein ...." in K. Rahner, "Frömmigkeit früher und heute"in *Schriften der Theologie* (Benziger, Einsiedeln – Zurich – Köln 1966) 22. The English translation is, "the devout Christian of the future will either be a 'mystic', one who has 'experienced' something, or he will cease to be anything at all". K. Rahner, *Theological Investigations, VII*,1,15.

[3] Cf. A. Staring, "Fr. Titus Brandsma and St. Teresa of Avila", in: AA.VV., *Essays on Titus Brandsma*, ed. R.M. Valabek, Rome, 1985, 205-213.

[4] Het leven van de heilige Theresia: naar de Bollandisten, hare verschillende geschiedschrijvers en haar eigen werken, Amsteerdam 1908, 's Gravenhage 1941.

first are written on regular pages with the letterhead of the prison, but at a certain point he was forbidden to smoke (which cost him no little sacrifice) and his paper was taken away. Father Titus, with Frisian stubbornness, did not give up. He continued his "work" between the lines of the other book he had. That was the life of Jesus by Cyriel Verschaeve that was recovered after the war and is now preserved as a relic by the Dutch Carmelites in Boxmeer.[5] The writing, in the first chapters is clear and firm but breaks down as the pages progress. Jesus, Teresa and Titus are united in a place of suffering and their "lives" were drawn together in a astonishing way.

This devotion to and intellectual knowledge of Saint Teresa appears again and again in many of the articles in this volume. His study of the concept of "mysticism", despite its brevity is one of the most important articles of this compilation and an indispensible work for whoever wants to know the thought of professor Brandsma. In it, almost as an obligatory point of reference, he considers the *Interior Castle* as the masterpiece of all mystical literature, and quotes it constantly. In other works he called it "the glory and pride of Spain". Moreover, Professor Brandsma strongly reacts against those who consider her a sentimental and emotional writer since for Saint Teresa of Avila, the intellect and understanding are also important and she never loses sight of the practice of good works and the virtues. This defense is very important, even in our own day, since, as is well known, in certain theological quarters in central Europe a certain prejudice exists that accuses the great Spanish mystic of the 16th century of falling into a kind of merely affective and sentimental psychology. As Father Titus noted, nothing is further from the truth.

Brandsma dedicated a whole article to the comparison between the spirituality of Teresa of Avila and that of Ruusbroec. Apparently, Father Luis Martin, later Superior General of the Jesuits, in

---

[5] His biography of St. Teresa of Avila would be published in 1946 by P. Meijer, in *Spectrum*: T. Brandsma – B.Meijer, *De groote heilige Teresia van Jesus* (Utrecht-Brussel, 1946).

an article published at the end of the 19th century, defended (as indeed Titus Brandma also did) the position that the "four steps" of Ruusbroec coincide with the last four dwelling places of the *Interior Castle* of Teresa. Likewise, Titus also mentions how the Benedictine Dom Willibrord Verkade already mentioned this comparison. For these authors, and also for our author, both Teresa and Ruusbroec start with the necessity of interiorization, in order to encounter the Beloved in the depths of the soul. From there, from this total and radical experience, all is relativised and diminishes in importance.

Ultimately, Father Titus' admiration for St Teresa of Jesus was a constant in his academic and intellectual activity, and his devotion to her was a constant in his own spiritual journey. Intent on knowing the environment of the Saint better, he traveled to Spain in 1929 in order to know the Teresian places. The friars who looked after him in Spain affirmed that he knew *Las Moradas* (the mansions) by heart. That is why this Dutch Carmelite travelled with passion to the Teresian places and planned one more time to continue the publication of the works of the Saint in Dutch, as well as write her biography. All of this, however, was frustrated again by his various other activities, and he could only get back to it when he was in the prison cell of Scheveningen.

I also think the article that Titus Brandsma dedicated to Geert Grote is very interesting and worth mentioning in this introduction. It is the text of a conference given in Deventer on the centenary of his birth in this city.⁶ Beyond an extensive study of the author, his life, his work and his spiritual development (something that could detain the experts on the topic), I want like to recall that this date explains in part why he chose this topic for his "conference" to other prisoners on Good Friday in 1942 in Amersfoort.

---

⁶ In this city where at that time there was a Carmelite house, Fr. Titus gave his very interesting lecture on peace in 1931. That lecture, in which Fr. Titus hinted at what was going to happen in Europe, and spoke out against the culture of violence and revenge that was being imposed, was translated into various languages and is a real jewel in the thinking of the author.

It was a dominant topic and one that he had recently studied (the result is the text of this conference). Certainly this was not the only motive. Geert Grote could easily be presented as a Dutch writer and in this way avoid the strict laws of the camp that prohibited the treatment of religious or political themes. Brandsma also thought that the mysticism of Grote would allow him to speak about what he really wanted to speak about: the passion of Christ which was in some ways being re-lived by the denigrated, suffering and humiliated prisoners[7]. But, there is no doubt, that this fact (his recent study of the author) contributed to his choice.

Moreover, in his conference on Geert Grote, in the selection of certain elements and aspects of thought of the Dutch mystic, one can see traits of the personality of Brandsma. So, for example, Brandsma stresses how Grote courageously confronted the spirit of his time, especially the corruption, and how he gave an appropriate and firm responses to its problems. It was Grote's special merit that he understood those times and responded to their needs. We might recall the phrase of Father Titus: "He who wants to win the world for Christ must have the courage to confront it with him," to see the closeness between the two. However, Brandsma, as one who was always sensible, moderate and opposed to anything that smacked of excess or fanaticism, criticized on not a few occasions the exaggerated tone of the 14th century author. He thought that it was a consequence of his being a convert that even though he sought an uncompromising gospel radicality, something very worthy of note and praise, he did not know how to live with human weaknesses and with the poverty of every spiritual experience and succumbed to a kind of exaggerated reaction to the things he criticized.

---

[7] See: Mom Wellenstein, *Nummers die een ziel hebben* (Numbers who have a soul). Persoonlijke ervaringen in Kamp Amersfoort, een concentratiekamp in Nederland, Amsterdam 2013, 27-28. The author, who was part of the same transportation of prisoners from Scheveningen to Amersfoort, was an eyewitness of this "conference".

Another feature of the personality of Blessed Titus that frequently appears in many of these writings is his "ecumenical spirit". We have already shown elsewhere[8] that Titus Brandsma was a profoundly ecumenical man, even at a time (Vatican II was still in the distance) when ecumenism was not very prevalent in Catholic environments. The Dutch Carmelite participated in the so-called "apostolate of reunification" with those of the East around which he was a great enthusiast.[9] When he organized the Marian Congress in 1932 to celebrate the 15th Centenary of the Council of Ephesus, he immediately wrote to clarify the intent of this, trying to avoid any sense of Catholic exhibitionism and trying not to hurt the sensitivities of the Protestant world. Moreover, and in a totally different way, his appreciation of the Discalced Carmelites is well known. He loved St Teresa of Jesus and would try to avoid disputes and sterile polemics.

This "ecumenical mindset" goes even beyond the limits of Christianity. He appears like a forerunner of the modern inter-religious dialogue. In his study about the concept of mysticism, when describing the essential features of mystical events, while Brandsma considers the Catholic Church the more correct place, or the place for true mystical experience, he does not reject the possibility that this experience can be known in other religions and confessions. He respects and values them and considers them as an higher manifestation of a religious spirit toward God. *Thus, mystical phenomena in other religions are to be respected, because they very often indicate an exalted ascent of the human spirit to God. While the founding of the Church points to the fact that only in the Catholic Church will God usually share the abundant graces that we see shared in mysticism, we may not altogether discount mystical graces outside the Catholic Church.*

---

[8] F. Millán Romeral, *Tito Brandsma* (Madrid 2008) 66-70.

[9] In the process of beatification, a number of different family members and friends spoke about how Fr. Titus urged them greatly to lend support to this "apostolate of re-unification".

The ecumenism of Father Titus was not only an intellectual stance towards a determined group. It was more a personal, vital and, indeed we might say, spiritual stance. He was always a man who was an enemy of barriers, of divisions, of systematic and useless confrontations. In a number of places he was known as the "reconciler". Some of this spirit is found in the academic writings that we present here. In them, not infrequently, Brandsma sought the middle ground in academic and intellectual disputes.

Generally, he showed how in relation to a particular topic, when faced with a concrete and problematic question, two tendencies can be found, two solutions, two opposite and generally extreme positions. Brandsma could normally see the truth and value of both and he normally went for the middle course towards a solution.

Curiously, we can see this same type of thinking in another great Carmelite of the 20th century, Father Bartolomé Xiberta, the well-known theologian, who is today in the process of beatification.[10] In several theological topics of great importance and scope (the conscience of Jesus, the supernatural, primacy and the episcopacy), Xiberta proved also to be somewhat "eclectic" (in the best sense of the word) and he offered theological solutions that were intended to save the best of the two positions at stake. It would be an exercise in "historical fiction" to attempt to see a kind of common style of Carmelite inspiration,[11] but it is not unreasonable to recall the spirit of restraint, realism, and balance of the Carmelite Rule that ends making this call to live this spirit of moderation: *Utatur tamen discretione, quae virtutum est moderatrix* (n.º 24)[12]

[10] F. Millán Romeral, *El talante teológico del P. Xiberta*, en: AA.VV., *Cerni essentia veritatis. Miscelánea homenaje al P. Xiberta de la Región Ibérica Carmelita*, ed. F. Millán Romeral, Barcelona: Claret, 1999, 157-187.

[11] In this same line, the theological positions of the Carmelite scholars who formed part of the "eclectic Carmelite school" are worth remembering.

[12] See, in this regard, the interesting commentaries by M. Plattig, "The Rule and Spiritual Growth", in AA.VV., *The Carmelite Rule* (1207-2007). Proceedings of the Lisieux Conference (Rome 2008) 451-470 (especially, 467-469).

By way of an example, in his famous writing on the concept of "mysticism" the professor of Nijmegen asked if one could really talk about a "Dutch school of Spirituality". Van Mierlo, a Jesuit, said yes while Dom Huyben said no. Brandsma positioned himself in the middle of both: *With reference to the question (...) whether historically one may speak of a distinctive Netherlandish school of mysticism, I feel I should follow the middle of the road...* So, with Van Mierlo, Brandsma recognized that there could exist a school of spirituality proper to Holland, but at the same time, with Dom Huyben, he recognized that this school would only emphasize certain aspects that are part of the common backdrop of Christian spirituality.

That does not signify that he was lacking in firmness of opinion, either in his academic activity, or, much less, in his personal attitudes, or that he was happy to accept anything for the sake of peace. Indeed he was often seen to be firm, and even obstinate, when it came to defending basic and unrenounceable principles[13]. Christine Mohrmann[14] detailed this very well in her declaration for the process of beatification when she affirmed:

His well developed sense of the just and the unjust, would prevail over his spirit of pacification and conciliation. Not even on the grounds

[13] This steadfastness in decisive moments is evident in his responses to the interrogation conducted by Sergeant Hardegan (the record of which is still extant). By way of an anecdote we might recall that this was portrayed very well in the RAI (Italian Television) film, Le due Croci (The Two Crosses), on the last years of Brandsma's life. The film was directed by Silvio Maestranzi, and the actors included Heinz Bennet as Titus, Pamela Villoresi, Jacques Breuer, William Berger, etc.

[14] The famous philologist was first a student and then a colleague of Titus in Nijmegen. Her works are still fundamental in the study of the sacramental terminology of the early Church (from *mysterion* to *sacramentum*). Her testimony to the beatification process is, without doubt, one of the most interesting and illuminating. Regarding this author, see the tribute dedicated to her in 1963 under the title, Mélanges offerts à Mademoiselle Christine Mohrmann (Spectrum, Utrecht – Anvers 1963). The review, Sacris Erudiri, A Journal on the Inheritance of Early and Medieval Christianity (Brepols Publishers), devoted a whole issue to her (Vol. 32 in 1991).

of friendship was he willing to give in, when he was convinced that something was right...[15] Therefore, when we speak of the ecumenical disposition of Father Titus, we must conclude that more than *irenicism, centerism* or diplomacy, it speaks more of a "deep epistemological conviction" that made him listen carefully to various opinions and discover the truth that can be found in various theories, however contradictory and irreconcilable they might appear.

Finally (and I think most importantly) we should note how the writings of Father Titus combine on the one hand serious academic work of a high quality (a critical apparatus, notes at the foot of the page, attention to the latest bibliography, etc.) and on the other hand a passion for what he was intent on explaining. These writings reveal some of the profound personal spirituality of the university professor. We don't want to enter here into the topic (amply treated by other authors) of whether Father Titus was a mystic and in what way we can affirm that he was,[16] but it is clear that the treatment that is given to the diverse spiritual topics (union with God, the mystical transformation, the spirituality of the passion, identification with the suffering Christ, etc.) makes us think that these were all part of his life. These themes are not only in his class notes or in his investigations, they are also in the depth of his heart and in his personal experience.

---

[15] We have translated this directly from the Italian edition of *Summarium super dubio beatificationis seu declarationis martyrii servi dei Titi Brandsma*, Buscoducen, Roma, 1979, 69-81 (72).

[16] Cf. B. Borchert, "The Mystical Life of Titus Brandsma", *Carmelus* 32 (1985) 2-13; A. BREIJ, "Life in the Spirit", in: *Essays on Titus Brandsma*, ed, R.M. Valabek, Rome 1985, 87-99; J. MELSEN, "Mysticism: the aim in life of Fr. Titus Brandsma (1881-1942), in: *Essays*, 100-114; O. Steggink, "Le R.P. Titus Brandsma. Son âme contemplative": *Vinculum Ordinis Carmelitarum* 1 (1948) 49, 294-297; Idem, *Mehr als ein Wissenschafter. Mystiker und Akademiker*, en: AA.VV., *Titus Brandsma, Mystiker des Karmel, Märtyrer in Dachau*, ed. G. Geisbauer, Köln 1987, 28-39; y, sobre todo: A. Staring, "The mysticism of the passion", in: *Essays on Titus Brandsma*, ed. R.M. Valabek, Rome 1985, 115-128, in which Staring poses the question: *Was Titus Brandsma a mystic?*

Even more, Brandsma is not only a scholar of Spirituality (like those who end their experience of God when they close the folder of their class notes) but also one who brings the experience of God to real life. Professor Brandsma is very far from spiritualities that are not embodied, but remain isolated, locked in a kind of "mystical bubble" (a clean, light spirituality more than a spiritual life). For the Carmelite (in the most genuinely evangelical way) the test, the proof, the confirmation of the mystical experience is in living a holy life and only the practice of virtue and its relationship to real life gives true value to the spiritual life. Some expressions of his dense article about mysticism are truly proof of this sense:

Likewise, in general, the Church credits only a private character to the mystical life and its phenomena, and only in very clear cases, which are moreover confirmed by a particularly holy life, does she acknowledge a mystical character accepted by all (...) Secondly, mysticism must be seen from the point of view of its meaning for life, that is of its relation to the practice of virtue.

This is perhaps what made Titus Brandsma not only an intellectual, but also a prophet of his time. Sometimes an intellectual knows how to analyze profoundly and critically a determined situation, but this does not make him committed to it. He looks from the outside with a certain academic coldness, like someone who dissects an animal in a laboratory or mixes chemical products. It was not this way with professor Brandsma, who was totally involved in what was happening, and committed to it, to the point where he would give his life defending the same ideals that he had philosophically and theoretically analyzed in his classes at the University.

On more than one occasion I stressed that it would be interesting to do a comparative study between Martin Heidegger's address when he was named rector of the University of Freiburg im Breisgau in 1933 and Titus Brandsma's address when he was named Rector of the University of Nijmegen one year before. Professor Heidegger (even though his words have been interpreted and reinterpreted in thousands of ways) praises the new laws of education that were coming from the National socialist government and offers a glowing expression of nationalism (German *dasein*, German destiny, German youth…). Father Titus on the other hand, with an intellectual approach that was doubtless inferior to that of the great German philosopher, was alert to something to which Heidegger did not advert: the omitting of God (both cite Nietzsche) becoming an invitation to occupy God's place, and the frightening possibility of making ourselves into gods and then into owners of the lives of others. Heidegger analyzed the reality with a more finesse than Brandsma and with a much superior philosophical capacity, but he was not aware of the danger and did not stand with the possible victims of what was happening. One is a philosopher of unmatched excellence. The other is a prophet, a witness, a martyr … a saint.

*

* *

There are many other aspects and characteristics of the personality of Titus Brandsma that we could describe through these writings and which are worth mentioning and carefully studying. We think of the influence of Christine Mohrmann in his definition of mysticism, through the work of this student on the concept of mystery (mysterion). Undoubtedly there was an interesting interchange of ideas between them and a mutual influence that deserves further study.

We also think of the "spiritual wisdom" that always characterized Father Titus and that he demonstrated in very complicated and striking situations like those of Teresa Neumann (the stigmatic of Konnersreuth that is referred to in his article about *Saint Lidwine of Schiedam* published in 1939 in *De Gelderlander)* or of Elisabeth Kolb. Both cases led him to write previously some considerations about the theme[17], which demonstrates that he was very interested in it. Titus proves to be very respectful of the experience

---

[17] T. Brandsma, *Teresia van Konnesreuth en Lidwina van Schiedam*: Jaarboek van de St. Radboudstichting (1931) 52-56; ID., *Teresia Neumann van Konnersreuth; waarde der verschijnselen*: Het Schild 13 (1931) 5-17, 49-58.

of stigmatics, but at the same time did not consider it important or essential to mystical experience:

A second group of accompanying phenomena have a more corporal character, such as the appearance of stigmata in confirmation of uniformity with Christ (…) Naturally, these phenomena are fundamentally less important, although they may particularly impress others, and the Church in word and attitude warns against setting too much store by them…

We can think of the pedagogical and didactic ability and care that seems to have guided the structure of the articles of Professor Brandsma. He wrote (let's not forget) quite frequently on very lofty topics in journals and in popular reviews. He was, undoubtedly, a communicator, in the best and most beautiful sense of the word. That is why the style of these articles is usually pedagogical, methodical, academic, using classifications, divisions and subdivisions in various stages, periods and trends, etc., in order to help understanding or even the memorizing of the material being treated.

We might think, finally, of the reference (brief but very interesting) to the "Servaes affair" when Brandsma mentioned the discalced Carmelite Jérôme de la Mère de Dieu in his article about Maria Petyt. As is well known, he commissioned the Belgian expressionist painter to make the 14 Stations of the Cross for the new chapel of the monastery in Luythagen.[18] This resulted in a certain amount of scandal because of its "realism", not so much because of its genre, as much as how it reflected the helpless humanity of Christ. The controversy took on international dimensions and the Holy See intervened, finally making them remove the stations.[19] Titus suggested they obey the Vatican order, but

---

[18] Cf. AA.VV. *Ecce homo, Schouwen van de weg van liefde*, (Contemplating the way of love), ed. J. Huls, Leuven 2003, 49-73. This work, beautifully produced, includes the fourteen Stations of the Cross of Servaes and the texts by Fr. Titus, as well as well as a number of explanations. I wrote about it in El Padre Tito Brandsma… la santidad de la humanidad (Father Titus Brandsma… the holiness of humanity. Fonte 3 (2006) 77-100, especially in the section titled, *La gracia de Dios entre dos pintores*.

[19] *Acta Apostolicae Sedis* XIII (1921-5) 197.

went on to publish the paintings in a recently founded magazine accompanied by a beautiful commentary.[20] In these articles we can see (apart from the specific issue of Servaes) many elements that are helpful in understanding Professor Brandsma and his devotion to the suffering Christ, and his regard for the real humanity of Jesus (probably influenced by Saint Teresa), for his suffering not to be understood in a masochistic or macabre fashion way but as a demonstration of his total loving gift to humanity.

I think that the publication of this selection of articles represents a qualitative leap in the understanding of the works, the thought and indirectly, the biography of Blessed Titus Brandsma. I hope that this translation into English makes it possible for the works of Titus Brandsma to be translated into other languages, thus making it possible for his thought, his greatness (both academic or intellectual as well as spiritual) to be known and appreciated more widely. I hope that it serves also as a first step towards the possibility of one day seeing his complete works in a critical and well catalogued edition that will allow us to have a global view of his importance in the Carmelite world of the 20th century and his testimony and inspiration for the Carmelite world of the 21st Century.

Fernando Millán Romeral, O.Carm.
Prior General

---

[20] In a certain sense we are indebted to this affair for the fact that Titus wrote the first of his commentaries on the Via Crucis. He wrote the second while he was in prison, as he thought about the chapel dedicated to St. Boniface in Dokkum, in the place where the saint is believed to have died.

Mysticism[1]

Mysticism, a special union of God with man, whereby the latter becomes conscious of God's presence and on his part also unites himself with God. Mysticism, therefore, has a two-sided character. The special, fervent union of God with man, so that the divine no longer hides itself behind the human but is felt inwardly, may be called the divine essence of mysticism; while the receptiveness of man to this divine grace, its experience by man and its influence on his life constitutes its human dress. At the present an excessive use is made of the word mysticism. One need not always take it in its strict and proper sense, and figurative language may be allowed a wider meaning; nevertheless, that freedom should be restricted in such a way that mysticism should always be taken to mean a secret communication or experience of the divine. Although one may speak of mysticism long before the cult of the Greeks, the word mysticism is taken from the Greek. In the Greek cult the celebration of the mysteries, the identification with the mysteries of the Godhead, evoked human conditions in which the individual, turned inward upon himself, experienced interiorly the presence, the working, of the Godhead. Here mysticism may be summed up by the terms inward turning and experience of God. The verb *muein* means to close the eyes and turn inward upon oneself; *musterion*, the sharing of divine knowledge, secret knowledge; *mustes*, the initiated, one filled with God.

The divine and the human in mysticism.

From the nature of mysticism it follows that two aspects are to be distinguished, and that now one, now the other, will come to the

[1] From the *Katholieke Encyclopedie*, VIII (1937), 199-206.

fore: the divine and the human, more specifically defined as the theological and the human element.

Important as the divine element in mysticism is, the human side of the mystical life compels one to consider, besides what is thrust upon the human being as of divine origin, what he can produce on his own. It is often most difficult to distinguish between the divine and the human. This need be no reason for denying or casting doubt on the divine character of mysticism, any more than the difficulty of distinguishing the dividing-line between life and non-life, between matter and spirit, justifies denying the existence of life or spirit.

While God bestows his gifts on whomever he wills, and we may not altogether discount mystical graces outside the Catholic Church, the founding of the Church points to the fact that only in the Catholic Church will God usually share his abundant grace which we see shared in mysticism, and we therefore see a wonderful mystical life flourish in her. However, we find paralleled in other religions the physical conditions which accompany this mystical life; they show us how far in this direction self-development and industry can go. In various Indian religions, in the ancient Greek cult, in the separated Christian Churches, we find ecstasies which have a certain resemblance to those we see in the mystical saints of the Catholic Church. Parapsychology demonstrates at what notable conditions humans, led by their own ideas or those of others, can arrive by means of suggestion, telepathy, clairvoyance, etc. Even stigmata, living by almost total abstinence from food, occur under the influence of suggestion. This makes it very difficult for outsiders to establish with certainty the mystical character of such phenomena. The Mystical Doctor, St. John of the Cross, adds that in the mystical life there is almost always need for greater clarity; it usually seems to be enveloped in mist, especially to the uninitiated. In this, he sees an indication that God wishes to see the certainty of faith placed above that of the mystical life. St. Teresa points out besides that for the person concerned God's presence and influence is often so clearly discernable as to remove all doubt that God often seizes the faculties of the soul with irresistible force. However, she also admits that the danger of being misled always exists, and that a person gifted with mystical graces should submit all divine inspirations and revelations to the judgment of an experienced spiritual director, and that obedience to his guidance and insight is a first and foremost requirement. Likewise, in general, the Church credits only a private character to the mystical life and its phenomena, and only in very clear cases, which are moreover confirmed by a particularly holy life, does she acknowledge a mystical character to be accepted by all. Of the many instances of stigmata, the Church permits liturgical celebration only in the case of St. Francis of Assisi, St. Teresa, and St. Catherine of Siena. This does not exclude the fact that the Church shows great reverence for the mystical life and considers it the highest development of the life of grace.

Meantime, it is quite incorrect to call meaningless, or even morbid, human activity that leads to mystical conditions, even though there is no question of formal mystical graces; or, in other words, even though these conditions remain entirely within the order of nature. Concentration of the spirit on the highest and noblest object of its contemplation, so fervent that it leads to ecstatic conditions, is basically more noble than the strongest poetic inspiration or the ecstasy of a artist painter. The fact that exaggerated or even morbid conditions can occur there, just as in the case of a poet or a painter, is not to be denied, but then the light will outshine the shadows. Thus, mystical phenomena in other religions are to be respected, because they not seldom indicate an exalted ascent of the human spirit to God.

A great distinction is to be made in mysticism between doctrine and life. One can describe the mystical life without oneself participating in the mystical experience of God. But since there is no lack of persons gifted with mystical experience, and these have also, either from inward urgency or upon command of their director, described their experiences, a description will still have to build on their witness and instruction. Thus, those personally gifted with mystical graces, such as St. Teresa, St. John of the Cross, and in the Netherlands Bl. Ruusbroec, are at the same time the most authoritative authors about the mystical life. It goes without saying that the mystical life can exist without finding expression in literature, and can also live on in literature, though it is no longer experienced.

Intellectualistic and Voluntaristic Trends. Mysticism and Asceticism. Conformity to God.

In the nature of things, mysticism manifests itself in many ways. In the first place, however, it is a union between God and man, in which the higher human faculties, intellect and will, play the most important role. Here, however, there is again occasion for distinction. There is, first of all, a more *intellectualistic* trend, in which contemplation of the mysteries of God is the highest element; the foretaste of heaven, as well as the happiness of heaven itself, are seen above all in the *visio beatifica*, the vision of God. Describing this vision of God, when all images are set aside, is most difficult. There is also talk of entering into the *divine darkness*. Besides this intellectualistic school, there is the more *voluntaristic* one, also called the school of love, of which, especially for our regions, the great masters are St. Augustine, St. Bernard, and St. Bonaventure. In the Netherlands, Hadewijch and Beatrice of Nazareth are the outstanding representatives of this school. If in general the Dominicans are more attracted to the intellectualistic trend, the Franciscans with their Seraphic Father and the Cistercians with St. Bernard as leaders are to be reckoned rather as adherents of the voluntaristic school. One often sees St. Teresa, the Seraphic Virgin of Avila, counted in this school, and she most certainly lays very strong emphasis on love, but rather as a means than as a goal. With Ruusbroec and John of the Cross, Teresa and the mystic school of Carmel occupy a more moderate position, which in the case of the first two perhaps still leans somewhat toward the intellectualistic trend; in Teresa's, toward the voluntaristic one; but which may still count as a notable harmony between the two schools. That is why these mystics also generally count as leaders in the mystic life.

Secondly, mysticism must be seen from the point of view of its meaning for life; that is, of its relation to the practice of virtue. Here, too, there is considerable difference of direction; one must avoid wanting mysticism to be too uniform. The essential and general virtues are those like obedience, humility, love of God and neighbor, purity, detachment from worldly things, and conformity to the will of God. These virtues must also shine in the most withdrawn and quiet contemplation. The Church condemns a degeneration of this sort of life into Quietism, according to which a person, underestimating all human activity out of an unsound humility, places himself in the hands of God and expects from him only grace. After a mysticism leaning too much toward Eckhart's intellectualism, there arose in the Netherlands under Ruusbroec, but still more under the influence of Geert Grote, a trend, the Modern Devotion, in which the practice of virtue took a prominent role, perhaps too much so. While highly esteeming mystical graces, emphatically regarded, however, as a gift of God, this movement stressed the need of making oneself receptive to it, not placing any obstacle to it, and on man's part doing all that God desired, without wishing to see these efforts result in mystical graces. The result was that mysticism was rarely spoken of, and there was regard only for asceticism. Legalism was the ideal. This led, though only very gradually, to the externalization of religion, against which, with Protestantism, a reaction toward interiority set in. Yet the Modern Devotion was a mystical school, because it regarded mysticism and asceticism as a whole, of which mysticism was above all divine and asceticism above all human. Thus, especially in the early years of the Modern Devotion, we find many of the devout with mystical gifts, and in their works a mystical background. In this light, by this method, the *Imitation of Christ*, although strongly ascetical, is to be called a mystical work. After this perhaps too strong a show of legalism there followed Protestantism with its elimination of good works. With the Carthusians of Cologne and the school of Oisterwijk and Nicholas van Esch, St. Peter Canisius contributed much toward again making the norm a harmonious concept of interior communion with God joined to exterior virtuous living. This brings forward a third element of the mystical life.

Thirdly, mysticism strives toward conformity to God. If at first this was given a principally spiritual interpretation, in the 13th century, with the emergence of popular devotion and its various forms, conformity to God-made-man came more strongly to the fore. Whereas earlier the main effort was to free the spirit from the body, now God was seen more as descending to man, and man as called to mirror himself in Christ. This idea flourished in the Modern Devotion, exemplified in the *Imitation of Christ*. Such imitation sometimes degenerated into an excessively material craving for likeness and imitation. Still, the idea contained much of beauty, blessed by God with various gifts. Particularly under the influence of this idea, we see emerging such phenomena as stigmata, not reported before St. Francis. All sorts of devotions to the humanity of Christ arise, to the manger, the way of the cross, the sacred wounds, the holy face, etc. When this movement degenerated and lost its appropriateness, a new form of spiritual and mystical life arose with the Reformation and Counter Reformation, known as experiencing Christ. The leader of this new trend, Cardinal de Bérulle, seems to have been influenced in his ideas by the Spanish Carmelite nuns, newly arrived in France (Anne of Jesus, first in Paris, later in Brussels), and by the *Evangelical Pearl* of the school of Oisterwijk. The imitation of Christ was to a great degree interiorized. "I live, no, not I, but Christ lives in me." Here the idea comes especially to the fore that, just as the life of Christ on earth was a sacrificial suffering, so too mystical union with Christ, which above all strives after conformity with God, should make ample room for suffering in the following of and union with the suffering of Christ.

It would be quite incorrect to regard mysticism as primarily enjoyment; such enjoyment is to a great extent paired with suffering; which, however, is gladly borne out of love of God and, with God, of neighbor. This suffering is intense, not only for the soul, but also for the body, and serves to purify and detach it from all earthly pleasure.

Classification into Stages and Forms of Prayer.

Since the mystical life is to be conceived as an ascent to union with God, it is classified into several steps or states. The most common division is into three steps or ways: the *purgative way*, also known as the way of mortification or the mortified life, in which purification of all sin, detachment from earthly things, penance and mortification are foremost. The second step is the *illuminative way*, of the practice of virtue, the adornment of the bride for her encounter with the bridegroom. The third step is called the *contemplative life* by Ruusbroec and Mande, elsewhere often the *unitive way*. It is the life of the most intimate union with God; intimate, because God himself takes possession of the faculties of the soul, and the soul thus falls into a passive state. It is remarkable how Ruusbroec and Teresa divide this matter in more or less the same way. After the prayer of recollection, the prayer of quiet follows, a succumbing as into sleep in the Beloved, followed by a spiritual death to self, in order to rise to a life with God. Both mystics here add the image of the spiritual betrothal, crowned by the spiritual espousals of the most intimate and steadfast union with God.

In Ruusbroec as in Teresa, we find the older division into seven steps, of which the first ones include the remote preparation for the mystical life, turning aside from creatures, turning toward God, the practice of virtue, and active contemplation; these steps lie more in the domain of asceticism, while the four highest rather describe the more mystical life. Teresa pictures these seven steps in her description of the seven mansions of the Interior Castle, *El Castillo Interior*, which certainly deserves to be called the masterpiece of all mystical literature.

If one regards more the form and manner in which communication with God is sought and found, if one sees the mystical life primarily as a form of prayer, then *meditation* constitutes the first step; pouring out of the heart or *affective prayer*, the second; while the ascent to contemplation, called the *prayer of simplicity*, forms the third. Contemplation is the transition to the mystical life, inso-far as active turns into passive contemplation, and the latter leads to the *prayer of quiet*, which as a rule is considered the fourth step. Then, as the fifth step there follows *ecstatic prayer*, in which the soul is taken up into God and raised on high. St. Teresa here distinguishes three states, simple ecstasy, rapture, and flight of the spirit, distinguished from each other by the vehemence with which the soul is raised up to God. The sixth step is the prayer of complete *surrender* and dedication to God, a spiritual betrothal, which in the seventh step leads to the more intimate and lasting union of the *spiritual betrothal*.

Growth of the Mystical Life.

A controverted question is the distinction between mysticism and asceticism, closely associated with the question as to whether all are called to the mystical life, and whether this is to be looked upon as the ordinary development of the ascetical or virtuous life. The distinction between the two has been sharpened more than is desirable, because in regarding the ascetical life attention has been too exclusively confined to the human element, and not enough consideration is given to the fact that God is equally active here through his grace, though more hidden behind the human; while in the mystical life the divine activity becomes more pronounced and is no longer hidden. This no doubt formally summons up another situation, which however is not so different as is sometimes alleged. A life of virtue must also aim at the highest union with God, without this implying that God shares his grace so abundantly with everyone that a mystical life would be destined for all. This has certainly been the particular position of the Netherlandish school of mysticism, which honors Ruusbroec as its father, and always required a more than ordinary life of virtue for all mystical life.

Accompanying Phenomena.

The material-spiritual nature of man implies that the mystical life, although it should be seen in the first place as a higher spiritual life, produces bodily, or rather psychosomatic symptoms, which may best be called accompanying mystical phenomena, and should never be considered essential. The phenomena most immediately connected with mysticism are ecstatic conditions. In some mystical conditions, the mystic is unresponsive to the usual stimuli of the senses and entirely removed from ordinary life. Strong concentration can in this respect already lead to remarkable conditions; especially in Indian religions, this gradually total ascent in a spiritual sphere, often of unconscious existence, assumes extreme forms. In Christian mysticism, the phenomena are more closely bound to a more positive attitude of the soul, which, directed to the divine, contemplates the divine. This leads to visions which can have a three-fold character: perception by the exterior senses, in which there is danger of hallucination in merely apparent mystical conditions; perception in the imagination, in which there is danger of purely subjective imagination; finally, a purely intellectual vision, an enlightening of the understanding, in which there is least danger of being misled, according to St. Teresa. Naturally, these three forms of vision can occur together or successively.

A second group of accompanying phenomena have a more corporal character, such as the appearance of stigmata in confirmation of uniformity with Christ; not needing food or even drink or also sleep or rest, accompanied or not by nourishing or strengthening oneself with Holy Communion alone; being raised up from the earth (levitation); diffusing the "odor of sanctity" (see Sanctity); clairvoyance and its related phenomena, etc. Naturally, these phenomena are fundamentally much less important, although they may particularly impress others, and the Church in word and attitude warns against setting too much store by them. In this connection, Catholic scholars even reject the demand to submit such phenomena to strict scientific examination, because too much importance may thereby be given them. Naturally deceit should be guarded against. When this is thought to be excluded, the question as to whether these phenomena are natural or supernatural is of secondary importance, since in the opinion of the Church they are not essential to the mystic state.

The Netherlandish School of Mysticism.

With reference to the question, answered positively by Mierlo, S.J., and negatively by Dom Huyben, whether historically one may speak of a distinctive Netherlandish school of mysticism, I feel I should follow the middle of the road, which leads to the recognition of a distinctive school, though without sharp differences from other schools and with emphasis on what in the various Catholic schools of thought must be put forward as common to all. The fact that the high points in the mystical life in the Netherlands occur in times when, not an individual, but the people themselves felt attracted to it; that the beguine movement and the Modern Devotion are specifically Netherlandish; and that the masterpieces of the Netherlandish mystics, such as the songs of Hadewijch, the *Spiritual Espousals* of Ruusbroec, the *Evangelical Pearl*, are written in the vernacular, shows that the Netherlander, moderate and an enemy of contrast, needs a popular movement in order to rise to the heights, and gives to Netherlandish mysticism a middle position between the strongly intellectualistic school of Eckhart and the strongly affective one of St. Bernard, as a moderate and harmonious bond between both trends, intelligible to wide circles; while the sober and practical character of the Netherlandish people, though prone to theologizing and not averse to speculation, also sees a particular value in the practice of virtue, and therefore "methodical prayer" also found in the Netherlands a fertile soil for its highest development. The leading work and the best representative of the Netherlandish school is the *Spiritual Espousals* of Ruusbroec.

Lit.: St. Teresia, Werken (I and III Hilversum 1921 ff.); St. John of the Cross, Werken (3 v. Hilversum 1932 ff.); Bl. Jan van Ruusbroec, Werken (4 v. Amsterdam-Mechelen 1932 ff.); A. Tanquerey, Kort Begrip der Asc. en Myst. Theol. (1932); P. v. d. Tempel O.P., De Wetenschap der Heiligen (1926); Joseph a Spiritu Sancto, O.Carm. D., Cursus Theol. Myst. Schol. (6 v. 1924 ff.); Th. a Vallgornera O.P., Mystica Theol. D. Thomae (2 v. 1927); R. Garrigou-Lagrange O.P., Perfection chrétienne et Contemplation (2 v. 1923); A. Gardeil O.P., La structure de l'âme et l'expérience mystique (2 v. 1927); J. de Guibert, S.J., Etudes de Théol. mystique (1930); A. Poulain, S.J., Des Grâces d'Oraison (1922); A. Saudreau, L'Etat mystique (Paris 1921); H. Brémond, Hist. litt. d. Sentiment religieux en France (10 v. 1923-'32); P. Pourrat, La Spiritualité chrétienne (4 v. 1917-'28); A. Farges, Les Phénomènes mystiques (2 v. 1923); dom. C. Butler O.S.B., Western Mysticism (1927); E. Hendrikx O.E.S.A., Augustins Verhältnis zur Mystik (Würzburg 1936); J. v. Görres, Die Christliche Mystik (5 v. n. d.); H. Jaegen, Das mystische Gnadenleben (1934); A. Stolz O.S.B., Theol. d. Mystik (Regensburg 1936); A. Auger, Etude sur les Mystiques des Pays-Bas au Moyen Age (1892); E. Bruggeman, Les Mystiques flamands (1928); Ons Geestelijk Erf (periodical, 10 v. Antwerpen 1927-36); Dom Huyben O.S.B., Y-at'il une spiritualité flamande? (in La Vie spirituelle, XIX 1937). – Non-Catholic: W. J. Aalders, Mystiek (1928); idem, Grote Mystieken (2 v. 1914); A. Hyma, The Christian Renaissance (1924); W. James, The Varieties of Religion [sic] Experience (1922); P. Janet, L'Etat mental des Hystériques (1911); B. J. v. d. Zuylen, Mysteriën en Inwijdingen in de Oudheid (1927).

The Spiritual Literature of the Netherlands – Its Phases[1]

I

It would be quite incorrect not see our spiritual literature as subject to various trends and powerful change. Least of all is it uniform, although a basic characteristic remains.

Besides periods when we see it blossom into expressions of the most exalted mysticism, there are others in which mysticism withers and makes room for a much stronger earthy, ascetical way of thinking. At one time, God and heaven are the center of attention; at another, man upon earth, wrestling and striving to be what he is and can be. There is also a great difference with regard to the expressions of the different faculties of human nature. At one time, the expression of love, the strong power of the will directed to God and the divine predominates; at another time, the intellect and reason occupy the prominent place, the culmination of which is the contemplation and speculation of the loftiest and most intimate mysteries. These expressions also are again replaced for expressions in which imagination, painting, graphic representation are of the most importance, and in place of the expressions of intellect and will, effusions of love of God and the divine, touch the sentiments of the heart, and feelings and their expressions occupy the foreground.

It is naturally not entirely correct to make the beginning of Netherlandish spiritual literature coincide with its expression in the Netherlandish language. Long before that, there existed not only a flourishing spiritual life in the Netherlands, but it found

---

[1] From *De Gelderlander*, Apr. 26, May 3, 10,17, 24, 1941.

expression in various literary forms. But in the first centuries, Latin
was so much the written language of writers that no one thought
of putting expressions of the spiritual life into the vernacular of
the country; it was even difficult to find the words and proper
expressions for this. Where the vernacular existed, it had such a
limited influence that it was not transmitted or retained. More
important works were translated into Latin to make them accessible in wider circles. Geert Grote, who in the 14th century performed great service in the matter of the use of the vernacular in
spiritual literature, has left only a few letters in the vernacular
besides a great many in Latin. His biographers, by way of something unusual, relate that he once preached in the vernacular in
Amsterdam and thereby broke with the general custom of preaching in Latin, which he himself almost always followed. He translated the beautiful Netherlandish works of the great Jan van Ruusbroec into Latin, in order to make them available in wider circles,
even of Netherlanders.

However, we shall not object if a special place is given to Netherlandish works in the history of the spiritual life in the Netherlands; if they are treated separately; and if the history of Netherlandish spiritual literature is confined to them, thus placing the
beginning of that literature in the first half of the 13th century.
Although we know that there were earlier examples of the vernacular, and we are still discovering traces of them, it seems that
in the 13th century there was such a development in that genre that
it becomes a well-known phenomenon and is expressed in works
of such artistic feeling that these were conserved and handed
down.

If Blessed John van Ruusbroec was long considered the Father
of Netherlandish mysticism, if later he was still regarded as the
father of spiritual prose, for the past ten years, we have known that
the school of Hadewijch flourished a century before him, and that
this noble lady by her lofty love songs and rapturous letters became
the leader of a trend in which love (*minne*) – aspiration to the
heart's Beloved – predominates over all else to such an intense
degree that Hadewijch may be called the songstress of love *par*

excellence; and all those belonging to her school emphasize the primacy of the will, the dedication of the heart to God, and affective prayer.

This bridal mysticism, this love-lyric, which echoes the Song of Solomon of Sacred Scripture, flourished to an unprecedented degree around the middle of the 13th century. It also takes on courtly forms; a prominent place is allotted to the cavalier, who defends the honor of his chosen bride and sings of his love for her.

Gradually, with the progress of education among the ordinary citizenry who still had to be taught their letters, a more educational trend, a more didactically inclined school, began to illustrate the spontaneous lyric with a variety of often very beautifully chosen images. Beside the will, the reasoning intellect gradually took first place, without yet replacing the will's effect. In the realm of philosophy, St. Thomas with compelling force of reasoning proved that concepts derive from sensory images and are not independently infused in us. The new trend of thought certainly met stiff resistence; especially as the new system of thought further developed, there were many who opposed St. Thomas, but even his opponents gradually accepted his basic principles and opposed him more on secondary points.

Aristotle won over Plato, as Thomas won over Augustine. The strongly affective Franciscan school, with St. Francis and St. Bonaventure, in Scotus, the famous schoolman, seems to accept the Aristotelian principle of the origin of our ideas in the images of the senses and thereby supports the new trend, which makes abundant use of images. In the beginning of the 13th century, in which the Cistercians of the southern Netherlands led the spiritual trend, St. Bernard with the love-lyric and bridal mysticism was the master *par excellence*. This school readily assumed effective leadership over the young flourishing Franciscan school. In proportion as the latter grew stronger, it turned ever more to images, dear also to St. Francis, who used them to teach the poor and to form his first simple brothers in devotion. Not only was the Christmas crib built, but the representations of the incarnate God were popular, and where picturing the actual was not possible, the symbolic was resorted to, in order to illustrate ideas. Two things are to be distinguished here: on the one hand, the progress of the intellect, reason, elucidation; on the other hand, and closely connected with it, the ever more frequent use of images and metaphorical language.

Maerlant[2] introduces the second period. He is the great didactic poet of the end of th 13th century, and the didactician, too, in his often beautiful utterances of the spiritual life. Already in his day, there are those who are unwilling to follow his lead, and, according as image and sensory representation gain influence, seem further inclined toward rejecting it. The so-called miscellaneous poems of Hadewijch – which, however, are not hers, but of a late representative of her school – already speak of the *ongebeelde* (unimaged). Through the new trend, [sensory representation] gains not only through giving the image an ever more influential role, but also by introducing it into the reasoning intellect, giving it an ever larger role; to the extent that in the beginning of the 14th century, the spontaneous lyric seems to be dying out and only faintly echoes.

If to the perhaps too strong exaggeration of the effect and action of the will, a natural reaction was that the reasoning intellect again assumed its rights, we now soon see a new reaction set in. If the intellect chose the image, in order gradually to resume its place, and if the image was greeted as the dawn of a new and plentiful light, metaphorical language became so profuse that it no longer made an impression and above all was applied in so unhealthy and unnatural a manner, that it more and more lost its appeal for the ever more developing intellect. Many examples may be quoted, especially from the beginning of the 14th century, of exaggerated, unhealthy, unnatural metaphors, so it does not surprise us that a reaction set in ever more strongly, by which the intellect in the nature of things took over the leadership.

---

[2] Jacob Maerlant, *ca* 1235-1300. See: Frits van Oostrom, *Stemmen op schrift*, Geschiedenis van de Nederlandse literatuur vanaf het begin tot 1300, Amsterdam 2006, 502-550.

If the first period extended from 1225-1275, we would like to place the second from 1275-1325. In the former stand the great figures of Hadewijch and Beatrice of Nazareth. In the latter, Jacob van Maerlant and Jan Praet, surrounded by a whole crowd of allegorical-didactical poets and prose writers. After this, however, comes the spiritual literary storm of images (*beeldenstorm*),[3] which the mysticism of Eckhart, so strongly intellectual, introduced into these lands.

II

A literary spiritual attack on images ushers in the third period. In round numbers, we would like to place the duration of this period from 1325 to 1375, although we must immediately note that here, too, we must state that this unprecedented trend emerged before 1325.

If our knowledge of both the first periods is slim, we know even less of the third. It would be very worthwhile for someone to undertake a deeper and more extensive examination of this notable period of our spiritual literature.

We spoke of a spiritual, literary storm of images, and we think we may be permitted to do so. It is a period of strong reaction to metaphor, overused and too focused on the imagination, in spiritual literature. The intellect reclaimed its rights, an urge for more abstract contemplation arose, a more metaphysical, a more philosophically pondered reflection exercised a greater attraction than something that was nothing more than an elaboration of the imagination. Greater education prevailed in the circles of the devout, and these required food for the mind. Spiritual literature became more elevated in outlook, without this implying that it radiated more fervent life, although this condition sometimes accompanied it to a large degree. Metaphysical speculation, exalted thoughts confined spiritual literature somewhat to a smaller group of the

---

[3] The allusion is to the *beeldenstorm* of 1566, during the religious wars in the Netherlands, when Calvinists destroyed the statues in the churches.

elect, but not to the extent that smaller and simpler folk did not enjoy it, up to a certain point, with profit. It is remarkable how comparatively little educated persons can manifest understanding of thoughts, which have religious truths for an object; can often better grasp their gist than the trained philosopher.

Here, in an often striking manner, the truth is realized that divine wisdom is kept hidden from the wise of this world, and the little and uneducated folk show understanding of it. But, on the other hand, a serious danger and disadvantage is involved. While there may be a certain receptiveness for the sublime, an often remarkable comprehension of the divine, there are limits, and those limits are soon reached. Then there come misunderstanding and straying from the truth on the part of those who feel themselves still attracted; aversion, on the part of the majority. In this way, a temporary success can be realized, and in a small group, a splendid spiritual life; but people soon ask for other forms.

Around the middle of the 14th century, this more intellectual trend in spiritual literature underwent the powerful influence of German mysticism; actually, it rings in German influence in our country. After the French unmistakably influence the first two periods, and St. Bernard is the great master, German mysticism, led by Eckhart, comes to the fore.

Born in 1250 in Hochhelm, Thuringen, Eckhart was the outstanding figure in the German province of the Dominican Order. He was twice elected provincial of Saxony, to which a great deal of the Netherlands also belonged. He died in Cologne in 1327, but his death did not end the great influence he exercised, especially in the realm of spirituality. Eckhart stayed in our land on several occasions and certainly did not fail to exercise his influence in sharing with others the thoughts that inspired him. He was a celebrated preacher, who long lived on through a great number of sermons, also translated into Middle Netherlandish. The research especially of Professor de Vooijs[4] and of various others has shown

---

[4] C.G.N. de Vooys, "Meister Eckhart in de Nederlandse mystiek," *Neerlandsch Archief voor Kerkgeschiedenis, Nieuwe serie*, 3 (1905), 50-92, 176-194,

the extent of Eckhartian literature in our country. But then, attention has concentrated principally on his sermons, yet there is still a great number of anonymous treatises that strongly breath the spirit of Eckhart.

These are immediately recognizable by their excessive recommendation of "un-imaged" communion with God; their solicitude to suppress metaphor and imagination, in order to commune most intimately with God alone in the spirit, in the inmost center of the soul, where God himself dwells and lights the fire of his love in the soul; where he has ignited the "spark of the soul" as the source of light and warmth in communion with him. That spark must flare up into a blaze, in order better to know the divine Being and in its glow to be kindled to love of him. We must seek God, not in creatures that reflect him only dimly, not in various images, but in himself, as he reveals himself to us in the innermost part of the soul. We must enter into ourselves, suppress the imagination, and seek to ascend into the spiritual light that radiates in us from the Godhead, a light that at once attracts us like the sun, but is also accessible to our weak faculties. We must live in God, who fills our being with his own; we must be one with him. We ourselves emanate from God who dwells in us, so that in us, with us, who come forth from God, the emanation of God the Son must be seen, with whom we have emanated from the Father for all eternity.

The indwelling of God in us and our eternal emanation from God, so that we may be called children of God, and are such, the extraordinary election and blessing of man by God, are the favorite subjects of contemplation in this period. These writers have been suspected of Pantheism, and Eckhart has been accused of and indicted for heresy. In our country, charges were also made against some of the members of Eckhart's Order because of their subtle and exalted preaching, causing people to fall into error. But Eckhart's orthodoxy may well be considered above all suspicion, although a list of theses has been taken from his works, which, when understood in a certain sense, must be deemed heretical.

265-190.

It should surprise no one that opposition should soon arise against such a trend, and that a reaction set in. This manifested itself first of all in a moderation of the Eckhartian terminology and at the same time in a proposal to match exalted contemplation with the practice of virtue. Against the accusation of propagating a pantheistic, quietistic mysticism, the followers of the Eckhartian school explained that they intended no quietism and gradually began to emphasize the practice of virtue in their sermons.

In Jan van Ruusbroec, the great Netherlandish mystic, we see represented in a wondrous manner this moderate intellectualistic mysticism, closely allied to the practice of virtue. Although Eckhartian mysticism as such can be found in our land, it reached its heyday in a modified form, blended with the practice of practical virtue to a greater degree than in Eckhart. It would be unjust to claim that Eckhart neglected the practice of virtue, but it cannot be denied that he places greater emphasis on theoretic contemplation and the happiness it confers. His mysticism is outspokenly intellectualistic. The intellect and contemplation predominate over the working of the will, the imagination, and application to life situations.

Although these are the characteristic traits of the reigning trend, it does not mean that therefore imagery disappeared entirely from the spiritual literature of this period. It has too prominent a place in the Gospel and also in human language for this to happen. But it was much more soberly applied and used in a much more rational manner. Gradually, it resumes its place and recovers it more and more. Ruusbroec himself, who with regard to knowledge of God strongly insists on freeing oneself of images, emptying oneself, stripping oneself of all impressions and influences of created things, nevertheless uses all sorts of images in his works, taken from Nature especially. The title of his principal work shows that he leads the soul like a bride to the festival and adorns her with all virtues, to be worthy of the heavenly Bridegroom. He looks to the animals and flowers of the field, to the mountains and the clouds, to the sun and its light, in order to borrow images for the ascent of the soul to God. In his *Tabernacle*, the ark of the covenant and all its appurtenances is the model for a grandiose, full-dress allegory. Yet, these images are no more than a preamble of the lowest faculties, in order gradually to arrive through the higher faculties at the "un-imaged," where God is known in "unknowing"; that is, not under well-defined and determined images, forms, and ways, and is enjoyed in "dark stillness." The image has received a very subordinate place. Yet, his use of images shows that Ruusbroec does not slavishly follow Eckhart, to whom he is very related, but pays more attention to the natural foundation of knowledge and its origin from images. Eckhart himself rests on that Aristotelian foundation, but he rises from it so quickly and thinks he can thus rove about in the world of thought, that he can hardly be recognized as an Aristotelian anymore, and by his assumption of many elements from pseudo-Dionysius is thought to belong rather to the neo-Platonist school. This is only partly true, and does not apply to his point of departure. Though Eckhart already preceded him, Ruusbroec more effectively brings the spiritual literature of our land from Platonism to a gradual acceptance of the Aristotelian point of view; a fact that should be first of all kept in mind for the understanding of the metaphorical language of the 15th as against that of the 13th century, although we will not deny that nowhere more powerfully than in spiritual literature does the Platonic influence continue to linger and flourish.

III

If we look back on the first three periods which we distinguished more in connection with the concept of God and its related manner of communion with him, then we note a great difference, which, however, should not be seen apart from the signs of difference already alluded to.

We pictured the first period as that of bridal mysticism, of the cavalier love-lyric. There God is seen as the object of our love, who attracts us to himself by his lovableness. It is still the period of the ascent of the soul to God, who attracts her, the flight of the bride to the bridegroom. Man ascends upwards. Love drives him up to God.

In the second, didactic-allegorical period, a clear transition is observable to greater prominence of the incarnation of God, of God's descent to man, of God's communion with him in images and figures. The communion becomes more familiar, more person to person. Many are the dialogs between God and the soul, the master and the pupil. In place of being high above us, God is with us. He has become man with mankind, in order to be our teacher and by his example to show the way to the most intimate union with him.

In the third period, this concept is developed further and, in accordance with the nature of this more intellectual era, is made more intimate and abstract. Not so much as in the first period, there now appears the loving and lovable Father in heaven; also not as in the second period, the incarnate God, like to us in all things, and our model. Now God is represented as seen in himself or in the entire Trinity, according to whose image we have been created, and who lives and thrones in us. It is the period of the divine indwelling in us; not God with us but God in us is now the preferred concept. Related to this is man's seeing himself as God's image; he must not only see God's image in himself, but must more and more bring it to expression. This exemplarism thus acquires a double side.

Not only does God's image live in us, created in us by him, but we also have the task of setting it off to full advantage. So we see arise here a gradual transition to a more practical cultivation of the spiritual life that cannot remain confined to contemplation by the intellect, to the formation of beautiful ideas and words, but according to God's word itself must be accompanied by the act of fulfilling the divine will. If we are created to God's image, then it is not only a truth that charms and captivates our mind, but also a truth that reminds us of the necessity of causing that image of God to be revealed.

Thus, we gradually arrive at a fourth period that we may call the period of practical cultivation of virtue, already ushered in by Ruusbroec as a transitional figure, but above all brought to perfection by the radical, anti-intellectual, practical mysticism of Geert Grote and his school.

Here there is indeed question of a new reaction. The moderate attitude of Jan van Ruusbroec actually already ushered in this period. His preaching and picturing of the practice of virtue already lies along the line later extended by Grote. But Ruusbroec is still too much the principal figure of the preceding period that we would want to place him in this. Yet he is really a figure that demonstrates how periods overlap each other.

Naturally, the image now again appears, because through the strong anti-intellectual trend, greater importance is accorded to the representation of the object of the senses. The further development of the idea of being the image of God is to be understood in this sense. If we want to express God's image in us, we must mirror ourselves in the God-Man, who came upon earth precisely to teach us how to express that image of God in ourselves. The exhortation to more intimacy is at the same time a call to the following of Christ. Christ our model is now the dominating idea. Introduced by Geert Grote, this period reaches its culmination in the *Following of Christ*, which in design and preparation could have appeared earlier, but actually appeared only in 1425, written by Thomas à Kempis, a complete delineation of the way to the most intimate union with God. Thus, this fourth period extends from 1375 to 1425.

In the *Imitation of Christ*, meditation on the sacred Passion occupies a very special place and thereby also a sharing in the Passion through penance and mortification. But of its own, the image now again appears in full strength, perhaps even more plentifully and more richly than in the second period at the end of the 13th and beginning of the 14th century. The *Imitation of Christ* requires not only the depiction of his life and Passion, but involves the depiction of the saints who are an example to us in that imitation of the way we thereby have to tread; also the depiction of the many symbols with which God has willed to make that way known. Now imagination resumed the place from which it had been forced during the intellectual period. Striving after the "unimaged" was declared to be dangerous, as will later again be done by St. Teresa against the quietistic trend in Spain. When God himself had willed to assume human nature to show us the way to heaven, would we dare to ban the object of sensory contemplation from our spiritual life? Imagination and memory vied with each other to help our spirit lead us to God and give our ideas the foundation from which alone they can be derived. The image receives an entirely new function. It is no longer introduced into spiritual literature from the natural need also to attach a sensory image to a concept, in order thereby to grasp it more easily; no, it now receives a place given it by God himself in his incarnation; namely, as the source of understanding and foundation of contemplation. The image does not crown the train of thought already determined by the understanding; the image itself is the foundation and point of departure. The sensory representation, which is desired and sought for its own sake, is gradually further developed. In this period, the image obtains, although gradually, the place which is its due; the place which corresponds to its functional importance in our thought process. That decidedly does not mean that we no longer meet improper use of metaphor; the opposite is true. But it tells us that we do well to distinguish the double tendency which the image can have, and in fact has had, in our spiritual literature.

It cannot be denied that in this way a certain externalization did not enter into the spiritual life. The retreat of purely intellectual contemplation to reinforce sensory representation has certainly done damage to the interiority of concept of the spiritual life. In the first years of this period, there certainly still occur many interior expressions, often very profound. Nevertheless, interiority gradually disappears to make room for much that is charming and attractive, dear and soft, much that speaks to the senses, but no longer penetrates so deeply, only moderately satisfies the intellect. It is also reflected in the graphic arts, which begin to gravitate to the representation of all that is amiable in Our Lord's life, the atrocious in his Passion, the realistic level, which is suited for affecting feelings, but hardly leaves room for deeper reflection or at least is not inspired by such reflection. Legend occupies an important place, without there being a question as to whether the mind is thereby satisfied. And this exteriorization goes further. Realism grows more and more, the spiritual life becomes ever more systematized and methodical, and that to such an extent that one asks oneself whether that pernicious development of the graphic does not rather damage the deep interior than nourish it, as is intended.

IV

The fifth period, which we would like to date from 1425 to 1475, is one of striking contrasts, which, however, resolve themselves in a "unity of opposites," characterizing this period as one of the richest and most fruitful in our spiritual literature.

We encounter opposites like Father Brugman and Denis the Carthusian, worldly humanism and strict religious observance, the revival of Latin spiritual literature with an often strongly idealistic tendency together with the emergence of strongly realistic Netherlandish popular art. And so we could go on. There is such a wide variety and so rich a gradation that at first glance it seems difficult to discern a unity that might characterize this period. The period has sometimes been referred to as autumn.[5] It seems to me that we do it an injustice so to designate it, though I freely admit that autumnal tints are to be discerned in it, as for that matter are to be found in mid-summer, and over the bloom of health falls the shadow of death. At this time, there is so much unfolding of new life, there is so strong a renewal, so many flowers bloom of such unprecedented beauty, that I would mark this time precisely as an age of highest achievement, a flowering of our spiritual literature, in spite of all who see it in another light.

The Burgundians did not relinquish the idea of a distinct Netherlandish culture, and its efforts in that respect were not without results. They were able for something other than fighting, even

---

[5] No doubt a reference to J. Huizinga, *The Waning of the Middle Ages*, New York, N.Y., Doubleday Anchor Books, 1954, to cite one of its many editions. The original Netherlandish edition appeared in 1924.

though they are immortalized in our country's history as warlike heroes who sought to construct the fatherland through conflict. They had a large share in the renewal of spiritual life, which they promoted in many areas. Not only did they preside at the great religious plays in the Grote Markt in Brussels, of which we still have the First and Seventh Joy (*bliscap*) of Mary; not only did they patronize more than one Flemish painter, who in an unsurpassed manner recorded the mysteries of religion on canvas and there live on immortally, but they themselves through their subordinate superiors promoted the reform of monastic life and thereby also the spiritual life of the people. In all religious Orders, through their protection and often through their insistence, religious observance was restored, and caused the renewed spirit of the Orders to bud forth in richness of spiritual flowers.

The Modern Devotion continues to linger on and develops further through the use of methodical prayer and the practice of virtue. It becomes more and more an ascetical school. We may regret that mysticism is repelled by it, but we should not see only the dark side; we should not hesitate to acknowledge and appreciate the rich development of methodical prayer and the practice of virtue, which are of great value in the spiritual life. They are not so prominent that we do not see next to them an ascending wave of mystical life, inundating and fructifying the smaller stream of less important phenomena. Was not this the precise time of the appearance of the "Mystical Doctor of the Netherlands," "the *Doctor ecstaticus*, Denis the Carthusian, author of the finest and most exalted treatises, filled with idealistic contemplation of God? Because, unfortunately, he did not write in the language of the Netherlands, he may not have assured himself of a niche in Netherlandish literature as such, but in our spiritual literature, where we also have to attend to the Latin blossoms springing from our native soil, as typical of this period, he appears as a leading figure, as one who climbed to a height a Ruusbroec does not seem to have attained. Denis' works, comprising more than forty volumes, witness to his prolific output, but upon examination also strike one by the exalted flight of thought expressed there.

It is a pity that in this period so much Latin was written, that the example of Ruusbroec was not followed, who knew how to describe these exalted matters in beautiful Netherlandish, but it was the time of Humanism, of growing international communication. The Modern Devotion turned the Netherlands into a focus of spiritual life, and everywhere the Netherlandish level-headed, practical approach to the spiritual life asserted itself. Everywhere, reformers of the spiritual life fan out from the Netherlands over the whole world. With the convents of the Netherlands as a firm base, the reforms in the various Orders spread to the surrounding countries. At no other time, did the Netherlands exercise more spiritual influence. Father Brugman, for instance, appeared not only in northern France, Belgium, the Rhineland, and Westphalia, but outside the narrow boundaries of our country. But similarly, a number of others of all the well-known Orders might be cited. This was bound to lead to a frequent use of the Latin language.

The use of it is no indication of poverty of spirit on the part of the people, but a revelation of a more vital life than ever. This explains how, besides the increase of Latin as a medium, the rhetoricians make their appearance with their philosophical prose, the expression of their native Netherlandish school of philosophy, with Louvain as the center and the various religious schools as vehicles and offshoots. The rejection of philosophy by the school of Geert Grote had been defeated, with the result that, although foreign universities were still frequented, philosophy was cultivated locally in rhetoric circles, and teachers who had been trained abroad were fain to concentrate on questions of local interest. This was under the enduring influence of the still strongly moralizing and logical-didactic Modern Devotion. *Elckerlyc* is a good example.[6] But the *via moderna* here also tempts to a more concrete way of thinking, which by the nature of things leads to one more symbolical and idealistic, no matter how paradoxical this may seem at first sight. If in this period Aristotle is still the dominating figure, gradually the Platonic influence begins to supersede Aristotelian

---

[6] Among editions see for example *Everyman*, New York, Dutton, 1920.

thought – not at once, but gradually, and only in the beginning of the following period decisively. The rise of Denis the Carthusian in mystical contemplation, of such great influence at the end of this era, shows how strong Platonic thought becomes, already in this period. Yet, there is still scarcely any opposition, because Platonic thought here is built only on an Aristotelian foundation of appreciation of true reality. Only later is there also acceptance of the Platonic principle of a more subjective knowledge, built on inner experience and enlightenment. The period is still preponderantly empirical; that is, still built on experience, proceeds from it, and – especially from a point of view of the promotion of methodical prayer and contemplation – is focused on the description and dramatization of the lives of Our Lord and the saints. The effect of contemplation issues, by way of sympathetic attraction, in the outpouring of the heart and to a lesser extent, in intellectual reflection. A typical example is Father Brugman. Next to him, there is Thomas à Kempis with his pious reflections, interspersed with the most ardent effusions. We think further of Hendrik Herp,[7] Dirk Coelde of Münster,[8] Cornelius van Sneek,[9] and the founder of Carmelite nuns, John Soreth.[10] Quite in this framework are the miracle plays, the mystery plays, all the spiritual rhetorician literature. The representation of God that predominates here is that of the God Man, but more than in the previous period interwoven with pious and often compassionate rather than intellectual reflection, exaggeration and legends. A prominent figure here is St. Liduina of Schiedam.[11] The practice of virtue through a gradual, often excessively materialistic following of Christ and desire for conformity with him, promote, first of all, the reform of religious observance, then, however, also a richer and more romantic representation of Christ. The *docta ignorantia* of Nicholas de Cusa,[12]

[7] Hendrik Herp, O.F.M., *d.* 1477.
[8] Dirk Coelde, of Munster, *d.* 1515.
[9] Cornelius van Sneek, O.P., *d.* 1534.
[10] Jean Soreth, O.Carm., *ca.* 1395-1471.
[11] See below, the chapter on St. Liduina
[12] Cardinal Nicholas of Cusa, *d.*1464, famous humanist and reformer.

the bankruptcy of the old concept of the world with the earth as its center, also promote, with regard to the concept of God, the neo-Platonic, negative idea of our knowledge of God, which is again held in honor by Denis the Carthusian. God is seen in Christ as so human that for the real representation of God only negation remains. The way is cleared for the idea that God himself must enlighten and inspire us, in order to achieve true contemplation and adoration of him.

V

If, as I believe, we may call the period of 1425 to 1475 in many respects an age of highest achievement in the spiritual life of the Netherlands, even though, as a result of the recent flourishing of Latin as the medium, the finest literary products are not written in the Netherlandish language, the period around the beginning of the 16th century seems to me of less importance and, in general, a time of decadence, although there are signs which point to approaching renewal.

In this period, the rhetoricians carry on with the dramatization of the spiritual, without rising to profound lyric expression. In their moralizing and didactic works, they are satisfied to preach the usual practice of virtue. Still, the era is not entirely wanting in noble and enthusiastic souls who seek the heights and break with the world. An example is Bertken of Utrecht in her hermitage near the local church in Utrecht; she wrote verses not only melodious in sound but also profound in thought and also occasionally bursting into flames of emotion.[13] But on the whole, what one finds is really ordinary, good, not bad, but nothing extraordinary. Most outstanding is Cornelis Everaert[14] with his plays, which do not lack attractiveness, yet excel more in graphic wealth than in the bright effusion of a heart wounded by love. Virtue is learned and is no doubt practiced, but ecstasy is missing, and life is regulated

---

[13] Suster Bertken, *d.* 1514.
[14] Cornelis Everaert, *d.* 1556.

and measured to avoid being special and unusual. There seems to be much formality, which is also shared by the spiritual life. True, there are still focuses of a higher life. The Carthusians especially maintain their influence. There is a craving for depth and intimacy, for a more conscious and spontaneous dedication to God and the divine, but there are yet no inspiring figures in that direction. There are as yet only rising voices, calling for more love, more desire, more spirit.

A Dirk Coelde of Münster especially makes himself the herald of love and preaches interiority and renewal, but his word does not arouse the echo he had so earnestly hoped. The Observant Movement around the middle of the century, which was so powerful and generally vibrant, flared up only temporarily, if powerfully. It declined around the end of the century almost as quickly as it had suddenly risen to an unprecedented height around the middle of the century. Brugman had already written his *Spiegel der Onvolmaaktheid* (Mirror of Imperfection) as a warning. His concern became reality. The bloom of the reformed convents faded, at least was not as hardy as was expected at the beginning of the Observant Movement. Still, the conventual reform continued, and in this matter the Netherlands were not without influence on the surrounding countries, but toward the end of the century reform came to a standstill and gradually slid into decadence. Of the convents of the period very little scandal can probably be reported, but they did not live up to high ideals.

The same may be said of the further methodizing of mental prayer, which was exaggerated. Brugman already showed a leaning toward this with his endless lists of kinds of virtue and vice, but at the end of the century, a Wessel Gansfort[15] and after him a John Mombaer[16] systematized the spiritual life in an even more minute manner. The *scalae* (ladders), *graden* (degrees), *trappen* (steps) run riot and are applied to Holy Communion, meditation on the

---

[15] Jan Wessel Gansfort, *d.* 1489.
[16] Jan Mombaer, canon of Sint-Agnietenberg, *d.*1501.

Lord's Passion, all religious meditation.[17] Wessel Gansfort met John Mombaer in the Sint-Agnietenberg, and the former transformed the latter into a teacher wholly taken up with method in the spiritual life. The Carthusians, too, seem receptive to this trend, though perhaps they were the first to incline to a more interior depiction of the divine in us. Under the influence of the new philosophic trends, a subjective idea of the spiritual life, a personal determination of what unites us to God, gained strength, until at length a gradually increasing number of souls, abandoning the forms that had been handed down, turned down new ways of union with God.

What has been said so far should not be construed as a condemnation of methodical prayer. It is a merit of the Netherlandish Modern Devotion that it forcefully insisted on that form of prayer and showed the way to it. At this very time, we see an Abbot de Cisneros of Montserrat[18] introducing the Netherlandish devotion into Spain, with the intention especially of calling attention to methodical meditation besides liturgical prayer. When we see the salutary effects of the activity of John Mombaer in France, we understand that what he perhaps exaggerated in his writings, he nevertheless fruitfully propagated as a general idea.

In a few previous articles, titled *Nederdalingen*, we have sufficiently indicated the importance of methodical progress in the spiritual life, and how the idea which is at its basis is continually renewed.[19] This does not mean that the Modern Devotion with its practice of the virtues and its methodizing did not eventually bring on a certain rigidity, a certain formality and exteriority which called for renewal. It should not surprise us that in the beginning of the 16th century, a reaction set in that broke with the old routine, called externals useless, disparaged good works, in order to assign the first place in the spiritual life to intimate union

---

[17] See below, the chapter, "Gerard Zerbolt of Zutphen (1367-1398)."

[18] Garcia Ximénez de Cisneros, 1455-1510.

[19] We know of no other articles on this subject besides that on Gerard Zerbolt, already referred to.

with God, faith in him, his grace before our works. Like many reactions, it quickly outstripped its goal and discarded much that could have been saved. In nascent Protestantism, we can observe in many a sincere desire for interiorizing the spiritual life, for eliminating many externals, which had become a hindrance rather than a help; but it is also whole-heartedly to be regretted that many went too far and, instead of renewing, destroyed the spiritual life. A great deal of opposition arose against the old ways. A reaction in favor of the interior life occurred, but also a terrible decline, because many under pretext of reform joined battle against all forms of religious life. Not only in the ranks of the Protestant reformers is meanwhile a tendency to interior life alive, but also in Catholic circles where vitality still lurked, and the expression of the interior life was not forcibly suppressed, a notable interiorizing of the spiritual life arose. In this respect, the Counter-Reformation is given too much credit. Fortunately, in the spiritual life much endures, which was not touched or damaged by the Reformation, but must be considered a natural further development of what was alive in the Church. That there are tendencies to be found which are related to Protestantism cannot be denied. Is this phenomenon itself also not a child of the times, related again to notable currents in other countries? The return in France to the Gospel; in literature generally, the return to the sources; the new establishment of man on the foundation of life in antiquity – these are trends which also inspired Luther to preach a return to the pure, unadulterated Gospel, to the practices of the early Church, to the rejection of much that had been added subsequently. In our country, also, in a time when there was as yet no mention of the Reformation, an interesting trend arose that was drawn to evangelical living. Worthy of mention in this respect is the circle of Oisterwijk, comprising Nicholas van Esch, Maria van Oisterwijk, and the writer of the *Evangelische peerle* (The Evangelical Pearl) – all living and writing under the influence of the Carthusians of Cologne. The imitation of Christ becomes interiorized into an experience of Christ: not a Christ for us, as in the first period of the *Imitation*; not a Christ with us, as in the subsequent perhaps too difficult and too little interior period around the end of the century; but Christ within us is the leading idea. The God who fills us with his grace, leads us through his inspiration, with whom we must associate in the still solitude of our heart – this is now the ideal. This interiorization of the spiritual life has as a consequence that methodical prayer is also renewed and perfected. The Carthusians of Cologne and Trier enthusiastically write to each other that in Mainz, Peter Faber is making known a method of prayer in the *Exercises,* which surpasses everything of the sort we have ever had, and they also introduce both Canisius and Nicholas van Esch, who are under their guidance, to the method. The religious strife, it is true, stimulates the love of God and gives occasion to fierce polemics, but also to beautiful utterances of faith and love. The *Refreinen* (Refrains) of Anna Bijns[20] are probably the finest, though she is by no means the only representative of the genre. When Luther and his school appeal to Tauler, and the *Deutsche Theologie* is published by Luther as a condensed version of Tauler, Canisius produced as his first work an edition of Tauler, from which Tauler's significance for this time becomes eminently clear. Besides the propaganda for the sacred Scriptures in Protestant circles, we see appear among the Catholics themselves two translations of the entire Bible: besides the better known and more official one of Louvain, there is the no less important though less circulated one by the pastor of the St. Nicholas Church in Utrecht, the Carmelite, Alexander Blanckaert, published in Cologne.[21] We may call the period from 1525 to 1575 the "evangelical period."

The Middle Ages are hereby closed. The Reformation introduced a new period, which contains so many contrasts that a synthesis becomes much more extensive in scope. We think we must postpone until later an attempt at a tentative synthesis.

---

[20] Anna Bijns, *d.* 1575, poet, native of Antwerp.
[21] Alexander Blanckaert (Lat.: *Candidus*), *d.*, 1555.

The basic idea of the Spiritual Life according to St. Augustine[1]

Doctor gratiae. This honorary title of St. Augustine already tells us that he was unable to contemplate Man in isolation, but that he who liked to plumb the depth and breadth of relationships, delighted to contemplate Man in his relation to God, with whom he saw him bound with the bonds of the most intimate union.

Tracing the mysteries of that union was his favorite task, and the love with which he undertook that contemplation caused him to intuit and surmise, to know and understand more of this mystery of love than any other of God's saints and lovers, at least in so far as it was given to them to share this with others.

So, St. Augustine has become the doctor of the life of grace, as well as the master of the spiritual life. There lies the secret of his mastery, acknowledged and honored throughout the ages. St. Augustine was rich and prolific in word and deed. His works follow one upon another with great speed, and in his works we continually meet new ideas, original images. There is a richness, a profusion of metaphor and simile that overwhelm one, and when a question seems to be exhausted, cause new viewpoints to be discovered, new light to be cast upon the subject. Just as, after the example of Plotinus, his description of the divine rule of the world unfolds for us the works of God in a great painting, in a grandiose panorama, so also his doctrine about our spiritual life is like a colorful mosaic, in which tiny stone by tiny stone are inserted and glitter at us, image after image rise up at us to a wondrous group,

---

[1] From the *Thomistisch Tijdschrift voor Katholiek Kultuurleven*, 1 (1930), 681-701.

like Angelico's rows singing and dancing angels, of whom we dare
not say who is the Strong One, Michael, invisibly leading and
conducting all before the throne of the Lord. St. Augustine's lessons and images of the spiritual life are many.
Efforts of many kinds have attempted to synthesize his doctrine
concerning this point. For most of them, this doctrine is to be
summarized with the one word: love. To express this idea, iconog-
raphy has by preference represented the saint pen in hand, writing
his beautiful works, while his left hand offers God his heart,
pierced by a shaft of love. Love led him in his work and love made
him write so beautifully about life, which is preferably described
in his words as a life of love.

It cannot be denied that St. Augustine assigns first place to love,
that he preaches love as the bond which binds us to perfection. It
would be difficult to point to a doctor of the spiritual life who lays
greater emphasis on the beauty and necessity of love. Thus, St.
Augustine as a matter of course becomes the grand master and
leader of the schools of a more affective tendency.

And yet, to my mind it is not there that the key lies to the great
synthesizer of Hippo's mysterious teaching about our spiritual life,
our ascent to God, our union with God. No matter how great the
significance that St. Augustine assigns to love, that love in its basis
as well as in its driving force, according to his idea and presentation, has caused us to discover a mystery that reveals its wondrous
might: our oneness with God.

Oneness with God touched Augustine's heart, and the contemplation of that oneness caused him to develop ever more strongly
the consciousness of it, in order to adhere to God in the awareness
of that oneness, and to dissolve ourselves in God with an untamed
force, ever more untamed in proportion as the awareness of that
oneness becomes more lively, in proportion as nature better understands that it is established in God, that it is created in oneness
with God, and that the obscuring of that awareness has become
the origin of all evil. As soon as Man lost sight of his divinity, he
could listen to the seduction of the devil, to the temptation of the
pride that propelled him to his own divinization.

In his teaching about original sin, in his fight against Pelagius, this concept has already grown in Augustine. Against the exaltation of human nature in itself, the glorification of the absolute in man's nature, he placed the glory of the relative, the lustre of man's relation to God. What is Man for St. Augustine, if he can only contemplate him in the abstract vision of his independence, his autonomy? He needs to see man in the fullness of life which is rooted in God as in a rich soil that bestows true fruitfulness; man shone upon and illuminated by the sun which surrounds and encircles him with its ray; man filled inside and outside with the might and glory of God. The vision of Man in the closest union with God and in the greatest dependence on him caused Augustine to turn his head from the prideful stoic ideas which made everything be expected of an all too rigid egoism, to which Man by nature was supposed to be called and obligated. For that reason, God gave Man the will and the power over himself. That power he was to exercise with all the strength which his nature had placed in his power. He was to rule himself with severity, repress his evil inclinations forcefully, and so keep himself free from all wrong. Man should be conscious of that might and that strength and not expect of God's help or grace that which God enabled him to do by nature. Pelagius would not hear of an original sin, which was supposed to have broken that strength and made necessary God's salvation and action of grace. Preaching such a doctrine struck Pelagius as dangerous, because it must cause Man to lose trust in himself and would confirm him in a temerarious trust in God.

How differently St. Augustine sees Man! True, for him there is in fallen Man nothing but weakness, corruption, and misery, but that dark shadow is not able to hide the light which bores through the clouds. However injured and wounded through original sin, nature has retained its receptivity to the help and grace of God, even if darkness has intruded, but a darkness which does not betoken a lack of receptivity to light; on the contrary, it cries out for the rays of God's sun of grace, in order in the light of that sun to be re-created to a new lustre, a new life.

That more humble concept of self raises Man to the spheres of the Godhead and makes him find in God the strength to lead a new and higher life than, left to himself, if that were conceivable, he would be able to attain. United to God before original sin, after that sin he was again united to God through the redemption and was plentifully restored to his former glory. That glory is none other than his union with the Godhead: more than an external union, it is a union which God makes a principle of mutual action with Man, which makes Man inconceivable unless he lives in and through God. This has by no means implied the denial of the autonomy of man; only that St. Augustine has managed so brilliantly to unite the autonomy of human nature with the need for the divine cooperation and help; has known how to picture the relation to God as a bond of the most intimate union and oneness without falling into the pantheistic concepts of the Neo-Platonists. This achievement has made him throughout the whole of the Middle Ages the highly respected and generally followed master of the spiritual and mystical life, whose doctrine concerning grace explained the teaching of Pseudo-Dionysius in the correct sense, and made the lovers of God so receptive to it. And not only in the Middle Ages but also today, he is still the *doctor gratiae*, who even in the most exalted expressions of the mystical life proceeding from the ordinary order of grace, remains the leader bestowed and enlightened by God. Our Lord's statement that without him we can do nothing is understood by St. Augustine, not as an elimination of our own activity, even less as an impossibility to arrive at beatitude because it is entirely dependent on God's grace; he sees God as the infinitely good bestower of all good, who overwhelms us with his benefits, about whom it would be the greatest injustice to his goodness to imagine that he could withhold the help someone might need. However, Man must cooperate with the grace that is given to everyone, and in that possibility of cooperating with God St. Augustine sees the greatest glory of our nature, otherwise so weak and enfeebled by original sin. The proper understanding of this cooperation saved St. Augustine from the quietistic conclusions which, already in his time and also in later ages, some have drawn from St. Augustine's glorification of the action of God and the necessity of grace which he preached. Those who have called upon St. Augustine in this sense have to their detriment neglected to read what this same great doctor has written about the cooperation of Man with the indispensable action of God. Particularly when he writes about the gift of perseverance, it becomes abundantly clear that although he is speaking there about a gift, he by no means at the same time leaves out of consideration steeling of the will, control of self, willing and doing good with all one's strength. But in the background of this scenario we always find God, who takes his pleasure in the fact that Man uses the strength given him with such overflowing goodness, seizes the strong hand of God, in order, thereby led and supported, but with no less exertion of his own powers, to perform good works.

So we understand that for St. Augustine the spiritual life, the living and striving for perfection, could be nothing else than an ascent to God, an ever closer union with God, an ever stronger consciousness that in our oneness with God we must see our most exalted glory and at the same time our greatest perfection, our strength. Our concept of that oneness is too weak and vague, particularly much too barren. When the saint preaches and glorifies love to the extent that many think that for him love is the summing up of the spiritual life, then we must have a proper understanding of the sense in which he speaks of it. When the soul becomes aware of what God means for it, then it can do nothing else than cling fast to him, fly into his arms from a sense of self preservation, cherish and love him as the source of all good, and unite itself to him ever more intimately. For love is not something original, predisposed; it springs out of the deepest ground of God's union with Man. God has fashioned a relationship with Man of such a kind that Man can neither be nor live without him, and his goodness made him unite himself so intimately with Man that Man not only has life but has it in the most abundant measure. Thus, God constituted himself a good for Man, which Man can never sufficiently appreciate, the contemplation of which must necessarily inflame him with love, to a love which is a necessary

consequence of the realization that one can fully live only in union
with God, or rather in bringing to full fruition that union which,
on God's side, is constant, but which we, alas, on our part hinder
in its completion in countless ways.
Toward that union with God we are *viatores*, travelers, who
ascend to it. To attain it, we must allow ourselves to be led by an
appreciation of that highest good, to be led by love. Our life is a
way to God, and only as we draw near to him, unite ourselves ever
more intimately with him, approach him in the inmost region of
our soul, are we good travellers. We can never be united to God
in a sufficiently intimate manner. Our love can never rest satisfied.
Our self-knowledge, our examination of conscience will always tell
us that we are still living too far removed from God and must ever
again turn to God in humility and trust, in order that he may
accompany us ever further on our life's journey. The motto that
Bl. Ruusbroec once chose for his main work, *The Spiritual Espousals*, (which we would like to rephrase as "the bridal gown for the
marriage of the soul"): "See, the Bridegroom comes, go forth to
meet him," we could also set as a motto above the works of St.
Augustine on the spiritual life. God is the Bridegroom of the soul,
united to it by bonds as intimate as those of marriage, so that both
are one. The soul must keep her eye fixed on God and see how he
comes to her to accomplish that union. But she should not remain
quietly seated until he is near her; she must go forth to meet him.
This ascent to him is her love. Thus, we can see in love the bond
of perfection, in so far as the desire for union with God therein
finds expression. But to truly understand that love we must, in
order to penetrate the spirit of St. Augustine, understand that love
in the sense that God and the soul are attuned to each other, a
oneness wonderfully conceived by God's wisdom and goodness of
two autonomous entities who, although remaining themselves, see
in the union with each other the crown and at the same time the
ground of their mutual love. In this sense, God, by enclosing himself in Man as co-principle of his being and his works and by
pouring himself into human nature, also poured into that nature
love for himself as a gift, without which that nature could not be

for God what he in his goodness wished to make of it. Saint Augustine has God say: Love me and you will possess me, because you cannot love me without possessing me. It is as though he wanted to say that to us our love seems to be the point of departure of our ascent to God, but in reality our oneness with Him is the ground of that love. In the practice of love, we shall come to realize and develop in ourselves the consciousness that we are powerless without God, that he is the deepest ground of our being and actions, that he is the only one who deserves to be loved, the highest good, the only good in itself, which however causes its goodness to be shared. All that shares in that goodness, that may be receptive of that goodness must come to realize that it exists for no other reason than to receive that goodness and to remain united to that source from which it is sprung. If the weight of bodies may be explained, says the saint, as the manifestation of the attraction they exercise on each other, then the weight of our soul is our love of God to whom we are irresistibly attracted, because we belong with God, because he wants to be with us and has so made us that only in our union with him are we complete, are we what we are.

And if that truth applies to each of us, then it goes without saying that we must first see in our neighbor, as in ourselves, the God who lives in him, comes to us in him. That is why St. Augustine speaks of the love of our neighbor as identical with our love of God. In God, specifically in God-made-man, in Christ, we all form one mystical body. Not to love one's brothers would be like not loving the body of Christ. Not to love the body of Christ is not to love Christ, who is its head. And not to love Christ would be not to love God, the Father of Christ. St. Augustine also recalls Christ's word that the commandment to love one's neighbor was equated by God himself with the commandment to love him. The idea that we are all one in God and rediscover each other in God occurs very often in St. Augustine; it dominates his whole line of thought. God is the center of all life and being, in which we all meet each other as in our common point of departure.

St. Augustine is the great guide in the spiritual life. Throughout the ages, men have had recourse to his teaching, have gone to God by his hand. But among the many, the countless many, who have had St. Augustine as their guide to God, perhaps no one has better understood the profound meaning of that guidance and more trenchantly expressed it than our Hadewijch. It may seem paradoxical, when we see her rejecting precisely St. Augustine, but that is completely in keeping with his teaching. Hadewijch clearly had the highest respect for St. Augustine. If anyone were to lead her to God, it would be Augustine, but she refuses to go to God by his hand, in order to rediscover Augustine in God himself and with him to enjoy God. She accepts St. Augustine only as a gift of God, designated by him as a playmate. Only in and through his union with God does he have meaning for her. Union with God is the touchstone by which she tests his guides. How can someone bring us to God in whom union with God is not reflected? Saint Augustine reduces pastoral care, preaching, to one thing: leading souls to God, awakening in them the consciousness that they have been created by God. Religion, which he likes to call devotion, in short, consists in nothing else than striving for God, love of him, effective striving toward union with him. Therein love, therein also devotion and religion, find their crown. All prayer is a yearning for that union to the extent that the soul already possesses it and has become conscious of it. In this connection, we can understand that one who knows how to pray properly, as St. Augustine assures us, will know how to live properly, because it is unthinkable that where love reveals itself in prayer as a striving of the soul to God, this same striving would not find expression in deeds. Praying and working, the soul is in the same passionate pursuit of God.

For the soul, the awareness of that union is a source of great joy, disturbed only by the realization that it is constantly weaned away from that union by its own weakness and the temptation of the world. The soul would like to be in heaven, never more to be parted from God, but to a certain extent, it already enjoys a foretaste of heaven here on earth, when it knows it possesses God and by an act of love enjoys this highest Good in itself. Life for a soul that knows herself in her relation to God becomes a blessing, to the extent that she already enjoys God to a certain degree and at the same time a severe trial, because she does not yet fully possess him and, worse yet, is continually drawn away from him. Nothing, in short, can bring her rest and happiness but the thought of God's goodness, which already holds her joined to Him. The soul then throws herself completely in God's arms, surrenders herself entirely to him, to arrive by the way he has chosen at complete union with him. But this rest is hardly our lot here on earth. The intellect cannot understand God as he is; we actually know only what he is not. That negative character of our limited knowledge of God, the only one we can really attain, for God is unutterable to our faculty of knowing, causes us constantly to long for the more positive knowledge of heaven, where we will behold him as he is. And what applies to the intellect obtains no less with regard to the will. In spite of the strictest self-control, the suppression of all besides God that can tempt it and try to draw it away from God, in spite of the most faithful practice of virtue, the will can only briefly arrive at the rest of soul which is the immediate introduction to the vision and the enjoyment of God, deriving from that vision. Ruusbroec's *"crighen en ontbliven"* (having and lacking)] is borrowed from Augustine's never satisfied craving for God. When the soul thinks she is enjoying God, she feels her at the same time hopelessly far removed from him in knowledge and love; yet only again to understand in that feeling of separation that God, so far away, is yet close to her, lives in her innermost being, and asks only that a dwelling be kept free there for him. That image of the soul as the abode of God is particularly dear to Augustine, but he likes to make it rather mean, quite in keeping with the truth, that God is at once the abode and paternal home of the soul. The soul must find God in herself but no less herself in God. From this favorite idea of the holy father Augustine, Hendrik Mande of Windesheim borrowed the thought which he developed in his *Boecksen der vercieringhe onser inwendigher woninghe* (Little Book of the Ornamenting of our Interior Dwelling). So also have many others who have pictured the spiritual life in the same spirit.

If in this connection, one mystery of revelation was dear to St. Augustine, and in the contemplation of that mystery the basic idea of St. Augustine again finds expression, it was (it cannot be otherwise) the mystery of the Incarnation of the Son of God, by which God made himself visible and in the most intimate manner united himself to human nature. St. Augustine sees it especially as a union with human nature in its Platonic sense of oneness, and although he by no means overlooks the material body of Christ, he nevertheless prefers to contemplate his mystical body, in which we are all one and united with him. To him, this union is, as it were, the foundation of the other. Our union with Christ should follow his example, should make us like him. Augustine sees everything as mutually connected and preferably in as profound a connection as possible. In this way, he has really deepened the concept of the spiritual life, and it is certainly regrettable that the once so flourishing Netherlandish school of the *Devotio Moderna*, which originally attached itself so strongly to Augustine, should under the influence of the times have failed to retain that interiority and profundity. May our own times, which have again turned to St. Augustine for counsel, learn of that counsel that precisely that profundity and interiority, that perception of fundamental bonds, and attention to the highest relationships constitute the strength of St. Augustine's doctrine and mastery.

I must call attention to one final point, now that I am speaking about Augustine's preference for the image of the mystical oneness of Christ with us, the members of that Body, Holy Church. That is, that he also sees therein the ground for Mary's motherhood over us. At the moment that the Holy Spirit made Mary the mother of the body of Christ, he made her the mother of his Mystical Body, of all of us, who are its members. But at the same time, Mary is herself a member of that Holy Body, and we are one with her in it, so that those words can be applied to us that whoever does the will of the Father may be called the mother of Christ, with Mary gives life to this Body of Christ; life, nevertheless, that we receive from Christ and cause to live in us. Thus, Mary is our mother and at the same time our model for receiving Christ in us. If later a St. John of the Cross will see in the incarnation of the Son of God in Mary's womb the image and model of the mystical life, then centuries before him St. Augustine was the masterful expositor of that idea. And then we have therein a new proof of how well he John understood the mystical life, and how oneness with God may rightly be called the basic idea of the spiritual life according to St. Augustine.

Saint Augustine seen by
Denis the Carthusian[1]

Now that voices are everywhere heard paying grateful and joyful homage to St. Augustine and making him come fully alive for us after 1500 years; now that writers and speakers of every land and tongue vie with each other to give him praise; now that I have been invited to contribute an essay to this commemorative volume, I hardly know what I can add to honor the great Doctor of the Church that has not already been more thoroughly and better said by others. The whole world is full of his praise.

Gladly do I range myself among the long ranks of his devotees, for I am animated by no less reverence and esteem than they. At the same time, I would prefer to remain silent and quiet, for what I might manage to say would add little to that chorus of praise.

Therefore, I shall let another speak for me with a voice the like of which no one in The Netherlands has raised before or after him; a voice that understands the saint, because it rings true to him and reminds us of his words and richness of thought, his countless works and teachings. He who achieved such prominence in The Netherlands that he came to be called the Augustine of Holland may justly be added to the chorus of his devotees on this centenary and at the same time remind us that the praises of St. Augustine were sung no less enthusiastically five hundred years ago than they are now.

Of Pope Eugene IV it is told that in an introduction to a work of Denis the Carthusian he declared, "The Church should rejoice

[1] From Miscellanea Aurgustiniana; gedenkboek samengesteld uit verhandelingen over S. Augustinus bij de viering van zijn zalig overlijden vóór 15 eeuwen, CDXXX-MCMXXX [n. p.] PP. Augustijnen der Nederlandsche provincie, 1930.

to have such a son."[2] This joy may again be ours, because we now have access not to just one volume but to the long series of his works, where we may find what he, the *doctor ecstaticus*, has to say about our great St. Augustine.

The amount the Carthusian from Roermond[3] read and assimilated is beyond belief, and among the writers whom he eagerly took in hand St. Augustine holds a very prominent place. He cites St. Augustine very often, but not always literally; with the relatively defective tools he had at his disposal he had to depend largely on memory, but by comparison we again have to admire his wonderful memory.

If we call St. Augustine the preeminent *doctor gratiae*, the enlightened teacher of the ways of God with men, the name which Denis acquired as the *doctor ecstaticus* shows quite clearly that he must have spontaneously sought the counsel of this elucidator of the divine mysteries.

"Exalted contemplative and most fruitful writer," my Carmelite confrère, Arnold de Bost, calls him, "united to God, yet working tirelessly for humanity; exhausting himself in works of fraternal charity, yet always attending to conversation with God: *in otio negotiosus et in negotio otiosus*."[4]

There is no lack of other witnesses. The Oratorian, Thomas Bozius, is of the opinion that the Low Countries may be proud of a man such as hardly any other country or any other time have produced.[5] St. Francis de Sales recommends the writings of

---

[2] Odoricus Raynaldus, *Annales Ecclesiastici*, Romae,1663, t. 19, ad annum 1471, no. 83.

[3] Denys Rijkel, ca. 1402-1471.

[4] Arnoldus Bostius, O.Carm., *De illustribus viris Ordinis Carthusiensis*, ch. 39. He describes Denis here in a remarkable manner in terms taken from St. Augustine, where in the 19th chapter of *De civitate Dei* he calls the contemplative life *vita otiosa* and the active life *vita negotiosa*. Denis himself refers us to this place in St. Augustine where he speaks of the union of the contemplative and the active life. *Enarratio in cap. X Lucae*, art. 28, *Opera omnia*, tom. XII, p. 25.

[5] Thomas Bozius, *De signis Ecclesiae Dei libri XXIV* (2 v.,Coloniae Agrippinae, 1626), II, 51.

Denis in words that remind us of a St. Augustine, when he reckons them the best that have been written about the love of God, inspired as they are by the noblest devotion.[6] The rule of the Society of Jesus lists the *Opuscula* of Denis among the works the master of novices must consult for their formation.[7] Cardinal Manning praises the works of Denis for their particular beauty and true doctrine, in which depth of meaning and precision of expression, proper to scholasticism, are paired with enlightenment of the spirit and sweet satisfaction of mystical theology.[8] Finally, let us quote the words of the Dutch historian, Prof. W. Moll, who writes in his *Johannes Brugman*, "Among the eminent men who were an ornament to The Netherlands in the 15th century, Denis occupied an outstanding place, and it would be difficult to understand how in our time, in place of being known and famous together with or even above Thomas a Kempis and others, he is relatively unknown, had not his works, no matter how numerous, almost become literary rarities. But neglected as he now is, he was all the more esteemed by the best of his contemporaries. Denis was known here in our land and throughout Europe."[9]

Meantime, things have changed. His works, it is true, have by no means yet become common coin of the realm, but a new edition of his writings has been produced, which has made them available to those who wish to make their acquaintance. In forty-three large volumes the works of Denis the Carthusian once again lie before us, in order, thus collected, again to inspire amazement at his tremendous energy.[10]

---

[6] St. Francis de Sales, *Philothea*, pt. II, ch. 17.

[7] *Regula Societatis Jesu*, Romae, 1582, p. 99.

[8] Henry Edward Manning, *The Internal Mission of the Holy Ghost*, London, 1883, p. xi.

[9] W. Moll, *Johannes Brugman en het godsdienstig leven onzer vaderen in de vijftiende eeuw* (2 v., Amsterdam, 1854), I, 71.

[10] *Doctoris Ecstatici D. Dionysii Cartusiani opera omnia, in unum corpus digesta ad fidem editionum Coloniensium.* Cura et labore monachorum sacri Ordinis Cartusiensis, Monstrolii, 1896-1901; Tornaci, 1902-1913, 43v.

In them, we learn to know Denis as philosopher, theologian, exegete, and spiritual writer. In each of these four capacities, although he cites a great many other writers, he seems to have attached the greatest value to the authority of St. Augustine. Although perhaps St. Jerome enjoys greater authority with regard to Sacred Scripture and pseudo-Dionysius the Areopagite with regard to mysticism, after these, he accords the place of honor to St. Augustine. If we take all his works together, then St. Augustine is for him the universal doctor, whose opinion he always takes into consideration with the greatest respect.

Although Denis, who also reproached himself with having neglected God in his youth and looked upon his entry into the Carthusian Order as a farewell to the idle pleasures of the world, as a conversion to God, sees in St. Augustine an example for his own life,[11] he does not emphasize this aspect of Augustine. For him, St. Augustine is above all the God-given teacher and guide on the way which love has traced for humanity.[12]

One might argue about what constituted the basic idea of Augustine's synthesis of the spiritual life. In an article I contributed to the special number on St. Augustine of the *Thomistisch Tijdschrift*, I attempted to show that love, which is so often regarded as the summary of St. Augustine's doctrine, has deeper roots in his idea of our oneness with God.[13] Even granted this to be so, love remains its natural fruit and external manifestation, and

---

[11] See, for instance, *Exhortatorium noviciorum*, art. 4; *Opera*, vol. 38, p. 531; *De vita et fine solitarii*, bk. 1, art. 30, *ibid.*, p. 337. So high does he here each time exalt St. Augustine that he proposes him only as an example to be followed from afar, endowed with graces in such a special manner that, unless God favors us with extraordinary graces, we are not in a condition to attain the holiness of a St. Augustine. On the other hand, however, he sees himself so graced that he cannot praise God's goodness enough. *De munificentia et beneficiis Dei*; *Opera*, vol. 34, p. 295-325, *passim*.

[12] He calls him among other things the "greatest doctor of all" in his treatise, *Contra pluralitatem beneficiorum ex dictis authenticis*, in which he cites in succession the witness of many saints and learned writers, among them the "*magni doctores*," Sts. Thomas and Bonaventure; *Opera*, vol. 39, p. 256f.

[13] *Thomistisch Tijdschrift*, 1 (1930), 681-701, reproduced in this volume.

the doctrine of our divinity can be made to coincide with that of the love which springs and flows from it in God as well as ourselves.

If Denis regards Augustine as the model of the most ardent love of God and the incarnate Son of God,[14] nevertheless two distinct attitudes, seen as exchangeable, clearly appear. On the one hand, Denis considers Augustine's love to be the basis of his enlightenment by God; on the other hand, the great graces, the enlightenment bestowed on him, inflame his love. To Denis, he is one chosen by God, whom God draws to and unites with himself, but one who cooperates with that grace, glowing with the purest love of God. Entirely in keeping with Augustine's own ideas, Denis sees Augustine not in himself but ever with God in the background; or rather, with God who lives and is active in him.[15]

A beautiful idea of Denis is that in Augustine God is with his Church, and that in Augustine we should first see God who is wonderful in his saints and who bestows these on his Church, not so much to make it great and holy through them but as a proof of its holiness, a sign that he is with his Church. In this context, Denis says that Augustine did not make the Church great but that the Church made Augustine great, and that to us his greatness consists in the fact that the Church speaks in and through him.[16] Here, I again recall the words of Pope Eugene about Denis, that the Church should rejoice to have such a son.[17] This thought is also found in Denis with regard to St. Augustine. He is a son of the Church, sprung from her bosom like a lovely flower, led to God and bound to him by her union with God.

[14] He continually refers to him with a name characteristic of St. Augustine himself: "*ardens Dei amator.*" See *Opera*, vol. 39, p. 256f.

[15] *De laude et commendatione vitae solitariae*, art.8, *Opera*, vol. 8, p. 336.

[16] *De praeconio sive laude Ordinis Cartusiensis*, art. 8, *Opera*. vol. 38, p. 425; *Directorium vitae nobilium*, art. 33, *Opera*, vol. 37, p. 599. In the appendix to the treatise he calls him, "*beatissimus doctor et lingua Ecclesiae illuminatissimus et profundissimus Augustinus*," *Opera*, vol. 40, p. 311.

[17] See note 2.

In Augustine, the Church speaks; of her he is the "tongue" or "language." He speaks on behalf of the Church and brings us her doctrine, her words. In this way, he guides and nourishes us and as father takes the place of our holy mother. He is entirely in the service of the Church, and Denis strikingly points out that long before Pope Gregory, Augustine, quite in keeping with the task God entrusted to him, called himself the servant of the servants of God.[18]

Therein lies Denis's recognition of the providential significance of St. Augustine for the Church. God who loves the Church, God who loves us, driven by his love, has bestowed graces and privileges on Augustine; and that election, that love of God for him and us, or rather, for all of us together who are one in the Church, has made Augustine the greatest of all the Church Fathers, the teacher of God's most profound mysteries, and at the same time, the ardently loving animator of the spiritual life, the unrecognized propelling force which drives us to the Source of our love.

Entirely in line with this reflection is Denis' wonder at the way St. Augustine could delight in tracing and contemplating God's decrees and providence with regard to the salvation and redemption of the human race. The delightful satisfaction which the contemplation of God's wisdom afforded him left him always unfulfilled; he could never sufficiently appreciate and praise God's work in the salvation of humanity.[19]

From this contemplation flows St. Augustine's great love for Christ, our Savior, in whom in the first place he sees God, come to unite himself and lead us to himself. No matter how prominent the humanity of Christ was in the mind of the devout in those times in which Denis lived, still under the influence of the Modern Devotion, it was the influence of St. Augustine especially that made them, and more than them, Denis the Carthusian, to keep their eyes fixed on the divine nature united to the human and on

---

[18] *Enarratio in tertiam regulam S. Francisci*, art. 2, *Opera*, vol. 38, p. 442.

[19] See De contemplatione, bk. II, art. 4, *Opera*, vol. 41, p. 229f., and especially *Enarratio in cap. 7 Lucae*, art. 18, *Opera*, vol. 11, p. 546.

the operation of grace. With the strong exteriorization which the Modern Devotion underwent in the course of the 14th century, as a result of the excessive emphasis on the human element in mystical union, the increasing tendency to replace mysticism with asceticism, while in the design of God it was intended to be the normal preparation for this never to be overlooked ideal, we may regard Denis as a flower which in all its twisting and turning follows and points to the position of the sun and reflects its glory.[20] This we may well ascribe to his veneration of St. Augustine, because he quotes him by preference in reference to that contemplation. We could also say that they met each other in that desire of their souls for God and in that enjoyment of beholding God.

To see God was for both the ideal. And in his longing to attain that ideal, Denis must have seen in Augustine not only a model but a teacher as well. He is partial to Augustine's, *De videndo Deo*, and in various works comes back to it, as if especially in the beautiful but difficult art of seeing God Augustine's guidance was for him of the highest value. He quotes this work particularly to confirm with the authority of St. Augustine that it is possible to be raised to the sight of God already in this life, albeit in a mystical state, in which the life of the senses loses its influence on the spiritual faculties through the strong action of spiritual forces. Following St. Augustine, Denis traces the way in which this special gift of grace fell to the lot of Moses and Paul, not in order to confine this gift to these two, but because in the opinion of both authors the Sacred Scriptures attest to this gift in the case of Moses and Paul, while such great certainty does not exist with regard to others.[21]

---

[20] In his discussion of the Incarnation Denis quotes the beautiful expression of Augustine: "*Conditor solis conditus sub sole,*" while he calls the incarnate Word the first of creatures. He explains this further with the words of St. Augustine. Placed with Christ under the sun, we look up to the creator of the sun. See *Enarratio in cap. I libri Ecclesiastici,* art. 1, *Opera,* vol. 8, p. 5.

[21] *Enarratio in cap. XII Numerorum,* art. 21, *Opera,* vol. 2, p. 390; *Enarratio in cap. XLV Libri Ecclesiastici,* art. 45, *Opera,* vol. 8, p. 296f; *Enarratio in cap. I Joannis,* art. 5, *Opera,* vol. 12, p. 295; more fully in *Enarratio in cap. XII epistolae II B. Pauli ad Corinthios,* art. 12, *Opera,* vol. 13, p. 254f.

With regard to Augustine himself, Denis sees in him not only a providential figure in whom the action of God visibly, although only indirectly, shines forth and is revealed; he sees him also as gifted with the grace of direct enlightenment by God and for that reason so firm and unshaken in the faith and our reliable guide.[22] It may seem unusual that he relates these graces and enlightenments to Holy Communion and regards them as its fruit. But this again is quite in keeping with the all-pervasive idea that God's love is revealed in the redemption of the human race, and that that redemption fills humans with love of God. That redemption is unthinkable without the incarnation of God's Son, who in the Mass and Holy Communion continues the sacrifice of the cross and the dispensation of its fruits until the end of time. Thus, for Denis, led by Augustine, Holy Communion becomes the source of all good.

His intimate union with God, according to Denis, gave Augustine those great insights, but on the other hand, we also see in his wondrous enlightenment the proof that God united himself to him.

This is of no slight significance for Denis' concept of the contemplative life, which with St. Augustine he definitely sees primarily as a gift of the Lord, an infusion of God's grace, but so narrowly connected with our searching and striving toward God, requiring and presuming it, that we may not see one without the other. This is very strongly brought out in Denis' reflection on Augustine's conversion, which with Augustine he again sees primarily as God's work, but nevertheless is full of praise for the spirit and courage of the convert. He does not overlook St. Augustine's former sensuous life, but he describes it precisely to bring into greater relief the profusion of God's grace in his conversion; yet no matter how highly he assesses this grace, he by no means loses sight of the human cooperation involved. Neither, with regard to the highest mystical graces, do we see him, certainly under the influence of St. Augustine, emphasize the action

---

[22] *De sacramento Eucharistiae sermones sex*, sermo 4, *Opera*, vol. 35, p. 469f.

of God more than the Modern Devotion generally does, and accord prominence to that action as an outgrowth of the life of grace, least of all in such a way that he would abandon the way of methodical ascent to God, so characteristic of the Modern Devotion. Although he sees in St. Augustine a miracle of God's love and election and almost opposes the grace he received with his aptitude for it, on the one hand he sees him lifted to the highest degrees of the mystical life, on the other hand he sees that grace as a reward for his search for God and obtained through his ardent love. He is for Denis the "*ardens amator*," the ardent lover, whose love God in his generosity cannot leave unanswered but answers it with the most abundant gifts, while he, again as creator and redeemer infused love in Augustine's heart. Thus, God is the beginning and the end, but in between lies the co-operation of Augustine, who did not smother the call of love; on the contrary, made it resonate more loudly in his interior and allowed himself to be led by it and, led by it, thereby to receive its most abundant blessings. It cannot be denied that nevertheless Denis, as well as Augustine, lays strong emphasis on the action of God, and that expressions are to be found in both in which the unmerited nature of all mystical graces, the slight value of all our human efforts to attain them, are quite emphatically pointed out. Both are seers of God and by preference look to the divine side of things and to the insignificance of us tiny creatures, who can only be great through our union with God.[23]

Certainly, Denis places high value on Aristotle and theoretically prefers him to Plato, but when we hear him say that Pseudo-Dionysius is his favorite author,[24] see him write his penetrating commentaries on that author's Mystical Theology,[25] hear him praise negative theology, and, in what concerns God and divine

---

[23] See particularly the beautiful treatise of Denis, *De contemplatione, passim*; *Opera*, vol. 41, p. 133-290, in which he treats this subject in so many places that it is difficult to cite them in detail. Here we render the general impression.

[24] He calls him "*doctor meus electissimus*" in the list of writers he has read: *Protestatio ad superiorem suum, Opera*, vol. 41, p. 626.

[25] *Opera*, vols. 15 and 16.

matters, see him place little trust in our human intelligence, which must reach understanding through images gained through the senses, then we see once more that not all who call themselves disciples of Aristotle are really such in heart and soul. Picavet has given evidence of acute insight into the currents of medieval philosophy, when he asks himself who is the more followed of the two famous Greeks, whom we sometimes too strongly oppose to each other in the history of philosophy.[26] Philosophy in the Netherlands, in the Middle Ages and thereafter, is called Aristotelian, but the nominalistic tendencies of a Geert Grote and his school, and perhaps even more, the rising reaction against the exteriorization of the interior life, tended, especially outside the schools properly so called, toward ever more subjective Platonic views of knowledge and action. Denis indeed calls Aristotle the "princeps philosophorum,"[27] he says his philosophy is more in harmony with Christian revelation, yet there are points in which he prefers Plato, especially in the matter of the final destination of the human soul.[28] And in another place, he dedicates an entire chapter to the question as to whether under a certain aspect one should not agree with Plato that the soul constitutes the proper being of humans. He refers to similar expressions of St. Albert the Great and Hugh of St. Victor. There follows a detailed explanation of the fact that the most real and proper element in the human being, also according to Aristotle, is the intellect, and that under certain aspects it is to be considered independent of the body. Accordingly, he distinguishes a lower and higher being in the soul; a lower, by which she actualizes the possibility of the body; a higher, by which she is in a condition to raise the body to her nature and existence. In this higher being, he sees with Avicenna and Plato a conformity of the soul with God and pure spiritual

---

[26] François Picavet, *Esquisse d'une histoire générale et comparée des philosophies médiévales*, Paris, 1907, pp. viii, 85-116.

[27] *De lumine christianae theoriae*, bk. 1, art. 50, *Opera*, vol. 33, p. 292; *ibid.*, art. 77, *Opera*, vol. 33,p. 327. Aristotle is "the" philosopher: *Elementatio philosophica*, prop. 7; vol. 33, p. 29f.

[28] *De lumine christianae theoriae*, bk. 2, art. 92, *Opera*, vol. 33, p. 498.

being; and this higher being he calls with Aristotle, though beyond his intention, the divine in the human being.[29] Thus, in more than one place Denis tries to give a Platonic sense to Aristotelian doctrine, in order to see in mystical theology almost solely this divine element in human nature as the subject of knowledge of God and to seek that knowledge in the non-concrete and unknown by way of divine enlightenment and inspiration. Pseudo-Dionysius especially might have brought our Carthusian, for the most part unconsciously, to Platonic views. His veneration of Augustine had already earlier brought him to study the opinions of Plato and with the Church Father often to accept them in a Christian sense. He states specifically that he is examining Plato more closely out of reverence for Augustine.[30] With Augustine, he expresses his wonder at the way the Greek philosopher more clearly and distinctly than Aristotle describes how only after this life is true happiness laid in store for human beings, and that this is a happiness that is bestowed on the soul, in which the body does not share. The happiness of the soul consists in union with the highest Good, Goodness itself; and described more exactly, it consists in the contemplation of the divine, that is, of the ideal forms of being; and in its highest degree, in the contemplation of God in himself, the highest Good.

Precisely with regard to this knowledge of God, the highest and most desired, the goal of all philosophy according to Denis, does he find difficulty in agreeing with St. Thomas, and by way of Pseudo-Dionysius and St. Augustine, prefers Plato, whom he has St. Augustine say that God, who is not even in part to be contained or described by our poor words, is barely seen by the truly wise who have freed themselves from the body by every means in their power – seen sometimes as a streak of lightning in darkest night, appearing suddenly as a most brilliant light. This, however, occurs only in cases of the greatest purity and of the most thorough disengagement from the material.

---

[29] *Ibid.*, bk. 1, art. 105, *Opera*, vol. 33, p. 368ff.
[30] *De puritate et felicitate animae*, art. 8, *Opera*, vol. 40, p. 401ff.

In this context, he calls Plato the great giant among pagan philosophers, rightly placed by St. Augustine above all others.[31] The important significance of this statement of Denis lies in the fact that he does not reject the Platonic idea that, though the soul animates the body, its highest and truest existence is an autonomous existence, in which it must find its own satisfaction in the contemplation of God and of divine truths; God directly enlightens the soul and, if it manages to free itself from material things, sometimes infuses the clearest knowledge of his Being without the intermediary of the senses or speech. In this view, lies the germ of the doctrine that human beings must find the way to God in themselves without recourse to exterior images – without recourse even to the contemplation of Christ. Neither Augustine nor Denis go that far, because their point of view is corrected and modified by their contemplation of God as the God of love who made himself human, in order through that humanity to assume us all into himself as into one mystical body. But Denis' return to this Platonic-Augustinian concept is a symptom of a process of development, which in its later one-sided form will earn the warning of a St. Teresa.

If I speak here of a process of development, I by no means intend to exclude Denis himself. The order in which he composed his works is not known with sufficient certainty, but an examination of them confirms the impression that he did not remain quite as unchanged during the long years of his literary activity as his stout unruffled nature and the firmness with which he usually speaks would lead one to suppose. Influenced especially by his own spiritual experience, he gradually came to be more strongly influenced by Platonic-Augustinian thought, to a great extent unconsciously, yet with thrusts of which he became aware. Thus, he himself recounts how, instructed in his youth in the philosophy of St. Thomas, he accepted a real distinction between being and existence, but later felt obliged to abandon

---

[31] *Elementatio philosophica: de anima rationali*, prop. 45, *Opera*, vol. 33, p. 58.

the Thomistic position on this point.[32] Under the influence of pseudo-Dionysian mysticism, as we just mentioned, he also came more to favor Platonic ideas in epistemology. The austere Carthusian who had no interest in food and drink; who had preferred to retire into the strictest solitude; who desired to commune with God in spirit and be free of created things; who desired to listen to God in his inmost soul; who in the detachment and mortification of his senses hardly had need of the play of the imagination to feed his spirit; who, sated with earthly things, sought nourishment only in the divine – this man did not live in a state of mind which would have confirmed him in an Aristotelian philosophy, in his time already debilitated. Against the exteriorization of the spiritual life of his time, as a beginning of an expected reaction wholly in keeping with his way of life, he began to emphasize more immediate communion with God and the action of his grace, thereby increasingly making St. Augustine a leader not only in name but in fact; not only in the spiritual life and in doctrine concerning grace but in connection with them also in epistemology and in all of philosophy.

What in Denis might be called a refinement of his nature, which nevertheless had received an Aristotelian-Thomistic training, was later, when disengaged from that basis, developed in too one-sided a manner. When the Protestants later appeal to Augustine and gradually allow their philosophy to be completely dominated by Platonic thought, they will do this in an entirely different manner than Denis, and their onesidedness will lead them to consequences of which there was no danger in Denis' case, because by devoting ever more attention to Augustinian ideas, he broadened and enlarged his vision and increasingly saw the relative beside the absolute in creation, particularly the relationship with God, to the degree that he increasingly stressed the "divine" in creation, and more idealistic ideas supplanted originally more realistic ones.

However, one should not take this to mean that the great esteem Denis had for St. Augustine actually constituted a danger

---

[32] *In lib. I Sententiarum*, dict. 8, q. 7, *Opera*, vol. 19, p. 408.

for him – no more, I would say, than that Augustine's ideas constituted a danger for Augustine himself. We may rather speak of the contrary case and see in Denis one who was preserved by his Thomistic formation from a too one-sided idea of the Augustinian concept in philosophy and theology. On the other hand, through his great love and veneration for Augustine he developed that original formation into a harmonious attitude toward the divine and the created, toward the spirit and matter. He remained with his feet on the world of reality and of real relationships without neglecting the first and highest reality, continually fixing his gaze on God and seeing his work in all that happens. His close relationship with St. Augustine widened and uplifted Denis' view and together with election by God, so openly acknowledged by both of them, made him the "*Doctor Ecstaticus*," as we like to call him and as he speaks to us in his long series of writings, in which he, as it were, never comes to us alone, but always in union with God, whose words he desires to utter and does utter.

But what we say here of Denis he himself attributed to St. Augustine. He has left us three sermons on this saint.[33] The text with which he begins the first sermon already states this as clearly as possible: everyone in the measure in which he receives God's grace must share it with others, because, in short, all grace is a union with God whose being is love and a sharing of himself. Augustine showed himself to be united to God, says Denis, in that he indefatigably sought to make God known and shared by all around him. True, he had lived in sin for years, but for that very reason the abundance of grace God granted him is all the more evident in his conversion; an abundance so great that he was driven to celebrate the mercy of God and narrate his love to all. So much the more because, beside the work of God, he also saw his conversion as the fruit of the prayers and tears of his mother, St. Monica, and of the apostolate of St. Ambrose; and it also became clear to him that God only shares his grace by way of human cooperation and requested by human prayer. Denis here

---

[33] *Sermones de sancti*, vol. 33, p. 357-64.

quotes Ambrose, who ascribed Augustine's conversion to God as to the first mover. However, he places clearly in the light, as St. Augustine himself did, what great penance he performed and how devotedly he dedicated himself to uninterrupted prayer. Only then, Denis says, was Augustine in a condition to undertake the apostolate of which we are still enjoying the fruits. But he immediately adds as Augustine's greatest glory that God infused in him the highest wisdom, continually granted him more light and strength. If the saint sought God in a human way, God showed that he would visit him in a divine way. And filled with God, he could not be silent about God, but wrote and spoke with the result, intended by God, that he became the way to God for countless persons, and himself after a holy and most laborious life was admitted to the contemplation of God.

If the first sermon already strongly expresses Denis' emphasis on God in the life of St. Augustine, the second, preached to religious, places God even more in the foreground. Augustine is for him a mirror of God's goodness in the natural as well as in the supernatural order. While he is full of wonder at Augustine's gifts and deeds, he sees himself confronted with a miracle of God's endless generosity. And when he asks himself what St. Augustine has been and still is for the Church, he sees it as a proof of God's love for his Church, who exalted Augustine so highly and filled him with such great wisdom, because he wanted to enlighten the Church through him. However active Denis pictures Augustine's life to have been and though he presents it for imitation, nevertheless, he says, it was almost more passive than active. He goes on to glorify the saint, because God filled him and by this way of his elected ones led him to the highest virtue and purest love. He proposes the saint as an example in so far as he cooperated with God by humility and prayer, untiring activity, and strict mortification, but with the wise observation that whoever follows Augustine in his virtue and works of charity is not therefore assured of a similar exalted gift of grace. God bestows his grace as he wills, and notwithstanding the need of our preparation and cooperation, it must always be borne in mind that the higher graces of God's

enlightenment are, in short, gifts of God, who is free to give them
to whom he wills. And he here warns about self-deception and
overestimation of self, while he points to humility as the first virtue of such souls gifted with grace. This sermon of Denis, precisely
in its praise of Augustine, may count as an authoritative voice in
the controversy which at present exists over the value of methodical prayer, and is recommended for reading and reflection to all
who are interested in that controversy or are involved in it. Here
especially Denis shows himself to be a worthy pupil of the *Doctor
gratiae*. That it is just on his, Augustine's, feast that he raises his
voice is all the more meaningful.

The third sermon is in addition a confirmation of what in the
second sermon might still be misunderstood. Here, too, the text
again speaks for the content. The gift of wisdom is here presented as the fruit of prayer. If we admire in Augustine his burning love and most intimate communion with God, we are actually admiring his great wisdom, and our admiration must drive
us to seek the ways by which this saint arrived at this wisdom.
Then we must look first at his conversion, surely with St.
Ambrose to be praised as a work of God, but at the same time
as a work of dying and mortification; a dying to the world in
order to live with God. Then Denis describes for us what Augustine did to enjoy that union with God which God granted him,
in order to continue participating in it, and to make it bear fruit
in him. He explicitly calls Augustine an example for all who
strive to perfect themselves. Our conversion must be like his, so
that we no longer busy ourselves with all sorts of idle and worth-
less things, but also show by reflection and prayer, by reading of
good books, by study of what really has value that we want to
cling to God and seek him. It is not enough to abstain from evil;
we must strive to free our spirit of all that ensnares it, in order
that it might remain always united to God. Augustine, though
he was active, avoided various activities which he knew too
greatly captivated his spirit. For instance, he did not want to
become involved in building; he fled the office of bishop. Only
when such activities were necessary and clearly the wish and will

of God could he convince himself to undertake them. But then the thought helped that such activity would keep his spirit united to God. In that way, he did not wish to leave God because of God. Outwardly and inwardly, he further directed his entire life to keeping himself united to God. Augustine excelled in fasting and abstinence, in peace and order, in poverty and simplicity, in quiet and interiority, in tolerance and patience, and he is an example for us in our exterior life. And in his interior life of meditation on the word of God, of contemplation on the divine in all things, of devotion and love, he is an even more excellent example of ascent to God and of raising of the spirit to the highest heights to which it can attain in complete submission to God's paternal providence, and in closest union with our mediator Christ, become human in order to make that union easy; become near to us in the Eucharist, in order that we might already here enjoy him as a pledge of our being one with God in heaven, our greatest happiness.

Denis certainly saw St. Augustine from many aspects, but after having more carefully read through his works from this point of view (who will read all those forty-three volumes?) we arrive at this summary: Denis, who loved God and sought to trace the mysteries of the revelation of his love, in order to revel in them and so to be happy with God already here on earth – this Denis saw in Augustine the ideal of a seer of God, the God-given safe guide to go to God both in the hours of prayer as well as in the hours of scientific speculation, to God as to the key of all mysteries, the key-stone of the wonderful building in which we live.

Augustine made Denis happy because he showed him the way to happiness, already found here on earth in the contemplation of God and divine things, and led him into that paradise of delight. In the consciousness of that happiness, he rejoiced that God gave Augustine to the Church and so to himself. Must we not rejoice with Denis, because in and through the Church the same holy teacher was given to us no less than to him, so that our knowledge of him might also increase our happiness? And so we repeat the word of Pope Eugene IV, applying it not only to Denis, but according to his indication also to St. Augustine: "*Laetetur Ecclesia, quae talem habet filium*", let the Church rejoice, let us rejoice and be glad with a great festive joy at the remembrance – after 1500 years – that such a son was given the Church, that this Light has been given us which lets us see God.

THE RAMIFIED SCHOOL OF MINNE

Beatrice of Nazareth[1]

I

Closely related to Hadewijch, Beatrice of Nazareth appears toward the middle of the 13th century, a second mystical writer in our Netherlandish literature. If Hadewijch was most likely one of the devout beguines who in the 13th century lived in such great numbers in Belgium and also in our country; if she was of noble family and still living in the ambiance of nobility, in Beatrice we have a cloistered nun withdrawn from the world, a member of the Cistercian Order, which in this century was undergoing a flourishing period. Because of her virtue and wisdom, she was elected prioress or superior of her monastery, and when she died on August 29, 1268, her memory as a saint was held in honor. She came of a wealthy middle-class family. Although her father did not belong to the nobility, he was a man of influence because of the wealth at his disposal, which with pious generosity he bestowed on good causes. His name, Bartholomew van Thienen, also sometimes Bartholomew Vleeschhouwer (Butcher), is preserved in three monasteries as their founder. Her mother's name was Gertrude, but Beatrice had already lost her at the tender age of seven. After the death of his wife, her father seems to have devoted himself exclusively to good works. First, he founded the monastery of Cistercian nuns, Bloemendaal, or Florival, where little Beatrice was also taken in as an oblate. At fifteen years of age, she herself requested the habit of the Order, but the abbess found her to be too young and postponed her admission for a year.

---

[1] From *De Gelderlander*, December 9, 21, 1940.

After she had been received, she remained in that monastery for a year of probation, after which she transferred to a second monastery, that of Ramela, to learn the skill of copyist for illuminating choir books for the new monastery. After a year of practice, she returned to Bloemendaal. During that year, however, she had not only learned the art of copying but had enriched herself with the friendship of the highly gifted Ida van Nijvel, with whom she carried on an interesting correspondence until Ida's death in 1232. Meanwhile, her father had founded a second abbey of Cistercian nuns at Oplinter, called Maagdendaal. Beatrice transferred from Bloemendaal to this new monastery, where her two sisters, Christina and Sibilia, were also Cistercian nuns, while her father and brother, Wigbertus, resided there. The date of this second foundation is not known with certainty, but we know that Beatrice's father in 1235 founded a third abbey in the immediate neighborhood of Lier, dedicated to Mary and called Nazareth. In 1236, the founder and his children took up residence there, and Beatrice became the first prioress of the monastery. She herself in no way desired this, for she was shy and modest and did not seek the first place in anything. She held the dignity of prioress until her death, thus upwards of thirty-two years.

This is the external history of her life. Of more importance is the story of her spiritual life, described for us in an old Latin biography, ascribed to William of Affligem.[2] There she is presented as an ecstatic, who while in rapture could not always suppress the urgency of her heart and often gave expression in an unusual way to the joy that filled her at the thought of the love of God. Then she would become frantic with love and love's affliction, especially when she remembered that love was not returned.

Thirteenth century Netherlandish mysticism has a special expression for this condition, which we also encounter with Hadewijch:

---

[2] *Vita Beatricis; de autobiografie van de Z. Beatrijs van Tienen, O.Cist., 1200-1268*; ed. by L. Reypens, S.J., Antwerpen, 1964. English edition: *The Life of Beatrice of Nazareth*; tr. by Roger de Ganck, Kalamazoo, Mich., 1991. The biography is no longer ascribed to Willem van Afflighem (*d.* 1279).

orewoet, which William of Affligem, or whoever wrote Beatrice's life, sometimes translated as *furor* (raving), again as *aestus* (ardor), sometimes even as *insania* (madness). By these terms he clearly indicates that the fire of love in that condition so consumed the soul that it raged in the soul and made it unreceptive to any understanding of earthly things and forms. As David danced before the Ark, so she would dance through the monastery and seize the sisters to have them share her joy and jubilation, in spite of the requirements of silence and modesty. This reveals her as an open, spontaneous woman who needed to express what lay hidden and glowed in her interior. Thus, Beatrice became, like Hadewijch before and during her life, a mystical writer. Her language is not as vigorous as Hadewijch's. She is more didactic than lyric; nevertheless, she is also a singer of love, though she prefers to write in prose.

From her biography, we know that she wrote over many matters of the spiritual life, and this often in the form of beautiful and pregnant images. There must have been treatises by her which described the spiritual life under the figure of a garden, which needs to be cultivated; of a monastery, in which God is the abbot, and the various virtues fill the principal offices, etc. But of all those treatises we have only the short summary in Latin. The old Middle Netherlandish text seems to be lost. Of only one of her treatises has the text been preserved. And from this fact alone, it already deserves a place in our Netherlandish literature; not only because it is one of its oldest products, but also because of content, language, and style. It is the treatise, *Seven Manieren van Minne* (Seven Ways of Minne)[3].

The text recently became known, when in 1895 Prof. Dr. H. Kern published the *Limburgsche Sermoenen*, a collection of forty-eight sermons of the first half of the 14th century.[4] A portion of

---

[3] Jos Huls o.carm., *The Minne Journey*. Beatrice of Nazareth's Seven Ways of Minne. Mystical Process and Mystagogical Implications, Fiery Arrow 9, Leuven 2013.

[4] Johan Hendrik Kern, *De Limburgse Sermoenen*, Leiden, 1895 (Bibliotheek van Middelnederlandsche Letterkunde)

them seemed to be of German origin, but another portion was clearly originally Netherlandish. When the works of Hadewijch began to awaken more interest, it appeared that the end of Sermon 41 corresponded entirely with the tenth letter ascribed to Hadewijch. Sermon 42 appeared further nothing other than Beatrice's tract, *Seven Manieren van Minne*, the content of which was known in detail from the Latin. That it was an original Netherlandish text, the Hadewijch expert, Dr. J. van Mierlo, S.J., had already deduced from the close correspondence this sermon showed to the twenty-first letter of Hadewijch, *Twaalf Uren der Minne* (Twelve Hours of Love).[5]

It now seemed also to exist in other manuscripts. De Vreese found it as a completely independent tract in a Ruusbroec manuscript under the letters, Vv.[6] Dr. Reypens, S.J., discovered a later manuscript of it in the Kaiserliche Hofbibliothek in Vienna.[7] Both are of the 15th century in the dialect of Brabant.

The treatise has again attracted attention in our 20th century. We may indeed say that it enjoyed more than usual interest. Shortly after Kern had published the *Limburgsche Sermoenen*, this treatise already had the attention of Prof. Kalf, who wrote in his justly highly regarded *Geschiedenis der Nederlandsche Letterkunde*, "Here and there, this prose shows, in working with antithesis and parallelism as well as in the construction of long sentences, an artistic merit such as has hitherto not been seen in our prose."[8] He did not realize that the prose was from almost a century earlier. If Prof. Kern, as we said, published a first edition of the tractate in his edition of the *Liburgsche Sermoenen*, Dr. J. van Mierlo and L.

---

[5] L. Reypens, S.J., en J. van Mierlo, S.J., *Beatrijs van Nazareth, Seven Manieren van Minne*, Leuven, 1926, pp. 59*-60*

[6] Willem de Vreese, *De handschriften van Jan van Ruusbroec's werken 2*, Gent, 1902, pp. 639-663, 644-645.

[7] Reypens/Van Mierlo, *Beatrijs van Nazareth*, p. 61*.

[8] "Hier en daar toont dit proza in het werken met tegenstellingen en parallelism, ook in het bouwen van lange zinnen, eene kunstvaardigheit, zooals die tot dusver in ons proza niet gezien was." Gerrit Kalff, *Geschiedenis der Nederlandsche Letterkunde*, Groningen, 1906, I, 373.

Reypens in 1926 produced a better text with the variants in the above-mentioned manuscripts and an ample introduction. In the *Bloemen van Ons Geestelijk Erf*, 1929, Father J. van der Kun, S.J., reedited the text of the *Limburgsche Sermoenen* according to the manuscript in Den Haag with a modern Netherlandish revision.[9] Around the same time, in 1928, there appeared in *De Gemeenschap* a well-done translation in modern Netherlandish by Albert Helman, who translated the title of the booklet, *Over Zeven Soorten van Heilige Liefde* (Concerning Seven Kinds of Sacred Love).[10] We may also call attention to a French translation of the treatise in the supplement of *La vie spirituelle* (Vol. XIX, 1928-1929), by Dom Kerssemakers, O.S.B., who also prefaced it with a short introduction.[11] Still worthy of mention is the lecture on Beatrice delivered by Dr. van Mierlo in the Koninklijke Vlaamsche Academie and published in the *Verslagen en Mededeelingen* of the year 1926.[12] In a final article, we will attempt to provide a brief review of this interesting little treatise.

II

Beatrice titled her work, *Van Seven Maniren van Minne*. Albert Helman, as we have said, translated this as, *Over de Zeven Soorten van Heilige Liefde*. Father van der Kun, S.J., retains the still comprehensible Middle Netherlandish terms and writes, *Zeven Manieren van Minnen*. Although I can in every way approve the translation of *minne* by *heilige liefde*, I feel I must have some reservations with the translation of *maniren* by *soorten*. By this term, the impression is too easily given that there is question of seven ways or forms of loving of equal worth; while Beatrice definitely had the idea of delineating the "ascent" of love. We come closest to her

---

[9] J. van der Kun, S.J., ed., *Zeven manieren van minnen*, Antwerpen, 1929.

[10] Albert Helman, ed., *Seven manieren van minne*, Utrecht, 1928.

[11] Jules W.J. Kerssemakers, O.S.B., tr., "Des sept degrés du saint amour," *La Vie Spirituelle (Supplement)*, 19 (1928-1929), 320-332.

[12] Pp. 51-72.

thought, if we speak of "Seven Steps of Sacred Love." The idea is very much present in ascetical and mystical literature, namely, that as practical experience teaches, also in the matter of the love of God and the union of the soul with him, the ascent to God is gradual. The little treatise of Beatrice of Nazareth proceeds from this idea.

The first step, or "manner of love", is that one desires to do good. Fully determined and defying all opposition, the soul decides to cling to God and conquer his love. She knows that God desires to give her his love, but also that he places conditions, requires a sound temperament; demands the practice of virtue. The individual perceives that he is not as he could be; that God deserves more love than he shows him; that he allows himself too easily to be led away from God. That must and shall be changed. All at once, the ideal rises in his mind of elevating his soul to the highest nobility. (Brugman speaks of the *puurste edelheit* (purest nobility).)

Herewith, he already passes over to the second step. Love is so beautiful and glorious, as soon as it is understood, that already for its nobility alone a man desires to love God. The soul desires to grow in love, not to merit heaven or avoid hell, but only because it is beautiful and good to love God. She knows that heaven awaits her and is happy at this prospect. She fears only hell and trusts never to suffer its pains, but the love of God is already a foretaste of heaven, and love makes all suffering on earth light.

The third step is still an increase and enlivening of love, but it is now linked to the painful awareness of yet a lack of love. In proportion as love grows, the awareness grows that one cannot love God as he deserves. A storm arises in the soul. By main force, she would be perfect in every virtue and continual communion with God but lacks the strength. In the humble awareness of her imperfection, she feels herself all the more strongly drawn to God, as the one who can infuse that love in her as a free and magnanimous gift. But God awaits his time, and meanwhile the soul often suffers grievously. Hadewijch, the fierce singer of love, has likened this "manner of loving" to the suffering of Hell. Beatrice, too, uses this image. She speaks of a *hellegtech leven* (hellish life), of being *in de pine der hellen* (in the pain of hell), because in this third step the want of God is so powerfully felt. The soul flies up to God and desires to cling to him, grasp him, hold him fast.

Ruusbroec, in his turn, speaks here of *crighen en ontbliven* (receiving and lacking), because together with that grasp at God the souls feels that he still *ontblivet* (is lacking) to her; that is, he still does not completely bestow himself on her, and she still feels herself abandoned and separated from him.

But if a man does not become discouraged and, trusting in God, continues to strive with all his might for union with God, then God from time to time generously grants – and this is the fourth step – a beam of light in the darkness, and it comes about that love softly and sweetly feels liberated, and man knows God is near, so that he can freely and unencumbered cast himself into his arms. He is wholly swept up in that embrace. Life with God comes first with him. He is willing to give all for it.

But these are only weak feelings compared to the storms that in the fifth step suddenly rise up and violently draw the soul to God, tear her away from earth in order to fly up to God in irresistible passion. The body joins in. It has recovered from the stupor of the previous step and is at the bidding of the soul and swept up in its enjoyment. The body is able for everything, must be able for everything that union with God requires. It troubles the soul that it sometimes cannot keep abreast. It seems like a battle of life and death, such violence does love do to the body. But instead of feeling pain under this affliction, the body asks for no appeasement; there is no other sorrow but that at last strength fails, and the weakness of the body disturbs the soul in its flight on high. Man feels himself still human, bound to earthly things. He would like to shatter the bonds that still bind him, because stronger bonds draw him ever closer to God. And so there is suffering and at the same time gladness; because, on the one hand, the urge to God is most powerful and confers the sweetest satisfaction; on the other hand, weakness does not permit him to do what out of love for God he would like to do and feels he must do.

In the sixth step, love has conquered, and opposition no longer matters. Man knows he is united to God and is in his hand, and receives everything from him. His will is wholly united to God's. Man no longer decides what unites him to God. He is near God, and God now rules all his actions. It is the love of the most intimate union, whereby the beloved and the lover are one in willing and doing. The storm has given way to an imperturbable calm, in which nothing is feared, nothing is considered too difficult, because union with God bestows strength beyond all understanding, and no practice of virtue is too difficult. Therefore, that calm goes hand in hand with the greatest activity, and man in that awareness of union with God is in no way inclined to rest. Or rather, with all work his rest in God becomes more intimate.

But yet a higher step is conceivable in human love of God. That love can surpass human power in the sense that man himself cannot raise himself to that height; it lies within human effort in so far as man's nature permits that love to be brought to that height. Against the pull of nature, man is violently drawn to God and can no longer live without him. He pines away with longing and no longer finds rest in this earthly life, because God gives him no rest and, as it were, incites him to a new and different life. In this sense, St. Teresa wrote her famous poem with the beautiful refrain:

I die because I die not yet.

This is no longer the desire which in the fifth step fills the soul for dissolution and union with God, as a result of reflection on its inability to love God as he deserves. Here all reasoning breaks down and the attraction of love is, as Beatrice says, above human sense and reason. She then uses the words, which Father van der Kun thinks are best translated by *uitzinnig* (frantic) and *zinneloos* (insane), in order to express the fact that here only the gale of the greatest love blows and propels up to God, without man's being in a condition to force himself to express that love. The will abides in heavenly spheres and transfers man here on earth to the midst of the heavenly seraphim. Man casts and loses himself in the immeasurable greatness of God and finds there all things: angels and saints, human beings on earth, and all creatures. The earth disgusts him. Unspeakable is the suffering he endures from longing for God. Nothing can console him except the passage to eternal life. Then all obstacles disappear. Then he may joyfully enter eternal happiness.

Beatrice closes with the prayer, "there may God quickly bring us all."

The Mysticism of Hadewijch[1]

I

Hadewijch has been rightly compared to a garden, and if in the history of mysticism in The Netherlands I were to choose a flower in that garden which best symbolizes her, I would certainly give a moment's consideration to the lily, lifting its lofty head and blooming on its tall stem in silky whiteness, symbol of grandeur, of distinction, taking childlike, innocent, and pure delight in heavenly sunlight. I would also consider the colorful little violet, which is humble and hidden in the foliage, but once uncovered, presents for our enjoyment a riot of color, a downy velvet of richest variety, an image of Hadewijch's flight from the world in order to cling to God, but endowed by God with luster, so that she attracts the gaze of all because of her beauty. But no, neither lily nor violet sufficiently render her principal trait. If I search for a flower which symbolizes Hadewijch, it can be none other than the rose, and not exactly the tenderly white rose, though it is fair in its virginal appearance; not the pink, for it is fierce and strong in its color; it can be none other than the red, the deep red, in which there is the glow of fire, the darkness of profound contemplation. For Hadewijch is the singer of Love, set ablaze by love.

To say "Hadewijch" is to say "Love." The word is interwoven with her mysticism as with no other. And she not only enjoyed its delight but was given to picture and describe it. In numerous visions, she saw and tasted the luxury of Love, in verses she sang it, in letters described and taught it, in so far as love can be taught. Hadewijch does not teach it, first of all, by speaking or writing

<hr>

[1] From *De Gelderlander*, November 16, 23, 30, 1940.

about it, but by speaking and writing about it with a verve and fire that make the warmth be shared by all who listen to her. Hadewijch has a two-fold significance in the history of mysticism in The Netherlands. She is not only a writer about mystical grace, but is herself the recipient of mystical grace. Through her writings in the first half of the thirteenth century she stands at the beginning of our country's literature. And it is a joy that one of the oldest original works of our literature introduces us to the sphere in which Hadewijch lived; that already in the first century of its existence our literature so beautifully reveals the bonds which bind us to the Godhead, which depicts our human nature in the radiant light of its union with God.

But the great value of mysticism does not lie in words. No matter how beautiful it may be to read about or hear its splendor and profusion described, its value lies in its experience. And so we see in Hadewijch not only a woman of special talent, who with great mastery of a still developing language describes the sublime life which can lead the human spirit in the interior awareness of God's unfortunately uncomprehended love for humankind, but also a woman highly gifted by God, so receptive to divine grace that in the end she became withdrawn from the sight of created things and was raised to the highest contemplation, with the result that her love became more ardent, her drive to the good more strong, her sanctity and amiability so attractive to our spirit that we stand in admiration of her person, honor her as a luminous vision, which to behold is to be healed.

Hadewijch makes her appearance in a greatly agitated time, a time of repentance and conversion, a time of a new renascence of the spiritual life. The thought of her transports us to the years when in our area the influence of the Cistercians and Norbertines reaches its highest development; when, furthermore, the example of a St. Francis, celebrated by Jacob van Maerlant, a St. Dominic, extolled by the singer of the *Golden Legend*, attracted many to a new form of religious life; when already the first of the crusaders of the Netherlands sought a contemplative life in the hermitage on Carmel or elsewhere in the Holy Land, described with such praise by Jacques de Vitry in his *Annales*;[2] and particularly when in Belgium, in the vicinity of Nijvel, the Beguine movement brought hundreds of women to a new form of devout life in the world. Hadewijch is a leading figure in this movement. She is not the teacher in the spiritual life, as for instance St. Teresa was to become, who described her exalted gifts of grace, in order that others might thereby be instructed in the wondrous ways of God. She is not the academically formed woman, such as the illustrious women and men who were to systematize the spiritual life and try to transform human life into a continuous preparation for exalted mystical gifts. Hadewijch is a mystical soul who in the hours in which she is conscious of divine union, or recalls it, sings out the joy of her heart while still in a state of ecstasy; sings and sings again the beauty of love. She often begins the verses in which she unburdens herself with a description of nature, but it is not long before her spirit has ascended to the Creator, and she hovers in higher spheres, both to enjoy the beauty of union with God, and to share her enjoyment with others, so that they might experience it more intimately.

Some are put off by the fact that Hadewijch is so continually preoccupied with herself, and they get the impression that she lacks true humility. She seems to be enamored of herself, and sometimes her words seem stilted and snobbish. But Hadewijch's language is no longer ours. Not every word has still the force and accent it had when she wrote her letters and visions. She lived in an age which was somewhat different, and the concept, especially of the perfection of women, was strongly influenced by the ideas of chivalric honor, respect of women, who were to hold themselves ideal and pure as a queen. Cistercian nuns present themselves in beautiful white garments. Holiness adorns the thrones of queens. Sanctity has a certain eminence and distinction. The Crusades had given women a special social position. Blanca was not the only woman to rule a land in place of her son, Louis; many a noblewoman governed home or castle, while the knight fought in the distant East to maintain the holy places.

---

[2] I.e., Historia orientalis.

This gives a woman like Hadewijch a certain often unwitting self-consciousness, something exalted, which is yet more appearance and formality than truth and reality. She can also be quite simple, can abandon herself completely to the ardent unburdening of her heart, and above all express her consciousness in sincerely felt language that everything happens by divine election, so that we may ever serve him better, and others in him. Hadewijch can contemplate God under many aspects. She wrote letters which justify us in calling her a teacher of the spiritual life up to a certain level. In flowing verses, she sang of the love which was consuming her; an anthology of that poetry could charm us for hours, were we able at first sight to penetrate its deep meaning and beautiful expression. Her language, however, is not so easy to understand, especially in her verses. To enjoy its beauty one would almost need a translation or transposition into modern language.[3] And how poetry is diminished in translation! Although to those who understand Middle Dutch I must recommend reading Hadewijch's verses, which raise the spirit and fill it with fire and fervor for the Most High; for the many who lack sufficient mastery of Middle Dutch I must refrain from quoting her verses. I must confine myself to saying that seldom is the love which a person can feel – indeed, should feel toward God, if he properly understands his relation to God – more profoundly felt and more strikingly sung. She is not merely the singer of Love, because the word, as it were, lies constantly on her lips and she can speak of nothing else, just as St. John at Ephesus once repeated his "Little children love one another, and all will be well." No, she plumbs the depths of the riches of love. She describes its characteristics and sings of its beauty as the most lovely and beautiful thing that exists. She sketches its luxuriance in such a way that she counterposes heaven and hell. It is her heaven, but there is the fact that she does not yet completely possess that heaven, and the lack of

---

[3] More than one modern version has since appeared. To cite an English translation: *Poetry of Hadewijch*. Introduction, translation, and notes Marieke J.E.H.T. van Baest. With a foreword by Edward Schillebeeckx, Leuven, 1998.

that highest good, which together with the pain of fire and more than the pain of fire, constitutes the torture of hell, causes her to liken love to hell. The comparison has been made before, but although it may not be original, it renders so sharply the profundity of Hadewijch's concept of the life of love, the extent to which her heart was filled with the love of God, that she felt its lack as the most terrible suffering – so terrible that she could only compare it to the suffering of hell.

II

A particular characteristic of Hadewijch is her gift of visions. It would be a sign of a mistaken idea of mysticism were we to think that the mystical life actually consisted in this gift; that without visions that life were not yet fully experienced. The mystical life consists in the consciousness of actual union with God. This consciousness, however, is strengthened in large measure by the visions, which God can give us of himself, of heaven, of the saints. They are like the food enjoyed by the prophet Elijah at the indication of the angel, so that on the strength of that food he might make the long journey to Mount Horeb, there to see God face to face.

Under this aspect, the life of Hadewijch is particularly instructive. She writes of St. Hildegarde, whom she may yet have known, with whom she may have been in correspondence, by whom she may have been guided, that she "saw all the visions."[4] But this could be said of herself, at least in the sense that her visions varied most in form and color, and that every type of vision, from the lowest to the highest, were her lot.

When a person is called to higher contemplation, in order to distinguish the various forms in which it can take place, one must take into consideration the many facets of human nature: the human person, that is, possesses a very complex faculty of knowing. In the first place, one has the knowledge, which comes

---

[4] Hadewijch, *Visioenen*, vertaald door Imme Dros, Amsterdam, 1996, Lijst van de Volmaakten, p. 160, line 191.

through the senses. This is the lowest level, which gradually leads one higher. A vision can remain at this lowest level. A vision can be had, beheld with the eyes, felt with the touch, perceived with the hearing. Hadewijch describes such a vision in the seventh of her series. God approached her from the altar in the form which he had on the day he instituted the Blessed Sacrament of the Altar: gentle and loving as a servant who places himself entirely at the disposition of another. He gave her Communion under both species, as was customary at that time. Then he came to her side and embraced her, and she felt his embrace in all her members, but this lasted only a moment, because he became one with her and she with him, and they became indistinguishably one. First, she writes, there was an outward seeing, tasting, and feeling, such as one outwardly tastes on receiving the Blessed Sacrament; an outward seeing and feeling, such as a lover and the beloved enjoy seeing, hearing, and being wrapped up in each other. After this, however, this outward seeing disappeared. She was so completely united to her Beloved, and he to her, that she no longer saw anything outwardly; "that I," she writes literally, "melted into him and did not remain myself." Thereupon, her vision turned into a vision of the imagination, which showed her beloved as one with her; indeed, as closely united as possible. "I was carried away," she says,"and taken up in the spirit."In the spirit, she then saw a holy mountain with five roads, all leading to the sight of the face of God.[5] This is further described for us in the eighth vision, which may be considered a continuation of the seventh. However, she more clearly describes such a vision in the sixth, in which she also writes that she was"taken up in the spirit and led to where I was shown a high and mighty city."From this vision, she proceeds to a higher level, in order, after having enjoyed union with God on that higher level for half an hour, to return to the vision of the imagination.[6]

[5] For the seventh vision, see *ibid.*, pp. 78-82.
[6] For the sixth vision, see pp. 72-76.

Thus, we here distinguish two states: first, the vision which is still bound to material images, not impressed on the outward senses by an apparition able to be experienced exteriorly, but on the inward sense, directly in the imagination and memory; that is to say, impressed without the cooperation of the outward senses. Further, in the second place, when, overwhelmed by those images, she is carried out of herself, the sensible images pale in the light of divine clarity, and without an image of the imagination, the intellect, without being able to find a word for it or form an image of it, knows that it is one with God. She sees nothing more with the senses or the imagination, but she knows more *clearly than before that God is with her.*

Through the richness of what I saw in him, she writes, I was carried "out of the spirit, since I had seen all that I sought," and when in the sweet consciousness of my happiness I knew my august Beloved was at hand, "then I was carried out of my spirit and of all that I had seen in him, and I became lost" in the enjoyment of his love. "I remained swallowed up in it," she continues, "deprived of all consciousness of all there is to know or to see or to understand, other than being one with him and experiencing him." In other words, she was carried outside herself, entirely lost and taken up in love, without knowing, seeing, or understanding anything other than that she was one with him and enjoyed that state.[7]

Thus, here we have the strong awareness of the intellect, which is conscious in the clearest manner of being united with God, but no longer under the influence of sensible images. It is a conceptual vision, a vision of the intellect, which raises the soul a step higher than that of images. This knowing without images has always been the symbol of the knowledge of God in heaven, where God is seen in himself; that is, in his infinity, not as he is reflected in images. Hadewijch also regards this as the foretaste of heaven, as a privilege already to see God here on earth as he is in himself, no longer in his creatures, imperfectly, under all manner of images.

[7] Ibid.

I will not here enter into the question of the extent to which it is possible already here to enjoy the vision of heaven. It goes without saying that God can raise a soul to this state and has also, in fact, so raised a St. Paul, a prophet Elijah. Whether this gift is given to others in its fullness may be subject to doubt, but it is certain that the soul can be brought to a state which so approaches that heavenly contemplation that it may count as a foretaste, though not complete, of the happiness of heaven. It is a purely spiritual enjoyment of union with the Godhead, an enjoyment which often has its reaction on the body and also fills it with enjoyment, without the bodily faculties producing the enjoyment or even cooperating in it. They share in it, but without any effort being demanded of them.

In the fifth vision of her series, Hadewijch describes the same transition of a vision of the imagination, or of an expressed image, into a vision of a concept or of the understanding. There, too, she begins by saying that she was taken up "in the spirit." And in the spirit, that is to say, in her imagination, she saw what she describes in that vision. It would take us too far afield to repeat it all. But at the end of her description, she says that the Beloved lifted her up "beyond the spirit in the highest experience of wonders no words can describe" – thus drawn beyond the imagination in the highest enjoyment of all those wonders without it being described in the spirit. And she adds, "There I enjoyed him as I shall in eternity." And after she also says that this lasted briefly, she further relates that afterwards she returned to herself, and that her Beloved again appeared to her under a certain form in a vision of an expressed image, or of the imagination, and told her that she had now had a foretaste of heaven: "And so this experience you will have forever."[8]

It ought not to surprise us that a spirited woman, who realized that she had been so exalted, who put such great value on her union with God that she thought she had been transported to heaven, who thus was wholly taken up in the love of God; it is

---

[8] *Ibid.*, pp. 68-70.

not surprising that she was – I would almost say – violently seized by Love and must needs sing of it every time. The cry of St. Francis, urging that love be contemplated and appreciated, his complaint that love was ignored, later so passionately repeated by the Carmelite mystic, St. Mary Magdalene de Pazzi, who rang a bell to tell people that they should recall God's love – the same complaint we hear in the verses and visions of Hadewijch.

In Hadewijch's time, there was a devout woman, a kindred spirit in the great beguine movement at the beginning of the 13th century, called Aleydis. On one occasion, she heard a wine merchant peddling his wares about the city. He cried, "Good wine, best wine, exquisite wine!" When she heard this, she called to the man, who evidently had a strong voice, that she found it a pity that wine was so publicly praised and God was forgotten. She asked him also to cry out that God was good, that God was merciful, that God was good beyond all understanding. And she gave him so much money that he again went down the street, and what he had before cried out about his wine he now called out about God. This touched Hadewijch to the heart, and she spoke of true love and defended Aleydis, even when highly placed persons condemned her. Likewise, we also should not be able to bear that something or someone be more loved than God.[9]

III

A great deal of theorizing has been done about the time in which Hadewijch lived and wrote. The time is not that long past, when she was identified with a certain Bloemmardine of Brussels, against whom Ruusbroec felt obliged to take action because of her excessively free ideas and practices.[10]

---

[9] For this story about Aleydis and the wine merchant see Titus Brandsma, O.Carm., "Wanneer schreef Hadewijch haar visioenen?" *Studia Catholica*, 2 (1925-1926), 244.

[10] Axters, Geschiedenis van de vroomheid in de Nederlanden, I, 346-354.

Dr. C. Serrure of Gent was the first to cast doubt on this opinion and advanced the conjecture that Hadewijch should be placed in an earlier period of our literature. He proposed the idea that Hadewijch should be identified with an Abbess Hawidis of Aywières in Wallonia, who actually died in 1248.[11] This theory at once advanced her dates a hundred years. From a contemporary of Ruusbroec, beside whom she was completely eliminated because of her alleged heretical stance, so that in the literary history of the Netherlands the former was long considered the Father of the Mysticism of the Netherlands, she became a significant and in every respect orthodox writer, who at least a century before Ruusbroec by her beautiful writings won a place for mysticism in the literature of the Netherlands.

What for Serrure remained a hypothesis, only gradually given general assent – although he added a few arguments in its support – became, with regard to Hadewijch's dates, certainty through the extensive research on the person and work of Hadewijch performed by Dr. J. van Mierlo, S.J.[12] Although it is not yet quite certain who she was; although it is debatable whether she was a distinguished beguine, born in Antwerp and apparently living in the environs of that city, rather than a devout cloistered nun, I personally am strongly inclined to the opinion of Father Dr. van Mierlo, who counts Hadewijch a beguine and places her outside the cloister. It was certainly the right time for it in Belgium. Her works seem to indicate this in several places, although those passages could, if need be, be taken in a different sense. It is certain that a Beatrice of the Cistercian monastery of Nazareth is closely related to her in language and imagery, but that still does not make her a nun. She does not appear among the devout Premonstratensian nuns, of whom we have a series of biographies of that time.[13]

---

[11] C.A. Serrure, "De Klooster-Zuster Hadewig, dichteres der XLV liederen uit de XIIIe eeuw," *Vaderlandsch Museum*, 2 (1858), 141-145.

[12] On the writings of Van Mierlo about this question, see Axters, *Geschiedenis van de vroomheid in de Nederlanden*, I, 452-456.

[13] Reference not found.

Although it is not entirely proved, we are inclined to see in Hadewijch one of the many beguines, who at the beginning and middle of the 13th century with their center at Nijvel enjoyed such an unusual expansion in Belgium and left their stamp on the spirituality of that century. Still, we must grant Dr. Plassmann, who devoted an important study to Hadewijch in Germany, that Van Mierlo's most important argument against Serrure is not to be taken too seriously.[14] Van Mierlo is of the opinion that the Flemish Hadewijch would hardly have been at home, as abbess, in a Walloon monastery, and that a nun versifying and writing in Diets can have had little understanding and acceptance in that Walloon milieu. Dr. Plassmann points out that there were other Flemish nuns in that monastery, and one reads in the life of Saint Lutgard that she was welcomed in that monastery, while it is recounted as a wonder that she, who knew no Walloon, conversed with a sick Walloon woman.

On the other hand, I must say that Dr. Plassmann attributes rather a good deal of weight to the occurrence of "*orewoet*" (impetuosity) in Hadewijch and Willem van Afflighem, who wrote the life of Saint Lutgardis, in which he mentions the Abbess Hawidis, in order to identify Hadewijch with Hawidis.

Be that as it may, although we do not know who Hadewijch was, at least not with sufficient certainty, certain it is that after Van Mierlo's researches her life span is to be placed around the middle of the 13th century. Van Mierlo bases his argumentation especially on a list of "perfects" inserted after the last vision of Hadewijch, a list of persons living in spiritual communion with Hadewijch. Here there is mention of a beguine, whom Master Robbaert killed because of her true love, which places us in the years 1235 and later. I have attempted to show, on the basis of old chronicles, that here there can be question only of a certain beguine, Aleydis, who according to a chronicle of Alberic of

<hr>

[14] J. O. Plassmann, *Die Werke der Hadewijch*, (2 pts. in 1, Hagen i. W., 1923), pt. 2, p.114.

Trois Fontaines was tried in 1238 by the inquisitor, Robert, called "*le Bougre*."[15] Then there is mention of a "Sir Hendric of Breda," sent by Hadewijch to an anchorite. Principally on these grounds, Father van Mierlo places Hadewijch's information about her visions between the years 1246 and 1256, because Hendrik was Lord of Breda during these years. However, I have already noted that the term "Sir Hendrik of Breda" does not mean that this Hendrik at the time of being sent was actually Lord of Breda. Long before that time, he is recorded and given the title "Dominus" or Lord. In 1231, he already appears as a witness in the will of his sister-in-law, Lutgardis, and is also already called "Dominus."[16]

We would like to limit and fix still a bit more closely the time in which Hadewijch had her visions. We found a welcome and hitherto unused argument in the record of a series of mystical friends who lived in prayer and contemplation in the solitude of the Holy Land. "Of the living, seven dwelt on the wall in Jerusalem as hermits, and three in the city; they are women, two are maidens, and the third a prostitute enclosed in a wall."[17]

If we look at the circumstances in which the Christians of the Holy Land found themselves around the middle of the 13th century, it is clear that hermits can be said to be living on the walls of Jerusalem and virgins and a walled-in anchorite dwelling in the city only at a time when Christians enjoyed a certain liberty in the Holy City, which leaves only the period of the ten-year truce from 1229 to 1239 agreed upon by Emperor Frederick and Sultan Malek el Kamel of Egypt, by which Jerusalem, Bethlehem, and Nazareth were restored to the Christians, and a truce of ten years was agreed upon. At the end of the truce, the king of Navarre,

---

[15] Brandsma, "Wanneer schreef Hadewijch haar visioenen?" pp. 244-147. See also the reference to Bl. Titus' opinion, H.W.J. Vekeman, *Het Visioenenboek van Hadewijch*, Nijmegen/Brugge, 1980, p. 244.

[16] Van Mierlo himself cites this text on p. 317 of his study in *De Visioenen van Hadewijch*, Leuven, 1924, v. 1, and further refers to *Bijdragen tot de Geschiedenis*, 5 (1906), 334.

[17] *Visioenen*, tr. I. Dros, p. 160, 212.

Thibault of Champagne, and his crusaders tried to retain the conquered territory for the Christians, but his army was defeated at Gaza, and still in the same year Jerusalem fell under the power of Malek es Saleh. The truce of 1240 returned the Holy City to the hands of the Christians, but the end of the Christian hegemony was at hand. In 1244 a battle was again fought at Gaza, and the might of the Christians was completely broken. Shortly thereafter, Jerusalem again fell under the power of the Saracens, who laid waste the city in a frightful manner and spared not even the Holy Sepulchre. Worse still were the Kwarismanian hordes, summoned from the coast of the Caspian Sea to the army of Malek es Saleh. The devastation wreaked by them defies description. Everything that showed the least sign of Christianity was burned and destroyed. These bands roamed the Holy Land for two years, until Sultan Malek es Saleh was constrained to take measures against these too savage reserves and to drive them forcefully from the Holy Land. We need foster no illusions with regard to hermits on the walls or devout virgins dedicated to the contemplative life within the walls of Jerusalem. A Carmelite chronicler, who lived in the Holy Land in the last half of the 13th century, William of Sandwich, states among other things that pilgrimages to the Holy City were no longer possible after 1244, and that the religious of Jerusalem who were dependent on alms for their living were forced to flee to Phoenicia and abandon their houses in Palestine, with the exception of the Carmel near St. Jean d'Acre, which remained a stronghold of the Christians until 1291. The Carmelite Order, he states, was completely expelled from the Holy Land.[18] Under pressure from these persecutions many habitants of the religious houses in Palestine and Syria returned to Europe. In Belgium, one of the first foundations was made in 1235 at Valenciennes in Henegouwen, and mention was expressly made on that occasion of the unfavorable conditions in the Holy Land. Certainly, more favorable passing conditions occasionally

---

[18] "Chronica Guilelmi de Sanvico," *Analecta Ordinis Carmelitarum*, 3 (1914-1916), 302-315.

occurred, but they cannot be considered important enough to allow the restoration of the peaceful practice of the contemplative life in Jerusalem and be assumed to be such in the Christian world outside. Even between the years 1239 to 1244, this seems unlikely.

On the basis of these considerations, I think that the time Hadewijch ended her visions with the List of the Perfect must be placed between 1236 and 1244 and most likely between 1236 and 1239.

The Growth of the Mystical Life according to St. Teresa and Bl. John Ruusbroec[1]

If I may write a few pages here about the growth and flowering of the mystical life in St. Teresa and Bl. John Ruusbroec, it goes without saying that I shall not be able to enter into much detail, and shall have to confine myself to a few leading ideas, which in my opinion, on the one hand, typify the mysticism of both mystics and, on the other hand, show a striking agreement between them.

I do this gladly, even though the temptation exists to enter into greater detail on a given point. I do this all the more gladly, because I regard this agreement as a credit to both. We enthusiasts of Ruusbroec like to see that his doctrine which we find so attractive finds an echo and favor, is confirmed by the high authority which beyond any doubt is universally conceded to St. Teresa. But as a child of Carmel, dedicated to the study of mysticism, I am happy to be able to demonstrate briefly that what God showed her to be the way to him had already been grasped by Ruusbroec, and is a way which we Netherlanders may follow, pointed out to us, as it is, by one of ours.

I quote here what the Dutch Benedictine, Dom Willibrord Verkade, writes in his introduction to the *Brulocht (Spiritual Espousals)*, for I am not the first to draw a parallel between these two great mystics:

> For those who are familiar with the writings of St. Teresa, it will be a satisfaction to compare her doctrine on the four degrees of prayer with Ruusbroec's exposition. In the twenty-fifth chapter of the first Book, they will find a guide to the first degree of prayer,

---

[1] From *Ons Geestelijk Erf,* 6 (1932), 347-370.

meditative prayer. In the eighteenth chapter of the second Book, the second degree of prayer, the prayer of quiet, is described, after there has already been a discussion in the ninth chapter of the prayer of recollection. Chapters nineteen to twenty-eight treat of the third degree of prayer, of spiritual inebriety. Interwoven is an important chapter on 'raptures and divine revelations.' The last degree of prayer, the prayer of union, begins with the thirty-fifth chapter of the second Book and culminates in the sixty-first chapter and the two following.[2]

Fifty years ago, on the occasion of the third centenary of St. Teresa's transit to eternal life, the later general of the Jesuits, Father Luis Martín, then still professor at Salamanca, delivered a truly magisterial address, not only praising the great Saint of Avila, glory and pride of Spain, but also presenting a profile of her teaching. This address has been translated into various languages. In the introduction to the German translation it is called "a solid treatise on the mystical doctrine of St. Teresa as well as a charming portrait of her great soul."[3]

Most remarkable is the way in which Father Martin, when at the end of his long address he sets out to summarize briefly, as he says, St.Teresa's description of the last four Mansions of the Castle of the Soul – the first three Mansions in his opinion refer rather to the ascetical life – reproduces those brief contents in almost the same words as those with which Ruusbroec describes the last four steps of the mystical life in his summary work, *Van den blinckenden steen* (The Sparkling Stone):

> In the prayer of recollection the faculties feel themselves, as it were, drawn to the interior of the soul by the sweet invitation of the divine Shepherd, but they can and must still apply some of their natural energy, in order to reply to that divine call. In the prayer of quiet, God suspends the faculties, and the delight they experience from the

[2] Jan van Ruysbroeck, *Die Zierde der geistlichen Hochzeit*. Aus dem Flämischen von Willibrord Verkade, O.S.B., Mainz, 1922, Vorwort, 6.

[3] In the new editions of the standard biography of St. Teresa, Ribera's *Vida de Santa Teresa de Jesús*, published in Barcelona in 1908, that address is included as an introduction to the mystical life and doctrine of the saint.

presence of their Beloved is so great that it raises them to a state of rapture, which renders languorous their natural energy. Union with God has an even more powerful effect; it causes the faculties to sleep the sleep of peace and love. Reduced to this condition, they find themselves powerless to shake off this sort of mystical lethargy. Finally, they die to the world and to themselves in the spiritual betrothal, which is celebrated in the Sixth Mansion, and rise to a new life in the Seventh Mansion, to devote themselves entirely to the service of their heavenly spouse, to whom they have united themselves by an indissoluble bond of love.[4]

Besides the three first stages, likewise of a more ascetical tendency, Ruusbroec also knows three higher stages, above which there is, finally, a *gemeen leven*, which can best be described as life in the most intimate communion with God. Thus Ruusbroec, like St. Teresa, sums up the actual mystical life in four states of the soul. After he has described the three lower stages in the chapter on the enjoyment of God, he continues literally as follows:

There are three more points,which are higher and which make man steadfast and able to always enjoy and experience God whenever he is willing to dispose himself accordingly. The first of these points is to rest in the one you enjoy. That is where the beloved is conquered by the beloved and the beloved is possessed by the beloved in bare, essential love, there the beloved has fallen into the beloved with affection and each is utterly the other's in possession and in rest. There follows the second point and that is to fall asleep in God: that is where the spirit sinks away from itself and knows not how, or where. And there follows the last point man can put into words: that is where the spirit contemplates a darkness it cannot enter with its rason. And there it feels itself dead and lost and one with God without any difference. And where it feels itself one with God, God himself is its peace, its enjoyment and its rest. And therefore it is all unfathomable in which the spirit has to die to its own self in bliss

---

[4] Luis Martin, S.J., in Discursos leídos en Salamanca el día 23 de octubre de 1882 en el acto de adjudicación de premios del certamen literario, celebrado para solemnizar el tercer centenario de la gloriosa muerte de Santa Teresa de Jesús en Alba de Tormes, Madrid, 1882, 41-127.

and return to life in virtues at love's command and touch. And look, if you experience these six points in yourself, you experience all that I have told you before, and all that I could ever tell you. And if you turn inward contemplation and enjoyment are as easy and as accessible to you as if you live in nature. And from this wealth derives the common life I promised to tell you about in the beginning.

The man who is sent by God down from these heights, into the world, is full of truth and rich in all virtues. And he seeks nothing for himself but only the honor of the one who sent him, and therefore he is just and true in all his actions. And he has a rich, mild foundation wich is grounded in the wealth of God, and therefore he must always flow into all those who need him, for the living fountain of the Holy Spirit is hid wealth which cannot be exhausted. And he is a living, willing instrument of God with which God does what he wants, the way he wants; and he does not claim this for himself, but gives the honor to God. And therefore he remains willing and ready to do all that God commands, and strong and courageous to suffer and bear all that God allows to befall him. And therefore he has a common life, for contemplation and action come just as readily to him and he is perfect in both. For on one can have this common life unless he is a contemplative man.[5]

Both St. Teresa and Ruusbroec speak to us here of turning inward, of introversion, of the necessity of entering into oneself in order to find in the inmost depths of the soul the God who dwells within us, thus to arrive at the experience of intimate communion with him. For both mystics, that turning inward, that introversion, that entering into oneself, leads to a state of rest and satisfaction, of enchantment with what the soul, entering into herself, finds in herself as her greatest treasure, her Beloved who dwells in her and whom she need not seek outside herself. The consciousness of carrying the Beloved of her heart within her and having him near gives her a quiet enjoyment, ravishes her faculties, draws all attention to him, turns her aside from whatever up till now fascinated and occupied her. Her faculties, as it were,

[5] The Sparkling Stone, lines 763-793, Vanden blinkenden steen, lines; *Opera omnia*, ed. by G. de Baere, (*et al.*) Tielt/Turnhout, 1991, X, 178, 180, 182.

become independent of the impressions other objects would want to make on them. They seem blunted for the world outside and entirely taken up in the contemplation of him who exceeds all else in worth and requires complete attention to himself. They seem to be in a spiritual sleep, in which the soul dreams of the Beloved, and although individual impressions of the outside world still threaten to disturb and interrupt that sleep, the soul is nevertheless independent of all those impressions and also tries her best to sink away into that sweet slumber and devote herself entirely to the contemplation of her Beloved. Often that spiritual sleep overpowers her, and she is no longer in a state to occupy herself with the things of the world about her, or to shake off that slumber. She sinks away entirely in the contemplation and enjoyment of the object of her love and seems to be dead and lost to the world. She casts herself, as it were, into the arms of her Beloved, betroths herself to him, and would like to stay with him always. The world can no longer enthrall her; she has neither ear nor eye for it. God is her only treasure; in him she wants to rest and never leave him again. If in that state her faithfulness is tried, the Beloved strengthens her in his love and celebrates with her the spiritual marriage of indissoluble union and of the most interior communion, worthy to be called by Ruusbroec common life (*ghemein leven*), because she then lives only in and through the Beloved. The soul has devoted herself entirely to her Bridegroom and has become a willing tool in the hands of God, whose hands she no longer leaves, from whose embrace she is no longer withdrawn, not even through contact with the world. She has awakened and risen to a new life, a life in which the natural and supernatural wonderfully blend, in which nothing can separate the soul from the contemplation of her Beloved, whom she adores in herself and surrounds with expressions of her love, whom she beholds in everything that happens or exists in the world outside her, whose will she adores and glorifies in everything, with whom, in a word, she lives in indissoluble communion and to whom she has not only delivered herself entirely, but who has drawn her wholly to himself and will never release her again.

Introversion and quiet, drowsiness and spiritual sleep, awakening and death, resurrection and new life experienced through God – these, according to Teresa and Ruusbroec, are the four steps of the mystical life, pictured in four consecutive psychic states of ever more intimate union with God.

Both agree especially in seeing the mystical life as something that develops in the soul in keeping with its natural inclination, as a realization of a potentiality embodied in her nature by God himself, which will be realized if the soul is conscious of her potency for perfection and, in order to arrive at that highest of conditions, surrenders herself completely into the hands of God who alone can raise her to the highest heights and therefore requires nothing else of her than that she conduct herself according to his wishes and desires, trusts him, and places in him her only happiness. He desires an ordered love and wishes to order love in her himself. He does not deny her the love of creatures, but he wants her to love him above all and other things in, through, and with him. Because her love is all too inordinate, and she loses herself in the enjoyment of perishable things, he wants her, first of all, to begin to enter into herself and to reflect that he lives in the innermost depth of her heart and in that most interior dwelling stands at the door and knocks and invites her to come to him and no longer wander about in the outer buildings, as though he, her quest, had not yet arrived. She must abandon and leave all things instantly, and join him in the most interior part of her soul. Once she is admitted there, united to him, she may from that central point freely examine and wander through the whole castle. Then all is hers, just as all is his.

The mystical life, therefore, is an ordering, a directing of the faculties of the soul to the object of knowledge and love. Because God is the highest and accordingly the most satisfying object, which provides the most happiness and love, God must occupy the highest and first place in the ordering of love. That God must occupy the highest place in the ordering of our knowledge and love derives not only from the all-exceeding and infinitely perfect character and nature of the divine Being in itself, but also from the dependent nature of everything we know and love. God is the creator and conserver of all being, and his action and love are revealed in all things; in everything the finger of God touches us. But in nothing is God nearer to us than in ourselves. It is there that we must first try to find and see him. We must not allow ourselves to become lost in the imagery of Teresa or Ruusbroec. No matter how remarkable it might be that both attempt to picture the mystical life in its gradual development and steady growth in almost the same terms and in the description of almost the same psychic states, this agreement points to a much deeper one. The *recogimiento* of St. Teresa and the *inkeer* of Ruusbroec point to the fact that both concentrate on a wonderful faculty of our nature, which we usually call the faculty of abstraction, and which possesses the ability of penetrating more deeply the object of our sensory observation and perception, to discover an element of intellectual knowability which actually exists there. In the metaphysical contemplation of himself, and really of all creation, but in the first place of himself, man ultimately sees his inner and essential dependency and origin from God, who meets him there and reveals to him his love, wisdom, and power. And as he penetrates deeper and deeper into that dependency and origin from God's hand, there unfolds for him something of that groundless mystery of the birth of eternal Wisdom from the bosom of the Father, for in that eternal birth of the Son of God, God recognizes himself as the image and ground of all that will come into being. Together with the Son, we ourselves are born of the Father according to our image, and our creation and conservation in time is the remote revelation of our eternal, divine origin. Thus, the Blessed Trinity meets us in the depths of our being, just as it occupied itself with us from eternity and now in time causes us always to be what we are.

In his sketch of Ruusbroec's doctrine presented in the just published, excellent commemorative volume, *Jan van Ruusbroec, Leven, Werken*,[6] Father Reypens has rightly spoken of the stamp

---

[6] Leonce Reypens, S.J., "Ruusbroec's mystieke leer," *Jan van Ruusbroec, Leven, Werken*. Onder de redactie van het Ruusbroec-Genootschap Antwerpen, Mechelen/Amsterdam, 1931, pp.151-177.

of exemplarism which Ruusbroec's mystical doctrine bears and, by way of synthesis, of Trinitarian mysticism. These are only different expressions for what has been said above. He also sees the viewing of God in creatures as the basic idea of Ruusbroec's mysticism. From creatures, or rather in creatures, we must ascend to God, in order to rediscover all things in God. We must see creatures as coming from God's hand and as a reflection of the light that has its source in God. Following the rays of light, we climb to the source, the origin of those rays, to the sun, to God. In God, we find all things again, better and more beautiful than they are in themselves. Thus we learn to regard God as comprising all that is and can be. When God understands himself, he at the same time includes all that is outwardly possible, all that can share being with him, because he can bestow being in keeping with the perfect understanding he possesses of being, of himself. That is why there is such an emphasis in Ruusbroec's mysticism on the procession (*ute gaen*) of all creatures from the bosom of the Father through the birth of the Son, and on the need of trying to realize and understand this before all else. To grasp this idea, *inkeer* (introversion) entering into oneself, is necessary, in order to discover in oneself one's divine origin, to become aware of the divine indwelling, to understand properly one's sharing in the divine nature. If this "flowing out of God" is understood by the soul and at the same time seen as an image of the "eternal procession of the eternal Word of the Father" will the soul understand how the Bridegroom (*Brudegom*) comes to meet her, and how she in turn must go to meet him, for the further elaboration of the image, which in the Blessed Trinity gives her the "flowing back into the one nature of the Godhead." Like "the flowing out of the Son from the Father, and of the Holy Spirit from the Father and the Son, and the reverse flowing of the three Persons into the one nature of the Godhead," the soul must also see herself going out from God, and God coming to meet her, in order to turn herself to God and return to him as her ground and origin, with whom to be one is her highest glory, her greatest perfection.

And through the eternal birth, all creatures have gone out eternally, before they were created in time. Thus God has beheld them and known them in Himself....

This eternal going-out, this eternal life which we have and are within God, eternally, without ourselves, is the cause of our created being in time. And our created being is suspended in the eternal being, and, with respect to its essential (*wesenlike*] being, it is one with it. And this eternal being and life, which we have and are in the eternal Wisdom of God, is like unto God. For it has an eternal in-dwelling without distinction, in the divine being; and it has an eternal out-flowing, through the birth of the Son, into an otherness, with distinction, according to eternal reason....

And this is God's image and God's likeness, and our image and our likeness, for God reflects Himself and all things in it. In this divine image, all creatures have an eternal life without themselves, as in their eternal exemplar. And the Holy Trinity has made us to this eternal image and to this likeness. And therefore God would have us go out of ourselves in this divine light and supernaturally pursue this image – which is our own life – and possess it actively and enjoyably with Him in eternal blessedness.[7]

In the light of this text, we can better understand why Ruusbroec chose as the motto and leading idea of his *Spiritual Espousals* (Chierheit der gheesteliker Brulocht) the phrase, "Behold, the Bridegroom cometh, go out to meet him."[8]

The meeting of the Bridegroom as creator and conserver in the deepest center of created being is certainly not the only meeting (*toecomst*) with the contemplative soul. The light by which God appears before our eyes as creator becomes more glorious and radiant, when he is also seen as the incarnate Word, as the bearer of grace, as the rewarder of good with eternal glory on the day of judgment. This light becomes even fuller and deeper, when it

---

[7] *Spiritual Espousals Die geestelike brulocht*, lines c 112-114, c 116-123, c 129-136; *Opera omnia*, ed. by G. de Baere (*et al.*), Tielt/Turnhout, 1988, III, 586, 588, 590.
    [8] Mt 25, 6.

penetrates not only the senses and imagination, not only the higher faculties of memory, understanding, and will, but the soul itself. Ruusbroec then speaks of infused clarity and breathed-in heat, of an overwhelming by the light, which pours itself out over us and lifts us up in its rays and unites us with the source of light, so that we become one with it and feel ourselves penetrated and devoured by it. But although that mystical union far exceeds the intellectual contemplation of God by way of abstraction as creator and conserver, yet for Ruusbroec this contemplation constitutes the first predisposition, the foundation, the point of departure. The life of grace builds up on the life of nature, just as mystical gifts are the further outgrowth of the life of grace, its overflowing, immeasurable revelation. Contemplation in the natural order makes us see God living and working in us, and from this contemplation the soul advances in the discovery of God's glory, because God continually reveals himself to the questing soul in ever clearer and more radiant light.

Typical of St. Teresa is her insistence on the foundation of the mystical life in our nature, her representation in the *Interior Castle* of the ascent of the bride to the Bridegroom as a gradual perfecting, as a realization by degrees of what exists in the aptitude of nature and of what God can realize in it on the foundation of that nature and in keeping with it. Here, too, there is a wonderful harmony between the natural and the supernatural, between the life of grace and mystical gifts. God, as it were, extends his creature further and raises it to its highest perfection. The development is so gradual that one would take it for Nature's work, but at the same time there is such an exalted rising above all the faculties of nature that only a divine gift could effect an ascent to those highest heights, could conduct nature to the ideal set by God. However much that exalted perfection exceeds the capacity of nature, it nevertheless remains a true fulfillment of that nature, a realization of what God has placed in us as a potentiality, even though that perfection can be realized only through his direct intervention.

True, there is a difference in the description by Teresa and Ruusbroec of that foundation in nature. Although the basic idea is the same, it does not take quite the same form in each case. Ruusbroec is more metaphysical, more intellectual. He extends the foundation further, and shows us more clearly how we must make the necessary distinctions in the being of the creature, in order to project a philosophically correct image of the mutual relation of both. The intellect delights in analyzing abstrusely the ontology of the highest as well as of created being. Ruusbroec still betrays here a certain dependency from and affinity with the intellectual school of Eckhart. In such philosophical reflections, the intellect finds nourishment and satisfaction. The mystical life is more deeply rationalized, and intellectual reflection provides it a solid foundation. In Teresa, such intellectual reflection is much more reduced; it is, as it were, taken for granted rather than minutely demonstrated. Teresa is much sooner over the bridge and is very quickly on the familiar ground of mystical grace. The images she uses make it clear that she has the same point of departure, but she hardly finds it necessary to make this evident by a series of organized ideas. However, in her diamond palace of the soul the sun stands as the source of light in the inmost Mansion and shoots its rays into the numerous adjacent Mansions. Its rays penetrate only weakly into the outer ones, because all manner of impediments hold back that radiance. But in Ruusbroec that light shining from the middle beckons to open the eye and approach the inner mansions, to behold the light in all its clarity, and to be illumined by that light. Here, Teresa has the image of the opposing beam of light shining from the innermost and deepest part of the soul, as well as that of the Lord knocking and calling, inviting the soul to introversion, to the most interior mansion. That call reaches only faintly to the outermost ring of the mansions, but happy is the one who hears that call and follows it.

The first grace is the messenger of ever-greater graces. In Teresa also, the Bridegroom of the soul goes to meet her, and the first grace is that the soul is able to see that meeting (*toecomst*) of the Bridegroom, to understand his voice. No other way leads the soul to her Bridegroom than that of introversion into herself. And although the first seeing, the first hearing, is to be regarded as a grace from God, which at once causes his light to penetrate the soul, at once allows his voice to be heard by her, an answer must be given to that invitation of love, and the soul must detach herself from what hitherto attracted her. In Teresa as well as in Ruusbroec, the eyes must be wiped, in order to see more clearly and better what God already presents to be seen in the outermost mansions for those who have eyes to see, to be listened to for those who have ears to hear. God can and will draw and bind the soul, make her rest in him and drowse, but only after the soul has managed to tear herself from what attempts to hold her in the world, in the outermost mansions, in the world of sensory knowledge and satisfaction and of intellectual contemplation, directed only to perishable things. The soul must free herself and set out to the mansion where in her inmost self the Bridegroom calls her to himself. She must abandon herself entirely to God and place herself under the powerful rays of the Sun, which, in Teresa as well as in Ruusbroec, is pictured to us as able and fit to shine through and draw to itself whatever falls under its rays. Ruusbroec develops the images of sun and light more harmoniously and completely; with him the imagery becomes an allegory. Teresa is satisfied with a few casual strokes about this image, in order to choose another which clarifies the first, without working out details.

But the leading idea is the same in both. While Ruusbroec is often difficult for the unschooled mind to follow, when he – although not in an excessively intellectual manner – compares the procession of the divine Persons to the metaphysical contemplation of our being, in order to demonstrate as clearly as possible for human understanding how God comes to us and meets as the Bridegroom of his most beloved bride, all this Teresa manages to explain in the simplest manner for her unschooled sisters, without a great deal of metaphysics and in a way more suited to them.

> I began to think of the soul as if it were a castle made of a single diamond or of a very clear crystal, in which there are many rooms, just as in heaven there are many mansions. Now, if we think carefully over this, sisters, the soul of the righteous man is nothing but a paradise, in which, as God tells us, he takes his delight. For what do you think a room will be like which is the delight of a King so

mighty, so wise, so pure, and so full of all that is good? I can find nothing with which to compare the great beauty of a soul and its great capacity. In fact, however acute our intellects may be, they will no more be able to attain to a comprehension of this than to an understanding of God; for, as he himself says, he created us in his image and likeness. Now if this is so – and it is – there is no point in our fatiguing ourselves by attempting to comprehend the beauty of this castle.... The very fact that His Majesty says it is made in his image means that we can hardly form any conception of the soul's great dignity and beauty. It is no small pity, and should cause us no little shame, that, through our own fault, we do not understand ourselves, or know who we are.... As to what good qualities there may be in our souls, or who dwells within them, or how precious they are – those are things which we seldom consider.... Let us now imagine that his castle, as I have said, contains many mansions, some above, others below, others at each side; and in the centre and midst of them all is the chiefest mansion, where the most secret things pass between God and the soul. You must think over this comparison very carefully.... Now let us return (Teresa continues a few pages further on) to our beautiful and delightful castle and see how we can enter it. I seem rather to be talking nonsense; for if this castle is the soul, there can clearly be no question of our entering it. For we ourselves are the castle: and it would be absurd to tell someone to enter a room when he was in it already! But you must understand that there are many ways of 'being' in a place. Many souls remain in the outer court of the castle, which is the place occupied by the guards; they are not interested in entering it, and have no idea what there is in that wonderful place, or who dwells in it, or even how many rooms it has. You will have read certain books on prayer which advise the soul to enter within itself; and that is exactly what this means.[9]

I could continue, but these quotations from the first chapter of the *Interior Castle* of St. Teresa already demonstrate clearly enough that if her reflections on the mystical life are built on the tenet that God created and preserves the soul in being according to his image

[9] *Interior Castle, First Mansions*, ch. 1; *The Complete Works of Saint Teresa of Jesus*, tr. & ed. by E. Allison Peers, (3 v., London, 1946), II, 201-203.

and likeness, he himself has his dwelling in the inmost mansion of
the soul, and hence the soul must enter into herself, in order to
take the first steps along the way of interiority, to meet him who
invites her into the inmost part of her being to his embrace and
union with himself.

It is sometimes suggested that St. Teresa conceives the life of
prayer as purely affective, and hence forms a certain contrast to
Ruusbroec, in whom intellectual reflection, the rational element,
would be much more pronounced. The grandiloquent title,
Seraphic Virgin, bestowed on St. Teresa, has caused this idea to
be even more widely accepted. A favorite quotation in support of
this notion is her statement, "The important thing is not to think
much, but to love much."¹⁰ However, when one refers to the place
where she makes this statement, one reads how much value she
attaches to mental prayer, although she wants to see it interrupted
and alternated with feelings of love and gratitude, and admits that
a time may come when the Lord so fills the soul with love that it
is no longer necessary to arouse that love by the exercise of the
intellect. She expressly warns that, even when God fills the soul
with feelings of love and gratitude, of wonder and happiness, one
should not abandon meditation, which is the ordinary way to
move the will.

For that matter, one need only read the works of St. Teresa to
see that for her the rationalization and logical development of the
truth has a very important place, and that she accorded a significant role not only to the working of the intellect but also to
that of the imagination. In how many comparisons does she not
pour herself out, in order to bring her Sisters to understand the
most sublime things. True, she admits and explains her inability
to find the proper expressions to explain what God bestows in
mystical graces. She gratefully admits that God makes a soul
understand more in a moment of enlightenment than we can
come to know in years of study and reflection, but this never
betrays her into the neglect of mental prayer, or causes her to

¹⁰ Ibid., Fourth Mansions, ch. 1; The Complete Works, II, 233.

underestimate the judgment of a professionally trained director. She wants us to use the faculties of imagination and intellect, in order, even though slowly, to make as much progress as we can with our weak powers. Not that she does not abundantly admit that mystical grace is a gift of God, and that we can do nothing to reach the highest grades, but at the same time she requires continual cooperation and especially grateful correspondence with all our strength to the gift of grace. She puts the strongest emphasis on the removal of the hindrances we place to the working of God's incomprehensible goodness and generosity. She is miles away from Molinistic quietism. With all her might, she insists on the practice of virtue, even in the highest stages of mystical contemplation and profoundest union with God. For her, as well as for Ruusbroec, the first three stages of our ascent to God are not only the treading of the way of the practice of virtue, but she wishes to see this continued to the last, and considers it, first, as the best preparation and proof of our receptivity; next, as the worthy companion of the life of union with God, an ornament of the soul, which enjoys the privilege of being chosen by God as his dearly beloved bride, and, as such, of being overladen with proofs of his favor; finally, as the necessary crowning, the promised fruit of intercourse with God. Assuredly, here, too, there is often talk of infused virtues, of acting under the irresistible urgency of God's grace, but here Teresa warns more than once against delusion and expressly states that no virtue is to be called genuine which has not been proven by continual practice of one's own. She admits no elevation of the natural order through the divine indwelling, but rather a continual ennobling of the activity of the distinct faculties. Here and there, she will represent the activity of the imagination and memory, even of the will, as obstructive; compares them to the wild fluttering of bats, the mad leaping of untamed beasts that waylay and threaten us at our penetration of the mysterious castle, but here it is a question of the unbridled activity of those faculties, of which precisely the harmonious activity must be stressed. For this, precisely, introversion is necessary. In the end, God shows his sovereignty by fettering all the faculties in his service and seizing them without taking away their ability to work. The higher the soul stands on the ladder of mystical union, the more harmoniously the faculties work together, in order not only not to place obstacles in the way, but also, by directing themselves to the highest object, to make the soul's enjoyment as complete as possible. Then they all again take action and are all free to act, in order to give all of nature an immediate share in the enjoyment of the highest faculties, nay, of the soul. What Teresa stressed as strongly as possible in the beginning of the spiritual life; that, namely, the ascent to God must be a perfecting of nature, that she upholds, if possible, more strongly still, in her description of the highest stages. There we encounter human nature in all the lustre of harmonious development. This is also the great merit of Ruusbroec.

I am pleased to be able to call attention to this, because the notion is all too common that mystical grace is the destruction of nature. I shall not enter into details about views such as those of Otterloo who, whatever his merits for having in a lengthy dissertation brought Ruusbroec's mysticism to the attention of many in this land, nevertheless, gives an entirely mistaken impression of that mysticism.[11]

The incident is well-known in the life of Ruusbroec, according to which, walking through the streets of Brussels one day, he heard one passerby say to another that he would not like to be like Ruusbroec, and upon being asked the reason by the other, explained that he would then not have another happy day in his life. Ruusbroec replied most emphatically that only one who had no understanding of true mysticism could speak thus.

For him, too, mystical grace was the highest flowering of human nature, in which God certainly profusely communicates his light and strength, but in which the human being is spurred on and enabled by God to the highest activity. Nature is not reduced to

---

[11] Antonie Adriaan van Otterloo, Johannes Ruysbroeck: een bijdrage tot de kennis van den ontwikkelingsgang der mystiek, Amsterdam, 1874.

nothing. It realizes itself to its highest perfection, because God, who created it to his image and likeness, and wills that it be perfect as the heavenly Father is perfect, wishes to see that likeness made as striking as possible and nature's most profound potentiality realized, not by absorbing it into his Being, but by causing it, united to him and resting in him, to be itself in the highest development of its being. Not less emphatically than Teresa, Ruusbroec posits the harmonious accompaniment of mystical grace and natural activity:

> (God) demands of us enjoyment and activity, and that the one should not be hindered by the other, but rather always be fortified. Therefore, the inner person possesses his life in these two modes, that is, in resting and in activity. And in each, he is whole and undivided, for he is wholly in God, where he rests in enjoyment, and he is wholly in himself, where he loves with works. And he is admonished and bidden by God at every moment to renew both rest and activity. And, at every moment, the spirit's justice wants to pay whatever is bidden of it. And, therefore, every time God glances within, his spirit turns inwards, in action and in enjoyment. And thus, he is renewed in all virtues, and more deeply immersed in enjoyable rest. For God gives, in one bestowal, Himself and all His gifts; and the spirit, in each inward-turning, gives itself and all its works. For through the simple inward inshining of God and the enjoyable inclination and transport through love, the spirit is united with God, and without cease is transported into rest. And through the gifts of understanding and of savoring-wisdom, it is touched for action, and it is enlightened and enkindled in love at every moment. And all that a person might desire is shown and presented to him in the spirit. He is hungry and thirsty, for he sees the angels' food and heavenly drink; he labors greatly in love for he sees his rest. He is a pilgrim and he sees his homeland. He struggles in love for victory, for he sees his crown. Consolation, peace, joy, beauty, and riches, and all that can gladden (him) are shown to enlightened reason, in God, without measure, in spiritual similitudes, and by means of this showing and the touch of God, love remains at active.[12]

---

[12] *Spiritual Espousals*, lines B 1933-1935; *Opera omnia*, III, 532, 534.

How this "showing", this heavenly light, drives and urges to love and to works of love is described further on in the *Spiritual Espousals*, where Ruusbroec writes:

> ... through the inborn light; thus they are transformed and at one with that same light by which they see and which they see. And thus the contemplative persons are attaining their eternal image to which they were made, and they contemplate God and all things without distinction in a one-fold seeing, in divine brightness. And this is the noblest and most profitable contemplation to which one can come in this life. For in this contemplation, one remains sovereignly master of himself and free, and in each loving turning-inward, can grow in sublimity of life, beyond all that one can understand. And he remains free and master of himself in inner practice things and in virtues."[13]

When we read this, we see that in the harmonious development of the mystical life according to Ruusbroec, not only is there room, besides the divine activity, for the expression of perfected nature, but also that, besides the action of the intellect, ample room is given for the outpouring of love and for works in which the expression of love is predominant.

The suggestion is sometimes made that in Ruusbroec the effect of Eckhart's ideas is so strong that he has given an all too intellectual stamp to mysticism. If in St. Teresa the affective element is sometimes seen to be too onesidedly brought out, and it appears after a closer examination and reading of her works that this affective element, although strongly stressed, is supported in a healthy and harmonious manner by intellectual reasoning and reflection, a reading of Ruusbroec's works shows that, although here and there the intellectual element occupies a very important place in the moving of the will and the expression of love, his mysticism is nevertheless to be styled a love song, harmonizes with the love mysticism of St. Bernard, and in a happy manner causes the two principle faculties of human nature to come into their own. In this respect, there is certainly a difference between Ruusbroec and

---

[13] *Spiritual Espousals*, lines 156-165; *Opera omnia*, III, 592.

St. Teresa, but difference here should not be stressed to become opposition. There is a difference of nuance; the accent is in a sense different, but the melody is the same, and in this heavenly melody, in the case of Teresa as well as of Ruusbroec, the bass of intellectual speculation sounds together with the tenor of love's unbosoming. The fact that the Seraphic Virgin sings somewhat higher than the wonderful seer of these Lowlands does not bring them both into disharmony, but brings both together in a beautiful accord.

In the last passage we cited, we hear and note how also for Ruusbroec love crowns reflection, and the activity of the intellect bears its fruit in the expression of love. It is a great merit of Ruusbroec that he consciously assigns so prominent a place to the activity of the imagination and intellect, without losing himself in the idea, or paying too little attention, to the expression of love.

Father Reypens has somewhere quite correctly stated, "His entire work, no matter how speculatively extended, retains the full echo and sometimes the letter of autotochthonous love mysticism, the mysticism of the unbosoming of love, springing spontaneously from Ruusbroec's emotion-filled and love-fired soul; a mysticism which a century previously had reached its apogee in Hadewijch and its spring-fed profusion in Beatrice of Nazareth, and of which Ruusbroec had perhaps read more than is hitherto known to us or preserved."[14]

The very title of Ruusbroec's chief work, *Chierheit der gheestelíker Brulocht* (The Spiritual Espousals), places us in the bride-mysticism to which St. Bernard gave such beautiful form and attractiveness by his commentary and application of the Song of Solomon. A Beguine of Tongeren in an ardent dialogue between the soul and God had already anticipated the beauty of the *Gheesteliker Brulocht* (The Spiritual Espousals). The Cistercian, Gerard van Luik, in his *Bereydinghe des Harten* (The Preparation of the Heart) already described the bridal gown of the bride who goes in to her Bridegroom, and, as it were, prepared hearts for the clear expositions with which Ruusbroec would consolidate this love

---

[14] This reference not found.

mysticism and preserve it from onesidedness. It is as if Ruusbroec, in the face of the upcoming exaggerated intellectual idea of mysticism, thought of the Beguine of Tongeren and the doctrine of the heart of the Cistercian of Reims/Liège and wanted to point to them, when he set about elaborating the same image in a comprehensive and thoroughly studied work.

Striking in many respects is the agreement between Ruusbroec's *Chierheit der gheesteliker Brulocht* (The Spiritual Espousals) and Teresa's *Interior Castle*, both classic works. I would like to point this out again for a moment, not only as I did in the beginning, because of their similarity in presenting the psychic states, but especially for the way both works direct the mystical life toward most intimate communion with the Beloved in the embrace of love.

If Ruusbroec speaks of nuptials, Teresa also traces the way to the highest heights through espousals to marriage. Ruusbroec's common life is nothing more than the new life with the Beloved in the mysticism of St. Teresa. Dead to what was hindrance for that intimate union, prepared for it by the practice of virtue, in the human being under the influence of God's grace, God's overflowing infusion of his strength and cooperation, a new enobled life finally finds expression, in which God and human, joined in indissoluble oneness, share a single common life, in which the most perfect harmony between the divine and human exists. In this union, rapture, ecstasy, flight of the spirit are only accidental conditions, which, it is true, are a revelation of union with God, but are not the first or substantial part. They are, so to speak, although high yet imperfect conditions, because there is not yet complete agreement between Ruusbroec's *"rastene en werken"* (rest and activity); not yet such a union with the Beloved according the whole of nature, which nothing is able to sunder. Both Ruusbroec and Teresa, in fine, admit the possibility of a union with God, in which he rules our whole life without our natural activity being hindered.

To reach that goal a long way will have to be traversed. In the beginning, introversion will be seen to necessitate a hard struggle;

much in us will have to die, in order that God might live in us free and unhindered. There is a life which in the first stages ought rather be called a death. But neither of our mystics wanted to regard the way to union with God as wholly negative; death should be a passage to a new life. While death is inflicted on everything in us that stands in the way of God's kingdom, at the same time the heavenly Gardener should be sowing the seed of virtues, and we should be planting and caring for the garden of our hearts, in order that soon, when the sun is at the zenith, the flowers may shoot up as a sign of the new Spring-like life. The care, the watering of the garden, is to a large extent placed in our hands. We must not only weed but also plant and water, but the Great Gardener helps us, or, to use a favorite expression of St. Teresa, he guides the water of his grace along several brooks and channels to the garden of our heart and lets his abundant rain fall at the proper time, thus rendering unnecessary the work of watering. However, we must continue to work at the adornment of our heart, even though the Bridegroom offers his help. Ruusbroec's *Chierheit* (The Spiritual Espousals) demonstrates in the clearest possible manner that the bride must clothe herself in the bridal gown of the most beautiful virtues. To this theme, he devotes the greatest part of his work. Teresa makes the same point when, drawing upon the old medieval treatise of the *Spiritual Chess Game*, she says that we must play a game of spiritual chess with our Beloved, with the King of our heart, and checkmate him. She adds that he cannot avoid being checkmated and does not wish to do so. By this, she lets us know that although we must do our best, the game is rigged in a way that makes the checkmate of the King inevitable, as long as we play as we should. The King will lose all the sooner according as the Queen – that is, our humility – is given freer play and can checkmate him. Ruusbroec begins by pointing out that we must nevertheless keep our eyes open, wipe our eyes clean, in order to see how the Bridegroom comes. We must go out from ourselves, we must do all we can to meet him, but he will come. Whoever does not withdraw from his embrace, by continuing to wander about amid earthly things and not opening his heart for him, will in the end discover his overflowing love. It all comes down to the fact that, although mystical grace is a pure gift of God, in the representation of both mystics God is so good, so full of love for us, and so driven to union with us, that the way to that mystic grace consists in the enlargement of our receptivity, the removal of obstacles, and the practice of the virtues, after which God, in the abundance of his love, will not withhold the awareness of union, nay, of union with him.

This is why both mystical systems, no matter how lofty in the description of the sweet commerce of the soul with God, on the other hand are so sober and matter-of-fact, so realistic and practical, and besides the exuberant wonder at the goodness and love of God – a wonder which especially in Ruusbroec no longer finds words and becomes a *stummer Jubel*, an eloquent stammer – at the same time lay the greatest emphasis on our preparation and cooperation.

Thus, both mystical systems have a strong didactic character. Both mystics are masters of the spiritual life, who did not in the first place gave utterance to something which in itself drove them to utterance, although both admit that here and there they were driven to write, but they wrote above all so that others might know the ways along which God is wont to lead souls to union with him. They both founded a school and in the plans of Providence were both given to us to enlighten many on the winding path of the mystical life. We may be grateful to God, it is a privilege to acknowledge the leadership of persons so obviously enlightened by God, it is a grace to see in them masters whose lessons we gladly follow. It is fortunate that at this time the figure of Ruusbroec again shines in glory, and that in him we may acknowledge the safe guide, the wise father, the proven master of the spiritual life. Oh, perhaps it was not necessary still to place that image beside that of the *Mater spiritualium*, the Mother of the Spiritual Life, revered and followed in the whole Church as the virgin enlightened by God, but it guarantees him more followers, a more loyal following, to know that the idea of the mystical life which led him is by and large the same as that of the Seraphic Virgin of Avila.

Finally, one other thought. God working and living in us is the point of departure of the mystical life. In that working of God, we should see the continuation of God's creation, just as the latter is again the continuation and further revelation of the eternal procession of the Son from the Father, and of the Holy Spirit from the Father and the Son. The awareness of that life of God in us, of the indwelling of the Blessed Trinity must again be awakened in us. God must live in us again, must be reborn in us. God's Son took on human nature, in order that we might again share in the union of our nature with the divine. We must unite ourselves to Christ, and in and with and through him to the entire Blessed Trinity.

No creature shared that grace more than Mary. She, our mother, is our model for the way in which God is also to be born in us, must live in us. We must on the one hand know ourselves to be her children, because her Son, Christ, is our brother; on the other hand, she must teach us how we also must receive and carry Christ in us, and how he must be born in us.

Thus, Mary is the Mother of the Spiritual Life, of the life of awareness of God, of the experience of God.

I conclude this short reflection by pointing out that in keeping with their mystical doctrine both Teresa and Ruusbroec have seen Mary in this light, and in their ascent to the highest heights have always wished to be her simple and true children. They tell us expressly that we can arrive where Christ calls us only clasping Mary by the hand. And this concluding observation includes a prayer that all of us, children of Mary, may learn from her what her image inspired in the seer of the Soniënbosch and in the seer of Avila. Her "Behold, the handmaid of the Lord" is another way of saying, "Behold, the Bridegroom cometh, go out to meet him," which again sounds different, but means the same as entering, at the sweet fluting of the King, the castle in the innermost mansion of the soul, in order to abandon oneself entirely to the call of the Bridegroom.

Nicholas van Esch[1]

I

Spiritual Director of the Young Canisius

The 16th century, which saw the rise of the Reformation in the Northern Provinces, and which is consequently regarded as a century of serious religious decline among the Catholics of our country, was not as dark a time as it is generally thought to be.

It is the century of the beginning of the Counter-Reformation, a term used to show that, while nascent Protestantism interiorized religion and opposed the many abuses in the Catholic Church, the Catholics themselves proceeded to a profound reform, and in the resulting fierce struggle not only did great and mighty defenders of the Church arise, but also serious and fruitful efforts were made to remove abuses which reform had highlighted.

No matter how praiseworthy it may be to set forth the glory of the Counter-Reformation and to regard the 16th century in this light, nevertheless, there is danger that thus this difficult and complex time will not be seen in a broad enough context.

There was still so much of beauty in our low lands by the sea; in many places, there was still such deep devotion and inner experience of what for centuries had been our heritage; what the 15th century especially had established upon elements of the "Modern Devotion" – not only in the Netherlands but far beyond – as the foundation of a new and flourishing spiritual life was so powerfully and splendidly continued, that it would be a pity if the Church of 16th century Netherlands were regarded as though the

---

[1] From *De Gelderlander*, April 30, May 9, December 3, 10, 17,24, 1938.

Reformation on the one hand and the Counter-Reformation on the other had initiated an entirely new spiritual life.

Deserving of every attention is a third respect under which this period of the church history of our country may be regarded; namely, how the old traditions were perpetuated; how the tree of the Church of its own inner vitality constantly sprouted new branches of piety, intimately joined to the old trunk and strong enough to weather the storms of the Reformation. A blossoming of religious life can be perceived and a constant development of forms of devotion, which the Reformation by no means interrupted.

Many expressions of religious life in the first half of the 16th century could be pointed out, which may be regarded as a further blossoming of the "Modern Devotion" of the end of the 14th and of the 15th century and which at least reveal the deficiencies to which other developments of the Devotion led. But as a particular glory of the Netherlands of that time may well be counted the devout "School of Oisterwijk," which has probably had an even more remarkable influence within and outside the Netherlands than that of the "Modern Devotion."

When we speak of the "School of Oisterwijk," we think of the *Evangelische Peerle* (Evangelical Pearl), the *Margarita evangelica*, which carried its influence throughout Europe; of the devout Maria van Hout; but above all of the father of that school, Nicholas van Esch.

He was indeed a remarkable man, a providential man for those troubled times. Born in Oisterwijk, he lived, without forgetting his birthplace, for months and years in Cologne, finally to crown his rich life as pastor of the beguinage of Diest in present Belgium. In all three countries in which he lived and worked, his presence brought blessing, and his memory has continued to be held in honor.

Nicholas van Esch was born in Oisterwijk in the year 1507. Jutta, the former domestic of his parents, shared a few details of his early life with his successor as pastor of the beguinage of Diest, Arnold Janssen, who wrote his biography after his death.[2] She related that the one who later became the saintly pastor of the beguinage, already as a child was remarked upon because of his special devotion. He often rose at night to pray, like some religious in their night clothes. Sometimes he stole quietly from the house, either at night or early in the morning, to betake himself to church. When he found the door closed, he would kneel down outside the church door. The sexton more than once found him thus, kneeling on the ground with outstretched arms, sometimes covered with snow.

He was about fourteen or fifteen years old, when like another John the Baptist he decided to retire into solitude, in order to live there alone with and for God. He had already managed to acquire a hair shirt, when his mother learned of his plans and adjured him not to leave her. She told him she could not do without him and would lose her reason as a result. Out of love for his mother, he renounced his plans at the time. He understood that it was the will of Our Lord.

Yet he felt himself particularly attracted to God. He first experienced that special vocation on the occasion of a Golden Mass, when the school children of the place acted a biblical play about the annunciation of the angel to Mary and he had that year to fill the role of Mary. It seemed to him that he was drawn into ecstacy, and that God's grace and the light of the Holy Spirit were infused in him. From that day onward, he directed his life entirely to God.

Although he remained in the world, he tried to live as much as possible as a religious. When meat was eaten at table, he often managed handily to hide his portion in his sleeve or pocket. In his bedroom, which he had for himself and could lock, he had exchanged his pillow for a large stone, until once when he had left his room unlocked, his mother came to him and threw the stone as far away as she could. This, too, he regarded as the will of God and thereafter never again slept on a stone. Later, he granted that in those days he had sometimes acted unwisely and imprudently

[2] Arnoldus Janssen, *Venerabilis Nicolai Eschii... vita et opuscula ascetica*, ed. P.F.X. de Ram, Leuven, 1858, pp. 1-149.

and was not to be imitated in that matter; but these small traits are nevertheless characteristic of his deep sense of piety and fervor.

Once, he received some money from friends. While praying in church, it occurred to him that he had better lock it up, because his brothers might take it. He had a profound experience at the same time of distraction at prayer and of the need to suppress in himself concern about money. He went home, took the money, indignantly threw it on the ground at a corner of the town square, trod upon it with his feet, and returned to the church, no longer concerned with money and for the rest of his life freed of excessive concern over it.

He wore only the plainest clothing. He wanted no fine raiment. He preferred an old suit to a new one, which might draw attention to him. Once, when he had been given a new suit and he felt a stirring of vanity, his reaction was as radical as that over money. He threw himself down in the mud and then triumphantly told himself, "He look better this way, Nick, my lad; better mud on your clothes than mud on your soul." All his life, he observed utmost simplicity in his clothing.

When he had grown older, he was sent to 's-Hertogenbosch in order to pursue further studies there with the Brothers of the Common Life, usually called the Brothers of St. Jerome. He was not only one of the best students, but because of his modest, friendly character and sincere piety was soon the friend of many. In due course, he outstripped all others in the composition of themes and poems. He even came to write an explanation of the Our Father and the Hail Mary so good that his teachers expressed their astonishment and looked up to their pupil.

The elder Van Esch, a linen merchant, though a good man, was less pious than his son. He noticed, not without concern, that Nick, whom he intended should later succeed him in his business, only had eyes for heavenly things and in no way seemed to bother himself about his father's worldly and material business. Nevertheless, he did not abandon his plan of assuming him into his business and having him accompany himself on his trips to Holland. When it seemed to him that his son had studied

enough in 's-Hertogenbosch, he came to the Brothers with a fine
new suit of clothes and told Nicholas that he should take off his
student's uniform, in order to go traveling with him on business
in normal secular clothing. It was a sad day for Nicholas. It
occurred to him that the vocation to which he felt himself called
was endangered, and that his father wanted to steer him on a
path entirely at variance with what he considered to be the voice
of God. Now a scene was repeated in 's-Hertogenbosch not
unlike one which had been enacted three centuries previously in
Assisi. Conscious of his vocation, Nicholas very decidedly told
his father, "Father, if I have to wear those clothes, I am your son
no longer. I have a Father in heaven who has given me the kind
of clothing I like. Take your clothes and give them to someone
else." He did indeed declare himself ready to go on a trip with
his father, provided he could retain his school uniform, which,
though not strictly ecclesiastical, nevertheless distinguished him
from the ordinary worldling.

How little he cared for the world and its beautiful things is clear
from the attitude he adopted, when he once came to a beautiful
city in a coach with his father. "Look, Nick," his father said, "how
beautiful this city is." Instead of looking about him freely, the
young man closed his eyes and did not open them until they had
again left the city. In his mind, he imagined the heavenly Jerusalem and reflected that the city of God must be much, much more
beautiful than the city they were traversing and much more deserving to be seen. Full of that sight, when asked what he thought of
the city, he answered, "Magnificent," but he was thinking of his
city, the city of God.

No, he was not made for the world, for business. His father
soon realized this and allowed him to return to studying. He
wanted nothing more than through study to be united to God as
intimately as possible. To be a priest became his ideal.

One time – it was Mardi Gras, then also in 's-Hertogenbosch a
time of fun and pleasure – he was watching a furious battle between
two turkey cocks, then, it would seem, a favorite entertainment of
the people. By chance, the former domestic of his parents, the

above-mentioned Jutta, happened to pass by. She had since become a nun and the bursar of her convent. Surprised to see Nicholas in that place, she asked him, "What are you doing here, Nick?" "Oh," he said, "I'm looking to see if amid all those noisy people I can find God, the Lord of Angels." "But," he asked immediately after, "tell me, Sister Jutta, what would you prefer: that God were in you or that you were in God?" She replied with another question, "What would you rather be?" "As for myself," Nicholas said, "I would rather be in God, because if God were in me, I would be able to lose him; but if I am in God, he cannot lose me."

From 's-Hertogenbosch, Nicholas went to the university of Louvain to study philosophy, theology, and canon law. Here, too, he was a model, particularly in the frequent reception of the sacraments. From this period dates the story that once while he was asleep in his room, a prostitute quietly drew near and awakened him, caressing him and addressing loving words to him in order to seduce him. But as soon as he became aware of her and her intentions, he sprang up and gave her such a blow in the face and belabored her so roughly with his fists that she would not try it a second time. This radical reaction was also not without effect in his later life. With regard to purity, he always practiced a strict reserve and was a stranger to frivolity. He also made it a habit to pray to God for the gift of purity.

At the end of his higher studies, Nicholas was ordained a priest by the current auxiliary bishop of Liège. He offered his first Mass in the church of All Saints outside the walls of Diest, the city where he was to pursue and end his priestly career in so marvelous a manner. Afterwards he went to Cologne. This city appealed to him for many reasons. There he thought he would find opportunity to lead a devout life dedicated to God and at the same time satisfy his desire for further study. Moreover, he felt himself attracted to the guidance of studious youth. He rejected an offer to take upon himself the education of the young Duke of Gulik, because he feared that life in court, no matter how attractive it might appear to many, would offer too great dangers to his spiritual life.

But he accepted with so much the greater enthusiasm the offer to take up quarters with Andrew Herl, of Baardwijk, a learned and devout canon of St. Gereon, then rector of the university of Cologne. Herl had taken in a small group of students. Of these, Nicholas van Esch now became the autonomous director. He supplemented the lessons which the students followed in the University with lessons of his own. Soon thereafter, he was also entrusted with teaching philosophy in the Gymnasium Montanum, a Dutch institution. Of the students, either of Andrew of Baardwijk or of the Gymnasium Montanum, who thus came under the direction of Nicholas van Esch, there were especially two, who by his own witness not only attracted his particular attention but also derived special benefit from his lessons and above all from his exhortations to a holy life. These were Saint Peter Canisius and his good friend, the famous Carthusian, Lawrence Surius. What Nicholas van Esch meant to them Peter Canisius fully described in his *Liber confessionum*.

II

The Testimony of St. Peter Canisius

Canisius was in the full flower of youth, when he went to Cologne for further study and there came under the direction of Nicholas van Esch, then still a young priest, who had come to the university of Cologne a couple of years previously and had been received in the house of Andrew Herl of Baardwijk, rector of the university of Cologne. In 1534, Canisius came to Cologne to the Collegium Montanum. If he thereby came into contact with Nicholas van Esch who taught philosophy there, their relationship became more intimate, because Canisius also resided in the house of the rector, Andrew of Baardwijk, where Nicholas was especially entrusted with the direction of the young student boarders. All his life, Canisius retained the most pleasant recollection of the years spent under the direction of Esch, especially because of his formation in the spiritual life. We may confidently assert that Esch was an important instrument in the hands of Providence in leading Canisius along the way which God had traced for him.

At the end of his life, Canisius wrote a *Liber Confessionum*, "confessions" about his life. It almost goes without saying that, when he writes about his youth, he does not leave the name of Nicholas van Esch unmentioned. But that he dedicates so many pages to him, and with such earnestness and gratitude, gives us understand that he felt himself in great measure indebted to him and was inspired by feelings of a very special esteem for Nicholas van Esch up to the end of his life. We present the testimony of Canisius in its entirety, not only because it is so flattering to his director, but also because it casts so beautiful a light on Canisius himself in his youth and old age. He had a God-sent director, but he deserved to receive such a one from God. He corresponded to grace. If Van Esch planted seeds of piety and virtue in him, his heart was a fertile ground in which those seeds could luxuriantly germinate and produce fruit.

The testimony of Canisius about Esch is a hymn of thanksgiving to God.

> To return again to my director, or rather my father, Esch," Canisius writes, "praise, my soul, the Lord and do not forget what he has given you by bestowing on you a director and daily exhorter to piety; one who sought not himself but me and my eternal welfare and always made that his study. Under his direction, I gradually began to seek less my own satisfaction and more and rightly that of you, O God, whom I in the bloom of youth still knew so little and feared even less.
>
> His advice, habits, and example gave my ears and eyes, as it were, new light. Upon his authority, I broke and suppressed my sometimes impetuous resolutions and idle youthful caprices.
>
> Satisfied with the confidential companionship I enjoyed with him, I dropped all other needs and society. No one, as far as I know, was more dear or more intimately bound to me, and upon his judgement I conducted myself as well as a father could ask of his son. And not only under the seal of confession did I open myself entirely to him,

and that often, but my confidence in him was so great that, before I went to bed in the evening I also revealed the shortcomings, faults, and blemishes of my soul, in order to give him as my director an account of my aberrations and of all I had done that day and to perform one or other penance for what was wrong, if that was his wish.

I acknowledge and reverently praise your mercy, because you, O God, watcher over mankind and protector of my life, have always and everywhere so leveled the path of my life for me.

It seems to me that according to the fixed plan of your Providence you destined this man to instruct me in Cologne, like another Ananias and to draw me closer to you. His constant concern for me was as follows: he prayed for me, complained about me or praised me, he warned me and stimulated my zeal, not only by word of mouth but also in writing. And when I was away somewhat longer and while in my native land gave in to myself a bit more, and it seemed as if I wanted to embrace an easier life, through him – he traveled for this purpose to see me – you awakened me like a sleeping child, reproved me for my remissness, upheld me when I threatened to fall, recalled me, a weakling, to you, and through his care and effort strengthened me on the way to you.

He knew how to set my heart on fire by teaching me aphorisms, such as,

To serve God is to rule.

Our sole duty is to serve God; all the rest is deceit.

To know Christ well is enough, even though you know nothing more.

A wise measure I also received from him was to read a chapter from the four Gospels every day and to select a memorable sentence from them, to be meditated on from time to time during the day and to be kept in mind. Added to this, was a reading from devout authors, through whom you, O God, showed me how to fear and love you. I found no less profit in the example of the saints he proposed to me, and in the study of history, to which I often applied myself. By these means, my faith and hope were roused, and I learned to look to what was best. By these means, the fear and love of the world grew ever weaker in my heart. By these means, the evangelical commandments and counsels provided me with a keener incentive and awoke in me an ardent desire for them. You, O Lord, in your mercy have taken every precaution, have prevented my falling into serious sin, and have withheld my steps from the broad way which leads the sinners of the world to their undoing. Let all innocent beings and saints thank you, O Lord, that you have laid your hand upon me and have had continual care for my weal and being, especially in the years in which youth, through the allurement of the world and given over to the satisfaction of their bodies, deviate from your law and pervert themselves, fall into a thousand traps which the devil spreads before them, and often bring upon themselves serious diseases which they never in their life time manage to overcome or know how entirely to remove. I bless your name, O God, light and strength of my soul, who have pastured and guided me from my youth, and for whom all the hairs of my head are counted. I thank you for your gifts and for all that you have deigned to do in me, through me, and for me. You have sheltered me day and night in the shadow of your wings, and protected me as the apple of your eye, not unlike the eagle who teaches its young to fly and, flying above them, stretches its wings over them and, taking them up, carries them on its shoulders. You have foreseen all my ways; have governed my loins, namely, the inclinations of my body; have carried me from my mother's womb; have placed your hand in the way of my enemies and have preserved me, not on account of my righteousness but because your hand and your mercy have saved me. To them be praise and honor from age to age.

I beseech you, O Lord, faithful watchman and lover of the human race, to bestow on many others the grace which you gave my unworthy self as a boy, which you make grow and bear fruit in them, so that, removed from the bustle and dangers of the world, they may have good and devout spiritual directors, through whose instruction and example they may find the strength rather to flee and abhor the faults of their conduct than the barbarisms of language. Let them learn what is to their benefit rather than what is only vain; to study what is certain, not what is a mere notion. I pray you let them all keep their destiny in mind, so that they want and can use a well-founded knowledge in a proper and becoming manner, first of all, for the exaltation of your name, to which all is to be subservient, but also for the prosperity of your Church, to which they have more to be grateful for and to which they must be of greater use than to native land, friends, or relatives.[3]

The fruit falls not far from the tree.

With these quite effusive words, Canisius praises his young master. At the same time, the master's glory is that he had such a pupil in Canisius, and that he was the one chosen by God to lead Canisius' first steps.

De Ram points out what great esteem Esch had for the newly founded Society of Jesus, and what an intimate friend he was of Peter Faber, who was then living in Mainz and was there earning a reputation for conducting the Spiritual Exercises of St. Ignatius. The reputation penetrated to Cologne and there struck a responsive chord with the Carthusians, to whose spiritual circle Nicholas van Esch also belonged: he even had his own cell there. When we read the testimony of Canisius over Esch, it is evident how great a share the latter had in Canisius' decision to go from Cologne to Mainz, there to be the first candidate in these lands to be received into the Society of Jesus by Peter Faber.

III

The Spiritual Exercises of Nicholas van Esch – I

We have already spoken of Nicholas van Esch, spiritual father of the Oisterwijk school, first entrusted with the spiritual direction of the Netherlandish students in the house of Rector Andrew Herl of Baardwijk, and hence director of the youthful Canisius, then founder of the beguinage of Oisterwijk, and finally reformer and

---

[3] Petrus Canisius, *Belydenissen IV*; *Werken*, uitgegeven bij gelegenheid van zijn heiligverklaring, Tilburg, 1925, pp. 17-20. *Een samenspel van geloof en liefde*: brieven en geestelijk testament van de eerste Nederlandse jezuïet, ed. Paul Begheyn, Kampen 1997.

father of the Great Beguinage of Diest, a post which became a source of honor and fame to him.

We return to him because of the "Spiritual Exercises" which he left to us and which still merit every attention.[4] His life transposes us to the age of "exercitia" or "practices." It is the time when the many "exercitia" which were current were all surpassed by the wonderful "exercitia" which St. Ignatius composed around that time, by means of which so many souls were won for God. Prior Kalckbrenner of the Carthusians of Cologne expressly wrote to the prior of the Carthusians of Trier that the *Exercises* of St. Ignatius were to be regarded as a higher development, a perfectioning of all the "exercitia" being practised at the time. Among the latter, the treatise of Nicholas van Esch no doubt has an important place in Kalckbrenner's train of thought. And although he considers the *Exercises* of Ignatius of greater value, his words also clearly enough disclose a high regard for the other "exercitia."

This is all the more clear from the fact that the treatise of Nicholas van Esch is dedicated to none other than Prior Kalckbrenner of Cologne, and from that dedication it appears that the Carthusians themselves, before the edition in Esch's name, had already published it among the works of their highly revered confrere, Justus van Landsperg. Nicholas van Esch playfully adds that Justus had never seen his *Exercitia*, which makes us think that he wrote them after Justus's death; that is, at the time Van Esch was already rector or pastor of the Great Beguinage of Diest.

In the preface, as well as in the treatise itself, where Esch treats mortifications and aspirations, he refers to the works of Hendrik Herp, but it is clear that he was also very much inspired in the Fifth Exercise by the treatise, *Over de hervorming van de vermogens der ziel; De reformatione virium animae* (On the Reformation of the Faculties of the Soul), by Gerard Zerbolt of Zutphen, which with Zerbolt's other treatise, *De spiritualibus ascensionibus*, or *Over de geestelijke opklimmingen* (About Spiritual Ascents), was reprinted

---

[4] *Exercitiae theologiae mysticae*, in *Verabilis Nicolai Eschii… vita et opuscula ascetica*, pp. 242-251.

in Cologne by Novesianus precisely at that time, or shortly previously, namely in 1539. The Carthusians, who at the time had Canisius translate Tauler, themselves later publish Tauler in Latin, mentioning that they and with them Nicholas van Esch, would like him (Tauler) to be translated into Low German and the language of Brabant. The Carthusians also published a Latin translation of Ruusbroec's works. They showed us how in their circle devotion sought a link with what Ruusbroec and after him the Modern Devotion had brought to our people.

The name Tauler might here create a misunderstanding, because it is known that the Reformers like to cite Tauler in a publication according to their ideas, but it is equally known that he was spread on a very wide scale in the circles of the Modern Devotion and like Seuse was held in high regard, quite in contrast to Eckhart, against whom the Modern Devotion took the field as "too subtle." Although Hendrik Herp[5] is a faithful disciple of Ruusbroec, he possesses elements of his own which bring him very close to circles of the Modern Devotion and cause him to be counted of its school.

The treatise of Nicholas van Esch compares favorably with the late 15th, early 16th century publications of the Modern Devotion. Already in the title he goes further than they later generally do and speaks of an introduction to the most interior life, the actual mystical life of union, the "contemplative life." One is reminded of some of the best works of the early period of the Modern Devotion, of such treatises as that of Hendrik Mande, *Van drien staten eens bekierden menschen* (Of the Three States of the Converted Person), in which, as in the *Exercises* of Nicholas van Esch, there is mention of the three already defined states of the spiritual life: the way of "purification", the way of "interiorization" or of "illumination", and finally the way of "union", or "contemplation".

---

[5] See: Bernard McGinn, *The Varieties of Vernacular Mysticism (1350-1550)*, vol V of The Presence of God: A History of Western Christian Mysticism, New York 2012, 130-136.

In the last two *Exercises*, great stress is laid on union or congruence with God. They are two hammers with which the soul knocks on the door of the interior life filled with the Holy Spirit. By this image, Esch expresses in a workable form how the mystical life requires prayer and practice on our part, even though it is then carried into effect and realized in us through the Holy Spirit.

The last two exercises give to the little book its distinctive character. They constitute it a typical representative of the devotion of the Oiserwijk circle, which is distinguished from the Modern Devotion by the fact that the emphasis is placed on "letting Christ live in us" rather than on the "following of Christ." Yet one should not look for too sharp a distinction here; both circles flow into each other. It can perhaps better be called a difference in emphasis than actually a different approach to the spiritual life.

Likewise, it is striking in this time of the rise of the Reformation that in connection with the desired intimate union and congruence with God such stress should be laid on works and actions in the service of God. We are taught to lead at once a contemplative life in one of activity. We are taught not to find it a difficulty that we must daily work and exert ourselves in order to achieve what is needed for the most intimate union with God. One's own industry is promoted to a high degree, no matter how great a place God's grace may occupy. We are shown how in order to achieve union of intellect and will with God we shall each time have to put up with great effort. Even in the highest degree of the spiritual life and of union with God, mortification and resistence to our passions are deemed necessary. It is also pointed out that we must strive to obtain through our conduct and prayer that other persons, like so many angels, stand before the throne of God and live united with him. We should not only work for our own salvation but also for that of those with whom we are more closely united, for the peace and tranquility of the Church, and for the deliverance of the souls in Purgatory.

The Seventh Exercise is also of particular significance, even though it belongs to the treatment of the "illuminative" life, because it is directed to teach us the virtues of Christ in his Passion through its contemplation. Still, this contemplation may not be omitted in the highest degree (of the spiritual life); on the contrary, it must be repeated daily. The Passion of Christ must remain our school of the virtues which are indispensable for a close union with God. In this way, it is made clear that according to Nicholas van Esch the practice of virtue must precede our union with God, must accompany, and even follow it; that this union with God is unthinkable without the practice of virtue.

The harmonious combination of the contemplative life with the continual practice of virtue, and that above all by making Christ live in us, makes of the little book of Nicholas van Esch a treatise of particular value, which may be called a happy and healthy reaction to the all too one-sided emphasis on works of later Modern Devotion, without its falling into the opposite extreme at which the Reformation arrived, of a divine union and pardon on which human activity has no influence; neither is there mention of a connection with the Passion of Christ in order to earn God's grace for oneself and others.

It seems to me incorrect in this connection to speak of a Counter Reformation work. It is rather a harmonious development within the Church itself, of which for that matter earlier indications are to be found. One lived entirely in a spiritual ambiance of the finest early expressions of the school of Ruusbroec and of the Modern Devotion, developed further and more profoundly in the sense of an even more beautiful experience of Christ, a most natural development arising from the doctrine of the *Following of Christ*. It is a time of deepening rather than of imminent mediocrity.

IV

The Spiritual Exercises of Nicholas van Esch – II

Upon closer examination of the *Spiritual Exercises*, or *exercitia*, of Nicholas van Esch, one is immediately struck – already by the dedication to the prior of the Carthusians of Cologne – by the fact that they no doubt served for Esch's personal use, but that he also expressly wrote them for the use of others, because, as he states, it seems impossible to make progress in true piety without certain practices of devotion. He is sure that whoever practises these exercises, as he has composed them, will make progress in the grace and friendship of God and will have no regrets. They are very simple, but we must also seek God in simplicity of heart. They will require effort, but what art is learned without trouble? If one is past the age of learning, one no longer feels the trouble, and one is glad with the acquired proficiency and the reward one thereby receives. And, in this case, the reward is not fickle change but eternal happiness in heaven.

In the preface, Esch again emphasises the need not only of personal effort but also of prayer. Without these two we will get nowhere. Then he insistently recommends the need of introspection, strengthened by a sense of guilt and an awareness of our need of help. We acquire that introspection if we keep our eye on God, who is ever near and in us. More in particular, he requires the observance of his *Exercises*. Eight, ten, twelve, or more days should be set aside for this purpose. On those days, if at all possible, one should retire for an hour in the dark, in order to dedicate oneself entirely to these *Exercises*. All those days, one should omit the otherwise customary practices of devotion, in order to keep one's attention fastened on the principal truths and guidelines of the spiritual life. Besides, we should unite ourselves as intimately as possible to God, ascend to him, and endeavor to leap over all that stands between ourselves and him. However, during those days it is also good to accept the guidance of a few spiritual writers, and by reading them to awaken correct ideas in oneself. He mentions in particular the meditations and soliloquy of St. Augustine, but more as an example. In the same way, he advises reading about the contemplative life, and recommends Henry Herp. Just as we gather honey from flowers, so we must know how to draw forth the sweetness of God's Spirit from those authors. Although he begins with reflection on our sins and shortcomings and considers a sense of guilt to be necessary, still he would not have us in anyway depressed. Contemplation should make us go to God with so much the more trust, he being our mighty but above all infinitely loving Father and Redeemer. To cling to God, to open ourselves entirely to him, to live with him, is the most wonderful thing there is for a human being; or as the Latin verse which is inserted in the preface expresses it:

Est amor his animae vita beata tuae
Love of these things is the happy life of your soul.

Of the fourteen exercises of which Esch's manual consists, four are dedicated to the first step in the spiritual life, the life of purification, the *via purgativa*.

Of these, the first exercise should give us a better idea of God; the second, of ourselves; the third, of the evil of sin; the fourth, of the need of the mortification of the senses.

The knowledge of God is the greatest gift for which we must pray and on account of which we cannot make enough effort. In this context, Esch quotes the words of Christ, that eternal life consists in this, that we know God and Jesus Christ, whom he sent to us, in order to unite us to himself. He impresses on us that we must not only contemplate God in his infinite goodness but also in his manifold relationship to us. He is our all. Therefore, we must praise God in his being, in the Holy Trinity, and all that this great mystery comprises. We should be mindful, firstly, of his might, then of his wisdom, finally and above all of his love, to be admired and praised. We should be mindful of how we have been lacking in this matter, with the most fatal consequences for our soul's life. Were we regularly to contemplate those three attributes of God, what different persons we would be!

The second exercise is aimed at acquiring a better knowledge of ourselves. If we consider how God created us, and what an exalted destiny he has given us; how, when we misused that gift of God, he has again saved us and drawn us to himself; how we are still intended to know and contemplate God and to be happy in that contemplation – then we should appear to ourselves stupid and shortsighted, if we do not turn to him with all our heart. Then earth must indeed become a place of exile to us, and our longing for heaven and God be more alive. On the one hand, we perceive the incomprehensible greatness and magnificence of the soul; on the other, we see how the soul does not realize and overlooks its own worth. This last reflection should stimulate us to conversion and improvement of our lives, to the acceptance of humiliation and penance, in order to atone for all those shortcomings and to share in the suffering and humiliation which Christ has deigned to bear in order to atone for us.

Esch then quotes the words which Ruusbroec chose as the motto and guideline of his *Chierheit der geesteliken brulocht*: "See the Bridegroom cometh, go out to meet him." He closes this exercise with a call to humble prayer out of the depths of our misery, both in order to be aware of this misery, and to be raised from it through God's merciful love.

The third exercise carries on from its predecessor. It is a call to sorrow with a strong resolve to change a life which has hitherto been so thoughtlessly led. We must try to realize what we have deserved, were God to apply his full justice to us. Realizing as much, we should be willing to suffer any unpleasantness the world or our life could bring, not excepting contumely and contempt. We must place ourselves in the sight of God and ask ourselves what God's judgement of us will be. To understand this, we must try to review our lives with all its shortcomings, in order thereupon to cast ourselves in the arms of Christ, our Savior, of Mary, and of all the saints to ask their intercession for God's mercy upon us. The thought of God's endless mercy should prevent our becoming discouraged; on the contrary, should rouse us to begin a better life and make everything good again with God's help and grace.

After this contemplation of our sins, as the second act in this exercise, Esch asks the entire oblation of ourselves. We must offer to God our body as well as our soul in atonement for our sins, declaring ourselves prepared for anything God might send upon us, though he were to deprive us of all that we think we need of body and soul. He proceeds further and in a third act of the exercise requires the dedication of our entire body and all its members, with all the greater readiness according as we have misused them in the service of God. A very detailed examination of conscience, aimed more at the neglect of good than at sinful deeds, should make us, he says, eat the bread of sorrow, before we may seat ourselves as chosen children full of trust and unabashed at the table of the Father.

The fourth exercise, which concludes the way of purification, bears the title, How we must mortify and reform our five senses, but actually treats the way in which we must arrive at introspection and self-mastery. For this, attention to simplicity and purity is first of all required. We must learn to limit and conquer the use of our senses, in order to enter into ourselves, there to see God and listen to him. No act, no motion of our body should take place, without our asking ourselves what God thinks of it, without our constantly consulting him as to his wishes in our regard. This life with God is the foundation of the spiritual life. Its continual practice will cost us somewhat, but the result is wonderful.

Upon reading this chapter of Esch's *Exercitia*, we understand what a self-mastered man he must have been. Introspection is the threshold of the mystical life. His *Exercices* are calculated to cross that threshold.

V

The Spiritual Exercises of Nicholas van Esch – III

After sketching the way of "purification" in the first four *Exercises*, Nicholas van Esch attempts in the following six to provide a further description of the way of "illumination." In the four last *Exercises*, he considers the way of "union." More about that in the final section of this article.

One often hears the Book Of Life spoken of, which everyone writes for himself and which contains the virtues he has practiced in the course of the years. In the 14th and 15th centuries, the art of writing flourished, especially here in the Netherlands. True, printing existed since the first quarter of the 15th century and toward the end of the of the 15th and the beginning of the 16th century developed very strongly in the Netherlands. We have our beautiful incunabula dating from this time and from the first forty years of the 16th century, the post-incunabula, among which, to the honor of the Netherlands be it said, there were also many spiritual works. But from this same time, we possess in even greater variety our marvelous parchment and paper manuscripts, written with such devotion. Particularly the spiritual books, the Bible, missals, books of Hours, were ornamented with special care. The loveliest decorations were added; page by page they were ornamented to the utmost with the most loving care. Especially at the beginning of a new treatise or chapter the first letter was decorated. The art of ornamenting books was called "illumination." The beautiful first letters were called "initials."

The idea of decorating books was transferred in the spiritual life to the writing of one's Book of Life for God. It, too, must be illuminated with the rich practice of virtue; there one must begin each time with a beautiful new deed. Quite in the spirit of the times, Thomas à Kempis insists that we must daily begin anew. And so our Book of Life should be filled with marvelous initials. So also the term, illuminative way, is used for the time when we must especially apply ourselves to the practice of virtue.

In the first of the six exercises, Nicholas van Esch insists after Gerard Zerbolt van Zutphen on the re-formations of the three faculties of the soul, intellect, will, and representational faculty, led by the imagination and memory. Weakened by sin, the faculties must with God's grace be continually directed to him by constant practice. First of all, the intellect should busy itself with the contemplation of God's love and wisdom, might and goodness, in order that through that contemplation the love of God might be interiorized and deepened. The will must, as it were, violently subject the individual to the will of God, and keep him directed to God as to his highest end, while imagination and memory must be kept free from so many idle and useless ideas, in order to nourish itself with pious images and feelings. This may require patience, but the infinite love of God will not suffer our efforts to go unrewarded.

It is striking that Nicholas van Esch follows Zerbolt only in a general way, and unlike him does not descend to practical details. This must be attributed to the abbreviated structure of Esch's work, for a comparison of both writers reveals that he is closely linked with Zerbolt's tract. This is particularly evident from his reference to the reform of the representational faculties. Although he does not treat extensively the three steps which Zerbolt distinguishes in this connection, he summarizes what Zerbolt treats successively in detail.

Dr. Joannes Soreth van Rooij, O.Carm., in his practical survey of the works of Zerbolt, which is doubly valuable because that author's writings are unavailable for many, lists these three steps as follows:[6]

1. With every effort, bridle the representational faculty, keeping from it all improper distractions, nourishing it with divine and useful thoughts;
2. Occupy yourself with good meditation material without untimely distractions.
3. As it were, be absorbed in God and rest in him through devout meditation, without any noise of flitting thoughts, images, and ideas.

If one compares this likewise abbreviated summary with that of Nicholas van Esch, one will immediately see the great similarity and recognize the dependency.

In the following exercise, Van Esch speaks of the twelve ways in which we must starve out the roots of evil in us. Here, as we have already remarked, he very closely follows Hendrik Herp, O.F.M. In the fine edition of Herp's *Spiegel van volcomenheit* (Mirror of Perfection) by Father Lucidius Veschueren, O.F.M.,[7]

[6] *Gerard Zerbolt van Zutphen, I: leven en geschriften*, Nijmegen, 1936, pp. 104-105.

[7] Hendrik Herp, *Spiegel der Volcommenheit*, ch. 1, lines 22-37; ed. Lucidius Veschueren, O.F.M., Antwerpen, 1931, pp. 17-19. A Mirror of Perfection, Part 4, in: *Late Medieval Mysticism of The Low Countries*, ed. R. van Nieuwenhove, R. Faesen & H. Rolfson, Paulist Press New York * Mahwah 2008, 144-164.

we find these ways summarized by Herp himself. There he says, "There should be in us perfect mortification, namely, in twelve ways. First, from all desire of earthly things. Second, from all desire of *eyghensoekelicheit* (self-seeking) – a fine Middle Netherlandish word – to be done in all works of devotion and to omit in all evil deeds. Third, from all desires of one's own sensuality. Fourth, of all desires of true, natural, and acquired loves. Fifth, from all desires of the society of creatures. Sixth, from all cares that are not truly necessary and are temporary or spiritual. Seventh, from all bitterness of heart. Eighth, from all idle glory and pleasure in one's self and desire of praise and worldly honor. Ninth, from all desire of interior pleasure, sensual or spiritual. Tenth, of all scrupulosity of conscience. Eleventh, of all anxiety to do one's own will." Nicholas van Esch almost word for word takes over Herp's description of mortification.

Esch presents the following exercise in four forms. The first is a simple explanation of the manner in which we must contemplate Christ on the cross, in order to draw from his wounded members the virtues of humility, wisdom, love, justice, and strength. From the wounds in his feet, humility; and emerging from it, the virtues of obedience, patience, and silence. From his pierced head, true wisdom with her three daughters, fear of the Lord, temperance, and simplicity. From the pierced heart, love with her three companions, faithful trust, hope, and perseverance. From the wound in his right hand, justice, with her three children, mercy, truth, and gratitude. Finally, from the wound in his left hand, fortitude, and the three virtues joined to it, purity, temperance, and poverty. We must extend ourselves with Christ on the cross and through the practice of the abovementioned virtues conform ourselves to Christ.

Esch subsequently presents the same exercise in the form of five prayers to the members of the Lord. In a second series of five somewhat shorter prayers, he repeats the exercise, while finally in nine quatrains he summarizes the exercise in yet another manner.

He attributes great value to this exercise. He wants us to return to it again and again, to repeat it constantly. That is why he repeats it in four forms.

In the fourth exercise, he further returns to the desire of conforming ourselves entirely to the crucified Christ. We are the members of his body and must share in his Passion. If we do not do this, we are not Christians. We must crucify ourselves and practice suffering: firstly, to imitate Christ's Passion; further, to show our compassion with the indescribable, divine Passion; third, to admire God in that suffering; fourth, to rejoice as intimately as possible at the marvelous Passion; fifth, to conform our hearts to the divine heart of Jesus and to become completely absorbed in him; sixth, to find rest in embracing the crucified Christ.

There follows a brief exercise, recommending that we cast from us all that is superfluous and remove anything that separates us from God, in order that we may live with God with as little hindrance as possible. He further emphasizes a very sober way of life, strict self-mastery, and continual listening to the voice of God.

The last exercise in this "illuminative" way is a call to love of neighbor, as Christ has loved us. In addition, Christ must above all live in us, and we must live and suffer with him, to the sanctification of our neighbor. We may not foster antipathy, or prejudge; we must continually keep our heart united to God and see our neighbor with his eyes.

VI

The Spiritual Exercises of Nicholas van Esch – IV

The last four exercises concern the way of "union." An excellent and for that time typical ending.

Nicholas van Esch feels that he may, indeed, must crown the *Spiritual Exercises* with uniting himself as intimately as possible with God for a few days, to detach himself body and soul from the world and to cling to God. Once and for all, we must free ourselves of worldly and perishing things, in order to see God, our beginning and end and to direct ourselves entirely to that end. We must realize that we are called to higher things. Therefore, it is necessary that at least now and then we earnestly contemplate that life with God, that most intimate union with him, of which we are capable through our spiritual gifts of understanding and will. Van Esch seeks that union more in the exercise of the will than of the intellect. Love must impel us to God. The intellect must lead the will, but once love inflames our heart, then the contemplation of the intellect may freely be dispensed with, and we have nothing better to do than, disregarding further contemplation and relinquishing all images of God, simply to seek and rest in him. The child that seeks its mother, insinuates itself into her arms and loses itself in her embrace without seeing her any more.

In this matter, Esch first requires the greatest purity of heart and complete detachment from all creatures. The spirit also must not occupy itself with creatures and must free itself of all images, in order, without any mediation of images, to dwell in the company of God with as little interference as possible. It goes without saying that one must remain free of all deliberate sin.

Also, one must know how to remain free of all irregular pleasure in food or drink and other bodily affection or enjoyment; how to lift oneself above enjoyment deriving from the contemplation of the beauty found in creation, especially feminine beauty, which so easily fascinates. Of course, we must eat and drink and satisfy other requirements of nature and appreciate that the means given to satisfy them affords us pleasure, but we must not seek them for the sake of pleasure. We should be indifferent to whether the food is tasty or not; we partake of it out of necessity. If we experience pleasure, we should not dwell on that sensation, but should raise our thoughts to God, who is so wise and good as to give us food in this form, and then we should give the matter no further thought. Fastened with Christ to the cross, we should accept the bitter as well as the sweet, contumely as well as honor, poverty as well as plenty.

With constantly repeated sighs and aspirations we must dwell in the company of God. Our companionship with God should consist in effusions of love rather than excogitations of the mind. We must be on fire. We must burn and glow with love of God. That inflaming of our heart is the basis and root of the contemplative life. We must know God is in us and feel ourselves fortunate in that posses-sion. Every time, our spirit must return to God and be united to him, seek him without ceasing. This exercise of united love is the beginning of all perfection.

With four hammers Esch has the soul knock on its inmost interior, where God abides. The first hammer is a continual offer-ing of self and surrender to God. The soul places in God's hand all honor and pleasure, all sociability on the part of others, all gratification of natural inclinations. In return, she wishes to receive from his hand loneliness and sickness, shame and misunderstand-ing. This complete surrender is already a mighty means of opening the door of the heart to a more intimate relationship with God.

The second hammer is a continually more insistent prayer. Knock and it shall be opened to you. We must ask God to bestow himself on us and help us to enjoy and love him, purely and free of all that is not he. To a prayer for a more perfect, an ever more perfect knowledge of God we should join a prayer for an ever more perfect knowledge of ourselves and also for a more correct under-standing of what prayer is, so that we do not mislead ourselves, and so that we may ever progress on the way of virtue.

The third hammer is a growing conformity with God and God's will under the impulse alone of the love that burns in us. Every tendency in us to estrangement from God must be cast in the glowing furnace of the love of God, and our desire to conform entirely to God must set us completely on fire. The soul must adorn herself with the bridal gown of all virtues and must petition it of God. In that state, we will achieve more by ardently pouring out our heart, prompted by sincere love, than through our own labor. We must place ourselves in the hands of God, so that he may recreate and reshape us. We must especially mirror ourselves in Christ and unite ourselves to him. He must live in us with all the virtues of which he has given us an example. God does not leave our loving sighs unanswered.

The fourth hammer, which opens the door of the heart to the most intimate communion with the Beloved dwelling there, con-sists in losing oneself and resting in God, completely conforming to the divine pleasure, whereby nothing can any longer perturb us or disturb our peace of mind. The soul seeks nothing more besides God and finds its all in him. Made pliable and receptive by these exercises, the soul, like impressible wax, receives the stamp of divinity. Her life with God presses its stamp on her whole being and all her activity. She lives in God and in that union is capable of everything. Nothing is too difficult for her. But she understands that what she is able to do she can achieve only united to God, so that she does not aspire to higher things on her own, but contrariwise is aware of her own impotence and deficiency and thus is immune to all disillusion. She does not regard her insufficiency as such, but sees it as the recognition of the correct proportion according to which she signifies nothing, God everything. She consequently buries herself ever more deeply in God. God then admits her to his presence and frees her of all earthly cares, gives her the wine of his love to drink and inebriates her with love.

The last exercise (the fourteenth in the whole book, the fourth of the third part), the way of "union," should be seen as the crown of the whole work. It is a renewed call to continually practice living in God and resting in him. This ultimately comes about through nothing more effective than the practice of the virtues of faith, hope, and charity.

It is not enough to have God in you – you could lose him again – but you must be in God and remain in him. The best guarantee for this is Holy Communion, of which God himself said that we thereby remain in him and he in us. Living and dwelling in God, however, is again nothing else than causing God to live in us. "I live, no, not I; Christ lives in me," should ever be our motto and ideal.

We must often kneel before the crucifix and contemplate Christ, who said about himself that he was the door through which we must pass. We must embrace and kiss his feet, contemplate all his wounds, arouse ourselves to share in his Passion, not only avoid all sin but follow the example of all virtue. We must seize his hands and allow ourselves to be led by them. As witnesses of his love, we must also place all our trust in him. But above all, we must unite ourselves to God through a three-fold act of love: love which makes us forget all earthly things; love which is directed to God as purely as possible, unmixed and undeflected; love, finally, which is ardent and puts us in a condition to give ever new proof of love.

Nicholas then returns to the four ways along which our heart must go to God, the four hammers with which we are to knock on the door of his dwelling place in us, so that he will let us in. These four images, as I have already said, Esch borrowed from Herp. The latter speaks of "aspiration" (*toegeesten*), in which, as he says, "four exercises are contained." The first is sacrificing (*offeren*), the second is requiring (*eijschen*), the third is resembling (*gheliken*), the fourth is uniting (*verenighen*).

Nicholas cannot insist enough that we must over and over again direct our spirit to God. Thence must all our "aspiration" come.

As the breath of our mouth, our aspiration to God must rise from our heart. If we persevere in that exercise – Esch would like us to devote thirty-three days to the entire exercise – and meanwhile receive Christ in Holy Communion with sincere devotion, then, he concludes, I anticipate abundant fruit.

May the joyous feast of Christmas unite us in that way to God; make us live in God, and God in us. (The article appeared in print on Christmas eve, 1938.)

The Evangelical Pearl[1]

I

Among the spiritual writings of the first half of the sixteenth century, the *Evangelical Pearl* (*De Evangelische Peerle*) occupies a very special place. It is not only a typical work, which must be termed the best expression and reproduction of the school which then flourished in the Netherlands and had its starting-point and center in Oisterwijk with offshoots to Cologne and Diest, but it is also a work which caused the Netherlands again to influence most favorably devotion outside its own borders.

It is a book of prayers and reflections written by a woman. It is a book of exalted mysticism, but at the same time, of fervent aspirations suited for everyone. It is related to the writings of Maria of Oisterwijk and Nicholas van Esch, and may be said, I think, to have inspired both.

No matter how great a significance both these writers have for the development of the spiritual life in the troubled times of nascent Protestantism, we think it may be said that not only the earlier date of composition, but also the greater diffusion of this book, mark it as the principal work of the school of Oisterwijk.

So much the more should it surprise us that the name of the writer is not known and that only a few vague details of her life have come down to us. She died on January 28, 1540, at the age of 77 without ever being married. She seems to have been of noble birth, although Father Dirk Loer, vicar of the Carthusians of Cologne, who prepared the first editions of the *Pearl*, writes in the first complete edition of 1537: "The one who wrote this book is

[1] From *De Gelderlander*, May 6, 13, 20, 27; June 3, 1939.

a notable enlightened person, noble not only by lineage but much more by virtues."[2] We are provided with the most information by Nicholas van Esch, who prepared the third edition of the complete, or "Great" *Pearl*, and who writes in a preface:

The book was written under inspiration of the Holy Spirit by a virtuous maiden, who herself has experienced what she describes and teaches, and from her youth until her death had chosen the King of heaven as her Bridegroom, and continued to follow him amid joy and sorrow. She lived in the home of her parents and in her youth had made a vow of spiritual obedience. With fasting, prayer, vigils, and other mortifications, she had subjected her body to her spirit. She had many fierce attacks and struggles to endure from the devil, but through repeated and severe mortifications, vigorous combat, and fervent prayer, she had won out over the many attacks and battles through the grace of God, and had acquired many virtues. She was often occupied with God for days on end and united with him in great fervor, so that she did not think of outward things and all her activity was suspended. On those days, she also did not go to bed, because all that time seemed to her only a day or an hour. She took every care always to preserve the greatest purity of heart, by which she earned so to be filled with divine light and joy that she was oblivious to everything else.

As gold in the fire, was she refined by ecclesiastical as well as secular persons with suffering, contempt, and persecution. But in this, she called on God's help and continued steadfastly to follow her hidden way, always equally friendly, merciful, and cheerful, and she prayed God for her enemies.

I do not mention the interior suffering and cross she carried at the thought of human aberrations and the damage souls suffered. What she suffered on that account is known to God alone. As a rule, she

---

[2] References to the old editions, because not always available for consultation, have been omitted. The Evangelical Pearl, Part III, in: *Late Medieval Mysticism of The Low Countries*, ed. R. van Nieuwenhove, R. Faesen & H. Rolfson, Paulist Press New York * Mahwah 2008,215-322. See: Bernard McGinn, *The Varieties of Vernacular Mysticism (1350-1550)*, vol V of The Presence of God: A History of Western Christian Mysticism, New York 2012, 143-159.

daily received the Sacrament of the Altar, leaning on the merits of her Beloved, and because he willed it. All her exercises were performed so that God would have honor, peace, and joy in her. Often she had on her tongue, and in the hour of her death declared, 'O Lord, may you have pleasure, peace, and joy.' In this way, she devoutly gave up her spirit in God, with whom she was already united.

In the preface to the first edition, Dirk Loer added that the writer "has practiced this for fifty years," which may be considered to concur with the age stated by Esch. Van Esch has circumscribed it even a bit more narrowly, stating that while she lived to be seventy-seven, "from her youth until her death" she led the interior life which she describes in her book.

If it is not yet obvious that the author absolutely wanted to remain unknown, this appears most clearly from what Nicholas van Esch writes in 1545 to Professor M. Burchard van den Berg in Cologne in the dedication of Surius' Latin translation. There he states about the author that he cannot reveal his name, because he has up to the present not allowed his name to be revealed, because he holds fast to the utmost to humility and unpretentiousness, that he does not want to derive anything of honor and fame from this work, but says he has received from God whatever of good and devotion it contains. He has composed this work to God's honor and glory, after having practised its doctrine most zealously for many years.

Esch is even silent here about what he expressly communicated in 1542 in the Netherlandish edition; namely, that the work was written by a woman, as well as the other details about her life he added there. There is thus evident, positive intent in the suppression of the name, a deliberate anonymity desired by the writer herself. We must respect it, but we have not abandoned all hope of discovering new details of the life of this gifted author.

In one of the final chapters, she herself evidently indicates in an effusion of gratitude to God for her consecration and election that she belonged to a circle of "pilgrims," a circle in which the concept of pilgrimage was very much alive. Among the "pilgrims," she mentions in accents of the most ardent gratitude a "lady friend" and a "friend" of God, sent by him to free her from her errors and lead her to God. They taught her to lose herself totally in Jesus, to become one spirit with him, to conquer nature and cause it to die, in order to be led by God to a new life. They taught her that God lives in her, and she accordingly prays that he will also work with, in, and through her. She asks for the grace of perseverance, not only for herself, but also for her "lady friend," her "friend," and for "all your friends in this circle." From all this, one rightly concludes that she belonged to a circle of spiritual friends, which could hardly be other than the Oisterwijk circle. In the "lady friend" we are inclined to see Maria of Oisterwijk, and in the "friend" none other than Nicholas van Esch. In this chapter, she also thanks God "because you have chosen me out of the thousands you have called to this place." Dr. Reypens sees in this an indication that the author herself is not referred to, because she continued to live in the home of her parents.[3] But I see in this expression absolutely no reference to moving, but much more to her predetermination to continue in the place in which she was living.

From the life of Nicholas van Esch by Arnold Janssen, his successor in Diest, we know that there was a circle of devout persons in Oisterwijk, who had not left the world, yet regularly gathered for exercises in the spiritual life.[4] Before she became mistress in the Maagdenhuis in Oisterwijk and thus acquired a permanent dwelling, Maria of Oisterwijk had already led a kind of religious life in the world. We also prefer to see in the writer of the *Evangelical Pearl* a devout woman living in the world, who had submitted herself to a "friend of God" by a vow of obedience, and kept up

[3] L. Reypens, S.J., "Nog een vergeten mystieke grootheid; de schrijfster der Evangelische Peerle," *Ons Geestelijk Erf*, 2 (1928), 52-76, 304-341; 361-392 (continued by J. Huyben, O.S.B.); 3 (1929), 60-70, 4 (1930), 5-26, 428-473.

[4] *Het leven van den eerweeerdighen vaeder, mynheer Nicolaus van Esch, oft Esschius... Eerst beschreven in de latynsche tale door Arnoldus Janssen... In het Duyts overgeset... door G.G. Met noch eeen profytigh tractaet van geestelycke oeffeningen van... vader Esschius.* Loven, Gillis Denique, 1713.

the warmest friendship with the beguines, or pious women, of the *Maagdenhuis*, but both before and after its institution continued to live in her own house. This is confirmed by a late, but to my mind dependable, reference by Geldolf van Ryckel, abbot of St. Geertrui in Louvain, who wrote extensively about the beguines of the Netherlands and Belgium and must have had access to a great many sources.[5] He bestows particular praise on the Oisterwijk circle and includes in it, the seventh member to be named, the anonymous author of the *Pearl*. True, he has the dates of her life and death wrong, but, considering the secrecy which enveloped her person, this is no reason for doubting the essentials of his information. This, to my mind, is also not negated by a letter the *Pearl* author probably wrote to Maria van Oisterwijk, when the latter was still living in Oisterwijk. Although the letter is hers, she could quite well have lived in Oisterwijk; at least have belonged to the Oisterwijk circle. Everything points to the fact that she lived and died there.

II

Contents and Purport – I

The subtitle of the *Pearl* already to some degree describes these: "Containing devout prayers, divine exercises, and spiritual doctrines; how we shall seek and find in our souls the greatest good (who is God), and love and possess him with all our strength."

Then there follows an aphorism taken from the Gospel: "The kingdom of God is like a person seeking good pearls, and when he has found a precious pearl, he sells all he has and buys it."[6]

A brief "foreword" further describes the intent of the book. This foreword is in some degree enlarged upon and further explained

---

[5] Josephus Geldolphus van Ryckel, 1581-1642, *Vita S. Beggae, ducissae Brabantiae, andetennensium, begginarum et beggardorum fundatricis, vetus hactenus non edita & commentario illustrata. Adjuncta est historia begginasiorum Belgii.* Lovanii, typis Corn. Coenestenii, 1631.
[6] Cf. Mt 13, 45-46.

by the forewords to each of the three parts into which the book is divided. The foreword to the second part is in this respect particularly instructive.

The three parts of the book treat the three steps by which, according to the ancient classic formula, the mountain of the spiritual life is ascended and climbed. In this case, they are further compared to the rising of the sun in its three phases of dawn, completed rising in the morning, and finally in its glowing blaze at noon, when it not only spreads abroad its full light, but its powerful rays also set the whole earth aglow.

A person begins by turning to God and orienting himself entirely to him. This introversion, also called conversion, has a much deeper meaning than our present word, conversion. It involves not only turning away from evil, but much more turning to good, a setting out upon the way which has as it goal the most intimate union with God. That full light is not yet seen but it is desired. It is still misty and dim. The consciousness of sin causes one's feet to drag, yet one has set out upon the way. With great reverence for the sublimity of God, but in such a way that distrust of self is conquered by trust in God's help, a person begins to understand that he must begin by detaching himself from all things and clinging to God alone; by abandoning himself to God through detachment from the world.

It is especially this abandoning that is described and taught in this first part. We are reminded of Jesus' word, "If you would be perfect, abandon all things, and follow me in perfect detachment.[7] This little book treats of this abandonment." This is more closely defined, according to St. Jerome, as no longer fixing one's senses on earthly things and detaching oneself from all one possesses; as keeping oneself untainted from all that the imagination can conjure up of carnal desires and inclinations and even suppressing images of the world, in order to rise up to God, who is the source of all things, and who has created all things as so many manifestations of his power, wisdom, and love. This upward glance at God

---

[7] Cf. Mt 19, 21.

on high will not sink us down in tranquil ease from that "abandonment of all things," but on the contrary will stimulate us to continuous activity, to the concentration of our spirit on that God on high, and to redirect our lives to him time and time again. It will soon become clear that we will not attain the contemplative life, the highest step, if we have not first experienced this laborious life to the full. Through this spiritual resignation, the author adds, the spiritual life is perfected, because the awareness of divine love lies as the foundation of this contemplation, as well as the recognition that all God's inspirations are prompted by this love, and that God thereby wishes to lead us to the highest Good, which is himself.

As an introduction to the first part of the book, the author further states that it is replete with fervent prayers, aspirations, and urgent ejaculatory prayers to help one converse inwardly with God, and to unite his spirit, soul, and heart with God in sincere love. The book is aimed not only at making us follow the Lord's life and passion, but also at making us lose ourselves entirely in God and ascend to him.

The book begins by calling upon the help of the Lord to learn to know him better and so to unite ourselves more closely to him.

May he look down complacently upon us! But for this it is necessary that we contemplate him in his life and Passion and conform ourselves to him. The way to achieve this is that at all the canonical hours, at all hours of the day, at attending Mass, at receiving Holy Communion, we truly and with equal fervor each time spiritually renew and quicken the love of God in us. Here strong emphasis is laid on what Hendrik Herp calls *toegeesting* (aspiration), and which is nothing else than repeatedly adoring God, beseeching his grace, and uniting ourselves to the Holy Sacrifice of the Cross for the forgiveness of our sins; thus making ourselves ever more conformable to God. The author wants us in this to follow the example of Mary, who so gladly pondered and preserved in her heart what was told her about and by God. God loves us and has chosen us to be his. We belong to his chosen friends. We must often think of him and inwardly and outwardly imprint his image on ourselves. We must pray to him with the words he himself has taught us to pray to Our Father and also daily repeat the greeting of the angel to Mary in the Hail Mary.

Just as Jesus was born of Mary in a three-fold manner, so must that three-fold birth be consummated in us. From eternity, God destined Mary to be the mother of his Son, and formed her spirit, that is, her most exalted and interior being, as a very special elected form of being. To that eternal destiny Mary answered in and through God's particular grace. A second birth took place when God filled Mary's soul, caused his only Son to be begotten in her, but on this account also caused her human soul, through the fulness of his grace, to correspond to the sublimity of that election. The third birth was that according to the flesh, consummated in a marvelous manner by God; in Mary it was the pledge and at the same time the reason for her fulness of grace. These three births are mutually inclusive.

And so we, too, must distinguish in ourselves how, according to the spirit, we were born in God from all eternity and, as the anonymous author expresses it in the language of a Ruusbroec, sprang from God formless, unshaped, ungrounded, without being; that is to say, that without any inner need for the definition of our being we sprang from God as he sees us, knows us, wills us. At this consideration, we sink away entirely in the Godhead. According to the soul, we were born in God, so that we would, according to our real being, receive our definition through and in him; and so that we would be what we are: exalted, elected beings, temples of the Holy Spirit, abodes of the Most High. But we must also be born in God according to the body, because all that we do, all that we say must be directed to him, so that we thus again find ourselves in him. In this our last birth in God, the birth of God in us takes place simultaneously, and he issues from us through our words and works.

There follows what the book still has to say about the three-fold life we are to lead in God. The spirit, which includes the highest faculties, must so lose itself entirely in God that, raised above all changeable things, we see everything through God's eyes, undisturbed and ever happy in being so gloriously chosen. The soul, dependent on union with the body and absorbed in it, will be subject to sorrow and sadness, and together with the soul of Christ must lament over the sins and ingratitude of men; must unite herself to the frightful sacrifice of Christ, while finally the body with Christ assumes the hardness of life and shares in the Passion of Christ. Thus, the book speaks of a happy life according to the spirit, a life filled with sadness according to the soul, and a life of pain and grief according to the body.

Mary is presented to us as a model of this three-fold life. By always keeping our eye directed to union with God, the heaven of the spirit, we will be able, in spite of the sadness which fills our soul, to introduce Mary into the paradise of the soul, because the soul, in spite of all her shortcomings and those of others, knows herself to be directed to God; while we, according to the body, in our fervent union with God make of our heart an enclosed garden, from which we tirelessly remove all that is not God; into which we no longer allow anything that does not have him as its source; and where the sacrifices we make are changed into flowers.

Finally, the book points out that by receiving the sacraments, by making ourselves available to the gifts of the Holy Spirit, by radiating the eight Beatitudes, by adorning ourselves with virtues and, arrayed with them, joining the nine choirs of angels, we possess a wealth and happiness which beggar all description and, in spite of the cross which God lays on the shoulders of his friends, fill us with gladness and render us happy.

The first part of the book ends with a meditation on the Gospel of St. John which speaks of the light which in Christ has come into the darkness of this world,[8] in order that it rise in us and become full day.

III

Contents and Purport – II

The second part of this remarkable book enters into detail with regard to the further development of the spiritual life, after its foundation has been examined in the first part. It deals with the

---

[8] Jn 1, 5.

way of enlightenment, or illumination, of the book of life; with
the life of adorning our soul with virtues, of further cultivation of
the garden of the heart by planting verdure and flowers.

The second step, according to the preface, signifies our further
progress along the path that is to lead us to intimate union with
God. Once one has purified his soul, he must make every effort
to adorn it with every sort of virtue. The writer points to Christ,
who for this reason was given to us as a model by the heavenly
Father. We must construct our life according to this model; we
must conform ourselves to him.

This is also the guiding principle of the Modern Devotion, but
it is worthy of note that the *Evangelical Pearl*, in developing this
idea, starts much further back and delves more deeply than the
Modern Devotion generally does. The dominating idea here is that
we were eternally known and willed by God, that we pre-existed
spiritually in God from eternity, that our image existed, formed
by God himself, which reflected what God intended for us, what
we should be, with what great splendor he willed us to shine forth.

We must return to that image. We must immerse ourselves in
that infinite ocean. We must place ourselves in that full light and
in the full glow of that eternal sun which penetrates and pervades
us with its rays. In order that we might again be able to do so and
with God's help actually do so, Christ came into the world. United
to him, we will again be able to return to our origin and rediscover
ourselves.

If in the Modern Devotion, Christ primarily represented for the
soul the God-given model of perfect man made to the image of
God, here the divinity of Christ is much more strongly emphasized, and we must unite ourselves to him, in order in and through
him to approach as closely as possible our original divine life. After
the humanity of Christ had been stressed – almost too much so
– for a couple of centuries, as a reaction there again set in a more
interior idea of Christ, as God made man, who lifts us to the
divinity. The life of grace – the placing of oneself entirely in the
hands of God, in order to be assisted and led by him – after the
era which emphasized human activity, again found a quickening

interest and appreciation. This is nothing new; we also find those ideas in the Modern Devotion. There is no real contrast, but there are difference and nuance. Thus Brugman, in one of his sermons, already speaks of "allowing and suffering, love and fear" – a theme about which we also find shorter treatises in manuscripts dating from the end of the 15th to the beginning of the 16th centuries; but it is very striking that in the *Evangelical Pearl* a very particular emphasis is laid on the *"laten,"* (let go or allow) and connected with it, there is a lengthy reflection on nothingness (*het niet*). Thus, what in the 15th century certainly is as much regarded as the foundation of the spiritual life, here receives a stronger emphasis, entirely in the spirit of Ruusbroec, who constantly points to receptiveness to the action of God as the foundation and starting-point of the spiritual life.

If we desire to make progress in the spiritual life, to adorn our heart with virtues, then we must as strongly as possible establish and nourish in ourselves the conviction that of ourselves we can do nothing, and that only the most intimate union with God puts us in the condition to do anything in that direction. Hence, the second part begins with describing how perfect God has conceived us, but the faculties of our soul are weakened and corrupted; they require a thorough reformation, and Jesus has come into the world to assist us in that work. We must turn away from creatures and again turn to him who is our origin.

This gives us to understand that the first need is of the divinely infused virtues of faith, hope, and love. After we have turned away from sin and the creatures which have so often led us to sin, we must form the starting-point of a new life in God, irradiated by his sun, cherished by his light and the warmth of his grace. Faith and the protection of God's Nature start us on our way. We cannot devote enough attention to what natural reflection on God and particularly Revelation can teach us about our origin and continued existence in God. We must exercise ourselves in faith in that most beautiful truth. From it, a boundless trust in God spontaneously springs forth, a firm hope that God will help us. That hope and love are no less the source of a growing love of

God, our Creator and Savior, our only salvation. Faith, hope, and love are three inseparably united virtues, which support and nourish each other. Our love, however, is quickened in a very particular way by meditation on the sacred passion of the Lord. There the divine love is most eloquently expressed. God himself has called that Passion the revelation of his love. We must continually gaze at the mirror of the suffering Christ. We must form ourselves like unto him: first and foremost, by living his life, making his feelings our own, interiorly being one with him, and that not only in his sacred humanity, but at the same time with his holy Godhead, who has loved us from all eternity, has created us and again redeemed us, in order that he might continue to work in us, and make us correspond to the image he has had of us from eternity.

To further that action of God, we must place ourselves entirely in his hands by a total "allowing"; that is, we must not interfere with God; we must allow him, who created and keeps us in being, reshape and perfect us through the action of his grace. With this "allowing," there is of itself connected a "suffering" in union with God. And in order that we may accomplish this, we must as much as possible be rid of ourselves and return in our own minds to "nothingness".

In a subsequent chapter, emphasis is laid on love, which makes all this possible in us. It is love of God that raises us aloft to him, makes us value in ourselves only what comes from God, and makes us consider good for our neighbor only what unites him to God and what comes to him from God. That love, that whole ascent to God, causes us to die to ourselves, and live the life of Christ. For this, great introversion is needed. Only one who in silent inwardness often ponders this and deeply imprints it in his spirit, can arrive at this state. With all my bustle and hurry, the writer says, I did not get there; only when I pondered all this in silence, did I arrive.

It may be considered worthy of note that the author, at the end of the 51st chapter – for that matter, quite in line with her idea of our emanation from God – dares to quote Master Eckhart as the again recognized master of the mystical life, who had been too much eliminated and avoided at the end of the 14th and during the 15th century, and reproduces from him the following beautiful dialogue:

> Meester Eggaert said to a poor man, 'God give you a good morning.' The poor man said, 'Sir, save that for yourself, for I have never had a bad morning; for all that God has ever allowed me to suffer, that I gladly suffered for God's will. It was better to consider myself unworthy, and so I did not become sad or afflicted.' The master said, 'Where do you come from?' He answered, 'From God.' The master said, 'Then where did you leave God?' He answered, 'In all pure hearts.' The master said, 'What sort of man are you?' He answered, 'I am a king.' The master said, 'Of what are you king?' He answered, 'Of my body, because for everything whatever that my spirit desired my body was ready to work and suffer, even faster than my spirit was ready to receive it.' The master said, 'A king must have a kingdom. Where then is your kingdom?' He answered, 'In my soul.' The master said, 'How so?' He answered, 'When I close the door of my five senses, and then long for God with all my heart, then I find him in my soul as clearly and full of joy as he is in eternal life.' The master said, 'You must be holy. Who made you holy?' He answered, 'That was done by my silence, my pondering exalted things, my union with God; these have bred me in God. I could find no rest in anything that was less than God. Now I have found God and have my rest and peace in him forever, and that is nobler than all the kingdoms of today.'

There follows further a short meditation on the commandments of God, because in their fulfillment love must become evident, a short discussion of the sacraments through which God's grace is communicated, followed by a short treatment of the eight Beatitudes, to be concluded with a chapter noteworthy in every respect, which attempts express the exercise of the seven Arts in the meditation of the seven words of Christ on the cross. As a concluding prayer, there follows further, as a crown, the doxology in honor of the Blessed Trinity, ascribed to St. Athanasius.

IV

Contents and Purport – III

The third part of this highly mystical work naturally has a predominantly mystical character. Its definite purport is to lead one still further into the life of the spirit, withdrawn from the ideas and thoughts which usually occupy one, in order to lose oneself entirely in God and to live only with God; that is to say, sharing in this earthly, material life, but always united to God, seeing things with his divine eyes, abandoning oneself to him, and in all things motivated by love of God.

Human beings remain human; they are actually never more human than in this form of life, for it is precisely then that they allow their highest faculties, their noblest feelings to govern their lives. Never is their sublime nobility more brilliantly displayed. On the other hand, in this third step of the spiritual life, the contemplative life or life of union, a person must more and more detach himself, must disengage himself from what is dear and pleasing to him on this earth, in order first and foremost, and each time anew to reflect and realize that from all eternity he emanated from the hand of God, from eternity existed in God according to the spirit, and all his life long must be nothing else than a reflection of that image of himself which existed in God from eternity.

In the depths of our being, we come upon the activity of God, whereby he maintains us in being, and leads and directs us. We must return to that profoundest point of origin in order to rediscover ourselves in God. There in our inmost soul we come upon the ground in which our being has its roots. On that ground, which is nothing else than the recognition of our bond with God, we must live, that is our native land, there we come into the kingdom of God which is promised us and to which we are invited, in which God has prepared a place for us already here on earth. In our inmost spirit we must adore God, converse with him, unite ourselves with him, lose ourselves in him, and ascend to him, in order completely to reform and reshape our being in harmony with God's image of us. In doing so, we must place ourselves in God's hand, so that he more than we can perform this work of reform.

God wills this too; he asks that we surrender ourselves into his hands, that we fly to him in the depths of our heart, each day anew, in the morning upon first awakening, in order to live united to him the whole day long.

And if a person looks around and observes not only his own lax ways, but how little other people bother about God, struck with the restlessness which is the consequence, he must be even more concerned for that total focusing on God, in order thus to find rest for his soul. What a pity it is that people do not more seek rest in this way! By it, one has such a simple means of living here on earth as though in heaven.

It seems to be a very sublime way of life, yet must be said to be very simple. To live it, no wisdom or knowledge in a worldly sense is needed; an unlettered person is just as apt for it as one who is preeminent in learning. Therefore, one should not regard it as something sublime and learned, but as something very simple, which God offers everyone – as it were, lets flow to everyone – if he only knows how to receive it. One can do this only if one opens oneself interiorly to God's grace, allows God's grace to flow into his heart. This, in turn, requires quietly abandoning one's self to God's action and keeping one's self free of all that in ideas and thoughts attempts to monopolize our spirit.

For this, the author repeatedly insists on the profoundest introversion. She warns against externality, curiosity, busy-ness – in a word, against the monopoly of the spirit by matters which do not keep us bound to God. Further, she warns very particularly against thoughts of self complacency, to which this exalted life so easily leads and yet which so treacherously undermines it that it is completely destroyed. One should keep in view one's great imperfection and avoid judging others as less perfect.

Meanwhile, one should carefully behold one's self in others and reflect that only a small number truly, sincerely, radically and absolutely seek this union with God, abandon themselves to him and live with him. Besides this group, there is another that realizes that it should and can live in this way, but has not the courage, the strength, the love for it; while a third group does not even arrive at seeing life in this way and loses itself in every sort of external matters.

We must cleanse ourselves in the precious blood of Christ and rise up with him to a new life. Christ is our ladder, with him we climb aloft. With the soul of Christ we must assume the suffering of the soul; with the body of Christ, all physical difficulties, in order, spiritually united with God, to be elevated above all suffering and to be happy in spite of all suffering.

The writer sees in the image of a ladder the ladder of Jacob, upon which angels climb and descend. So must we, with the angels around us, climb our ladder, who is Christ, and at the same time bring him down from heaven to earth. Our life upon earth must be heavenly. The earth must ascend to heaven; that is, our thoughts must ascend on high. Heaven must descend to earth; that is, we must live upon earth as though we were in heaven.

In that ladder, the author distinguishes nine rungs or steps, virtues which union with Christ causes us to practice in order to make us remain like him.

The first step is fear of the Lord, reverence, respect, humble adoration. On this step, the Angels greet us. In their midst, stands Christ, who is the finest example and truest companion in continual, humble adoration of God.

The second step is love of God. Union with Christ, who always acted out of love, also causes us always to act with him, above all driven by love. Here, we are greeted and inspired by the Archangels, aflame with love.

The third step is moderation in all virtues, of which Christ is again the most shining example, while the choir of Virtues adjusts our faculties in the most proper manner.

The fourth step is humble patience, the quiet and humble bearing of the yoke which Our Lord lays on our shoulders. The choir of Powers helps us, but above all we carry our cross with Christ and by his strength.

With this, we climb the fifth step, which consists in contempt of all the world offers. The choir of Principalities teaches us to assess the world at its true value; but especially once again Christ, whose reign was not of this world, shall help us to value at its worth what the world has to offer.

Then, the sixth step is introversion, self-mastery with the choir of Dominions, but above all attracted and enthralled by him who holds hearts and affections in his hand and inclines whither he wills.

With the choir of Thrones, we attain on the seventh step complete abandonment to the will of God. He must reside in our heart like a king on his throne. That is the kingdom of Christ in our heart.

The Cherubim raise us up to the eighth step of complete ascending to God, so that our intellect sees him in everything. All images are repelled so as to see nothing but God, the light of all light.

So we arrive at the topmost step, on which stand the Seraphim, directed to God alone, occupied with him only, one with God.

Let us often step into ourselves to see how high we have climbed up this ladder, acknowledging with regret that we have not fostered enough love to persevere and continue to climb, praying to God for help and grace, and opening our hearts ever wider to him, in order that he may enter with the fulness of his grace.

Let us also go to Mary, to see how she climbed these nine steps and to ask her to hold out her hand to us as we climb.

Early in the morning, our heart must be directed to God.

The seven times of the day, in which we pray the canonical Hours, should be so many hours of renewed climbing, together with meditation on the Passion of Christ, divided according to the Hours of the day. Evening requires an examination of the past day, but even during the night, our communion with God must continue. When we awaken, or when we are wakened in the morning, our first thought must again be directed to God, so that communion with him is never interrupted.

V

The Diffusion of the Pearl

The diffusion of the *Pearl* was extraordinarily extensive. It is surprising that this little work, after being published and in the following century reprinted and even translated, was thereafter as good as forgotten, and in spite of the many editions it enjoyed has become a rarity.[9]

The first two editions were quite incomplete, but were the occasion for publishing a complete edition. From the 39 chapters which Dirk Loer, vicar of the Carthusians in Cologne, published through Jan Berntsz in Utrecht 1535, and the following year already had to have reprinted by Simon Cock in Antwerp, the beauty of the contents of this *Evangelical Pearl* was revealed, with the result that two years later, 1537-1538, a complete edition appeared in Antwerp, this time by Henrick Peetersen of Middelburch. It consisted of 168 chapters and was titled, *The Great Evangelical Pearl*. The small edition was subsequently never reprinted, though the distinction, *The Evangelical Pearl*, and *The Great Evangelical Pearl*, remained. The addition, *Great*, was maintained until the last edition, but disappears in the translations.

Of the first edition of the *Pearl* (Utrecht, Jan Berntsz, 1535) it would appear, there are at the moment only five copies in public libraries: the abbey of Tongerloo,[10] the Rijksprentenkabinet in Amsterdam,[11] the Koninklijke Bibliotheek in The Hague, the Stadsbibliothek[12] in Cologne, and the British Museum[13] in London.

Of the edition of the short text by Simon Cock there are the following copies in public libraries: the library of the Capuchins

---

[9] The Nederlandse Centrale Catalogus lists 21 copies of the 16th and 17th centuries in The Netherlands.

[10] This seems to be the *Abdijarchief,* of the Premonstratensians; cf. P. O. Kristeller and Sigrid Krämer, *Latin Manuscript Books Before 1600* (Monumenta Germaniae Historica, Hilfsmittel, 13), München, 1993, p. 816.

[11] Not listed by Kristeller/Krämer, *ibid.*

[12] Now the Universitäts-und Stadtbibliothek; cf. *Ibid.*, p. 505.

[13] Now the British Library; cf. *Ibid.*, p. 538.

in Velp near Grave (pp. 199-200 wanting), in the major seminary in Gaesdonck near Goch (defective), and in the Provinciale Bibliotheek in 's-Hertogenbosch. This edition was printed only by Simon Cock, at the request of Adriaen Roelofs, "bookseller in the Corte Kerckstrate in den Vos," 's-Hertogenbosch.

Of the first edition of the "Great" *Pearl*, Antwerp, 1537-1538, there are copies in the Plantijn Museum in Antwerp,[14] in the Universiteits-bibliotheek in Ghent,[15] the Bibliotheek van de Maatschappij der Nederlandsche Letterkunde in Leiden,[16] Nazareth monastery in Oorschot, and the British Museum in London.

Already a year later, in 1539, a second, practically identical edition of this first complete edition appeared by the same printer in Antwerp. Of this printing, there are still copies in the Koninklijke Bibliotheek in Brussels, the Koninklijke Bibliotheek in The Hague (p. 244 wanting), and in the convent of the Friars Minor in Woerden.

The original editor of the *Pearl*, the Carthusian, Dirk Loer, in this last year, 1539, became prior of the Charterhouse in Hildesheim. The next printing was prepared by the great friend of the Cologne Carthusians and director of the Oisterwijk school, the well-known priest, Nicholas van Esch. It is not hazardous to conjecture that he prepared their first edition for the Carthusians of Cologne. In 1542, Nicholas van Esch took over the work of Dirk Loer and produced a third edition with a new introduction, printed by Willem Vorsterman in Antwerp. This edition is still preserved in the Stadsbibliotheek in Antwerp, the Koninklijke Bibliotheek in Brussels,[17] and in the Universiteits-bibliotheek in Ghent.[18]

In his biography of Nicholas van Esch, Mgr. de Ram mentions a printing of 1546,[19] but I take it that this is a misprint for 1551,

---

[14] Now the Musaeum Plantin-Moretus (Library); cf. *Ibid.*, p. 247.

[15] Now the Centrale Bibliotheek der Rijksuniversiteit; cf. *Ibid.*, p. 441.

[16] Cf. *Ibid.*, p. 522.

[17] Listed by Kristeller/Krämer under its French name, Bibliothèque Royale Albert 1er.

[18] Now the Centrale Bibliotheek der Rijksuniversiteit; cf. *Ibid.*, p. 441.

[19] P.F.X. de Ram, *Venerabilis Nicolai Eschii vita et opuscula ascetica*, Louvain, 1858.

because all the details he communicates fit this edition. The approbation by Simon de Planen, pastor in Antwerp, is first dated 1547, and hence hardly to be reconciled with an edition of 1546. Finally, no edition of 1546 is known, while in 1548 another edition was prepared by Henrick Peetersen himself, and only in that of 1551 is his name replaced by that of his widow. Hence, we make the fourth edition that of Antwerp, 1548, of which there are copies in the Trappist abbey of Westmalle and in the Plantijn Museum in Antwerp.

The fifth edition is that of Antwerp, 1551, referred to above and still preserved by the Jesuits of Louvain and in the parish rectory of Duivendrecht.

A sixth edition by the same printer appeared in Antwerp, 1556-1557, and is still preserved in the Koninklijke Bibliotheek in Brussel, in the Universiteits-bibliotheek in Leiden,[20] and in the Bibliotheek van de Maatschappij der Nederlandsche Letterkunde in Leiden.

Finally, the seventh edition was issued by Jan Roelants in Antwerp in 1564-1565, of which there are copies in the Plantijn Museum in Antwerp, the Koninklijke Bibliotheek in Brussels, and in the Universiteits-bibliotheek in Leiden.

There then follows a pause, in every way remarkable, in the rapidly successive production of editions. In sixty years, no reprint of the Netherlandish edition appeared, but then all at once two editions, one after the other. In 1626, the edition of 1542 was again printed unaltered by Peeter Bouvet in Kortrijk. The approval of 1547, which was maintained without change in the four last editions of the 16th century, is here replaced by a new one by Hieremias Baes, the then *censor librorum*. Of this edition, the eighth in the long series of editions, a rare copy is preserved in the Universiteits-bibliotheek in Ghent.

Three years later, a ninth edition appeared in Antwerp by Jan Cnobbaert. The edition is placed in 1629, though the approval is dated 1630; hence here, too, we assign the date 1629-1630. It is given a new introduction, taken for the most part, however, from

[20] Bibliotheek der Rijksuniversiteit; cf. *Ibid.*, p. 519.

the old introduction by Nicholas van Esch, but the author of the introduction adds in his own words a summary of the contents of the book. Of this last Netherlandish edition, there are copies in the Carmel of Nijmegen,[21] the library of the Ruusbroec Genootschap in Antwerp, the Universiteits-bibliotheek in Ghent, and in the convent of the Friars Minor in Woerden.

Since then, now already three centuries ago, this voice is stilled in our native language. Quite remarkably, at the same time that it is stilled in the Netherlands, this voice begins to be heard abroad. The Carthusians of Cologne soon came upon the idea of translating into Latin this little book, which was such a success.

They had translated Ruusbroec, circulated many excellent books; now one of them, the well-known Laurence Surius, probably at the request of Nicholas van Esch, set about translating the *Pearl*. This Latin translation already appeared in 1545 with an introduction by Nicholas van Esch, printed by Melchior Noveslanus, who among other works, had published Zerbolt of Zutphen in Latin. A copy of this edition is preserved in the library of the Bollandists in Brussels[22] and in the Universiteits-bibliotheek in Ghent. Worthy of note is the fact that in this Latin edition the third part is somewhat abbreviated by the omission of several effusions and prayers taken from St. Augustine; in their place a fourth part was added, which the *Pearl* attempted to adapt after the *Exercitorium* of García de Sisneros, particularly for the practical exercise of the virtues.

Surius also changed the order of the chapters and subjected the whole work to a sweeping rearrangement which did not affect its nature yet introduced considerable changes in the text.

It was the year 1609 before this Latin translation was reprinted, but when it reappeared in Dillingen, printed by Adam Meltzer –

---

[21] The Carmel in Nijmegen, to which Bl. Titus refers, was destroyed during WW II in 1944. This book is now found in the library of the Titus Brandsma Instituut (TBI, 231 d 10) in the Radboud University of Nijmegen. Another copy is in the central library of the University (641 c 70).

[22] Listed as the Société des Bollandistes in Kristeller/Krämer, *Ibid.*, p. 321.

as a work of Nicholas van Esch – its success was so great that already in 1610 it was reissued by the same printer; thus, the third Latin edition. A copy of the second Latin edition is preserved by the Jesuits in Edingen, or Enghien (Belgium). They also have a copy of the third Latin edition, as does the Universiteits-bibliotheek in Louvain.[23] In the beginning of the 17th century, the *Pearl* saw two printings of a French translation from the Latin by the Carthusian, Richard de Beaucousin, with approvals by Gallot and Quatresols, theology professors at the University of Paris. The first printing appeared in 1602 by the Widow de la Noue; the second, in 1608.[24] Copies of the first edition are preserved in the Ruusbroec Genootschap in Antwerp, by the Jesuits in Edingen and Louvain, and in the Universiteits-bibliotheek in Ghent. We have not found any copies of the second edition.

Only in the second half of the 17th century were two different German translations made. The first, printed at Glatz in 1676, is the work of the famous mystic, Johann Scheffler, better known as Angelus Silesius. His translation is also made from the Latin; the copy he used is preserved in the Universiteits-bibliothek in Breslau.[25] A second translation appeared in 1689, the work of the Friar Minor, Heribertus Hobbusch, also from the Latin. It was printed in Cologne by Johann Alstorff. We know of no copies of these two German editions. They should be searched for under the names, Angelus Silesius and Hobbusch.

Isn't it time to follow up the many reprints with a 10th Netherlandish edition?[26]

---

[23] Listed as the Bibliotheek der Katholieke Universiteit by Kristeller/Krämer, *Ibid.*, p. 525.

[24] "Loher," *Dictionnaire de théologie catholique*

[25] I. e., Wroc_aw, Biblioteka Universytecka; cf. Kristeller/Krämer, *Ibid.*, p. 918.

[26] Bl. Titus' wish, it would seem, has so far remained unfulfilled.

Maria van Oisterwijk[1]

I

In the circle of Nicholas van Esch we also meet the beguines of Oisterwijk. The reformer of the beguinage of Diest began his apostolate among the beguines with a similar institution in his birthplace. Its foundation is somewhat obscure and, as in so many other cases, probably developed gradually, so that it is difficult to fix its actual date of foundation. Oehl reports in his anthology of letters of German and Netherlandish mystics that already in 1532 there is mention of the beguinage of Oisterwijk. [2] This was no doubt an initial effort. From a patent of Emperor Charles V,[3] it would appear from the witness of the pastor, sheriff, magistrate, etc., cited there, that in 1539 Esch bought a house with lot in his native town as a residence wherein eight or nine young women might devote themselves to the service of God. Ten years later, the emperor authorized the pastor, sheriff, and magistrate to take over the house of Nicholas van Esch on behalf of the said young women.[4] It is quite certain that the Carthusians of Cologne played an important role in the founding of this house. A few devout women were already connected with the Charterhouse of Cologne, and it is not unlikely that the Carthusians prompted Esch to make this foundation and even assisted him financially. Thus, it is understandable that the foundation is ascribed to the Carthusians, as

[1] From *De Gelderlander*, May 28, June 4, 11, 1938.

[2] Wilhelm Oehl, *Deutsche Mystikerbriefe des Mittelalters, 1100-1500*, München, 1931.

[3] J.P.W.A. Smit, "Het Begijnhof van Oisterwijk," *Bossche Bijdragen*, 3 (1919-1920), 45-49.

[4] *Ibid.*

Ram does in the introduction to his life of Esch,[5] and that Nicholas van Esch is said rather to have confirmed the foundation and by buying the house to have given it a concrete existence. The abbot of St.Gertrui in Leuven, Joseph Geldolph van Ryckel, in his life of St. Begga, which imparts extensive information on every sort of beguinage,[6] states on the authority of George Garnefelt, Carthusian of Cologne, that the beguinage of Oisterwijk may be proud of its outstanding reputation and had housed many devout women. Among these women, Maria van Oisterwijk, also known by her family name, Marie van Hout (Lat. *de Ligno, Lignana*), occupies a wholly special place[7]. She seems to have been the first Mother of the beguinage of Oisterwijk. It is certain, in any case, that she was in charge from the earliest years of the foundation. How long she remained the Mother cannot be ascertained. All we know is that she went to Cologne in 1545 together with two other beguines, Ida and Eve. From that time, also, we know that St. Peter Canisius esteemed her highly and enjoyed listening to her. He is so enthusiastic in his praise that he does not hesitate to call her his "most faithful mother."[8]

Oehl dates her death in 1547, but the statement of Ram seems more correct. He records from the chronicles of the Charterhouse of Cologne that she was buried in that monastery on September 30, 1557.

The writings of Justus van Landsperg also witness to the high regard Maria must have enjoyed in Carthusian circles. Since then,

---

[5] *Venerabilis Nicolai Eschii... vita et opuscula ascetica*, ed. P.F.X. de Ram, Leuven, 1858.

[6] Josephus Geldolphus van Ryckel, 1581-1642, *Vita S. Beggae, ducissae Brabantiae, andetennensium, begginarum et beggardorum fundatricis, vetus hactenus non edita & commentario illustrata. Adjuncta est historia begginasiorum Belgii.* Lovanii, typis Corn. Coenestenii, 1631.

[7] Bernard McGinn, *The Varieties of Vernacular Mysticism (1350-1550)*, vol V of The Presence of God: A History of Western Christian Mysticism, New York 2012, 159-164.

[8] *Beati Petri Canisii, S.J., Epistulae et Acta*, ed. O. Braunsberger, S.J., Freiburg i. B., 1896, I, 21, 229, 249.

the biographer of Nicholas van Esch, Arnold Janssen, bestows on her the most ample praise.[9] His account clearly shows the influence she wielded. He calls her "enlightened in spirit and practised to the highest degree in the contemplative life." He writes that she composed many letters in the vernacular to many religious and friends of the Lord, wondrous in their content. Later they were printed anonymously in Cologne. After she had governed the beguinage in Oisterwijk for several years, she went to Cologne, either out of devotion or out of need. There she was provided for and supported by the Carthusians and other pious persons. Janssen also adds the reason; namely, because she was a maiden of high perfection and possessed a wonderful gift of bringing all, no matter who, religious or laypersons, to devotion and of attracting them to the spiritual life. By her holy counsels she was able to touch not only persons who had made vows of chastity and continence but also men and women united in marriage. These last she brought to the point that they seemed rather to be monks and nuns than persons living in the world.

The letters, of which she must have written quite a few and which were partially published in Cologne, have recently become more accessible. In 1927, Father Kettenmeyer published an anthology of her letters in the review, *Ons Geestelijk Erf,*[10] of which Oehl again included a great number in his above mentioned anthology of letters of mystics.

But besides these letters, very much worth reading and filled with spiritual doctrine and stimulation, we also have a book, which, to be sure, cannot be entirely ascribed to her, but in large part is from her hand. This is *De rechte weg ter evangelische volmaaktheid* (The straight way to evangelical perfection), already

[9] Arnoldus Janssen, *Vita venerabilis Nicolai Eschii*, ed. P.F.X. de Ram, *Venerabilis Nicolai Eschii... vita et opuscula ascetica*, Leuven, 1858.

[10] J.B., Kettenmayer, S.J., "Uit de briefwisseling van een Brabantsche mystieke uit de 16e eeuw," *Ons Geestelijk Erf,* 1 (1927), 278-293. Maria van Hout, Two Letters, in: *Late Medieval Mysticism of The Low Countries*, ed. R. van Nieuwenhove, R. Faesen & H. Rolfson, Paulist Press New York * Mahwah 2008, 365-369.

anonymously published in 1531 by Gerard Kalckbrenner, prior of the charterhouse of Cologne. In his studies about Maria van Oisterwijk, Father Kettenmeyer has pointed out that large portions of this work are decidedly to be attributed to Maria van Hout.[11] As such, he lists the explanation of the Creed and the Lord's Prayer, a treatise on the seven gifts of the Holy Spirit, a call to poverty of spirit, devout exercises in honor of the five holy wounds.[12] At that time, a second ascetical-mystical work appeared, *Paradijs der minnende ziel* (The paradise of the loving soul).[13] Father Kettenmeyer thinks it very likely that this work is also from the hand of Maria van Oisterwijk, but until now this has not been able to be established with certainty. Still another work is ascribed to Maria, *Over de negen trappen der enkelvoudigheid* (About the nine steps of simplicity), but no manuscript or published version of it is known.

We hope to return further to the letters and other writings of Maria van Oisterwijk, because it would be a pity, after having become acquainted with the few details of her quiet and simple life, not to learn more about what inspired her and what she tried to infuse in others through her books and letters. In a study of her mystical ideas and viewpoint, A. Möllmann has attempted to describe somewhat more closely and typify the mysticism of Maria van Oisterwijk.[14] The first thing that strikes us, he says, is the wonderful equanimity and harmony of her spiritual life; everywhere there is lucidity, assuredness, and quiet. The supernatural is founded as harmoniously as possible on the natural. Her instructions on the practice of the virtues are as harmonious as those on prayer. Beside and with the most profound humility and submissiveness there are decision and daring, only to be explained by a consciousness of a divine mission. In her letters, it is striking how

---

[11] *Ibid.*, 278-279.

[12] J.B. Kettenmeyer, S.J., "Maria van Oisterwijk (+1547) und die Kölner Kartause," *Annalen des historischen Vereins für den Niederrhein*, 114 (1929), 1-33.

[13] Cologne, 1532.

[14] A. Möllmann, "Maria von Osterwijk und ihre Schrift, 'Der rechte Weg zur evangelischen Vollkommenheit'," *Zeitschrift für Aszese und mystik*, 2 (1927), 319-333.

strongly the craving for suffering is expressed for the purpose of thereby preparing the way to God for others. Also noteworthy is her insistence on frequent, if possible daily, Holy Communion in such strong terminology that it seems that she was able to draw from this sacred bread the strength which left her free for a lengthy period to abstain from earthly sustenance. So powerfully did she see and feel the wonderful effect of Holy Communion on the soul that, according to her opinion, the body must necessarily experience a beneficent reaction.

Also deriving from the Oisterwijk circle is the *Evangelische Peerle* or The Evangelical Pearl (Lat. *Margarita evangelica*). It is undoubtedly the most beautiful work this group has produced. It was formerly thought that it should also be attributed to Maria van Hout. One would like to credit this most beautiful work to the one who holds first place among the women of Oisterwijk, yet it is not hers. In the preface to his edition, Esch states that the book was written by a devout maiden who lived in her father's house, (thus was no beguine) and died in 1540 at the age of 77.[15] These data do not fit Maria van Hout. However, this shows that there were others of this Brabant circle who deserve a closer look. In a subsequent article about these companions of Maria of Oisterwijk, we will have somewhat more to say, after having first examined her letters and works.

II

Her Writings and Letters

In her writings and letters, as A. Möllmann writes, Maria van Oisterwijk has left us a reflection of a simple soul, entirely and exclusively directed to God. First place among those works is occupied by the treatise, *Der rechte Weg zur evangelischen Volkommenheit* (The straight way to evangelical perfection), translated into German in 1531 by the Carthusian, Gerard Kalckbrenner. It is a

---

[15] *Dye Grote Evangelische Peerle*, Antwerpen, Willem Vorsterman, 1542.

little book in which actually four of Maria's tracts are collected, together with a number of letters written in that year. Although she raises the reader to the most intimate mystical feelings and thoughts, the book is, on the other hand, so simple and without pretension that she gives the impression of writing about the most ordinary matters in the world; as though the group of like-minded women for whom she writes was so large that she presumes a great many persons to be in a similar condition as hers.

The first tract starts with the Creed, and shows how the soul that seeks union with God can reach the most intimate union with God by the simplest means. The second speaks of the Seven Gifts of the Holy Spirit and shows how one can and must overcome the difficulties that occur on the way to the highest perfection. The third treats of poverty of spirit, by which she understands nothing else than humility. She describes the ever growing detachment from earthly things and therewith the ever increasing love of God. The fourth is a series of spiritual exercises of devotion to the Five Sacred Wounds.

Then there follow letters to the prior of the Carthusians in Cologne, Peter Blommevenna, her spiritual director; to Gerard Kalckbrenner, her brother and spiritual son; and to several others.

A quick review of the first tract already clearly shows us where she stands spiritually.

"I believe in God, the Father almighty." This statement is for her, and should be for all, a call to go to God with the warm-hearted simplicity of a child and unlimited trust in him whom we call our father. According as we place ourselves more completely in his hands, surrender ourselves to him, all the difficulties which can arise in our lives disappear. God is a father filled with love and care for us. With him we are secure and at peace. All that surrounds and affects us is also in the hand of God. Good things and pleasant come to greet and gladden us in the name of God. Unpleasant things bring us to knowledge of ourselves; we deserve nothing else. Our Father knows that unpleasant things are sometimes good for us. In due course, God will again give us the sweetest enjoyment of himself, the happy awareness of his presence.

And if we know we are with him, with the eye of a child directed to him, what can harm or disturb us? God created us out of nothing. He is the almighty, the eternal, the Lord of glory. What does creation not contain! But God's love is not revealed only in his creation. God goes on to regard us as the children of his love and predilection.

God sent his Son into the world to be human with us. How profoundly should we not bow to reach Christ; how fortunate should we not consider ourselves, now that he is with us! What wonder should we not have for his obedience to his divine mission, for the humility with which Mary received him! We must learn from Jesus and Mary to be equally obedient and humble. By means of these two virtues, we climb to the highest heights and meet them both. And when God meets a soul that has mastered these two virtues, he cannot resist her love. He chooses her for his bride, not only to give her pleasure, but also to make her share in everything he has suffered through obedience and humility, from the crib to the cross.

On the occasion when Christ was declared to have received the Holy Spirit, he petitioned the Father to send his Spirit to overshadow her (the soul), so that the divine Word would also live and dwell in her. Every time she contemplates this sacred mystery, the soul thinks of the wondrous descent of God's Son in the Holy Eucharist, which for her is a living image of Christ's conception in the womb of Mary. Through Holy Communion, she can receive Jesus with Mary. His birth from the Blessed Virgin Mary is realized in us when we completely submit to him the will which he has given us as a free will. We will achieve this by contemplating the Child Jesus, who humbled himself as profoundly as possible by descending from the heights of heaven.

The thought of Holy Communion reminds the soul of the miracle in Christ's life of the multiplication of the loaves. For her, too, the Bridegroom is multiplied. He gives her the bread of his teaching and then, the bread of his example. He feeds her, as he once did himself, with the hard bread of penitence, in order to make her die to all things and live for him alone. For this purpose, finally, he daily gives her the sweet bread of Holy Communion, so that she may begin a new life with him, a life of suffering and sacrifice on behalf of the world.

The soul must first be crucified and buried with Christ; that is, buried in the deepest humiliation, seemingly abandoned by God and man, trodden on like a worm, the last trace of *ongelatenheid*[16] (wilfullnes) and self-love wiped out, in order then to rise with Christ. Christ descends into Limbo, into which the soul imagines herself transposed, in order to carry her away in glorious resurrection and to rise with and in her. Just as Christ assumed divers forms from his resurrection to his ascension, so the soul must now become all things to all people, must speak of God to everyone she meets along the path of life, must bring them to God, must let God be seen in her actions. She must know how to enter closed doors; that is, continue to master and mortify her senses and thus move more freely in society. But although in the body she is wholly at the beck and call of people, she must let her heart travel to heaven and be so united to God that sin is no longer possible. The Blessed Trinity takes pleasure in her, comes to dwell in her, and works in her. She is wholly in God's power. She sits at the right hand of God and with him judges the living and the dead. The former she teaches more intimate union with God; the latter, by word and example she brings to penance and conversion. But the higher God lifts her up, the more profoundly the soul humbles herself and realizes that all is the work of God's grace.

In the depths of her heart, she adores God the Holy Spirit, who works all things in her and causes her to live one with the Father and the Son. She is alive to the fact that she shares in all those graces as a member of the mystical body of the Holy Catholic Church. Ordering her life ever more in the spirit of the Church, she goes to meet the resurrection of the body and life everlasting, in order to rest eternally in God.

The more intimate the soul's union with God, the more secret her life with him becomes. From time to time, he brings her to his wine cellar and gives her the wine to drink that begets angels and

---

[16] Titus leaves this term untranslated and places it in quotation marks.

virgins. He inebriates her with love. She can no longer hide her joy over her union with God. She must speak of him, praise and extol him, she is completely filled with him. She thinks only of him, and does everything with and for him. He lives in her and desires to be known and loved in her. But while she is so intimately united to God, he may try her physically and subject her to much suffering, while he also often withholds from her the sweetness of his presence, no matter how closely she remains bound to him. The bond with God here on earth is not primarily a pleasurable bond, but rather a share in the sacrifice designed to redress, in company of the Savior, the injustice done to God and to obtain graces for mankind. (This should never be forgotten in evaluating the mystical life.)

What beautiful, profound thoughts are those of Maria van Oisterwijk as appears from this treatise on the contemplation of the Creed! Each time, it brought before her eyes the whole development of her spiritual life and strengthened her awareness that whoever makes himself small enough to regard God as his father and leave everything to him, to trust him, to obey him, must share in the most wonderful interior life, because… because God just happens to be father to whomever makes himself entirely his child.

III

Her Letters

Besides the little book on the way of perfection, for the most part written by Maria van Oisterwijk and published in 1531 by the Carthusian, Gerard Kalckbrenner, in Cologne, there are eighteen letters written by Maria van Oisterwijk and one addressed to her. They are all very simple letters, originally no doubt written in Netherlandish, of which there are now only extracts, the rest translated in German of the Cologne dialect. Of these nineteen letters, Father Kettenmeyer has published fifteen, thus the majority.[17] Wilhelm Oehl has published a new German translation, so that

---

[17] "Uit de briefwisseling van eene Brabantsche mystieke," pp. 287-2

now the text is for the most part available to Netherlanders as well as Germans. Father Kettenmeyer is of the opinion that the letters, which naturally cannot have been written after 1531, in fact, date no earlier and all originate in that year. Five of the letters are directed to her spiritual director, two to the prior of the Charterhouse of Cologne, Peter Blommevenna, four to Gerard Kalckbrenner, and seven to members of apparently various nuns' convents.

In 1531, Father Kalckbrenner dedicated the book to Master Arnold van Tongeren, professor at the university of Cologne, noted for his opposition to Reuchlin.[18] In the dedication, Kalckbrenner writes that on a trip (to 's-Hertogenbosch in 1530) he made the acquaintance of some hidden friends of God, who in those disordered times shored up the Church of God by their prayers. He then refers especially to Maria van Hout as one enlightened by God and particularly united to him. He would be able to write a good deal more about her and her writings, which he says are inspired by the Holy Spirit, but he thinks that the time for that is not yet ripe. One thing, however, he writes, I cannot leave unsaid; namely, that in his whole life he has never been so deeply moved and drawn to God as by a conversation he had with her, by the reading of her writings, and by her prayer. He adds that his prior, Father Peter Blommevenna, his confreres, and other devout persons were also brought by her writings to a more profound love of God.

In her letters, Maria calls Father Kalckbrenner her spiritual son, and it is known that, not only several eminent Carthusians, but also the first Jesuits in Cologne, such as the first rector, Father Leonard Kessel, Father Peter Schorichius, and Saint Peter Canisius revered her as their spiritual "mother." These letters reveal that Maria lived with several young women and formed a small community. The devout women who constituted the community all remembered Father Kalckbrenner in their prayers and all offered Mass for him and his confreres. Maria adds that during the night of the feast of St. Peter, the apostle,[19] she had been wondrously

---

[18] Johannes Reuchlin, 1455-1522, German humanist.

[19] The feast of Sts. Peter and Paul is celebrated on June 29.

enlightened by God, and that Fr. Kalckbrenner had been given to her as her son. This had filled her with such great joy that she had been obliged to leave her bed in order to master her happiness. She predicts that God has elected him as an instrument of his plans and she urges him to rejoice. She then describes how valuable it is for one to place himself entirely in the hands of God and to abandon himself completely to him. She has done this, and in Father Kalckbrenner, who at the time was bursar of the monastery, God has given her such a good provider of her temporal interests that, in keeping with her desire and prayer, she is able to devote herself entirely to communion with God.

God has also provided a place in her heart for the prior of the monastery.[20] With both she must now go to God. The prior has also become her father. She enjoins on him to occupy himself to the best of his ability with the contemplation of the wondrous works of God and how God is still filled with love for mankind. She urges Father Kalckbrenner continually to picture the life of God's Son upon earth and to imitate his humility and simplicity; to serve others in his office of bursar and oblige each one in whatever way. He should bear in mind how Jesus let himself be led like a sheep or lamb without inner or external resistance. At the same time, she points to Mary, how she followed Jesus in weal and woe.

A second letter to Father Kalckbrenner begins with the wish that Jesus's life, so rich in variety, be ever kept before his eyes. Maria feels herself united to God and considers it her vocation to suffer with him and to pray for his apostles; that is, those who are called to imitate the life of [Christ's] apostles. She prays with Jesus in the upper room: "O dear Lord, just as you and I are one, so will that these my sons, whom you have given me, may also be one with you, as you and I are one." Gladly will she be crucified with Christ, in order that her sons might preach God's name in her place. She then describes how, while the monks praise God at night in Matins, she receives from God a share in his Passion and delivers herself entirely into his hands. Her head is day and night

---

[20] Peter Blommevenna

filled with pain, as though a cap of thorns pierced it on all sides. The pain in hands and feet and side is so great it cannot be described and wrings tears from her eyes. Her eyes hurt her so much that she can hardly open them. Above all, however, her feet sting, and her hair seems on fire. The most terrible thing is that this pain in her feet is accompanied by a feeling that she cannot and may not approach God unless she merits by her suffering to bring others to him. She desires to gather everyone in her heart, in order to carry them into the heart of God. She asks all the Carthusians in Cologne to pray for her, that God may give her the strength to be able to suffer much for her fellow human beings. (This is especially noteworthy in this time of nascent Protestantism, and shows how alive in Maria van Oisterwijk was the idea, not only of sharing in the Passion of Christ, but also of the tendency which this sharing has in the Catholic view of meriting on behalf of other persons. This social character of Catholic mysticism sharply distinguishes it from mystical expressions of a Protestant leaning, which always have a strong individualistic character.

Also noteworthy in this letter is what Maria van Oisterwijck writes about two Carthusians, who according to what she knew of God's ways, had died too little to their own wills. She makes it clear that a strict life without interior mortification of the will is of little or no value. Here it is also clearly expressed that holiness of works or virtue must above all be sought in the interior, and that the preaching of this doctrine had not died out in this circle and at this time.

In her appeal to her spiritual child, Maria also issues a warning against exaggerated care or fear, even though here and there he may be lacking somewhat in perfection. Surrender to God in humble receptiveness of his grace, the most childlike and simple obedience with mortification of the will hold first place in her estimation.

From a letter which she shortly thereafter wrote to her confessor, it appears that she abstained from all food for a certain period and lived only on Holy Communion. How long this privilege lasted is not clear. Later, in a letter we possess of the year 1531, she praises God that she can again partake of food. She can actually no longer fast, but she ascribes her need of food to the fact that she must be deprived of the food of Holy Communion and must now for want of anything better again use earthly food. She desires nothing more ardently than to receive Holy Communion, but I am wholeheart-edly satisfied, she writes, when love forces me to abstain from it. She knows that in either case she is in God's hand and gladly complies with his arrangements. She writes that she is enclosed in a cell, and that her confessor is the cell that keeps her enclosed. Whether this is to be taken in a literal and strict sense and whether this could be the reason for her deprivation of Holy Communion is not clear. In a following letter, however, she writes that her confessor allows her to receive Communion as long as she can do this in peace and that she may now receive Holy Communion for forty days. Farther on, she hints that her confessor sometimes makes difficulty about her receiving Communion, and that she then does not do so unless he tells her to. When she earlier reveals that her superior must force her under obedience to use earthly food, and on another occasion says that her superiors were always very strict with her and addressed few friendly words to her, one gets the impression that her superiors tried her in obedience by forbidding her for a time to receive Com-munion and that she was thereby forced again to partake of earthly food. In that case, her obedience was certainly heroic. That this supposition is not entirely unfounded is confirmed by the severe reproach Father Landsperg makes in the preface to the edition of the works of St. Gertrude[21] to priests who laugh at devout women and allow them only to receive Communion every other fortnight. One may not put limits to the Holy Spirit, he goes on to say, and it is not permitted to deny such women or other devout persons, who wish to communicate frequently.

At the end of 1531, Maria writes to a sister, full of delight, that the day has finally come for which she has suffered and prayed so much; namely, that she might receive Holy Communion daily.

---

[21] Cologne, 1536.

The Preparation of the Heart[1]

I

Among the spiritual writings of our Middle Netherlandish literature, the work, *Van der herten bereidinghe* (The Preparation of the
Heart), occupies a very important place. It is usually ascribed to
the Dominican, Gerard van Luik,[2] but it is becoming more and
more unlikely that the work is his. It is rather to be attributed to
the Cistercian school and is yet another witness to the wonderful
spiritual life that flourished in that Order especially in 13th century
Netherlands, and that infused such vitality and fervor into the
beguine movement. We do not wish now to enter into detail on
the question of the authorship of this treatise; for the moment, we
would rather occupy ourselves with the treatise itself.

It is quite a comprehensive work, and we do not wish to reproduce it in its entirety. We shall concern ourselves only with a part,
which to our way of thinking is the most important, and which
has not been without influence on the spiritual literature of the
Netherlands. It strikes me that when Ruusbroec wrote his *Spiritual
Espousals* toward the middle of the 13th century, he was also influenced by this treatise. Although the whole work may be considered
important, the part which compares the human heart to a bride is
particularly so; above all, because it is a fine example in our literature of the bridal mysticism of St. Bernard.

The book was originally written in Latin with the title, *Doctrina
cordis*, and has come down not only in a relatively large number

---

[1] From *De Gelderlander*, March 30; Apr. 6, 13, 27; May 4, 1940.
[2] D.A. Wilmart, O.S.B., "Gérard de Liège, un traité inédit d'amour de Dieu,"
Revue d'Ascèse et Mystique, 12 (1931), 349-359.

of manuscripts but also in a number of printed editions. Exactly when it was translated into Netherlandish is not certain. Indeed, there are several translations with rather strongly divergent versions. A very old translation is preserved in the Fideikomissbibliothek in Vienna.[3] The Instituut voor de Geschiedenis der Nederlandsche Mystiek at the Catholic University in Nijmegen,[4] as well as the Carmel in that city[5] possess photocopies, the latter also a transscript. In the Albertinum, the Dominican House of Studies in Nijmegen, there is another manuscript, but it is substantially more recent and strongly variant from the others.[6] We will follow the Vienna manuscript.

The treatise begins like almost all spiritual treatises which feature a somewhat complete introduction to the practice of a fervent spiritual life, including the purification of the soul. First, the soul must purge itself of sin and by mortifiction of the senses strive to arrive at introspection. So, The Preparation of the Soul begins with elucidating the need of cleaning the house of the soul through confession, in order to further adorn it. The house must be fitted up and locked. Watchers must be placed at the door. Turned inwardly, the spiritual person should then give thought to nourishing himself with the food presented by God himself: the Blessed Sacrament of the altar. Holy Communion should serve to make us similar to Jesus and to associate us with his own sacrifice. If the "inn" is clean and pure, everything well prepared, and the table set, then the soul can receive her Bridegroom.

Thereupon follows the symbol, often used in antiquity and in the Middle Ages, of Christ as a baked fish, or meat roasted on a

<hr>

[3] This library seems to have been taken up in the Österreichische Nationalbibliothek; cf. Nicole Marzac, *Concordance entre les cotes de la Fideicomissbibliothek et les cotes actuelles de la Series nova*, Paris, 1977 (typescript), cited by Paul Oskar Kristeller, *Latin Manuscript Books Before 1600*, 4th ed., München, 1993, p. 904.
[4] Now the Titus Brandsma Instituut, Toernooiveld 300, 6525 EC Nijmegen.
[5] Now in the Karmel, Steenstraat, 39, 5831 JA Boxmeer.
[6] Now found in the Koninklijke Bibliotheek in The Hague, M. 135 F 6, ff. 39ff.

spit. "Piscis assus est Christus passus (a baked fish is Christ suffering)," Tertullian already writes.[7] In the catacombs, we already find the image of the fish as a symbol of the Savior on the cross. Here in our land, in the Middle Ages, we hear Father Brugman more than once compare the sacred Passion of Christ with the roasting of his divine flesh in the fire of his divine love. The symbol has now become somewhat unusual and sounds to our ears even rather hard and crude; yet, we may not declare this formerly oft used symbol to be void of a deep and striking meaning. Thus, in our treatise, after the first abovementioned fitting up and preparation of the house, or inn, of the soul, we find a chapter titled, "That man is obliged to prepare himself to become food just as Christ prepared himself for men." Then, another follows, "How a person is to roast his heart with four tribulations and lard it with the grease of charity." A third chapter reads, "That one finds these three things in Christ: flaying, roasting, larding." A following chapter again treats of "The signs by which one may know when the heart is well roasted."

A more accessible image for us is the comparison, which then follows, of the human heart with the bride. I would like for a moment to look at this image more closely. After a reference to the Old Testament according to which priests may marry only virgins,[8] the writer states that, if we wish to marry the Great High Priest, we must be pure as virgins. If you wish to marry Christ and be his bride, you must, according to Zacharias,[9] cast off your soiled clothing and cleanse your spiritual garments of all stains. Just as a stain is more unbecoming and bothersome on a white garment, so the stain of sin is also more unbecoming to a virgin. So, in Sacred Scripture, we find virginity compared to white garb. Therefore, a virgin and bride of Christ must often cleanse her conscience, although it is not enough that she be free of stains. She

---

[7] The quotation is actually St. Augustine's, *In Iohannis evangelium*, tractatus 123, par. 2: "piscis assus Christus est passus."
[8] Cf. Lev 21, 13.
[9] Zach 3, 4.

must, moreover, nourish and foster the most fervent love in her heart toward her Bridegroom, love him, desire him, seek him. In the lamp of her life, the oil of good works must continually feed the flame of love. A virgin without love is like a lamp without oil. The treatise goes on to speak of four ways by which the Bridegroom recognizes the virginity of his bride. In medieval treatises, bridal mysticism, often with reference to the Song of Solomon and the liturgy of the Church, carries imagery rather further than we in our times consider fitting and proper. This particularly obtains in our regions, where various physical objects are kept hidden from view, which in other regions remain, freely and without scandal, open and uncovered. Although recently there has happily been a strong trend encouraging young mothers to feed their infants at the breast, nevertheless, here propriety demands that this organ be entirely hidden from sight. It is counted a proof of modesty that the swelling of the breasts of a young mother is not visible through a slit in the clothing. Picturing the divine Child at the breast of Mary, so popular in our native medieval art, is now avoided. Yet I would not want to say that the present moral sense of our country is more refined than it was in the fourteenth and fifteenth centuries. Be that as it may, certain it is that in medieval spiritual literature there is greater freedom in these matters than in our day, and we find in that literature allusions to bodily matters which we prefer to avoid today.

Thus, it need not surprise us that, also in this treatise about bridal mysticism, one of the signs of virginity is that in the young maiden her breasts are not yet swollen, and that accordingly both breasts are chosen as symbols of the cognitive and appetitive faculties, not yet cleansed and swollen with the acceptance of every sort of image. Thus, the bodily condition is used to show that, if we wish to go to meet Christ as brides, our understanding and our heart should not be filled with thoughts and desires which are not of Jesus. The second sign is poverty, because the bride has not yet received anything from the beloved, and she awaits all her riches from her heavenly Bridegroom. The third sign by which the Bridegroom recognizes the virgin is her voice; while the fourth is taken to be that the virgin – again, according to the morals of those times – still goes about with her head unveiled and thereby is a symbol of the soul that stands free and uncovered before the face of the Lord and freely ascends to the contemplation of him.

II

After the tractate has indicated the four signs by which Christ will recognize the soul as his bride, the devout person is impressed with the need to nourish in his heart a desire of the spiritual marriage. How can we find a wiser or nobler bridegroom?

No union is more profitable for us, none gives us more happiness, none lends us more honor and prestige. The bride will find no fault with this Bridegroom. God is everything to her heart: a model, a helpmate, a medicine for all her ills, a reward for all her efforts, a father, her Creator, her teacher, her love, her hope, the object of her continual praise, the one from whom she bears all things, the strength of her life. All that he has becomes the property of his bride. Should she not then confer on him all that she is and has? Christ has said, "When I am lifted up from the earth, I shall draw all things to myself."[10] Whom does he draw other than the human being? This being, therefore, is his all. Shall we, then, neglect bestowing ourselves entirely on him without any reserve?

The treatise then points out that this union with Christ comes about only through love. Through love we pay him the tribute which is his due from what he has given us. He asks nothing else. Were he to require of you great austerity of life, you would be able to excuse yourself by protesting your inability; were he to require of you wealth of earthly goods, you could point to your poverty; but you could not claim not to be in a condition to give him your love. To whom could we better give it; who would recompense us more lavishly? It is incomprehensible how often we thoughtlessly commit and give away our love.

---

[10] Jn 12, 32.

Next, the treatise employs an image which often occurs in medieval spiritual literature, that of the game of chess. How careful a chess player is to place even the smallest piece so that it is covered! How long he often holds the piece in his hand! And we carelessly set our heart on things which place it in the greatest danger. The chess player is ever intent on covering himself so as not to lose the game. So we, too, must fly from all those things to which we so easily lose our heart, in order to retreat to the inmost region of our heart and be without fear or danger.

Another image is borrowed from the game of dice. God has handed you cubes or dice. Take advantage of the occasion, for he has given you the power to make whatever cast you wish. Don't do as those who only keep the dice in their hands and lose time shaking them, but cast the die; that is to say, use the time given you to discharge your guilt and gain merit by doing penance for your sins.

Moreover, we should bear in mind the price God has been willing to pay in order to buy our love. He loved us first. And if the price of his precious blood is not enough for you, he has, besides, promised heaven to those who will grant him their love. How little he asks of us! How cheap is the exchange he proposes to us! Earthly love is maintained with little gifts as so many keepsakes; God gives us himself, and gave us that food as a remembrance, not only of the miraculous food with which he fed the Jews in the wilderness, but much more of the love he showed us in dying for us. I have graven you in my hands, he said;[11] that is, I still carry the signs of my wounds on my hands, so that I may not forget you. Nowadays, we make a knot in our handkerchief as a reminder. In the Middle Ages, there seems to have been a similar custom, but one made the knot on the belt, or cord, with which one was girded and which hung from the waist. The three knots in the cord of the Friars Minor still recall that symbol and signify that the friars do not want to forget their three vows and therefore have made three knots in their cord. Christ desired to make a mark on

---

[11] Is 49, 16.

his very body, in order not to forget us, and for that purpose chose wounds in his hands and feet and side. Never think that God abandons or forgets you.

Next, it is pointed out that three periods are distinguished in the contraction of matrimony. One begins with promising mutual love and fidelity in prospect of marriage in the future. When the time has come, both partners express their will to contract marriage. This is then crowned by living together in inseparable union. The same is true of the spiritual marriage, which is introduced by a probationary period, secured by vows, and crowned with union forever in heaven.

Because a person is inclined to do later in life that to which he had accustomed himself in his youth, it is of the greatest importance that we do not procrastinate, but as soon as possible set up our heart to love God and grow to maturity in the school of love. The lesson to be learned in this school is easy to remember. Christ teaches school hanging from the cross. Our heart must truly be of stone, if we could not understand the lesson he teaches us there, or if we could not remember it. Moreover, he has surrounded us with the works of his hands; heaven and earth speak to us of his love and do not cease urging us to return that love.

A fire grows greater in proportion as one brings more wood to feed it. The wood is stacked all around us, a heap piled up to maintain the fire of love in us, if we only want to use it.

Seneca points out that a dog loves his master who is good to it. Would you be outdone by a dog? He also tells the story of a lion that faithfully followed a knight who had saved it from a snake.[12] Can we, then, allow our savior and redeemer to walk alone?

A drop of water hollows the stone. Is our heart harder than stone that it is not softened by the continual proof of divine love?

In the Old Testament it is written that one who goes forth to battle and finds a beautiful woman among the prisoners, may take her into his house, but she must first wear mourning for a month, then remove the garments with which she was captured, and

---

[12] Wrong reference – not in Seneca.

finally cut her hair and nails. Only then may he take her to wife.[13] This is a symbol of Christ, who in a noble life and death struggle has captured the soul and desires to make her his bride. He has brought her into his house. There he has given her opportunity to mourn over her sins, to lay aside her garments and don new ones, to cut her hair and nails; that is to say, he has made her adopt new manners, freed her from what in the world was her pride and joy and from the outward aspects of luxurious living.

Again, the soul is warned not to do as Rachel, who, when she fled from Laban's house to belong to Jacob, took the idols of her father's house and hid them under the straw of the camels.[14] This is also the case of the soul, who, fleeing from the world in order to become Jesus' bride, would like to take with her the love of honor and pleasure and attachment to her own will – the idols of the world – and hide them under her spiritual gown. As children of the world, we must divorce ourselves from our mother, in order to live a new life with God, who causes us to be reborn to him.

After the probationary period of the novitiate, the time has come to bind ourselves for good to God through vows and to enter into spiritual marriage with him. We must have the fixed and expressed purpose of thenceforth living with God and of belonging only to him. It is in this sense that St. Paul says that love is the bond of perfection.[15] And although this state involves many duties, we may not complain, because each new duty binds us more closely to the Beloved. The bride should meanwhile not imagine that her marriage promises her an immediate entry into life. Her spiritual marriage is like the marriage of a knight who meets his bride in a foreign land and there secretly binds himself to her. Only when he returns to his own land after the battle is over, do his companions come to meet him, is a great feast laid

[13] Deut. 21, 10-13.

[14] Gen. 31, 19, 34. The English Vulgate has "the camel's furnishings"; the Revised Standard Version has "the camel's saddle."

[15] Col 3, 14.

on, and the marriage celebrated. So also the union of the soul with Christ here on earth is still often filled with sorrow and strife, and only later, when the Bridegroom has led his bride into his native land, which is heaven, does the joy of the eternal nuptials follow. Then will his companions the angels, come to meet him, and the eternal Alleluja echo.

The Jews arrived in the promised land through the wilderness and the Red Sea. In the Red Sea, their enemies met their fate, but God saved them from the waters and brought them to the land where he wished to make them happy. We, too, must traverse that Red Sea and that wilderness.

III

Treating in greater detail the image of the wilderness which the Israelites had to traverse in order to arrive at the promised land, the author sees in that image a figure of religious life, lying between life on earth and life in heaven to which religious life leads; just as the wilderness lying between Egypt and Israel led the Jews to the land of happiness destined for them. Further, the author sees in the impossibility of satisfying every human desire in the wilderness, an indication that one cannot expect as much in the monastery; that there luxury must be excluded and poverty and hardship experienced.

Next, the author attempts to show how, just as in earthly marriage, in the spiritual marriage of the soul with her heavenly Bridegroom, Christ, there are three things which make it beautiful and desirable.

The first is that bride and bridegroom swear mutual troth and belong to each other. Likewise, the soul must also give herself completely to God and place herself entirely in his hands. She knows that God has placed his all at her disposal, has given himself to her, and so may expect that she will reciprocate his faithful love with equally sincere fidelity. She must give him, and him alone, all her love, and open her heart completely to him. She must divest herself of all attachment to creatures. With a three-ply bond, which according to St. Paul is difficult to unravel,[16] she must bind herself to her Bridegroom; that is to say, she must think of no one and love no one but him; she must find no pleasure in the love of anyone whomsoever other than his; she must be intent on pleasing him alone. At her vows, the bride of Christ usually receives a ring as a token of her fidelity. The ring is made for her alone, and fits only her. So the heart of man must closely fit God and include nothing besides him. God has created you alone, says St. Augustine.[17] He also desires your love for himself alone.

The second good is that marriage is contracted in order to be blessed with children. So also must spiritual marriage be fruitful. Its fruits are the good works which must issue from union with God. They will bear witness for the soul on the last day. Wicked works and sin should be to her like bad and degenerate children, whom she must disavow in confession and penance, and dismiss from her house, lest they bear witness against her before the judge on the last day.

The third good contained in earthly marriage is that, contracted in church, it is a sacrament which binds bride and bridegroom indissolubly to each other. What God has joined together no one can put asunder.[18] This is an image of the constancy which in the end earns the heavenly crown for the bride. Many begin well, but only those who persevere to the end will be blessed.

The writer uses another apt image when, continuing to speak of the good works which must be the fruit of union with God, he points out that not everyone can or must do the same thing. Each one must do that to which Providence, or the authority under which he has placed himself, calls him. Even if a person were to practice strict penance, or perform actions at which the world wonders and for which it esteems him, it is no indication that union with God is producing the fruits of good works in him. In doing penance, one should follow, not one's own judgment, but

---

[16] Perhaps an allusion to 1 Cor. 13,13.
[17] Enarrationes in Psalmos, Ps. 127, par. 12.
[18] Cf. Mk 10, 9.

the guidance of the rule, statutes, and superiors. Likewise, it should not be thought that only they who follow all the community exercises in the convent can possess true religious perfection; those, too, who are dispensed from all austerity in the infirmary; or who, engaged in promoting the interests of the monastery, must neglect various exercises and even live outside the cloister, can be united to God and produce fruits of good work. These latter he likens to notes which are not, like present lined writing, written between staves, but according to ancient use of neumes, appear in open space; yet in music have the same sound. So also David wanted the booty shared equally between those who had gone forth to battle and those who had to remain behind to guard the camp.[19]

There now follows the description of the bride's attire. This is linked to a text of the prophet Ezekiel, in which God turns to sinners and tells them all he has done to cleanse them and bedeck them with ornaments. In the 16th chapter, Ezekiel pictures Jahweh's love for Jerusalem, which is represented as a bride: "And I washed thee with water and cleansed away thy blood from thee: and I anointed thee with oil. And I clothed thee with embroidery and shod thee with violet coloured shoes: and I girded thee about with fine linen, and clothed thee with fine garments. I decked thee also with ornaments, and put bracelets on thy hands, and a chain about thy neck. And I put a jewel in thy forehead and earrings in thy ears, and a beautiful crown upon thy head. And thou wast adorned with gold, and silver."[20] Thirteen ornaments are listed here, which for the writer of our treatise are so many symbols of God's love and benefactions.

He then enlarges on these thirteen ornaments in a series of chapters, and with that closes the first Book of his treatise. We would like briefly to sum up what he thinks all these ornaments and decorations symbolize.

First of all, Jahweh says he has already washed his chosen bride at her birth and cleansed her of the blood with which she was

[19] 1 Sam 30, 24.
[20] Ezek 16, 9-13.

defiled. The water with which he washed her was the water that streamed from the wound in his divine heart, opened by one of the soldiers with his lance. With this water, heated in the furnace of love, we were washed in baptism, and the soul was cleansed of the blood with which the wounds, inflicted by sin, had defiled her. Mixed with the Lord's sacred blood, it had become lye which removed all our stains. Once purified, the soul must strive to keep her conscience clean and pure. If at home you want the dishes for eating and the linen for your clothing to be clean and without stain, how much more then should you keep spotless your heart, which is much more precious. You must not allow it to be besmirched with evil thoughts. To maintain its purity, we must often bathe it in the blood of the Lord, which was shed, not only to wash and cleanse us, but at the same time to dye our garment in the most precious purple. Let us take care that it does not lose its distinctive color; after the example of Christ, we must often re-dye it. How often did he not bathe his body in this blood: at the circumcision, at the sweating of blood in the garden, at the scourging, at the crowning with thorns, at the crucifixion, at the piercing of his heart. That is why the bride in the Song of Solomon declared that her Beloved was at once white and ruddy.[21] And because a garment that is died in the wool retains its color better than if dyeing is postponed until the wool is spun into threads, so we must as soon as possible dye ourselves with the precious Blood and already sanctify our youth with it. Accustomed in youth is accomplished in old age, Solomon already taught.[22]

Secondly, Jahweh says that he has anointed his bride with oil. This is conceived to be an image of spiritual joy. God wants us to bear our yoke with gladness.[23] When you fast, anoint your head with oil.[24] It is an election. Thus, the soul must awaken happy thoughts in herself, her countenance should gleam with virtue,

---

[21] Song 5, 10.
[22] This popular adage is not found in the Wisdom literature.
[23] Ps 99, 2.
[24] Mt 6, 17.

because she has been called to the retinue of the King and may enter his apartment.

Thirdly, Jahweh says that he has clothed her in many-colored garments. This signifies that he has instilled in her a great variety of virtues. Not only has he given her a many-colored garment, which at once radiates a wealth of virtue, but he has also given her garments of various colors, to be worn on various occasions, and thereby to indicate that distinct circumstances of life should elicit new virtues. In meditating on the birth of the Lord, the soul must wear a garment of humility and modesty, because he was born so small and insignificant; in meditating on his Passion, a garment of penance and mourning; in meditating on his resurrection, a garment of gladness; in meditating on his ascension, a garment of hope and love. On the feast of a martyr, she must wear a garment of patience; on that of a virgin, a garment of purity. In this way, all her virtues are revealed.

IV

The fourth ornament, which God, according to the description of the prophet, bestows on his bride is footwear of the finest leather, studded with jewels. In the luster of the stones, the glow of heaven is reflected, and so the writer takes this symbol to mean that the soul that wishes to be God's bride, must arise in longing to heavenly things. The gait of the king's daughter is beautiful, when her shoes tread earthly things underfoot, and her whole desire is directed to heaven. Her foot may not step in the mire of sin but should be shielded against it by lofty desires. The liturgy of the Church expresses this symbolically, when it prescribes that the bishop, when he pontificates at Mass, puts on shoes embroidered with gold and so ascends the altar.

Fifthly, God says to his chosen one, I have girded you with a girdle of damask. This is a symbol of purity, not only because of the color of the fine white damask, which, purified at the cost of much effort, glitters and shines, but also because a girdle is made of it. The girdle holds the garment together and keeps the body from losing heat. It also ties off the upper part of the clothing, so that one can hold something in the bosom and keep it safe. So also must the bride of the Lord gird herself, so that she does not lose the glow of love through dissoluteness, but safeguards her love and the good thoughts which she receives from God. Finally, the girdle keeps the hands confined to the nobler parts of the body which lie above it. But then the person should gird himself after the manner of one going to battle or about to serve. If God grants you a girdle of finest damask, take that as a sign that he is calling you to battle and that he wants you in his service. Set great store by the fact that he binds you to his service, distinguishes you with the sign of election, girds you in order that, pure and chaste, you occupy yourself only with what he gives you to do.

The sixth ornament of the bride is a chemise of silk, for the writer a symbol of faith. It can also be regarded as a garment of finest weave lying closest to the body and, as it were, arms and protects it from any danger of error. Further, just as every fabric consists of warp and woof, so also this garment of the bride, who must weave her life from good thoughts interwoven with good desires.

As the seventh ornament, God gave his bride a festive garment. This is nothing else than love which he pours into her. Love gives luster to all other virtues. Without love, one is at the wedding feast of the Lord like the one who had no wedding garment and was ignominiously cast out.[25]

The writer assigns five reasons why the Lord was surprised to find someone in his festive hall without a wedding gown. The first is that he has gone to such pains to assure that his bride should yet have this gown. He did not make it of wool or silk, but of his own heart and dyed in his precious blood. The second reason is so that his bride should nevertheless know that this gown alone is able to make her pleasing in his sight. It is a symbol of the coat without seam that he did not want to see divided, although he allowed his body to be wounded and his heart pierced. So also the

---

[25] Mt 22, 12-13.

love, which must be the wedding-gown of the bride, may not be divided. The third reason the writer proposes is that the bride is to wear this garment in the train of the King, when he enters the heavenly court with her. The garment must already be woven; it will be too late then to begin to weave. Meditating on the benefits which she receives from the humanity and divinity of Christ, the soul must quicken her love, never to lay aside this garment of love. The fourth reason is that through love the soul covers all her imperfections and failings; only in this way is she in condition to remove her naked ugliness. The fifth reason, finally, why the Lord must be surprised to find in his festive hall someone without this garment of love is that the bride should know that no one is admitted into heaven without it.

The eighth ornament of the bride is the bracelets around her wrists. This denotes the fact that the Lord causes her to perform good works in order that she might offer him the work of her hands as a sacrifice. Not only exterior works of virtue, but also interior ones of prayer and contemplation are required of her. She must divide her work, and serve God interiorly as well as exteriorly. Although this service is a privilege, although the bracelets around her wrists are an ornament, the weight of that service and of those bracelets presses heavily. This is a symbol of Eliezer, who gave Rebecca bracelets weighing as much as ten pounds.[26] Here, Eliezer is the image of Christ, Rebecca is the bride, while the bracelets of ten pounds refer to the ten commandments of the Law, to the ten things that render religious life difficult.

The first of these ten things is the silence that must be observed after the example of him who allowed himself to be slaughtered like a lamb, who did not open his mouth. Again, the conception of St. John the Baptist at the time his father was dumb is described as showing that God's grace can only be received in the quiet of maintaining silence.

The second difficulty of religious life is that one must remain indoors. One should not resemble a bird in a cage, which has no

[26] Gen 24, 22.

rest, but constantly jumps back and forth. The soul should not consider the cloister a prison, in which she does not feel at home and is driven by restlessness.

A third difficulty may be the severity of the superior. A fourth, that there are so many regulations to follow. A fifth, that in any case freedom is cramped by the statutes of the house.

A sixth difficulty which religious life can involve is that not all religious are equally perfect, and that harmony is sometimes disturbed by persons who are dissatisfied.

A seventh cross can be that the food and drink are too frugal, and that superiors are not sufficiently concerned about the bodily needs of subjects.

Also, an eighth cross, clothing can sometimes be a difficulty, be harsh and uncomfortable, rough and shabby. One should reflect, however, that a tree is not appraised by its bark but by its fruit.

A ninth trial of religious life is the obligation of limiting bodily rest and of having to interrupt or end sleep on account of the hours of Matins and Prime.

A tenth rigor of religious life can be, finally, that the prayers and the recitation of the Hours last so long and weary the spirit.

But although these ten points are difficult and can be hard to observe, on the other hand, according as these heavy bracelets weigh more, they are also more valuable; and the loving bride gladly bears the weight, because she knows that with these ornaments she is more beautiful and pleasing in the sight of the Beloved.

As the ninth ornament of the bride, the prophet Ezekiel indicates a necklace.[27] This is a symbol of self-mastery in speech. We must erect a dam or sluice against the stream of words that would erupt from our throat, in order that the water issue from it in the measure we deem useful and proper. Also, the fire of anger should not become so heated in us that we can no longer hold the water of hard words in the vat which contains them, because it cracks under the influence of the fire.

---

[27] Ez 16, 11.

Next, the tenth ornament are the rings in the ears. They are symbolic of the correction administered by a wise man to a docile and sensible disciple. It is to the credit and honor of the soul that she heeds wise counsel. Her docility must show a double aspect, as rings are worn in two ears: she must not only follow wise counsel and shape her actions accordingly, but she must know how to wait and apply her ears to listening, in order not to act arbitrarily, but to be ever docile, and to be ready for anything. We should not wipe up earthly things with ears hanging on the ground like those of dogs; but with ears directed to God, we should open them to his words, so that they hear only his voice. Like the miser who loves money and finds the sound of it sweet, so we should love God's word and find our joy in it only; we should not allow it to go in one ear and out the other, but let it penetrate into our heart. We should not be intent on idle news, but on what brings us closer to God. And just as we cannot move our ears individually, but they follow the motions of the head, so our longing for news must follow the guidance of the intellect.

V

As the eleventh ornament of the bride of the Lord, Ezekiel denotes the crown placed on her head by the royal Bridegroom.[28] Here this is taken as a symbol of her virginal life. A crown is prepared for everyone in heaven, but the virgins will receive a double crown. Above the golden crown, with which the heads of all the saints in heaven are adorned, the virgins will receive a headdress of roses as a token of their victory in the struggle of life.

The Bridegroom further adorns his bride with gold. Gold is here a symbol of the wisdom and intelligence of the spirit. This means that a person will draw the lessons from the past which are hidden there for him; that he accepts the present, understanding what he must do; finally, that he foresees what the future has in store for him and is prepared for it.

[28] Ez 16, 12.

In the first place, a person should bethink himself of the benefits God has conferred on him; how God created and maintains him in existence; how God further surrounds him with images of his being contained in creation. But not only is God always near and in him as Creator; in the Blessed Sacrament, he is our food and our strength. This reminds him further of the sacred Passion of the Lord, of which Christ has preserved the wounds in hands, feet, and side. He has inscribed Christ in his hands, and as often as he shows his hands, he reveals how dearly he loves him. Just as the water of the spring of Bethlehem was especially dear to David,[29] because it had been won for him at the cost of so much courage and strife, so should the benefits of the Lord be especially dear in our eyes, because he has willed to suffer so, in order to bestow those benefits on us.

Further, we must consider what the Lord has commanded us to do, what commandments he has laid upon us; not in order merely to know them or speak about them, but to fulfill them promptly and faithfully. As the book of the Law lay in the ark of the covenant,[30] so must the book of God's law lay in our heart, and so must we be mindful of God's law day and night.

Then we must be mindful of the saints who have gone before us and should be an example for us. We should imitate them, just as young squires imitate knights, and as heralds impress upon them the heroic deeds performed in the tourneys. The Lord's sacred Passion and the courage and love with which the martyrs shared in it should fill us with the strength to follow their example.

Finally, we must be mindful of our sins. We should settle our account with God, but also verify how much we owe him. A frank and complete confession is necessary to begin a life of introspection and union with God.

But wisdom is not only a glance at the past; she must in the second place understand the present. Seneca has already said that we must indeed be mindful of the past, but we must above all

[29] 2 Sam 23, 15.
[30] Ex 25, 10.

make good use of the present.[31] It is harmful to postpone the good until later. We must give God what we have. What we will possess in the future we do not know.

Still, wisdom must also look forward to the future. If the ant diligently works during the summer in order to be able to live in the winter, then a much wiser human being should make provision in due time, in order to protect God's grace in the hour of danger. We must collect merit and acquire virtue and so provide the dwelling-place of the soul with what is needful for her life.

The thirteenth and last ornament listed by Ezekiel, besides gold, is silver. "With gold and silver have I adorned you."[32] Silver is here taken to be a symbol of the sweetness of the divine inspirations. The Lord's words written in the Gospel and addressed to our heart are a sweet melody and quiet enjoyment for the soul.

The bride is happy in sweet dialog with her Bridegroom, adorned with all the ornaments with which he could bedeck her. Thus arrayed, she may enter the wedding hall with him and be happily united to him.

This is the end of the first book, which, after treating the preparation of the soul as a dwelling-place for the Lord and as food, regards the soul more particularly as a bride, and in the light of this image explains how the soul should prepare herself for union with the Lord.

This is always regarded as the most important part of the treatise dealt with here. Of the three "preparations" of the heart, that presented under the symbol of the bride is certainly the most important. We have wanted particularly to call attention to it, mostly because we have in it, besides the beautiful work of Ruusbroec about *De Spiritual Espousals*, a second important treatise through which bridal mysticism has found entrance into these lands.

---

[31] Perhaps *De beneficiis*, lib. 3, cap. 3, par. 4: "Hoc loco reddendum est epicuro testimonium, qui adsidue queritur, quod adversus praeterita simus ingrati, quod, quaecumque percipimus bona, non reducamus nec inter voluptates numeremus, cum certior nulla sit voluptas, quam quae iam eripi non potest."

[32] Cf. Ezek 16, 13.

We shall still very briefly indicate how, after the "preparation" as "first *principiael*," six other exercises are presented, which affect the human heart in its ascent to the spiritual life. The second *principiael*[33] is that, after having prepared our heart, we must preserve it in its so laboriously acquired condition. Here, for the first time, the heart is likened to a vessel in which precious liquid is hidden; next, to a castle. After that, there is an explanation of the reason why a person often succumbs in the spiritual strife; why a person should guard his tongue, not only in a negative sense, by governing it, but also in a positive sense by speaking out, when the good of the neighbor requires it.

The third *principiael* is that we must open our heart. Here, first, the symbol of the book is used, which must be laid open to God and to those who represent him. Next, under the symbol of a door which is opened to the Lord, we are told how we must open our heart to God. Not only must God have entrance to our heart; we must also keep our heart open to our neighbor.

The fourth *principiael* follows, to the effect that we should make our heart strong and steadfast and by good thoughts strengthen its desire for the good. We must fortify our faith; then the power of faith will also render us steadfast in our desires and make us desire only what God wills.

As the fifth *principiael*, we are told that we must give our heart. God asks us, "My child, give me your heart." He has shown what great store he sets by it. His love on the one hand, his sovereignty on the other, must force us to grant him our heart with love and humility.

The sixth *principiael* tells us that we must lift our heart on high to God. This we do when we lift our hearts on high to God and heavenly things. For this, our heart opens up. Besides a good thought, hope will lift up our heart; thirdly, desire; fourthly, the good intention.

Remarkable here is a comparison of Jesus to Judas. Jesus, whose feet were nailed down, tells the spiritual person to remain

---

[33] Bl. Titus throughout does not translate or modernize this word.

in solitude and not to wander here and there; while his nailed hands symbolize that our hands must be bound and must do or give only what is permitted. His voice, however, was free to proclaim God's praise and to preach the truth. Judas' hands and feet were free, but the halter with which he hung himself prevented him from speaking and proclaiming God's praise, an image of the religious who allows himself the freedom to go about wherever he will, and freely to dispose of whatever is at his disposition, but thereby neglects to pray and to sing God's praise in the canonical hours.

To this is added that we must lift our hearts because our native land lies there on high; second, our treasure is there; third, our Father is enthroned there; and finally, all good things await us above.

The seventh *principiael*, to conclude, is the circumcision of the heart. In all-conquering love, man must suppress all earthly and worldly love, in order to adhere to God alone and commune with him in the sweetest enjoyment. However, he must remember that, although God gives him here a foretaste of heaven, this enjoyment is again interrupted here on earth, and he will find the kingdom of heaven only through struggle and suffering.

Gertrude van Oosten[1]

I

From the end of the 13th until about the middle of the 14th century, there lived in Delft a holy beguine, whose name is familiar enough, but whose life may be said to be practically unknown. Her name is inseparably linked to an old song, which is still held in honor, "*Het daghet in den Oosten*" (Day is breaking in the East). The holy beguine, whose name is Gertrude, is named after this song; not that she wrote it – the song must predate her – but because she not only liked to sing it, but also because she made it a short summary of her spiritual life. Although in its original form it is a not uncommon chivalric song, the biography of Gertrude specifically says that she sang it and liked to sing it, because she saw reflected in it the story of her own life; in particular, of her conversion and consecration to God. In one of the following articles, we hope to return to this song.[2] For the moment, we wish to concentrate on Gertrude's person. If we have a general idea of her life, it will be easier to comprehend how she understood this song, and how her name can be associated with it.

Gertrude was a beguine of Delft. She should not be called a little beguine, though Alberdingk Thijm may be forgiven, who called her by that name in one of his very beautiful narratives dedicated to her.[3] It is known that she was of a robust figure, of a tall stature and posture.

---

[1] From *De Gelderlander*, July 16, 23, 30; 20,27; Sept. 3, 10,1938.

[2] Titus' two articles on Gertrude's song, published on Aug. 6 and 13, 1938, in *De Gelderlander*, are not translated in this collection.

[3] Een Delftsch begijntje uit de XIVde eeuw," *Verspreide verhalen*, Amsterdam/ 'sGravenhage, 1909, I, 65ff.

Like many other cities, Delft at the time had its beguinage. It was dedicated to St. John, and so was called the St. John Beguinage. Later, it had its own church, but not while Gertrude spent her devout life there. Of the church also there are no remains. It was pulled down at the time of the Reformation, but the Beguinage still remains, though its purpose is changed. Standing in the great enclosed space of the courtyard, one can somewhat imagine how it must have appeared in Gertrude's time, how she dwelled and passed her life there.

The Beguinage is a large open courtyard, surrounded by various darling little houses, like cells around a great cloister, in the midst of which there was a large cross with the figure of the dead Savior, flanked by Mary and St. John, the patron of the place. A large, deep well formed the second focus in this great open area between the houses. These were more hermitages than houses, and whoever took up residence in one gave notice that she wished to live removed from the world. This does not mean that the beguines did not leave their hermitages; on the contrary, not just once, but several times during the day they went to church to pray; while one carried out this, another that sort of work in the city. Gertrude preferred going to the hospital to bestow her care on the sick; others found employment in a linen factory or offered their services to the citizens of the town; a few also worked at home at tasks commissioned by persons in town. Needlework was by no means neglected, for it did not withhold them from the most important reason for which they chose this form of life, prayer and communion with God. The work was rather a continuation in another way of their life of prayer, for in their work they tried not only to serve God in their neighbor, but also to sanctify this work by continually occupying themselves with God; also to accept the work from his hand as the task at the moment indicated by divine Providence as the means of showing their love.

Gertrude especially excelled in this practice. She already excelled in it before she became a beguine, in the simple service she had first performed in the home of a middle-class family in Delft.

She was a girl of the working class. Her parents were quite unpretentious farmers from Voorburg near The Hague. There she was born at the end of the 13th or beginning of the 14th century. The precise year is not known. Her needy condition required her at sixteen years of age to seek and accept employment. She went into service as a servant-girl and cheerfully attended to her duties. She became a model for all who are called to this way of life.

It is especially known about her at this time that as a servant she liked to sing while she worked and even after work was done. She must have had a fine voice and have lent a particular charm to songs by her melodious singing.

In a town as small as Delft, she became known for her singing and was often invited to perform. When work was finished, and folk would meet in small groups in the square or on the bridge, Gertrude was invited along, and it must have been a pleasure to listen to her singing. It is not unlikely that Gertrude, who we know was poor and all her life long admitted her poverty, even with a certain enthusiasm, sang her songs as a source of income. In those days, people gladly rewarded a beautiful song with a couple of coppers. There were even traveling or wandering minstrels who earned their living that way, and many a song has thus been preserved by our people.

Now there was a song that was her favorite and that she sang most enthusiastically. It was still one of those old songs of the age of chivalry, many of which are still preserved in the language of the people, and were later written down. It sang of a knight and his beloved, his death and her sorrow, her disillusionment and conversion. This song, as we mentioned, assumed a particular significance in her life, because she understood and converted it into a song about her beloved Jesus and her election as his bride. At first sung with no deeper meaning than it had in the old chivalric poetry, the song acquired in her mouth and in her heart a continually deeper and more fervent significance.

The year of her conversion, or rather of her consecration to God, is not known to us. We do know, if not already from her favorite song, from an old biography,[4] that during her service in Delft she soon won and returned the attachment and love of a young man. She ardently looked forward to marriage. The affair reached the point of their becoming engaged and the day of their wedding was at hand. However, she, too, experienced the transitoriness of much earthly love. Her lover jilted her for another woman. This grieved her sorely and she could not reconcile herself to her loss. She must have realized that the main fault lay with the woman who had cut her out and who held her lover in her power. She attempted to persuade her rival to release her lover and restore his freedom to make good his promise of marriage. But the love of the second bride was too strong to make her want or to enable her to give up her lover. The pair married, and Gertrude remained alone with her sorrow.

However, she as a religious young woman, who in her domestic service and in her response to the love of a young man, always kept Our Lord before her eyes in a special way. So great was her piety and love of Jesus that although she lived in the midst of the world and was called upon in many ways as a servant, she led the most intense interior life and communed so fervently with God that in this respect also she can well be proposed as a model to all persons in that walk of life. Best of all, she managed to keep hidden from all eyes that sweet and silent communion with God, during which she seems even to have been granted very special graces. Only much later, when she was many years in the Beguinage and could no longer hide the spiritual gifts bestowed on her, she had to admit that she had received them much earlier, already when she was a domestic, and that she had then been vouchsafed the most intimate company with Our Lord. Her love of Jesus also helped her to overcome her disillusionment; more still, she considered that earthly attachment as a trial for purifying and interiorizing her love of God. She also took that occasion to cling more closely to Jesus and live a life more dedicated to him as a beguine.

---

[4] *Acta sanctorum, Januarius*, Antverpiae, 1643, I, 348-351: *De venerabile vergine Gertrude ab Osten, beghina Delpjensi in Belgio*, cap. 1, par. 4, p. 349.

II

When we hear Gertrude speak of her conversion, it should by no means create the impression that at the time she was leading a frivolous life. The opposite is clear from her biography. But many devout persons, at the end of this 13th and during the 14th century, used this word, conversion, to mean nothing more than a more fervent dedication to God. In the circle of the Modern Devotion, the word is almost always to be understood in this sense.

But in her great love of God, strengthened by disillusionment, Gertrude regarded that brief earthly love and that desire of her heart to be married to the beloved of her heart as a temptation and a trial of her love of God. When that love again more strongly engrossed her heart, she was ashamed that she had allowed herself to be diverted from the sublime object of her supernatural love. Although she had not sinned, she felt guilty, because she had not immediately and more generously answered the great love of Jesus. We read in her biography that she spent fourteen days and nights in prayer and tears, allowing herself only the barest amount of nourishment, in order to obtain from God forgiveness of her infidelity. It was a happy satisfaction for her, at the end of those fourteen days, to receive a revelation from heaven that all was forgiven her.

In order to reinforce her conversion as strongly as possible, she resolved, not at all from discouragement or despair, but from the love of God, to seek admission of the beguines, who were still few in number, leading their retired life in the old Beguinage. She was warmly welcomed and saw herself shown one of the little houses, in which she settled with two friends, Dievertje and Lielte. Dievertje seems to have shared the same room with her. Besides Dievertje and Lielte, Gertrude's biography mentions as one of her companions a certain Catherine de Coudenhove, who evidently led a particularly devout and holy life in the Beguinage. She observed severe abstinence and sometimes for days at a time partook of no nourishment. She spent a great deal of time in prayer and, although of noble birth, was known for her simplicity and humility and for the generosity she showed to the poor and the church. Catherine had a special devotion to the construction of the new church. It was only completed in 1381, but long before this, the founding of this church was the object of particular devotion to more than one inhabitant of Delft. From the old *Miraekelboek* (miracle book) of the church, Dirk van Bleiswijck, recounts various legends relating to its foundation.[5] Catherine de Coudenhove is said to have provided for its foundation and have immediately contributed ten old golden *schilden* toward its construction. She is also credited a benefactor of the Beguinage.

Gertrude van Oosten is also said to have foretold the foundation of this church. In 1351, in a vision to a hermit of Delft, Brother Simon, the site was indicated for a sacred edifice; until then, it had been a place for the execution of criminals. Since then, on the feast of the Presentation,[6] devout persons – among whom Catherine van Coudenhove as well as Gertrude van Oosten are probably to be reckoned – saw lights like candles on that site, until the church was consecrated there thirty years later. The quotation from Dirk van Bleiswijck cited above adds that Gertrude often related to her confessor, the Reverend Claes van Hodenpijl, her vision of the future foundation of this church.

Although we do not want to accord great historical value to this prediction by Gertrude, which continued to live as oral tradition without being assumed in her biography, we must recognize in it another witness to the esteem in which she was held by her fellow citizens, and that they saw in her a person blessed by God. Further details in her life show that there is more than one reason to think this.

Once she had been accepted in the Beguinage, Gertrude devoted herself almost entirely to prayer. She became a recluse, who after having first served as Martha, now sat down to listen in silent contemplation to the Lord's words, which she not only

[5] *Beschrijvinge van Delft*, Delft, Arnold Bon, 1667, 2 v. Not available for consultation.

[6] February 2.

read and reread in the sacred books and sang in the canonical Hours, but also seemed to hear spoken by the Lord himself in her inmost being. She still sang her beloved song, but applied it entirely to her leave-taking of the world and her conversion to Jesus.

She begged her bread from house to house, and wakened all to whom she spoke to prayer and the practice of love. She allowed her body neither necessary nourishment nor even needed sleep. She did not deny herself all food and sleep, but limited them to the utmost. In the first seven years, she never allowed her body the full rest which it felt it needed.

She liked to speak to little children to tell them about Our Lord and to rouse them to devotion. But they were not allowed to disturb her at prayer. Then she considered their importunity as a temptation of the devil, who abused her love of children to keep her from prayer, and repelled the children. She also tried her best to suppress the distractions which arose in her mind and to ban them from her spirit and imagination as the work of the devil. Sometimes temptations took a violent form, and it seemed to her that the devil himself had a direct share in them. Then she would resist him all the more.

Her meditations particularly concerned the life of our Lord. She had a childlike devotion to the Holy Childhood and especially during Advent and Christmastide tried to enter into Mary's happy feelings, while she awaited the birth of her child, and after his birth busied herself with his needs and devoted her maternal care to him. Then she looked upon herself as another Mary, in whom Jesus desired to be conceived, in whom he desired to grow, from whom he wished to be born. It is quite remarkable how in her case, as in that of St. Liduina of Schiedam, whose life hers very much resembles, though she did not have such need for suffering, the devotion of conformity to Mary, the mother of Jesus was particularly fervent and even led to tasting the sweetest joys of motherhood: how with Mary she pressed the divine Child to her breast in order to feed him with the milk of her love. In this way, according to the old biography, the word of the Gospel was fulfilled in her, according to which Jesus said that everyone who does the will of the Father becomes his mother.[7] But God was not satisfied with making her also physically share the virtues of his holy and virginal mother; he wanted also to make her similar to himself and, according to a prophecy her companion, Lielte, had made concerning her the previous year, in 1348 imprinted his five holy wounds on her hands, feet and side. They were not painful wounds to her; on the contrary, they awoke in her a feeling of indescribable sweetness. It happened in the night of Pentecost in the year 1348. It is true that the old biography published by the Bollandists from a Utrecht manuscript,[8] assigns the year 1340 to the event, but Joannes a Leidis, the well-known prior of the Carmel of Haarlem, who includes in his *Kroniek van Holland*, if not the whole, large excerpts from the old biography, cites the year 1348.[9] We would have no right to hold his reading to be the correct one, if that date did not find confirmation in other sources. We have already spoken of the *Mirakelboek* of the New or St. Ursula Church in Delft. From that source, Dirk van Bleiswijk, in his *Beschrijvinge van Delft*, relates, after his account of the vision of Brother Simon in 1351, that Gertrude van Oosten "within three years, for the first time had the wounds of our Lord revealed in her side, hands, and feet, and had many ardent meditations and visions, among others, concerning our church here, as she often related to her confessor, the Reverend Claes van Hodenpijl."[10] Here, too, therefore, the year 1348 is proposed.

III

In the night of Pentecost, 1348, we may thus assume, Gertrude van Oosten received the Lord's five wounds. In a rapture of delight, she called Dievertje, who, as we saw, shared her room with her. She must

---

[7] Mt 12, 50.
[8] See footnote 4.
[9] Not available for consultation.
[10] See footnote 5.

see the glorious signs which God had vouchsafed her. And what could only partially be distinguished in the darkness of night by the dim gleam of weak artificial light, they saw in full daylight as a joyous reality. And Lieltje, who had foretold it for her, must soon have been made to share the holy joy. Seven times a day, we are further told, when Gertrude was accustomed to meditate on the Lord's Passion according to the canonical Hours, bright blood flowed from those wounds, and the flow of blood over her body suffused her soul with the most wonderful satisfaction and enjoyment.

One circumstance tempered for Gertrude the happiness which these holy stigmata afforded her. The phenomena soon became known, and she became the object of frequent visits. She could no longer apply herself undisturbed to her devotions. Moreover, she feared that vanity would steal upon her, and that, after having received such exalted gifts from our Lord, she might still be lost through that vanity. Therefore, she knelt in ardent prayer to ask God, if it was in keeping with his holy will, to remove those external signs, so that she would not be estranged from him through vain self-complacency or some other snare of the devil.

God answered her prayer. The wounds completely closed and left only a scar, but at the same time she lost the sweet pleasure that accompanied the flowing of the blood. The joy and luxuriousness she then felt gave place to a feeling of pain and insensitivity to heavenly things, to which she had formerly been so susceptible. Then she regretted having asked Our Lord to remove the wounds. "If he would only give them back," she often said, "I would no longer ask to remove them from me; even though I were to show them to everybody on a platform in the marketplace." But God left her the scars with a sense of abandonment and sorrow, in order thus to make her more conformable to himself, after he had strengthened and steeled her by allowing her special enjoyment.

It goes without saying that the impression of the five holy wounds made of Gertrude van Oosten a greater lover than ever of the sacred Passion. We may look upon this gift as an expression of her devotion to the sacred Passion. In particular, we may see in the seven-fold flowing of blood from her wounds at the times of the canonical Hours how acceptable to God was the devotion of the Hours of the Sacred Passion, so popular in the Middle Ages and so faithfully practiced by Gertrude. We know that it was also the favorite devotion of St. Liduina of Schiedam, from whose time we still have a striking Netherlandish Office of the sacred Passion. This devotion of recalling seven times a day a portion of the sacred Passion is little known in our day. In her six-volume work, *De Godsvrucht in de Nederlanden*, Sister Imelda has again called attention to this practice and has provided a tentative summary of the individual hours of the Sacred Passion.[11]

Besides these spiritual gifts, we also find mention in the biography of Gertrude van Oosten that she was so absorbed in contemplation that she sometimes did not leave her cell for weeks, and let food and drink stand untouched, in order to immerse herself in the mysteries of Jesus' life. It did not matter to her that the bread was mouldy and dry. She made no other demands and was easily satisfied. This points to ecstatic conditions. In any case, we find many other evidences of it in her life. When, during her begging tours through the city, she was admitted into the house by notable friends, it often happened that she fell into ecstacy on the spot and, once awakened from that state, spoke eloquently about the mysteries of the faith. Sometimes she was found standing in front of the door of a house, waiting to be admitted, wrapt in ecstasy while meditating on the miracles of the Lord.

The old biography also records various prophecies she made and revelations she received. She allayed the fears of some of the beguines who were uneasy about past sins by assuring them of God's ways; telling them that they certainly must do penance for their sins, but that nevertheless all was forgiven and they would one day partake of the happiness of heaven. To another, she prophesied her death, even though all signs indicated that mortal danger was past.

---

[11] Maria Mertens (Sr. Imelda, Ursuline), *De Godsvrucht in de Nederlanden*, (4 vol., Antwerpen, Standaard/Nijmegen, Dekker & van de Vegt, 1930-1934), I, 162-163: "Horologie der Passie."

Another notable incident is recorded, in which God even
wished to grant his servant maid physical satisfaction. Once, during her severe fast and abstinence, when she longed for bread and
cheese but had none, she sent her companion Dievertje to the gate
of the beguinage to receive bread and cheese from a countryman,
whom Gertrude saw had been led there with that food for the
poor without knowing for whom.

At the end of her life, she was in poor health. As we have said,
she was tall and robust of build, but she was now barely able to
attend church, so that on her way there, she was obliged to stop
several times to rest. But this did not stop her from visiting the
church each time anew. To the very last, she dragged herself along.
In 1358, her end was at hand. It was the feast of Epiphany. [12]
She lay on her deathbed, and the beguines gathered round to witness her end. She had been strengthened with the last sacraments
and well prepared to die. It is edifying to relate that in that last
hour, she suddenly lifted her voice and cried out, "I'm going
home!" "But, Gertrude," the beguines, who thought she was deli-
rious, told her, "you are home." "No," she answered, I am not
home. I want to be where the squares of the city are paved with
purest gold." She was referring to the heavenly Jerusalem in the
language of Revelations. [13]

The old biography ends with a beautiful comparison: just as the
feast of Epiphany, or revelation of the Lord, records how the three
kings of the Orient found Jesus, so on this day Gertrude found
her Child Jesus.

As we have already related, the beguines at the time did not
have their own church, so that they could not yet be buried there,
as was later the custom. Gertrude was buried outside the south
door of the entrance to the tower of the church of St. Hippolytus.
The great *Divisiekroniek* confirms this as follows: "And she died
in the year of our Lord 1358, on the feast of the Epiphany, and
she was humbly buried outside the door of the tower of the old

[12] January 6.
[13] Rev 21, 21.

church on the south side, because the beguines did not have a church or graveyard."[14]

From these words one can conclude that the burial before the door is conceived as a token of her humility, and Gertrude must have wished to be buried there, so that her body would be trodden on by all who entered the church.

He who humbles himself shall be exalted.[15] Because of the place where Gertrude was buried, it has not been possible to cover her grave with a monument. Not even a stone marks her grave. What was once regarded as hallowed ground, because the churchyard surrounded the church, has now become a public street, leading to and around the tower of the old church. Nor does a stone in the wall recall her burial on that spot. The many persons who still enter Delft's St. Hippolytus Church through the south door do not even know that they are walking over the place where Gertrude van Oosten is buried.

Yet, she is not forgotten. Her memory lives on, and her remembrance is held in higher esteem than that of many others on whose grave a great stone, or monument, serves as a reminder. We hope soon to devote a couple of articles to the remembrance and cult of the mystic beguine of Delft, and to make known the many ways in which she is honored.

IV

Noteworthy Spiritual Exercises – I

In 1631, Jozef Geldolf van Rijckel, abbot of St. Geertrui in Louvain, published a life of St. Begga, whom he regarded as the foundress of the institute of beguines, so that he added to the biogra-

---

[14] *Die Cronycke van Hollant, Zeelant, ende Vrieslant*, Dordrecht, Pieter Verhaghen, 1585, 23sten Divisie, cap. 5, "Van dat leuen suster Gheetruyts van Oosten tot Delft," ff. 131v-132v. The author of this famous work, generally known as the Divisiekroniek, is Cornelius Aurelius.

[15] Mt 23, 12.

phy a history of many beguinages and beguines in the Netherlands and Belgium.[16] Although his position with regard to the origin of the beguines leaves much to be desired, his work about the beguinages is nevertheless of no little value for the early history of devotion in the Low Countries.

In his work, Van Rijckel treats the Beguinage of Delft and, of course, the Venerable Gertrude van Oosten.[17] Important to note, after a short sketch of the life of Gertrude, he speaks of "Spiritual Exercises" ascribed to her. Her life, according to the old manuscript of Utrecht edited by the Bollandists, states that "this devout bride of Christ daily meditated on the life and Passion of Jesus."[18] It also mentions that in these meditations, called exercises, she followed the Church Year. Further reference is made to specific exercises for Advent, Christmas, etc., but no other indications are given regarding the form in which these meditations were couched.

Geldolf van Rijckel's information about these meditations thus finds a valuable confirmation in the old biography, so that what he relates regarding these meditations may be said to be a welcome complement to the scanty information provided by the old biography.

According to Geldolf van Rijckel the meditations were still extant at the time. In his so-called classic, but actually baroque Latin, he provides some further information regarding the content and form of the meditations, but unfortunately it leaves more to be guessed and conjectured. This is more to be regretted because what he relates can only whet our appetite for the meditations in their original form. In his enthusiastic admiration, Geldolf van Rijckel presents a free rendering, which he calls a commentary or paraphrase. However, it is to be feared that his rendering does not stay close to the original text, which was most probably very simple.

[16] *Vita Sanctae Beggae, ducisse Brabantiae andetennensium, begginarum et beggadorum fundatricis… Adjuncta est historia begginasiorum Belgii*, Lovanii, typis Cornelii Coenestenii, 1631.

[17] *Vita S. Beggae*, pp. 357-382. On p. 356 is a fine metal cut print of Gertrude.

[18] *De ven. vergine Gertrude ab Osten* cap. 3, par. 12-13; *Acta Sanctorum, Januarius* , I, 350.

Van Rijkel does not say in what language Gertrude's exercises were written, but from the very nature of the case, it appears to me as good as certain that they were composed in Netherlandish, because they served as meditation for an uneducated beguine. Also, in the case of an edition of a Latin text, Van Rijksel would have retained the original text. As I see it, he had recourse to a rendering a commentary, or paraphrase, because the text, a poem in Netherlandish, would not have been appropriately reproduced as such in a Latin work, and also it would have been difficult to translate literally.

Van Rijkel gives four different names to Gertrude's exercises. First, he calls them "reflections" or "meditations"; next, he names them "*theoremata,*" which in his language means "material for meditation." In his life of her, he speaks simply of "truths" or "*theoriae.*" Referring to her life of prayer, he states that she was sometimes engulphed in prayer and contemplation for six weeks, "*theoriis divinioribus intenta,*" "intent upon divine truths." Speaking of her meditating on the sacred Passion, he also wrote, "while she was entirely occupied with this truth," "*dum huic theoriae tota vacaret.*" Concluding his commentary or paraphrase, he ends with the words, "So far the materials for meditation – *de Theoremata* – of the Blessed Gertrude." When, finally, he begins the exercises proper after the introduction, he titles them, "Spiritual Exercises Used by Gertrude van Oosten," "*Asceses seu exercitia quaedam familiaria B. Gertrudi van Oosten.*"

Van Rijckel states that he is only reproducing in brief the life which he is taking from Abraham Bzovius,[19] in order to have more room for a somewhat more ample development of the exercises which have come into his possession. He says that there are still some poems in circulation, "*circumferuntur quaedam manuscripta rythmica,*" which provide ample material for a commentary. "Because they reflect her fervent spirit and the ardor of her reflections so acutely, I have thought, he continues, to reproduce their sense and concept, in order to give the little ones, if not bread, then at least a few crumbs fallen from the table or the hand of this

---

[19] *Vita S. Beggae,* p. 360.

rich spirit. However, I am certain, he says, that her feelings and thoughts about the Lord's Passion are not to be reproduced. Her ecstatic and inexpressible feelings are not to be expected of me, but only simple expressions which everyone can understand." He relates further that the maidens of the Beguinage of Brussels, old and young, have continued to beg of him to include in his work about beguines something about Gertrude's *theoremata*, or material for meditation, divided according to the seasons of the Church Year. Thus, he also dedicates his work to the beguines of Brussels.

Van Rijckel divides the Spiritual Exercises into three parts of fourteen mysteries each, and he suggests that Gertrude thus prayed a threefold rosary of fourteen mysteries. Each mystery comprised a decade. He adds that, on meditating each mystery, that is, each decade, Gertrude was accustomed to place herself in the company of one or more saints, who inspired in her a particular devotion in relation to that mystery. She engaged in conversation with them, revealed her feelings, implored their intercession, etc. However, in his commentary, Van Rijckel does not always indicate the saint with whom Gertrude discussed the corresponding mystery. Whether the fault is his or of the original text is difficult to determine, as long as the latter is not known.

Meanwhile, we cannot escape the impression that Van Rijckel's rendering was not very carefully done. His work does not correspond to the enthusiasm with which he announced it. True, some very beautiful thoughts are reproduced, here and there these are cast in good form, but in general the adaptation must be said to be slovenly. This immediately appears from his statement that at each decade a conversation was held with one or other saint, whereas of these saints in most cases there is no mention. He also speaks of a triple set of fourteen decades, but after the last of the first fourteen, he adds for the first of the second fourteen a mystery, "Christ's Invitation to the Wedding Feast of Cana," which is unnumbered. In the second fourteen, he jumps from the eighth to the tenth decade, and so arrives at an enumeration of fifteen. In the third fourteen, there occurs between mystery 11 and 12 another unnumbered mystery, so that we have here fourteen numbered mysteries, while in reality there are fifteen.

The handling of the material also varies considerably. In the third decade of the third set of fourteen, there is a fine address and prayer to Jesus. It does not seem to be a commentary or paraphrase at all. This prayer occupies an entirely singular place. In other decades, the material is so condensed that it can hardly even be called a commentary. In the second fourteen, one receives the impression that one mystery is divided without reason into two or more decades; or rather, those decades boil down to about the same mystery. It seems as though an attempt has been made to make fourteen decades out of a smaller amount of material in order to preserve the symmetry.

These are some of the defects of the reproduction of the original text. Until now, I have not been able to find the text. In a subsequent article, I shall attempt briefly to summarize Van Rijckel's quite extensive account. This may give occasion to experts in the field of spiritual literature to recover the original text. For today, suffice it to describe the general division of the three-fold fourteen decades. The material for meditation in the first set of fourteen was as follows: the promise, the expectation, and the coming of the Lord; of Jesus' youth and hidden life. Material for the second set: Christ's prayer and fasting in the desert, his baptism, his temptation by the devil, his miracles and gifts, his life of austerity and prayer. The third set of fourteen treats meditation on the Passion and death of Christ, his resurrection and ascension, the descent of the Holy Spirit.

V

Noteworthy Spiritual Exercises – II

In the first of the three sets of fourteen mysteries, according to which Gertrude van Oosten divides her meditations on the life and Passion of Christ, she speaks of the promise, the expectation, and the coming of the Lord, of Christ's youth and hidden life. She thus situates herself at the beginning of the Church Year, on the first Sunday of Advent, in order to traverse the entire Christmas cycle.

Gertrude begins with a meditation on the happy transgression of Adam, which earned for us such a Redeemer. This she does in the company of St. Gertrude of Landen, daughter of Pepin of Landen. In the second mystery, she considers how difficult was the redemption of the human race. No angel or human was equal to the task. This casts a particular light on the glory of the Incarnation, but also shows how severe the temptation of the angels must have been, when they saw how God had exalted human nature by his Incarnation. It also became the occasion of their fall. This mystery Gertrude discussed with St. Begga, whom she looked upon as her mother and patron.

In the third mystery, Gertrude considers how Christ did not hesitate to enter the womb of his mother and would not shorten the time before his birth, in order to bear everything that human nature involved. In this meditation, Gertrude used as a model St. Monegunda, who fled the world and enclosed herself in a little cell with a very small aperture, out of devotion to this mystery of Christ's early life on earth.

The fourth meditation is about the birth of Christ. All come to adore him. Gertrude engages in conversation with St. Joseph, who tells her about Jesus: see how everyone comes to him. What a joy that he can now live with Mary in the company of Jesus!

The fifth point is the Lord's circumcision. She asks herself who performed the ceremony, Mary or the priest, and addresses herself to both. The priest must have hesitated, and in the words of John the Baptist have said that he should rather be circumscribed by Christ. For Mary, Christ was the child of blood, who received his blood from her in order to pour it out for mankind. Here, Gertrude witnesses the flowing of the first drops.

In the sixth mystery, she sees herself as the woman who had grown bent, and could not see the shining sun, but being straightened by Jesus, beheld his beauty revealed.[20] With this woman, Gertrude prays, "Lord, have mercy on me!" She complains that

---

[20] Mt 15, 22.

she comes to him so late, and addresses the Three Kings, who also had to come to him through darkness from afar.

Gertrude's seventh point is Christ's presentation in the temple, the feast of Candlemas.[21] With St. Augustine, she joyfully cries, "Me, too, you have called to your light!"[22] She sees a three-fold light: God and humanity united, Mary identical with mother, faith in God's word united to the craving of the human heart. She converses with the grey-haired Simeon, of whom she envies his holy burden and who, after he has departed this world in peace, is asked to place the Child Jesus in her arms.

In the eighth mystery, she desires to participate in the flight into Egypt as a maid servant. In her imagination she addresses the cloud which gave light upon the road. In Egypt, the idols fall to the ground at the approach of Jesus. Jesus is now removed from our sight for a time, but he will return after seven years. She asks and begs him to return, so that she can behold him.

Upon Jesus' return in the ninth mystery, Gertrude again offers him her services and expresses wonder at his roving and humiliating life. Here she converses with St. Aldegonda, who fled the attentions of an earthly lover to belong to Jesus, and so attained the state in which God wished to sanctify her.

For the tenth mystery, Gertrude reflects that Jesus did not wish to have an abiding habitation here on earth. His own received him not, neither Nazareth, nor Capernum, nor Bethsaida. They did not understand the service being done them. Gertrude prays the angel guardians of Holland and Frisia to cause God's grace to rain upon those lands. Already she hears the woe Christ called down upon the three aforementioned cities also descend upon Holland; and she cries out that if so many signs had been shown to pagan islands, they would have done penance in greater mourning.

The eleventh mystery transposes Gertrude to Nazareth, where Jesus, having returned from Egypt after seven years, now begins the second seven years of his life. Here he grew up. What did he

---

[21] February 2.
[22] *Confessiones*, 9, 4: "Signatum est in nobis lumen vultus tui, Domine."

do? He trained himself in the rudiments of a lowly trade. She discusses this in all simplicity with St. Bonaventure, who has described this period of Jesus' life.[23]

For the twelfth point, Gertrude chooses Jesus' striking disappearance, when as a twelve-year old child he withdrew from the company of Joseph and Mary and remained behind, after they had left Jerusalem. She sees in the incident a prefiguration of Christ's death and burial, followed by the joy of the resurrection. At the same time, she sees thereby depicted how Jesus can from time to time withdraw his presence from the loving soul, in order later to make her doubly happy. She also reflects that Jesus is still hidden from the inhabitants of Asia and Africa, and asks herself why he has revealed himself to her. She carries on a conversation with her angel guardian, rejoicing at her election, but she also understands her responsibility. She praises God's mercy and resigns herself to his inscrutable ways.

In the thirteenth mystery, Gertrude joins the Jews in their wonder at Jesus' wisdom, while he had not attended any schools of earthly knowledge. Jesus frequented the school of Mary. Gertrude converses with the prophetess Anna, from whom Mary received her education in the temple, lessons which she in turn shared with the child Jesus.

In the last, or fourteenth mystery, Gertrude meditates on Jesus at his humble trade in the workshop of Joseph. She speaks with St. Justin, who devoted particular attention to this mystery in the life of the Lord. He has Jesus make a plow and other tools, and in many of them sees an image of the cross, upon which he would one day die.[24] Jesus lived hidden from everyone, so that the Jews would say, when he entered on his public life, "Is not this the son of the carpenter Joseph?" Filled with wonder, she ponders how Jesus rose from this humble trade, suddenly to become the Son of God.

One would expect to find here the end of the first fourteen mysteries. It is somewhat surprising, as I have already noted, that

---

[23] *Commentarius in Evangelium S. Lucae*, cap. 2; *Opera omnia*, Quaracchi, 1895, VII, 64-68.

[24] Reference not found.

Geldolf van Rijckel, before proceeding to the first of the second fourteen mysteries, inserts after these first fourteen still a fifteenth mystery, as a transition from Jesus' hidden to his public life; in fact, it is a meditation on Jesus' invitation to the wedding feast of Cana. She reads in this mystery that Jesus, by accepting the invitation, has hallowed the institution of matrimony. She asks St. Jerome whether he has not written about marriage in too severe a manner. She finds an explanation of his severe words in his conviction that the end of the world was at hand. In the miracle of the changing of the water into wine, she sees depicted Jesus' wish that earthly marriage should be elevated to a heavenly bond, and that this should be an incentive for making our earthly life a heavenly one.

VI

Noteworthy Spiritual Exercises – III

As we have already said, Geldolf van Rijckel's edition of Gertrude's Spiritual Exercises, divided her meditations in a triple set of fourteen mysteries.

In the first fourteen mysteries Gertrude meditates on the promise, expectation, and coming of the Lord, Christ's youth and hidden life, at the same time engaging in conversation with one or other saint. In the second fourteen, she meditates on Christ's prayer and fasting in the desert, his baptism and temptation, his miracles and gifts, his life of austerity and prayer.

In the first of these mysteries, she is dismayed at the hardness of humans versus God's goodness. How few of the Jewish people followed him! She speaks about this with St. John the Baptist and asks why he did not work miracles. Was it in order to make Christ's wondrous goodness radiate more fully, and to preclude his being honored more than Christ? We cannot sufficiently praise God's goodness and should not be as hardhearted as the Jews.

In the second mystery, she sees Jesus engaged in prayer before choosing his apostles. She reflects that Jesus is an example for us in this. We should never allow ourselves to be lead in our actions by our own strength or our own will, but we should always ask God for enlightenment. She addresses the apostles and asks how there could be a Judas among them, whether this was in order to protect us from scandal. If there was a Judas even among the apostles, we should understand that we, too, must live among the good and the evil.

When next, in the third mystery, she sees Jesus enter the desert, she asks herself by what sort of spirit he was led, and concludes that this must have been a good spirit who made him flee the world. She then sees that it was St. Hilarion who was the saint who particularly imitated Jesus in this. He trod the world under his feet and placed solitude above all else. Jesus, too, in his struggle with the devil rejected all kingdoms.

The fourth point is Christ's forty-day fast in the desert, prefigured by the fast of the same number of days of Moses and Elijah and the sojourn of forty years of the Jews, fed by the miraculous manna. Jesus thereby merited that the desert became the refuge of hosts of hermits; the convents, the home of countless religious, bound without chains by their love of Jesus. Then follows a conversation with the angels who came to serve Jesus and she asks them where they had obtained the food with which they fed Jesus.

The baptism of Christ by John is the fifth point. Gertrude sees notable antitheses in this mystery. They must have puzzled the devil. By allowing himself to be baptized, Jesus seemed to be a sinner, but the dove which came to hover over his head and the voice from heaven announced his goodness. She then addresses St. John the Baptist and asks him how he could say that he knew not Jesus and yet did not wish to baptize him but said he would rather be baptized by Jesus. For Augustine, too, she thinks, this was a also great mystery.

With Pope Leo the Great[25] she meditates, as the sixth point, how the Jewish people as well as the devil continued to doubt Jesus and how Jesus did not want them to give witness to him, unless they truly believed in him. Jesus avails nothing to the prince of this world, who does not understand that he is powerless against Jesus, and so continues to resist him to the end.

---

[25] See: Leo the Great, *Sermons*, Washington 1996, nrs 35, 56, 57 and 65.

In the seventh mystery, she sees Jesus' divine and human actions: the healings he worked, how he drove out devils, walked upon the water, divined the inmost thoughts of his hearers, stilled storms, and with a word commanded Nature, but on the other hand was truly human. Gertrude united herself to Mary his mother, about whom the Gospels say that she considered in her heart everything that Jesus said and did; she ardently desired to be able to do this also and in all things to be similar to Mary as God's mother. Reflection on God's miracles should above all lead to feelings of gratitude and praise of God.

As the eighth mystery, Gertrude sees how Jesus bears the discomforts of life, wearies himself by his journeying and preaching, his conversing with sinners. The sight of it should wring our hearts. Gertrude converses with the martyrs and preachers of God's word, who have drained the cup of suffering with Jesus and have feared no fatigue.

In the ninth mystery, Gertrude looks more closely at the hidden gifts which our devotion discovers in Jesus, even though the Gospels are silent about them. The devout soul reads between the lines of the Gospels and sees Jesus' great love of the cross, his magnanimity and long-suffering, the peace of heart that ruled his life, his devotion and fortitude. She understands that she, too, must serve God in secret, and that her beauty must be within. She speaks to St. Athanasius, who had been obliged to live so long in secret and patiently bore so much, knowing that God was with him.

Gertrude's tenth mystery concerns Jesus' miracles, whereby he made himself an instrument of the Holy Spirit. He assumed human nature in order that the divine power might be revealed. Thus, his touch worked miracles. Obviously, this meditation is meant to make us pray that God also touch us and fill us with his strength to our welfare and healing. Here, there is no mention of a conversation with a saint.

In the eleventh mystery, Gertrude reflects on the austerity that characterizes the public life of Christ. It knows no indulgence of bodily needs nor itch to be honored and glorified. Even at night, the body is allowed no rest and compels the spirit to pray. Here we can learn to know the spirit of Christ. This mystery, too, contains no conversation, perhaps because it leads to conversing with Christ himself.

For the twelfth mystery, Gertrude chooses the promises Jesus made us. Although he had no stone upon which to lay his head, yet he can promise us paradise and gladdens those who listen to him. To see and touch him is already a foretaste of heaven; to live with him, a pledge of eternal happiness. The thought of this suggests to Gertrude that Christ in his poverty knows what makes us rich.

Her thirteenth mystery is Jesus' prayer. He prayed, not out of necessity, but out of devotion, because prayer is so beautiful and lovely, a communion with his heavenly Father, who hears his prayer. Jesus uses few words, but they come from the fulness of his heart. Gertrude is enraptured and addresses herself to Christ as to the leader of her soul, asking that his devout and quiet prayer may be an example to her in which she mirrors herself.

As the last of this second set of fourteen mysteries, Gertrude chooses Jesus' words. They are like arrows that fell his enemies. She wishes to take them to herself, and that to such a degree that in the future Christ will live and speak in her. She wishes to breathe in his spirit, so that her mouth speaks his words. In this meditation, too, there is no mention of a conversation with a saint. Perhaps its place is taken by the words of the Psalmist, whom she quotes: "Your arrows are sharp, nations lie under your feet and the courage of the king's enemies fails."[26]

Herewith ends the second series of Gertrude's meditations. The third set of fourteen goes on to deal with Christ's Passion and death, his resurrection and ascension, and the descent of the Holy Spirit. A final article will consider these.

---

[26] Ps 44, 6: "Thy arrows are sharp: under thee people shall fall, into the hearts of the king's enemies" (English Vulgate).

VII

Noteworthy Spiritual Exercises – IV

In the third set of fourteen mysteries, Gertrude treats the Passion and death of Christ, his resurrection and ascension, crowned with a meditation on the descent of the Holy Spirit. She begins with a very remarkable meditation on the need of love that complements Christ's and with an appeal to share in the Passion of Christ. The manner of doing this she must leave to God and so she abandons herself entirely into his hands – in her words, like a slave or a hard stone – crying out, "Wound me or I die!" She finds her nourishment and refreshment in sharing in the Lord's Passion. In expressing these feelings, she converses with Job, the great sufferer of the Old Testament.

In the second meditation, she feels that reflection on the Passion sets her heart on fire and makes her desire to share in that suffering. She turns to the saints who have beheld the Passion in a state of ecstacy and have shared in the pains and wounds. She asks them to free her soul also, so that she will think only of the Passion and, like them, merit to receive the Lord's stigmata in her body and to share in that Passion.

Gertrude's third mystery is the departure of Jesus for the Garden of Olives. She asks him to take her with him, enthralled and bound to him by his love. May he wound her heart with the remembrance of that last night and Last Supper! May it always appear before her spirit, especially at the hour of death, before her last Judgment! She asks Jesus also to accompany her departure from life, just as she now accompanies his departure and death in her thoughts.

In her fourth mystery, Gertrude meditates further on Jesus' agony in the garden. She knows that he will not permit anything to be omitted that might conduce to our salvation; Christ submits to whatever avails for our salvation. Constantine the Great willed that appeal could be made from verdicts of the nobility of the realm, which he highly esteemed but thought imperfect, to those of the bishops. So also Gertrude willed to consider her judgment imperfect and to submit herself entirely to the judgment of God. She closes the meditation with the beautiful words of St. Augustine, "One never makes himself more similar to God than by willing what God wills."[27]

Gertrude's fifth mystery is really a conversation that Jesus holds with her. She is given to understand that her salvation lies in the acceptance of Christ's agony in the garden and of his death on the cross. The greatest hurt is done him by those who do not share in his Passion, while he bestows himself on them. He asks Gertrude to score her heart and arms with the signs of his Passion, and to understand that he, as a jealous God, cannot bear that she direct her love elsewhere than to him. On the cross, he took her as his bride and committed himself to her with the most exalted expression of love.

In the sixth mystery, Gertrude seeks to fathom the reason for Jesus' agony and she beholds him filled with anguish and fear, not so much on his own behalf as on that of his disciples. He awakens them to pray with him. Gertrude sees how Peter falls. When the pillars of the Church, the rock upon which she is to be built, totter, how weak must she be, unless Jesus strengthens her!

Then, in the seventh mystery, Gertrude sees Jesus rise up and after he has deigned to manifest our human nature in his fear of the Passion, he shows us his love for the Passion. He rose up and thereafter knew no rest until he had found it on the deathbed of the cross. He went from judgment seat to judgment seat. Gertrude asks Jesus to allow her to accompany him.

Continuing from the last mystery, Gertrude in the eighth meditates on the meaning of Jesus' words, that he will draw all beings to himself.[28] On the cross, Jesus' power is made manifest. The Old Testament types are fulfilled, prophecy becomes reality. The single Temple makes way for worship throughout the world. The cross becomes the source of blessing. With Pope Leo the Great[29], she

---

[27] *Epistulae*, 92
[28] Jn 12, 22.
[29] See: Leo the Great, *Sermons*, Washington 1996.

reflects how strength comes from weakness, honor from shame; life from death. The ninth mystery presents for meditation the strange contrasts offered by Jesus' death. While there should have been a full moon at the Passover, there was an eclipse instead. After three hours, the moon must have resumed her place in relation to the sun. The eclipse meant that, at Jesus' death, the Light that should have enlightened the world was extinguished. But at the same time, the phenomenon was a revelation of God's power. As against the indignity of Christ's death, the truth of his divinity shone forth. Gertrude addresses Nature and asks why she fled and hid in darkness; she asks sun and moon why they neglected to cast light on this great mystery; mountains and hills why they trembled and were rent.

In the meditation on the tenth mystery, too, she again confronts the great contrasts that were revealed at the death of Christ. He spoke his last words in a loud voice. He died willingly; he bent his head to die. He died at the ninth hour, the hour of the Paschal Lamb who had to be slaughtered that we might live. The veil of the temple was rent in two, the rocks were rent, but the hearts of the Jews were not. The earth trembled as a sign of the Lord's death. The dead arose, but only after the resurrection of Jesus, who is the first of those risen from the dead. She asks herself if these risen persons later died, but leaves the answer to Jesus, who knows all things.

Next, she meditates on the miracles that took place during the three days after Jesus' death. First, she cites the legend that the threshold of the temple was broken, the angels who guarded the temple fled, the temple doves flew away through the rent veil. From the blow of the soldier's lance, blood and water flowed from Jesus' side. The water was to wash us; the blood, to save us. They flowed from his side, because from the side of Adam was formed the woman who became the cause of sin. Thus, from where the guilt came there came also grace. What is purer than this blood, what more wholesome than this wound?

The resurrection of the Lord constitutes the eleventh mystery. He rose shortly after midnight before the rising of the sun. He was the new sun of justice. At that hour, too, he had seen the light of day. He was the new Samson who carried away the doors of his confinement on his shoulders. When the sun had risen, the women arrived. They could no longer find him among the dead. There follows a conversation with Mary Magdalen and the other women, whom Gertrude asks what they had seen.

The twelfth mystery is indeed a very remarkable meditation. A heretic could take the line that Jesus rose from his grave before the stone was rolled away and could ask himself if not an equal power is to be ascribed to God in the Eucharist, so that when we adore Jesus hidden in the tabernacle, he has already risen from it. Gertrude rejects the thought and addresses herself, "O my soul, redeemed by Christ's blood, do not restrict God's miracles with your intellect. Rejoice and partake of his banquet. The one who said those things is now converted." Praise the Paschal lamb! *Victimae paschali laudes.*[30]

For the thirteenth mystery, Gertrude meditates on the Lord's various appearances: first, to his mother, then to Mary Magdalen. Jesus did not want earthly love of Mary Magdalen – no touch, because she was alone with him. Perhaps he later allowed this, when others were present. One day in heaven, the most intimate union will occur, but on earth the greatest distance must be maintained. This incident is for Gertrude a symbolic example of the distance persons of the opposite sex must observe with regard to each other. Now that we cannot follow Christ physically, she says, we must unite ourselves in spirit to Jesus in heaven.

In conclusion, Gertrude reflects, in the fourteenth mystery, on Christ's ascent into heaven: how on the eve of his Passion he said, "Rise, let us go,"[31] and now, after forty-three days, he repeated these words and proceeded to heaven to send the Holy Spirit. With complete trust, we must await the coming of God's Spirit in us.

---

[30] Sequence of the Mass of Easter Sunday.
[31] Mt 26, 46.

FROM MODERN DEVOTION
TO RENAISSANCE AND BAROQUE

The Conversion of Geert Grote[1]

Grote lived in Deventer. There lay the focus of the work by which he became the glory of this city. Here he was born six hundred years ago. Here, too, he exchanged the temporal for the eternal life. Although some shadows darken his figure, it makes sense to place his likeness in the light and to rejoice over the fact that this man here saw the light for the first time six hundred years ago.

Grote not only obtained a special place in the history of this city but through the gathering of persons and things about him achieved a place in our native land as well as far beyond it. His name is associated with a new trend in the spiritual life, a new aspect of the service of God called "The Modern Devotion," which earned esteem for The Netherlands, and which exercised great spiritual influence. It would not be right to present the Devotion as a personal invention of Geert Grote. Both Geert Grote and the movement which was put in motion through his intervention are children of their times, but it is Grote's special merit that he understood those times and responded to their needs.[2]

Geert Grote was a renovator, a reformer, but one who himself had in no small measure the faults against which he inveighed. He is a convert, and his reforming activity in large measure bears the hallmark of a convert's work. I would like to go even further and say that it has the good but also the dubious characteristics of a conversion, a reaction.

---

[1] A Discourse Delivered in Deventer on October 16, 1940, on the Sixth Centenary of the Birth of Geert Grote (1340-1384), Mystic and Founder of the Modern Devotion.

[2] See: Bernard McGinn, *The Varieties of Vernacular Mysticism (1350-1550)*, vol V of The Presence of God: A History of Western Christian Mysticism, New York 2012, 96-100.

It makes no sense to place Geert Grote in a strong blinding light which conceals the shadows on his figure. It is very useful, especially in these times, to reflect on him, but we should mirror ourselves in him, not only to learn much from him – that we can do – but at the same time to learn to know the movement which gradually blossomed more harmoniously and beautifully in men like Gerard Zerbolt of Zutphen, Thomas a Kempis – in a word, in his immediate and close followers. He formed a school, awakened a movement. We must see him as such, in order to enter into the dynamics of that movement.

Geert Grote did not reach an advanced age; moreover, his short life was far from exemplary in its first years. Only the last twelve of the forty-four years of his life are worthy of particular appreciation. His father was sheriff of the city of Deventer. He came from a respectable family. He had the means to play the lord in the world and he did so too. He seems to have lost his mother early. He was only ten years old when the Black Death decimated the population of Deventer and, it would seem, deprived the young Geert of his mother. In time, the plague would also require his life.

At fifteen years of age, he attended the university of Paris. That one already went to the university at fifteen years of age was not unusual at the time, in fact it was quite usual. In those days, instruction did not extend over so many subjects, with the result that the few subjects that were taught could be mastered at a young age, in order to follow academical studies in the liberal arts. Thus we also see Geert Grote at seventeen already taking an examination in the liberal arts and at eighteen becoming a "master in liberal arts."

However, his academic career was by no means thereby concluded. He remained on in Paris for years, in order to continue studies in law as well as medicine. He applied himself to the study of astronomy, a study which, however, quickly degenerated into astrology. In fact, during those years he does not seem to have been a serious student. Although we should perhaps not take his later confessions too seriously, from his frank self accusations and the whole history of his conversion it is nevertheless evident that he was guilty of many irregularities and led a not very edifying life.

This is all the more blameworthy, because at the same time he continually petitioned the pope for ecclesiastical benefices, which clearly had more to do with obtaining the incomes involved than taking seriously the attached obligations. This points to very unhealthy circumstances against which he later loudly inveighed.

How long Geert Grote remained in Paris cannot be determined with certainty. He is still there in February of 1366, when he is recommended for the parish of Ouderkerk. The petition says of him that after his master's degree in the liberal arts he persevered for seven years in the diligent study of various sciences. The previous year, he had requested a canonry in Utrecht, three years previously one in Aachen. He obtained both, but in the request for Ouderkerk he seems not have known that Utrecht had been granted him, because there is mention only of Aachen. The church of Ouderkerk he did not obtain, perhaps because Utrecht had meanwhile been given him. It is not at all certain whether he enjoyed the incomes of the canonries granted him while he was in Paris. Often one had to wait years before one's turn came up. Papal approval often meant no more than that one's name was on the list to succeed in one's turn. As a rule, benefices were already requested during the years of study, not so much in order to draw the income while a student, as to have at one's disposition the necessary means of livelihood as soon as one's studies were completed.

It seems very likely to me that after he left Paris, where he lingered not so much as a student as to spend some time in its academic ambience, Geert Grote visited the cities of Prague and Cologne and there frequented the university circles. His stay in all these cities may not have been edifying; nevertheless, he came into contact with devout and virtuous men who led him back to the right path, supported him in his conversion, and moreover later became his followers. Student friends are often very influencial. Thus, among his fellow students in Paris was the later Carthusian Hendrik Eger of Kalkar, in God's providence the man who definitively led Geert back to the right path. In Prague, he almost certainly made the acquaintance, not only of the loyal Floris Radewijnsz, his right hand in the founding of the "Brothers of the

Common Life," but also with a closely related form of that way of life. It is not unlikely that in Prague he received his first inspiration for the establishment of a common life based on manual labor and also for his battle against the infringement of celibacy.

The twenty-four theses which he defended in this battle are taken one by one from Conrad of Soltau, who became a master of arts in Prague on February 27, 1368, and there taught philosophy and theology with great success until 1386 or 1387. Grote had already begun reconsidering his conduct in Prague. In Cologne, strong influence was again exercised on him, but it seems not to have been until 1372 that, in Utrecht, Hendrik of Kalkar – to use an expression of Thomas a Kempis – managed to land this great fish in the net of Christ.

The matter now became serious. A great change now took place in his life. He had acquired such a reputation for learning that it was said that it had been physically driven into his head. Thus, he went from one extreme to another. That radicalism characterized the rest of his life.

Grote laid aside his luxurious clothing and adopted very simple attire, approaching that of the poor. Who has the courage to do this? He seemed another Francis. He broke with all worldly habits and ended by crowning his conversion with the renunciation of his two benefices, which had not only obtained him esteem but must have also provided him with considerable income. He left Utrecht and retired to his house in Deventer. Here, too, he continued to live in a very simple style, withdrawn from the world. In order also to break with pseudo-science, he caused all the books about astrology which he still possessed to be publicly burned in the marketplace of Deventer, in order to show as clearly as possible that he did not wish to be hindered by them. Such an about-face by a respectable man did not fail to make an impression.

Naturally he was ridiculed and condemned by some, but others were impressed and felt themselves drawn by his radicalism, realizing that only in this way could the spirit of the times be successfully opposed. In this way, he acquired, if not many, at least some supporters, or at least admirers. Especially when he placed his house and means at the disposal of persons who had great need of help and when at the same time he established an organization to provide poor students of the Deventer school with the means of leading an orderly life, a few well-intentioned persons joined him. The organization consisted in providing the means of copying books, and selling them for a good profit. His efficient organization paid well.

By this means, he helped many young students, but his purpose was much broader and designed in this way to make good books widely available. Grote expressly proceeded from the idea that this work should at the same time be an apostolate for the young students. Thus, he gathered about him above all such young men as placed ideals at least as high as material goals, and who after the example of Grote and his friends – among whom Floris Radewijnz was one of the most prominent – were willing to lead a holy and edifying life. The conversations which Grote held with them (he paid them a little at a time, in order to come in contact with them often), the schedule which he arranged for them, in which hours of prayer and reading were alternated with work performed in retirement and silence, so fired the spirits of many youths that after a while Radewijnz approached Grote with the suggestion to pool all their income and thus to lead a life like the first Christians. They did not want to make vows, to found a monastery; they deemed themselves unworthy. This was not considered necessary, because Grote above all wanted the idea to penetrate, and caused it generally to penetrate, that sanctity should least of all be thought to be confined to the cloister or to the priestly state, but that a fervent life with God could and should be striven after in the world without a relation to the cloister or vows.

Thus gradually came into being the Brothers as well as the Sisters of the Common Life. If at first the home of Master Geert became the dwelling of the first Brothers, when Floris Radewijnz made his house available, the Meester Geertshuus became the home of the first Sisters. Soon, however, other houses were added, such as the Lammekens-huus, the Brandeshuus, etc.

The Sisters did not seek their means of existence by copying books, which was the chief occupation of the Brothers, although soon teaching and especially the conduct of boarding facilities for scholars were added. The women, that is, the Sisters, occupied themselves with spinning and needle work and also hired themselves out for household work in the city and environs. Geert Grote retained only a small portion of his large house for himself and lived there entirely separated from the remaining part. He had contact with the women only through a small hatch and received what he had need of from them through a revolving drum.

All this seems to have taken place in the years 1378-1380. In those years, the first Brotherhoods of the Common Life, of men as well as of women, seem to have been founded. For Grote, however, this by no means signified the end; it was rather a beginning.

I have already noted that Henrik Eger of Kalkar, prior of the Carthusians of Monnikhuizen near Arnhem, definitively converted Grote. Thereafter, Grote remained intimately connected with this monastery. He often stayed there for long periods and in the end decided practically to retire almost entirely there and to share the life of the Carthusians.

This is not the first such occurrence in the history of the spiritual life of The Netherlands. Grote was preceded by Ruusbroec, who was formed in the Carthusian tradition in the charterhouse in Herne and remained in close contact with them. In the renascence in the beginning of the 16th century, we see Nicholas van Esch, and St. Peter Canisius after him, receive their formation from the Carthusians. Van Esch had his permanent cell with them, as did Geert Grote.

However, Grote did not become a Carthusian. He was their guest, but this also meant that he shared their life. No doubt, he returned to Deventer now and then, but for three years Monnikhuizen became a second home to him. There he came under the direction of Hendrik of Coesfeldt, one of the great personalities of the Order. According to one manuscript, preserved in

Berlin,[3] Geert Grote translated Hendrik's little work on the conversion and the introduction of novices to the new life. If this is true – and there is more than one indication of it – the translation will have been a fruit of this time. Grote even gave serious thought to requesting a permanent place among the Carthusians of Monnikhuizen, but on the other hand he was attracted by the apostolate, the work of converting others. Especially when he was invited to set down his ideas about renewal of life and to take action against the abuses of the time did the urge to be an apostle come alive in him.

However, he was no priest, not even a deacon. It seems that he became a subdeacon in order by his ordination to belong to the clerical state and be able to enjoy the benefices of the canonry of Utrecht and Aachen. He may have had only minor orders, but all things taken together this is unlikely. But although he lacked the higher orders of deacon and priest, the lower clergy were also permitted to preach occasionally, provided they were invited by the pastor of the church to do so. Geert Grote expressly alludes to this practice in a letter of 1383, written by him or in his name to the bishop of Utrecht. Thus, in 1378 we see Geert Grote travelling from Monnikhuizen to Utrecht in order to preach there.

His knowledge, his zeal, his urge for renewal and fervor, joined to the outward talents which he must have had, no doubt made him a renowned orator. This became apparent enough later on. It should not surprise us, therefore, that the Carthusians, aware of all this, but with an eye to his health and their strict way of life, dissuaded him from becoming a Carthusian. They saw in the circumstances rather an indication that God had chosen another life-sphere for him and assigned to him a field of activity of reform and renewal of the world by preaching a new and hitherto unknown life in the world.

Geert Grote himself felt the call of preacher and reformer. He was radical enough to form an opposition to the world and strong

---

[3] Berlin, Staatsbibliothek, Ms. germ. oct. 430, ff. 19r-84r, *De institucione noviciorum*.

enough to defy its ridicule and judgment, spiritual enough to perform the work in the true spirit of union with God. The three years in Monnikhuizen had raised his spirit to great heights. What Ruusbroec found in the abbot of Herne, Grote found in prior Hendrik of Coesfeldt, a leader who led to the highest heights.

Jacobus de Voecht has described for us in a few words the whole ascent which Grote made there in Monnikhuizen: "He came as a contrite sinner, he left as a mystic contemplative, burning with love and glowing with zeal to share with others the fire that was alight in his heart." In his account of the founding of the convent of Zwolle, De Voecht by way of introduction speaks briefly of the founder of the movement of which the house in Zwolle would have such an eloquent spokesman in Thomas a Kempis.[4]

De Voecht describes for us the ascent of Geert Grote in the three stages of the spiritual life. In describing the first stage, which deals with detachment and mortification, with conversion, and the battle with evil, he says that in Monnikhuizen Grote exercised himself mightily in abstention and mortification, in order to discard and root out all the failings he possessed. Coming to the second stage, which treats of the illuminative way and the adornment of the soul with virtues, he indicates how Grote next dedicated himself with the same energy to the practice of the virtues which he had to acquire. To show that Grote also ascended the third stage, which concerns union and mystical contemplation, he says that Grote finally ascended to the contemplation of the divine mysteries. It can hardly be more clearly indicated that according to the idea of the first followers of the Modern Devotion Geert Grote traversed all stages of the spiritual life, including the mystical life, and that they regarded and experienced his ascent to God as the highest in his life. His later activity was for them the fruit of that lifelong preparation.

Before speaking of that activity, we think we should examine the Modern Devotion a bit more closely. From Geert Grote himself we have ample information regarding the resolutions which at

---

[4] Jacobus Trajecti, *alias*, de Voecht, *Narratio de inchoatione domus clericorum in Zwollis*, ed. M. Schoengen, Amsterdam, 1908.

the time he made and fixed. These were not vows, as he says, but firm intentions and resolutions for the reform of his life: *conclusa et proposita.*[5] With these, he makes a radical break with his past and wishes henceforth to concern himself only with eternity. He speaks, however, of a new calling, given him by God. He renounces all his benefices and whatever accords him temporal gain. He will no longer serve two masters and dedicates himself to God. Only from him does he look for salvation and happiness. Therefore, he also gives up every form of astrology and wishes to trust only in God's providence and to abandon himself entirely to him. He also discontinues the study of law and of medicine.

It is noteworthy that in regard to philosophy he chose the position of St. Bernard in his reaction to the dialectical intellectualism of his time. Among the philosophical sciences he is interested only in ethics. Philosophy should not make a person more subtle but more moral. No less noteworthy is the fact that he bypasses Aristotle and chooses as his teachers Plato and Socrates. This is all the more noteworthy because the Modern Devotion in many respects is truly oriented to Aristotelianism, and Geert Grote himself in the large role he assigns to representation by the senses and to the imagination seems closer to the viewpoint of Aristotle than that of Plato.

He was averse to all kinds of learned pretension. Disputations, which were quite usual in the scholasticism of the time, he considered evil. He no longer wished to write books or make journeys in order to win fame. Henceforth, the study of the spiritual life held first place. He did not even want to obtain a degree in theology. This would only tempt him to use it to his advantage. He was in favor of theological science, but this he could pursue without a degree, perhaps even better, because to obtain a degree one often had to study many things of little use.

However, he says that he does not wish to break with learning to the extent that he could not use it for the advantage of others.

---

[5] Cf. *Conclusa et proposita, non vota,* in Thomas a Kempis, Vita Gerardi Magni; his *Opera omnia* (7 v., Freiburg i. B., 1902-1922), VII, 87-107.

He desires the tranquillity of the contemplative life, but should charity require, he is willing to place his learning at its service. He next lists the many books which henceforth will constitute his reading: sacred scripture, the writings of the Fathers of the Church about the relationship of man with God, Bernard, Anselm, Gregory, Augustine.

Grote wishes to attend Mass daily, and it is remarkable how he adds: remain standing to the end of the gospel, silent adoration at the consecration, and spiritual communion at the kiss of peace. He shows particular devotion to the sacred host at the raising after the consecration and for that reason wants to sit close to the altar. At the Friars Minor's he had a small room adjacent to the church, from which he could hear Mass. In the wall was a hatch which he opened at the consecration and closed after the raising of the sacred species.

He is very severe in his resolution to help only the "most devout" to become priests. He thereby shows a great reverence for the priesthood, of which he finds only a few worthy, himself least of all. He finds it better that those who cannot positively be expected to conduct themselves in a manner worthy of that vocation should not become priests. Here too is a trait of likeness to St. Francis.

He is strict with himself in the matter of fast and abstinence. Yet he regards this more as a matter of mortifying the appetite than as a severe exercise of penance. He takes no meal without mortifying the appetite in some way.

Noteworthy also is his order of the day. Apparently, according to the custom followed by the Carthusians and borrowed from them, he rose very early, and in keeping with this same custom went very early to bed. He set his midday meal in the afternoon, around four or five o'clock, in order to be able to devote the whole day to prayer and study, and thereby not to be made heavy with food. After the meal came a period of rest. He seems to have gone to bed at least by six o'clock, in order to rise around two o'clock in the morning. The Carthusians also rise around two o'clock, to pray the nocturnal hours. This custom also existed among the

Cistercians. He considered this early retiring more healthful, because the food is thus digested while the body is at rest. Moreover, it has the advantage of permitting a full night's rest before the nocturnal hours without requiring sleep to be interrupted. With regard to drink he is also strict in the extreme. He would really like to give up the use of wine entirely, but he does not do so, because there may be sometimes need to drink something for reasons of sickness or hospitality; yet he does not wish to do so outside mealtimes. Wednesdays and Fridays he always fasts. He does not take a vow to do so, but he binds himself with a most firm resolution.

It is also striking that in all that he does, says, or writes, he is resolved not to be precipitous, but to force himself to be calm and quiet. It seems that his rather strong temperament had need of such a resolve, with the result that he was later able to restrain himself in a masterful fashion and excelled in modesty and self-control.

He made a point also to obey more promptly according as what was commanded was contrary to his inclinations. Humiliation and misunderstanding were welcome to him as an exercise in humility. His ideal in learning was to arrive at the knowledge that he knew nothing. The further one thinks to be removed from perfection, the closer one is. In prayer he emphasizes fervent, childlike communion with God. Especially on retiring we should arm ourselves with good thoughts, in order to have them with us on awakening.

In conclusion, he summed up all his resolutions – which he wished to review regularly – in one word: "I shall ever direct my eyes to God." All this can be said in a few sentences, but it is not so easily observed. Grote himself realized that this resolution required lifelong practice and that practice a resolute will. Thus, he became in the history of the spiritual life in The Netherlands especially the man of practice and method in the spiritual life. The tendency toward a more methodical way of prayer had grown continually stronger. Geert Grote very strongly recommended and impressed this on his disciples. He himself adopted it. He expressly warns against leaving prayer and the practice of virtue to chance.

He wants us to explore and sharply define the way along which we wish and will be able to ascend to God. If we do not do this and leave everything too much to the last minute, we run the danger, he says, of making little progress. This is evident, besides, not only from the *proposita* mentioned above. In his *Sermo*, "On the Nativity of the Lord," also called, "Treatise on the Four Sources of Contemplation," he shows the great importance of a systematic development and reflection, in which the imagination especially must help.[6]

I have lingered rather long on this more intimate portion of Geert Grote's life. Others, in the interest of history, will place more emphasis on his exterior actions. However, it is most important to know the inner being of the man who has had such a great influence. There lies the secret of that influence. There we have before us the convert staunchly resolved to reform himself thoroughly before proceeding to preach to others. Improve the world, begin with yourself. There we see how deeply he is impregnated with the desire to place the eternal above the temporal, the divine above the human, and so to call forth a reversal in himself and thereafter as much as possible in others. His motive in this was not so much the desire to judge others but especially to cause others to share in the beauty of a more spiritual life, to taste the sweetness of interior communion with God.

It is a characteristic peculiarity in the life of Geert Grote that before he travelled through The Netherlands as an apostle, he spent years in first forming and reforming himself, and so did not thoughtlessly proceed at once after his conversion to the reform of his environment. After he had nourished his spirit in prayer and the reading of good books in the quiet solitude of Monnikhuizen, he went on one occasion to Utrecht to preach in the open there. One invitation led to another. But because he was not a deacon, this had to remain confined to very special occasions. A pastor might allow him to appear once, but particularly as he attacked

[6] *Sermo de Nativitate Domini*, ed.A. Hyma, in *Archief voor de Geschiedenis van het Aartsbisdom Utrecht*, 49 (1924), 296-326.

the abuses of the time more and more fiercely, he quickly experienced opposition and discovered that without a higher calling, warranted by a higher ordination, he could not continue to preach. Thus we see him, late in 1379, requesting to be ordained a deacon, in order to be able to preach freely. It was then quite customary for deacons to preach, particularly on moral themes. Only after he was ordained a deacon in the beginning of 1380 did his apostolic labors begin on a large scale. He traversed Holland, Utrecht, Gelderland, and Overijssel, in order everywhere, where the occasion arose, to point out the abuses of the time and to rouse to conversion.

Thus we can understand Thomas a Kempis, when he writes that Grote, after having dedicated three years to reading and prayer (that is, after having lived for three years in solitude with the Carthusians in Monnikhuizen), began to preach to others. He is referring to Grote's leaving Monnikhuizen and his first sermon in Utrecht, the initiation of his apostolic activity, not to his extended work of preaching, which could only begin two years later, after he had been ordained a deacon, precisely in order to be able to do so more freely and extensively. Neither is there a contradiction between him and Dier de Muden, when the latter says in his chronicle that Geert Grote lived a hidden life for five years before he began to preach as a deacon.[7] Finally, there is no contradiction in the rhymed biography by an anonymous oblate of Windesheim, who says that Geert Grote bestowed eight years on the care of his own soul before he began the work of healing others.[8] Converted in 1372, Geert Grote waited eight years before beginning his work of reform as a deacon.

After the quiet years of reflection and meditation, there now follow those of strenuous work, hard fighting, disappointment and disillusion, besides satisfaction and contentment. He has

---

[7] Rudolf Dier van Muden, "Scriptum de magistro Gherardo Grote," ed. G. Dumbar in *Analecta, seu vetera aliquot scripta inedita*, 1 (Deventer, 1719), 1-11.

[8] Titus. Brandsma, O.Carm., "Twee berijmde levens van Geert Grote; *Ons Geestelijk Erf*, 16 (1942), 5-51. See also *De Gelderlander*, Feb. 1, 8, 15, 22, 1941.

indeed become a fighter, unrelenting and giving no quarter. He takes action against the school of the Free Spirit, which under pretense of union with God permitted itself much that did not conform to the commandments and the teaching of the Church. He dares to challenge its teachers who have found support in wide circles and does not rest before he has convinced the bishop of Utrecht to take measures against them and disavow their doctrines. He does not relent – and here we see how fierce he could be – before the one whom he considered to be the most dangerous leader of that school, and who had meanwhile died, was transferred from consecrated to unconsecrated ground, as a sign to all that the latter's teaching was not in keeping with that of the Church.[9]

From the writings Grote has left behind, it appears that he spoke on many subjects. Nevertheless, his quarrel was principally with two very serious abuses in the Church: the violation of the sanctity of marriage and of the priesthood and the pursuit of money and goods, which found its stongest expression in the search for ecclesiastical prebends and the exacting of usurious interest. His fight is first of all against abuses in the ranks of the clergy, but inevitably this fight led him to include the deeper roots of those spiritual failings, the spirit of sensory satisfaction and of greed in wide strata of the population.

It would be entirely unjust to regard Geert Grote primarily as a reformer of the clergy, although his activity reaches its zenith there. He well knows that the evil is rooted much deeper, and that the clergy are so little regarded because the people tolerate these abuses among the clergy, do not consider them very serious, because the clergy mirror what lives in all levels of the population.

Next to the *Sermo contra focaristas* – the powerful discourse Geert Grote preached against priests who so forgot the sanctity of their state and bond to a pure celibate life that they even

---

[9] Miewes (Mattaeus) van Gouda. See G. Epiney-Burgard, *Gérard Grote (1340-1384) et les débuts de la Dévotion Moderne*, Wiesbaden, 1970, 189-190.

maintained a concubine in their house[10] – we must place the treatise about marriage, in which he opposes with all his might the generally accepted idea that it is practically impossible for persons to live in abstention, and that marriage for them is first of all an adjustment for the appeasement of the sexual urge, which supposedly could not be suppressed.

We are transported to a society which has lost much of its spiritual strength, in which higher motives no longer work their noble influence on the human heart. Grote confronts this condition with proud, free human nature, which by vigilance, self-control, and willing cooperation with the grace of God must regain the strength given it by God; a nature for whom other and nobler satisfaction must exist than the mere gratification of sexual passion. He does not hesitate with his graphic style to point out to humans, the rulers of creation, the much less frequent gratification of passion by the animals, and hard is his reproof that humans have lost the sense of their own worth. Here Grote is also radical – perhaps like all reactionary figures, radical enough to exaggerate in the opposite sense. But we understand that and must accept it, though we judge him too strong in a few points. In any case, we have to admit that he grasped the evil in its deep and wide aspects and that he did not oppose it on merely juridical grounds, although occasionally this might seem to be the case. He understands that the evil has deeper roots and finds its ground in the spirit of the times, which he then attacks with indomitable force.

We need not think that he preached only once on this subject. From what has come down to us about his action against the abuses mentioned above, we may conclude that he addressed the general public outdoors and that he spoke at greater length and more insistently to the assembled clergy.

[10] *Sermo contra focaristas*, ed. Th. en J. Clarisse, "Over den geest en de denkwijze van Geert Grote, kenbaar uit zijn geschriften," *Archief voor Kerkelijke Geschiedenis inzonderheid van Nederland*, 1 (1829), 364-379; 2 (1830), 307-395; 8 (1837), 5-107. Gerardi Magni Sermo ad Clerum Traiectensem de Focaristas,ed. Rijcklof Hofman, *Gerardi Magni Opera Omnia* Pars II,1, Corpus Christianorum Continuatio Mediaevalis 235, Turnhout 2011.

Utrecht, the capitol of the diocese, is at the same time the place where he carried out his action most intensely. And, we are happy to say, not without success. He himself in his letters expresses his happiness in this regard, although he must also to his sorrow attest that some, after having first dismissed their concubines and begun a new life, again fell into their old faults.

Mention should be made here of the fact that Geert Grote, while establishing the existence of this coarse abuse among the clergy and waging his hard battle against it, strikingly expresses his reverence for the priesthood. What he has to say in the introduction of his discourse against bad priests about the proper life of a priest, and in praise of the good priest, belongs to the most beautiful pages of his writings and is also an example of a strong, robust manly lyricism.

His struggle reached its climax in the long discourse held on August 14, 1383, for the assembled clergy of Utrecht. By that time, however, his opponents seem to have had their fill and used their influence with the bishop to curb what they considered the ill-advised zeal of the immoderate preacher, as they called him, who was not even a priest but only a deacon.

Their principal grievance must have been that he, himself not a priest, was not called to judge and condemn priests, and to accuse them to the people. At that time, the feeling of rank and of trial by peers was still strong. We deduce this from the fact that, by a general interdict, preaching by deacons was thereafter forbidden; and even more from a statement by Geert Grote himself that, although the exalted dignity of the priesthood gave him pause out of reverence and humility, he nevertheless thought of requesting ordination to the priesthood for the sake of what he considered his vocation, namely, to be able to continue to oppose the abuses of the time, particularly among the clergy. This shows that he was attacked, not for what he preached, but because as a deacon he presumed to oppose priests in public.

A second abuse against which Geert Grote took a stand was the quest for and acceptance of as many benefices or prebends as possible; that is, the assignment by the clergy of positions such as canon, pastor, etc., in order to enjoy the incomes connected with them, while the attached duties were almost never personally performed; these being entrusted to generally ill-paid vicars or substitutes. This had the two-fold disadvantage that, first of all, these offices, which could be of such great significance for the spiritual life, were desired for temporal gain and, secondly, that their discharge and administration became a mere paid employment.

This abuse also had deeper roots than in the views of the clergy alone. It was related to the spirit of avarice and a material concept of life held by the entire populace, for whom money and possessions counted as the highest good. Hence it need not surprise us that besides Grote's more specialized discourses to priests about simony, the lease of ecclesiastical offices, etc., we meet a more general treatise on poverty and disdain for the possession of money.[11] In this matter, his example gave particular strength to his words.

He himself was clothed as one of the poorest. The rich son of a sheriff was not ashamed to wear cast-off and mended clothing and to spend all his money to help others. He himself occupied only a couple of rooms in his large house. The Meester-Geertshuus had become the house of the sisters. His meals were most simple and frugal. Although his followers professed no vow of poverty, by having all things in common and, though of a wealthy background, by earning their daily keep by means of manual labor, they formed such a contrast with the world of those times that their example could not fail to exert great influence. They were a living protest against the usury practiced by many, a painful embarrassment for all who, eager for earthly possessions, made every effort to gain a benefice or prebend. Over against this degenerate Christian world, Grote places the figure of the poor Christ and calls upon those who bear the name of Christ to follow him on the way of renunciation of the world.

---

[11] Probably the *Sermo in festo Palmarum de paupertate*, ed. by W. Moll, "Geert Grote's Sermoen voor Palmzondag over de vrijwillige armoede," *Studien en Bijdragen op het Gebied der Historische Theologie*, 2 (1871), 432-469.

Those who strove for the increase of their earthly possessions, and often did not hesitate to use strong measures to acquire incomes, felt it as a quiet but sharp rebuke, publicly declaimed against them, when Grote travelled about in order to raise his voice against these evils. We can thus understand that one of his supporters wrote to the bishop of Utrecht after the above mentioned restraint on preaching that now the usurers were laughing up their sleeves, and it appears that the abuse was widespread in Overijssel, particularly in Salland, so that there more than elsewhere there was rejoicing, now that Geert Grote was rendered harmless, nay, was entirely eliminated, in his battle against usury. It came to Geert Grote as a hard blow. What he considered his vocation had become impossible.

We can understand that he earnestly remonstrated with the bishop, requesting him to withdraw the promulgated prohibition, or at least still grant him permission to preach under certain conditions. His friends also, among whom were some of great power and influence, appealed to the bishop, and later even to the pope, in order to obtain permission to preach for a deacon whose work was so useful. But Grote obeyed. He did not want to give scandal. For the time being, he remained silent in certain expectation that permission would again come to continue his activity which seemed so necessary. The powerful discourse which is considered to be the immediate occasion of the prohibition, according to several manuscripts was pronounced in Utrecht on August 14, 1383. The prohibition as well as the remonstrance against it date from the fall of 1383. Geert Grote died on August 20, 1384. During all that time the bishop did not relent; at least no revocation is known to have been made. It even appears that a revocation was no longer expected, so that one of Grote's most influential friends, William of Salvarvilla, cantor of Paris and archdeacon of Liège, appealed to the pope. The permission granted by the pope did not reach Grote before his death. Yet he did not entirely remain silent. Shortly before his death, he travelled from Deventer to Zwolle in order to preach. Had Geert Grote therefore been disobedient?

This is unbelievable after the humble submission he openly made. We think the explanation for his action in Zwolle is to be found in the fact that he preached there on request of the pastor of Zwolle, in his church, and for one time only. It is to be seen as an example of the ancient custom by which one who was not even a deacon might preach a single time with the permission of the pastor of the church. Against such an explanation is the fact that Geert Grote in his petition to the bishop asks that, if the latter is unwilling to rescind his prohibition, he at least allow him, according to ancient custom, occasionally to preach with the permission of the pastor. This request of Grote would make no sense, one might think, if Geert Grote was of the opinion that this custom did not fall under the ban. However, this is not quite correct. Were the bishop to declare expressly that he did not wish to abrogate the custom by his prohibition, many a pastor who saw good in Geert Grote's preaching would have gladly given him permission on his personal responsibility. Without such a declaration on the part of the bishop, a pastor would no longer so readily consent, even though it was allowed by custom. Our explanation becomes even more acceptable through the very special relation of Grote to the pastor of Zwolle. The latter was one of his greatest admirers and friends. Perhaps a stronger argument in favor of our explanation is the fact that, in case Grote's action were to be regarded as an act of resistance against episcopal authority and of disobedience, Thomas a Kempis would not have included it in his life for the glorification of Geert Grote. Its inclusion in the life guarantees us that in this case Geert Grote was not disobedient.

However, we can understand that such an act by way of exception would not be able to satisfy Geert Grote, and that he went about with the idea still to request ordination to the priesthood, in order to be able to carry out his vocation. Meantime he did not remain idle. The months in which he could not preach a single time as an exception in order to continue his apostolate, Grote employed in another way through personal conversations or through writing letters and treatises. We may regard this as a special act of Providence. From his last year date, not only a few still extant letters, but one would like to place at that time several still preserved treatises, because Thomas a Kempis expressly writes that he used this time to continue his apostolate in person or through writing.

However that may be, the time of his silence did not last long. Before the year after the ban was completed, Grote was summoned by God to sing forever in another life the praise he had sung here. However, before we describe his demise, we must touch on a couple of points regarding his meritorious life.

I have already said that during his sojourn with the Carthusians in Monnikhuizen Geert Grote was raised up so high in communion with God that Jacobus de Voecht does not hesitate to call him a beholder of God's mysteries. Hence it cannot surprise us to see Geert Grote attracted by the father and master of Netherlandish mysticism, the great Jan van Ruusbroec, and unhesitatingly undertaking the long journey to South Brabant to visit Ruusbroec. Thereafter he wrote to the Brothers of Groenendaal that he regarded himself as a footstool at the feet of the master and would like always to sit at his feet. Grote translated the principal works of the mystic Ruusbroec into Latin and provided them with an introduction in which we can feel his admiration for the mystical life.[12] When we see with what taste and care he translated the *Spiritual Espousals* and also the *Zeven Trappen van Minne* (The Seven Rungs) of Ruusbroec, it sounds like a want of appreciation to say– as is frequently done– that Geert Grote was no mystic.

We cannot here go further into this matter. It seems clear to me that Geert Grote was a great admirer of the mystical life, that he regarded the silent, fervent communion with God who fills all things and dwells in us, an ascent in that union with God, as the zenith of human life on this earth. But he also emphasises the need on our part of making ourselves receptive to God's grace, which

---

[12] Cf. *Ornatus spiritualis desponsationis Gerardo Magno interprete*, ed. Rijklof Hofman, Turnhout, 2000 (Corpus Christianorum, Continuatio Mediaevaliis, 172). The translation of the *Zeven Trappen* is in preparation and will appear in the same series.

after all is a gift. He emphasises what we as humans have to do: first, conversion, which for him is synonymous with turning to God and at the same time turning away from what keeps us away from God; next, the practice of virtue, which must precede and accompany our communion with God and at the same time must be its fruit.

From a practical point of view, he considers these two steps more important, because grace itself is not in our power, and we must leave to God whether he will grant us mystical grace and the experience of God. We should not concern ourselves with this, we must not aim at it, as though we were able to do anything about it.

This practical, "businesslike," in a sense Dutch matter-of-fact, viewpoint did indeed somewhat withdraw mysticism from the consideration of the Modern Devotion. Not because it did not appreciate or reverence it; rather, too much so. It ranked it too high, too much something purely from God. And being silent about it out of humility, it left it rather much, perhaps too much, at least surely at the end, entirely outside the sphere of its attention. This unfortunate result came about in the course of the following 15th century. More and more we see the mystic school of Modern Devotion cooling into mere asceticism. But this had not been the intention of Geert Grote; on the contrary.

As a particular merit and at the same time another manifestation of his love of prayer and fervent converse with the Lord, we must credit Geert Grote with having done much to broaden and interiorize the prayer of his Brothers and Sisters, and no less of the faithful in general, through the use of the common spoken vernacular. With the purpose of spreading good literature, he had many Netherlandish spiritual books copied by his Brothers, but he also took in hand the translation of the most common Little Hours and Hours of particular devotions. Here, too, he is not always original and bases himself on earlier translations of hymns and psalms, but it is his great merit to have given by his translations a great impetus to vernacular prayer, which for a great many fosters fervor. How highly he valued the vernacular for its ability to speak to the heart is shown by the fact that, as we read in his life, he was the first to preach in Amsterdam in the vernacular.

One word more over the *Imitation of Christ* as a fruit of the tree of the Modern Devotion. This fervent, harmonious little book, so genuinely Netherlandish in design and tone, is most certainly a fruit of the school that honors in Geert Grote its spiritual father; perhaps more than of him who finally compiled it. An original work of Thomas a Kempis it can certainly not in part be called. Much of what was current among the Brothers and Sisters is brought together there, and most certainly many pithy sayings of Geert Grote, Floris Radewijnsz, and many others of the Devout are also fixed and preserved there. The harmonious collecting of all those *dicta* or "sayings" remains a credit to Thomas a Kempis, which amply compensates for the lack of originality, and still makes this little golden book his own. But the acknowledgment that his work is less original than was formerly thought extends the origin of this little work over the entire early period of the growth and rise of the Modern Devotion. Although it may be considered unproven to determine what part in that origin is to be ascribed to Geert Grote – it will presumably be confined to a group of noteworthy "sayings" preserved in the circle of the Brothers – Grote's own practice of collecting in that way good sayings which he came across in reading or speaking has augmented not only that collection but also the "gold mines" of others. Under the organizing spirit of Thomas a Kempis they have developed into what may well be called the finest fruit of the tree of this ascetical-mystical school. Thus, although we must almost certainly deny Geert Grote the authorship of the little book of *The Imitation of Christ*, this does not detract from the fact that through his movement he conferred prestige on it and that it must be called the fruit of his school. It remains a monument, not only of the writer, but perhaps more so of the school from which it derived and consequently also of him, who as founder of that school, shares in its glory because he prepared that glory.

A good life is crowned by a good death. *Sicut vita finis ita.* It can only be gratifying, at the end of this short description of Geert

Grote's ascent to God, wherein he sought to include so many others, to hear that his death was no less edifying than the final years of his life.

Pestilence was again rampant in Deventer, and many fell victim of it. One of Geert Grote's most intimate friends was also stricken. He asked to speak with his master in his last hour, all the more urgently because he wished to come to an understanding by which arrangements in support of the newly founded Brotherhood, already long ago mutually agreed upon, would receive confirmation and ratification. Even without this reason, Grote would have sought out his friend. He had already sufficiently shown that he no longer allowed himself to be led at all by craving for money or possessions. Still, he gladly accepted this last settlement in favor of his Brotherhood, because he welcomed every support and he considered it his duty to make every effort to insure the Brotherhood's continued existence and prosperity. Contact with the dying patient was to be Grote's death. He must have been alive to the danger, but he must have defied it for his friend and his Brotherhood. Thus, he fell a victim of his love.

The Brothers and Sisters stood about his deathbed grieving. He comforted them with the words of a saint who entrusted them all to God and promised them all good from him. In particular, he said to the Sisters who shared the house with him that he would cast down flowers on them from heaven, referring by this to the growth which their institution would have after his death. But not only the Sisters, the Brothers also grew in numbers and strength, so that only a few years after Grote's death the crown could be set upon his foundation. A convent was founded at Diepenveen for the Sisters and at Windesheim one for the Brothers, which took over the best of them in a religious community and gave support to the Sisters and Brothers living in the world. Windesheim especially lived and worked in keeping with this calling. That had also been Grote's intention.

He was not averse to religious life – on the contrary – but for himself and others he also wanted to be able to live a holy life in the world. In order to nourish and strengthen this effort, in the end he deemed the foundation of a convent necessary, so that therefrom guidance would be given. Particularly the priests who were chosen from among the best of the Brothers and gathered in Windesheim in a convent of canons regular, founded one convent after another or after reforming their religious community caused the spirit of Geert Grote to live on.

The Windesheim community contributed greatly not only to preserving the spirit of the Modern Devotion in many houses of the Brothers and Sisters but also to keeping alive the idea that outside the cloister, too, one is called to communion with God and can live a fervent life with God. To this renewal of the world, of the ordinary person in the world, to this turning to the Lord, Geert Grote summoned his generation.

Today he lives again for us. But he does not truly live for our spirit if we do not heed the lesson of his life, if we on our part do not turn to the Lord with him. In our turning to the Lord Geert Grote lives on in us.

The Garden of the Soul; or, The Little Garden of Devout Souls[1]

I

Exceedingly numerous are the spiritual manuscripts and books in which the soul is compared to a garden where Our Lord is to take his delight, where flowers spring up and scent the air, an image of the variety of virtues. The cultivation of the garden is a symbol of one's duties; its plan, of the knowledge and appreciation of the methodical and systematic nature of the spiritual life.

This allegory already appears among our oldest spiritual and mystical treatises, beginning with Beatrice of Nazareth, whose *Seven Manieren van Minnen* (Seven Ways of Love) assure her a place of honor among Netherlandish spiritual writers. Other examples are the spiritual treatises which see the soul as a garden and in this symbol find occasion for striking ascetical reflections.

In the second flourishing era of our spiritual literature, we see Hendrik Mande[2] following in her footsteps. Even better known is the fervent 16th century song by Bertken of Utrecht[3]:

---

[1] From *De Gelderlander*, Feb. 17, 24; Mar. 2, 1940.

[2] Hendrik Mande, canon of Windesheim, *d.* 1431.

[3] Bertha Jacobs, *known as*, Sister Bertken of Utrecht, *d.* 1514. This poem cited in Stephanus Axters, O.P., *Mystiek Brevier III: De Nederlandsche Mystieke Poëzie*, Antwerpen, 1946, p. 7980. A selection from her Songs: in: *Late Medieval Mysticism of The Low Countries*, ed. R. van Nieuwenhove, R. Faesen & H. Rolfson, Paulist Press New York * Mahwah 2008, 208-214. See: Bernard McGinn, *The Varieties of Vernacular Mysticism (1350-1550)*, vol V of The Presence of God: A History of Western Christian Mysticism, New York 2012, 137-140.

I had gone to my garden for herbs
But found nothing but thistles and thorns.

Known throughout spiritual literature is the wonderful way in which St. Teresa, under the symbol of the four ways of furnishing a garden with water, defines and describes the four steps of prayer. And so I could continue on and on.

Among allegories in our Middle-Netherlandish literature there is one which has a certain resemblance and relation to *De geestelijke Palmboom* (The Spiritual Palm Tree),[4] but develops the image of the garden of the soul on a broader basis and, in a way, occupies a special place among the numerous spiritual tractates.

In the Universiteitsbibliotheek in Amsterdam, there is a manuscript,[5] dated about 1500, containing four tractates of Henry Mande, followed by a sermon on perfect conversion, and finally by, *Een ghenuechelic hoefkin der devoter sielen* (A Pleasant Little Garden of Devout Souls).[6]

The tractates of Mande have all been published,[7] and Moll in his work about Brugman also edited the sermon which follows them,[8] but, as far as I know, the treatise of the garden of the

---

[4] See Titus Brandsma, O.Carm., "De geestelijke palm boom," *De Gelderlander*, June 24, 1939.

[5] Ms. I.F.II (556).

[6] *Ibid.*, pp. 129-188.

[7] Editions listed by Stephanus Axters, O.P., *Geschiedenis van de Vroomheid in de Nederlanden* (4 v., Antwerpen, 1950-1960), II, 524, 533. Th.F.C. Mertens, *Hendrik Mande (?-1431): Teksthistorische en literairhistorische studies*, PhD dissertation Radboud universiteit Nijmegen, Nijmegen 1986. Hendrik Mande: *Een boekje van drie staten*, bloemlezing uit zijn werken, samengest. en toegel. door B. Spaapen, Tielt 1951; *Alle werken*, ed. H. Vekeman, Th. Mertens e.a.Nijmegen 1977; *Van den licht der waerheit*, uitg. en toegel. door Th. Mertens, Erftstadt: Lukassen 1984; *Een spiegel der waerheit*, uitg. en toegel. door Th. Mertens, Erftstadt: Lukassen 1984; *Een minnentlike claege*, uitgegeven en toegelicht door Th. Mertens, Erftstadt: Lukassen 1984; Apocalypse (excerpts), A Love Complaint, and extract from A Devout Little Book, in: *Late Medieval Mysticism of the Low Couintries*, ed. R. van Nieuwenhove, R. Faesen and H. Rolfson, New York Mahwah 2008, 76-86.

[8] W. Moll, *Johannes Brugman en het godsdienstig leven onzer vaderen in de vijftiende eeuw*, Amsterdam, 1854, I, 263-292..

soul has so far remained unpublished. Yet it deserves a closer examination.

According to the theme of the allegory, the soul invites her bridegroom to see the beautiful garden she has laid out for him. The plan first of all involved planting flowers, but the charm of the garden is not limited to that. There is mention of a fountain, springing up in the middle of the garden, which not only waters the garden but provides coolness and freshness; of a mountain, or hill, which not only adds variety, but offers height and leads to beautiful vistas; further, of birds singing there. All these features have a symbolical meaning.

The first feature in the garden is the planting and blooming of the most beautiful flowers. Sad to say, there are weeds which threaten to suffocate the flowers, if the soul does not make every effort to uproot the weeds and bring the garden to the desired condition for making the sown seed germinate. She must moisten her garden with the water of her tears of the most ardent sorrow; by confession, cleanse it of all that disfigures it; and by doing penance, dig it up and make it receptive to the seed.

The first flower that must bloom in that garden is the little violet of humility. If it will not bloom, it is useless to plant other flowers. It is the first flower of Spring and the symbol of the virtue which is the prerequisite and foundation of all the others.

The second flower that must bloom is the little daisy. This, too, is only a small insignificant flower that requires little nourishment, but it knows how to protect itself from storms by closing its calyx, which, however, opens wide when the sun shines on it. It is the symbol of detachment from the world and of poverty of spirit. The human heart, like the daisy, must open up in the Sun and close before all the storms of the world.

If these two little insignificant flowers are willing to bloom in the garden, as a third flower the soul must plant a rosebush, the symbol of obedience. This virtue is like the rose. Sharp are the thorns that surround it, but all the more fragrant is the scent it emanates. So it is with the obedient person. His life appears hard and severe, but within, this virtue gives the sweetest satisfaction.

His model is Jesus himself, who bloomed on the cross like the most beautiful rose, sharply pierced with thorns. The perfume of his sacrifice rose like incense in the sight of the Father, when he obediently said, "Not my will, but thine be done."

In her garden, next to the rosebush, the soul will plant lilies of purity and chastity and thereby have fulfilled the requirements of her threefold vow of poverty, obedience, and chastity. The lily is the symbol of chastity, but also of pure love of God. It has a strong, deep root, and rises on high as a symbol of hope and trust in God. The white calyces symbolize the practice of virtue which shines with the most luminous glitter. The golden kernels of the calyx point to the gold of the good disposition of the heart with its good will. The six blades of the calyx symbolize the six radiations of the virtue of chastity: circumspection in company keeping, simplicity of dress, sobriety in the satisfaction of all bodily needs, custody of the eyes, gentleness of speech, calmness and restraint in gait. It is a pleasure for the Bridegroom to walk among such lilies and to enjoy their fragrance. They who do not have such tastes are to be pitied.

Lilies are the symbols of holy souls, of Mary, of John, yes, of Jesus himself, who is called the lily of the valley and who cannot be symbolized more purely than with this image of purity. Yes, all three Persons of the Blessed Trinity can be depicted by lilies, because of the glory that radiates from them. To be raised to the highest heavens before the throne of the Blessed Trinity is to walk among the lilies. In order that we may one day do this, we must now upon earth plant lilies in the garden of our soul, to walk among which God regards as a luxury to enjoy.

The fifth flower the *Hoefkijn* calls "Christ-eyes" (*Christ-oogen*),[9] "which are very pleasant and pure little flowers," the image of simplicity and innocence, which blush at the least thing that could wound purity. If the lily demands clear whiteness and radiates

[9] The Flemish term for the Netherlandish *koekoeksbloem*, variously called in English ragged robin, gillyflower, or bachelor's buttons; K. Ten Bruggencate, *Engels Woordenboek II*, Groningen, 1978, p. 409.

glory, these little blossoms symbolize by the blush they have on their cheeks, the delicate, pure innocence which is the loveliest ornament of the bride of the Lord. Blessed are the pure of heart, for they shall see God.

After the flowers have been planted in the garden of the soul and are full-blown, signifying that the soul has withdrawn her senses from the world and walks entirely in the love of God, as the bride of the purest Bridegroom, the flowers can open there that point to the contemplation of God and participation in the eternal Wisdom. The flower selected for this is the marigold, because gold is the symbol for wisdom, and no wisdom is greater than losing oneself in the contemplation of God. Then all that is earthly and temporal loses its luster. Compared to this gold of divine Wisdom, these things are as sand that has no value and is trodden under foot. This wisdom the soul must acquire, and therefore the manuscript says, "Take pains, O bride of Christ, to plant this marigold in your garden."

II

After that in the garden of the soul, cleansed of weeds, there have successively been planted the little violet of humility, the little daisy of poverty and detachment, the rose of obedience, the lily of purity, the bachelor's buttons (in Flanders locally called Christeyes) of lightly blushing innocence and tenderness of conscience, finally, the marigold of divine wisdom, the treatise names five other flowers, equally symbols of virtues, still to be planted in that garden. They are the violets of harmony, the carnation, image of the hope of heaven, the wildflower, image of the love of God, even of the Bridegroom himself, further, the rosemary bush with its fragrant flowers and leaves, which blooms twice: first, as an image of interior prayer, then of upright gratitude, finally, the columbine as symbol of constancy.

The violets in question here are not the little blue violets, which bloom in March and must be planted before all other flowers as a symbol of humility, but the much richer tri-colored little violets or violettes,[10] which continue to bloom until October and are an ornament of the garden for richness and variety of color. They suggest how people with their various gifts must live in concord and harmony, and that the beauty of the garden consists precisely in that the soul adjusts herself to all these people of various gifts.

The carnation on its tall stem raises its calyx high above the other flowers and spreads around the sweetest scent. Therefore, it is the image of hope and of the joyful anticipation of heaven which makes all suffering sweet. As this flower raises its calyx on high, so man lifts his head to God to hear his voice which already announces his eternal reward. If he listens to the voice of God, everything that can tempt him here fades away, and his soul takes delight only in the things of God. With Moses he goes into the desert and there sees the face of God.

The wildflower in Sacred Scripture is the symbol of the Bridegroom himself, who is called a lily of the valley and a flower of the fields.[11] His luster lends beauty to all flowers. This flower is thus also the symbol of the love of God, of union with God. Like sheep, we must enter the meadow to which God leads us in order to give himself to us. Jacob worked seven years in order to have Rachel; to have us for his bride, the Bridegroom worked thirty-three years in the direst poverty and in a state of most profound humility. How much love we owe him! We must bind him to us with the bonds of the most ardent love; wound his heart with fiery arrows over and over again and open it up to us. As a deer is driven by the hunter, so we must be chased by our love into the arms of our Bridegroom. Nothing may ever separate us from him again. Love must dominate us entirely, we must be unable to live without the Beloved, and always seek and long for him. He sees us seeking and lamenting and does not leave this unanswered. But he comes to us in the person of our neighbor, in order that we might love him in them.

[10] This synonym is added here because found in the text, but it does not exist in English.
[11] Song 2,1. English Vulgate: "I am the flower of the field, and the lily of the valleys." Revised Standard Version: "I am a rose of Sharon, a lily of the valleys."

The rosemary bush blooms in the spring and in the autumn. The flowers that bloom in May are the symbol of fervent prayer, in which our heart opens to God and receives the rays of his light, and the next step to contemplative prayer is prepared. Prayer is of greater value than spiritual reading, because in the latter, it is true, we hear about God, but in prayer we speak to him and listen to his own inspiration. Rosemary also blooms in the autumn and closes the season of flowers by looking back over them. It is thus an image of our gratitude for God's gifts. The beautiful rosemary leaves also suggest the tongue which sings God's praise, knows how to speak about him to people, and so lead them up to God.

Finally, there is the last flower which this treatise adduces for the ornamentation of the garden, the columbine or aquilegia, which by its beauty crowns the luster of the garden and enhances the value of all flowers. It is the symbol of constancy, which first confers full value on our virtues. He who perseveres to the end will be blessed. It is not enough, says St. Bernard, to have performed a good deed once; we must continue doing it.[12] We must not be withheld from the good by storms and north winds of discouragement or temptation; but just as the columbine keeps open it calyx in storms and rain and remains upright in full bloom, while other flowers close their calices, so we also must persevere in virtue and not allow ourselves to be dissuaded from the practice of virtue by any adversity.

After the garden has thus been planted with a rich variety of flowers, we should not forget that the garden must be regularly provided with water. Here the treatise refers to Sacred Scripture, where the first chapter of Judges records the request of Caleb's daughter, Axa, to be given springs in the upper and lower land of the field given her.[13] So, too, the soul must have water in the

---

[12] "... nequaquam sufficere semel vel secundo operari quod bonum est, nisi incessanter adda nova prioribus." *Sermones super Cantica Canticorum, sermo 47*, par 2.

[13] Judg 1, 14-15: "And as she (Axa) sighed sitting on her ass, Caleb said to her: What aileth thee? 15 But she answered: Give me a blessing, for thou hast given me dry land: give me also watery land. So Caleb gave her the upper and nether watery land."

upper and lower land of her garden. The water course in the low land is the symbol of her tears over her sins and shortcomings. This water of repentance must issue from the depths of her heart and make the dry ground of her heart fruitful. But water must also come into the high land; that is, on high. It is the symbol of the tears of happiness and well-being wept in the sweet embrace of the Bridegroom.

But the soul must not only do her best, on the one hand, through compunction, on the other, through awareness of her vocation, to be fruitful soil for the budding of the flower of virtue – she must also erect a fountain in her garden, which, when the two sources of water dry up in times of drought, will yet provide her garden with the necessary water. That fountain, that *fons signatus*, that marked or sealed spring, is the soul herself, if she constantly reflects on and contemplates heavenly things. Then inevitably those thoughts will cause springs of living water to erupt in her, which will irrigate and fructify the garden of her soul. The Bridegroom himself, who lives in her, causes that water to leap up, and he matches his strength with that of her thoughts. Therefore, the soul prays that her Beloved may always remain united to her and make his thoughts be hers, so that both together force her to loving deeds, and that all other flowers of virtue, drenched in this water, bloom and give forth scent unto ever more fervent pleasure in God.

Next to the fountain, and irrigated by its living water, the soul must plant a tree, which lifts itself up and receives in its branches a host of birds, in order by their singing and warbling to enhance the beauty of the garden. Two birds nest in that tree, which is the image of the tree of the cross. These are the nightingale and the turtledove. The former is the bird which, when death approaches, sings out the highest song on the topmost branch; and during its lifetime, in spring, daily announces the rising of the sun. The latter bird is the symbol of the contemplative life.

But first, we must call attention to a little bird which does not fly up into the trees but nests amid the greenery and flowers: the lark. Scarcely is the winter past, than it appears, loudly and joyously to announce the new year, which formerly began with spring.[14] It flies over the ground, crying out, "Dee, dee," to bring God honor and homage and to begin the year with him. Then it rises aloft in the air and cries, "Pee dee, pee dee," to glorify God's goodness and mildness, while it looks over his miraculous works. Then he rises higher and higher and now cries, "Tutti, tutti," to indicate that God, Lord of all and Lord above all, is praised and glorified by all creatures.

This points to three ways of contemplating God. The first is that the soul, allowing its glance to encompass all creation, sees things as so many miracles performed by God. But then she rises on high and sees there how good God is, how gentle, and full of love. Finally, she sees in all creation an image of God and rises from this to God himself, who is all in all. After the winter of life, after the darkness and cold of earthly existence, the soul sees a light rising, which is Christ; sees the sun rise, heralding the joyous, eternal day of never-ending contemplation of God.

III

After the most beautiful flowers have been planted in the garden of the soul, after the irrigation of the garden has been regulated by springs in the highlands and lowlands, and, besides, by a fountain in its midst, the garden has been rendered so beautiful and luxuriant that the lark builds its nest there — after all this, the plan of the garden must be further developed.

A tree, watered by the fountain, must rise, which in due time will produce the loveliest of fruit. It is the tree of life in the middle of paradise, the tree of the cross, upon which centuries later ripened the most beautiful fruit, which gave itself to us as food. In this tree, two birds sing.

The first is the nightingale. Folklore relates about the nightingale that, when it feels death approaching, it climbs to the highest branch in the tree and there sings out its last and highest song.

---

[14] In some countries of Europe the calendar year formerly began with the feast of the Annunciation, March 25.

Also, that in early morning, around the time the sun rises, it announces its coming. Its voice rings louder and louder according as the sun rises higher and higher. First, at the hour of Prime, it still sings softly; but later, at the hours of Tierce and Sext, it can no longer control itself and sings as loudly as it can, in order to give voice to its joy. It is a symbol of Christ, "that sweetest of birds, who during his lifetime outsang all the birds." He sang his loveliest song; that is, his most striking expression of love, when he preceded us in death and climbed to the highest branch of the tree of the cross. What sweet words are written in the story of the Passion; from the hour of Prime, when Jesus stood before Pilate, until Evensong, when at the fiercest burning of the sun of his love, he uttered the seven words on the cross and died.

To have this tree in her garden and have it bear fruit, the soul must make a hill or mountain as a symbol of Calvary, to express the idea that she lifts herself to God and from that chosen height overlooks the road she must travel.

This mount has many meanings. First of all, it is the place from which God instructs us and gives us his ccmmandments. Next, it is the place where sacrifice is offered to God. Thirdly, it is the place most fiercely warmed by the sun, and where its light and heat are best received. Fourthly, it is the mountain, shelter, and refuge whence comes our help and deliverance. Fifthly, it is the mountain of silence and listening to the Lord. Sixthly, it is the mountain, a town, from which we can climb as close as possible to God. The highest mountain must be found to unite ourselves to God.

Thus, this mountain or hill in the garden is a symbol of the contemplative life. On this mountain; that is to say, by applying herself to the contemplative life in union with God, the soul will be able to pluck the fruit of the tree growing thereon. This fruit is a remedy to protect her from the seven-fold evil which threatens her with eternal death.

The first evil is pride. We must climb the tree of the cross to pluck the leaf on which is written, "Learn of me, for I am meek and humble of heart," and, "I am come to serve, not to be served."

The second is envy. Climb into the tree of the cross and pluck the leaf with the lesson, "A new commandment I give you, that you love one another."

The third is discord and dissension. Pluck from the tree of the cross the leaf on which is written, "If you remember before the altar that your brother has something against you, first go and be reconciled with your brother and then come back before the altar to make your offering."

The fourth is avarice. Pluck from the tree the leaf on which is written, "Give alms." "Seek first the kingdom of God."

The fifth is gluttony. Pluck the leaf with the words, "They have mingled my food with gall." "Man does not live by bread alone." And, "Woman, give me to drink."

The sixth is sloth. For that evil you must pluck the leaf which instructs you, "You shall love the Lord your God with your whole soul and with all your strength." And that other leaf on which is written, "Why should this tree any longer encumber the earth, if it bears no fruit?" And also the leaf on which you read that Jesus used to spend the night in prayer.

Finally, the seventh is lust. For this evil you must pluck the leaf on which is written, "Whoever looks on a woman with the desire to sin with her has already done evil with her in his heart." And the words to the Bridegroom to hold him far from sin, "Follow me." And also the words to the adulteress, "Woman, sin no more."

Besides the nightingale, the soul must allow a second bird to sing and nest in the tree of her garden: the turtle dove. A contemplative soul must mirror herself in it to try to acquire its characteristics. The dove has bright, clear eyes and, while floating on the water, sees in time the goshawk which would like to catch and kill it. Then it finds shelter among the rocks. The eyes of the soul must also be open and clear and must assimilate the living wisdom in the running water of Sacred Scripture, whereby she sees through the snares of the enemy. In times of danger, she flees to the caves; that is, to the wounds in the Rock, which is Christ. The gray color of the dove is an image of simplicity in clothing. Instead of singing, she sighs and coos, in order to show that while the world tempts her to pleasure and idleness, the soul should rather lift her heart with sighs to God and to her heavenly fatherland. When the dove dies, the cock does not seek a second mate, but mourns in a thornbush until he too dies. This should symbolize for us that, when the soul has lost God's grace through sin, she should not seek comfort in strange creatures, but should do penance and fly to the arms of the cross. Likewise, her eye should be round like a dove's; that is, just as a round object touches the ground only at one small point, the eyes of the soul should also be round and scarcely touch the earth.

Once the garden of the soul has been arranged entirely according to the taste and wish of the Beloved, invite him to linger there with his bride. He will not have to wait at the door or knock on it for long. The soul comes to meet him and watches out for him.

The soul regards the Beloved as the light and reflection of the Father and knows that the contemplation of that Light is a foretaste of heaven. She knows that it is his delight to be among the children of men, but that he wants to be sought after, and she seeks means of finding and bringing him into her garden. He is her Beloved, without whom she cannot live, for whom her heart yearns. She verifies whether the flowers of pure and heaven-directed thoughts have actually blossomed; whether the tree has actually produced fruit of good works to satisfy the Beloved; whether the birds are actually singing out of gratitude and readiness to make sacrifices. She knows that the north wind of temptation often threatens to damage the bloom of her little garden, but she also knows that temptation is not sin, that the north wind again falls, and that struggle strengthens rather than weakens the practice of virtue. Therefore, she does not fear adversity and suffering, because these attract her Beloved rather than estrange him. All her desire is directed to having her Bridegroom come to brighten her garden with his luster, to protect it with his might. The Beloved cannot resist loving desire. He comes and in turn invites his bride into his heavenly pleasure-garden.

Meanwhile, the soul has one last task to perform. When she has arranged her garden so tastefully that it charms the eye of the

Bridegroom and he desires to come to her, in order in his turn to invite her to his garden, then she must take every care that, until the moment her Bridegroom arrives, her garden remains in the excellent state to which she has brought it. She must keep far from it whatever might impair its beauty; that is to say, she must lastly build a wall around it. She must allow access to her garden only to the Beloved of her heart, and at its gates place a Seraphim, an angel of true love, who will refuse admittance to all that is not God. The soul must live in herself in profound inwardness, take delight in the flowers and birds of her garden, and enjoy caring for it with loving solicitude, so that none of its beauty be lost, and its delight rather increase.

Gerard Zerbolt of Zutphen (1367-1398)[1]

I

Spiritual Ascents – I

After we have discussed methodical prayer in general, and in our previous article treated of the "ladders,"[2] which several authors have constructed to help us gradually ascend to the pinnacle of perfection and the summit of God's love, we would like to request a moment's attention to a writer of the late 14th century, whose name and work we only mentioned before, but who deserves to be more closely examined and discussed.

We refer to Gerard Zerbolt of Zutphen, who died in Windesheim in 1398. His death in the monastery of Windesheim would seem to indicate that he belonged to the Canons Regular of that house, but this is actually not the case. He belongs to the Brethren of the Common Life of Deventer, from which monastery, it is true, Windesheim was founded, and which considered Deventer to be the center of activity on behalf of the interiorization of devotion, yet expressly adhered to the common life with vows initiated by Geert Grote.

We know how highly Geert Grote esteemed priests, and what a demanding attitude he took, when it came to ordaining a priest. Only one of the Brothers was chosen for this distinction, and the choice was made with the utmost care and concern. Geert Grote

---

[1] From *De Gelderlander*, Jan. 11, 18, 25, 1941. See also Bl. Titus's article "Zutphen, Gerard Zerbolt van, 1367-1398)," *Katholieke Enciclopedie* (24, v., Amsterdam, 1933-1938), XXIV (1938), 713.

[2] See Bl. Titus's article, "Ladder (geestelijke)," Kalholieke Enciclopedie, XVI (1936), 113.

did actually receive a few priests into his brotherhood, but of the brothers he accepted, only Florens Radewijnsz was raised to the priestly dignity. Later, Gerard Zerbolt of Zutphen was one of these chosen ones, which must give us a high opinion of his learning and holiness. He lived only a short time: he was born in 1367 and already died in 1398.

Busch states that Zerbolt joined the Brothers while Geert Grote was still living.[3] Since Geert Grote had already died on August 20, 1384, Zerbolt must have been young when accepted among the Brothers. Before that, he attended the Deventer school, but not exclusively, for he also frequented other schools, perhaps even abroad. He spent the short time he lived in the Brotherhood to the greatest advantage both to himself and to the Brotherhood. He became one of the founders of the Modern Devotion, and may in fact be regarded as one who lent the greatest support to the work of Geert Grote and Florens Radewijnsz and hence to the movement introduced by them. He became the spokesman and advocate of the young Brotherhood, and by his writings, also in the area of spirituality, provided leadership and closer definition to the movement.

I have already referred to his principal work as "Spiritual Ascents," or from the opening words of the original Latin edition, *Beatus vir*: "Blessed is the man whose help is from thee (the Lord): in his heart he hath disposed to ascend by steps in the vale of tears, in the place which he hath set."[4] This text of Psalm 84 (83) is quite appropriate as a description of the return of fallen man to his original blessed condition.

Zerbolt had treated the same theme in a previous work, *Over de hervorming van de ziel* (Concerning the Reform of the Soul). The

[3] J. Busch, *Chronicon Windehemense*, rev. by K. Grube, Halle, 1886. Not available for consultation.

[4] Ps 83, 5-7. The RSV, Ps 84, 5-7:: "Blessed are the men whose strength is in thee, in whose heart are the highways to Zion. As they go through the valley of Baca they make it a place of springs; the early rain also covers it with pools. They go from strength to strength; the God of gods will be seen in Zion."

Middle Netherlandish translation, rediscovered in Berlin,[5] typically describes the title as, "*Wo wi die crachten der zielen weder seollen te rechte maken*" (how we must strengthen the forces of the soul). An excellent summary of both works has been provided by my confrere, Dr. Joannes Soreth van Rooij, O.Carm., in his broadly conceived and carefully elaborated dissertation on Gerard Zerbolt of Zutphen.[6] Particularly useful are the outlines, which he has drawn up as a general summary of both works and which allow us to see at a glance the underlying ideas of the Modern Devotion. It is beyond the scope of the present articles to repeat these outlines in their entirety. We must limit ourselves to what in a stricter sense more closely describes "methodical prayer" and reproduces it in its basic principles.

Zerbolt's principal work was often copied and printed in former centuries. Dr. Van Rooij has discovered and described 40 complete and 26 incomplete manuscripts of the Latin text; 12 complete and 5 incomplete manuscripts of the Middle Netherlandish text. The work was even more widely spread through print: known to be extant are 24 complete and 2 incomplete editions of the Latin text; six complete editions of translations into Lower German, Middle Netherlandish, and English. Yet, because the work is practically inaccessible to the modern reader of Netherlandish[7], and the time for a critical edition was not yet ripe – because of the large number of manuscripts and printed editions, this would require a great number of years – Father van Rooij has performed an unusually meritorious service by providing a rather detailed summary, based on a few of the oldest and best manuscripts and

---

[5] Berlin, Staatsbibliothek Berlin, germ. oct. 181. A photo of this ms. is found in the Radboud Universiteit, Nijmegen, Titus Brandsma Instituut, Album, 148-149.

[6] *Gerard Zerbolt van Zutphen. I Leven en geschriften*, Nijmegen, 1936.

[7] Gerard Zerbolt van Zutphen, *Geestelijke opkliommingen*. Een gids voor de geestelijke weg uit de vroege Moderne Devotie. Vertaald, ingeleid en toegelicht door R.Th.M. van Dijk o.carm., Amsterdam University Press 2011. See: Bernard McGinn, *The Varieties of Vernacular Mysticism (1350-1550)*, vol V of The Presence of God: A History of Western Christian Mysticism, New York 2012, 107.

printed editions, of Zerbolt's main work, and including it in his dissertation (pp. 124-164). These 40 pages alone already make his book a precious possession.

It is in the nature of things that Zerbolt begins with a depiction of the fall of man in order thus to make man understand, not only what he must recoup, but at the same time to point out to him what has led to that loss, and what he must avoid and oppose. He describes how the human powers have degenerated through original sin, particularly those of desire and striving; how because of the sinful tendency which now made itself felt, love becomes disorderly, in the first place, through an inclination to evil, then through repugnance to good, and in general through inconstancy. But that was not the end of it in the case of man. By mortal sin, the evil deed, man even went on to turn completely from his Creator and bestow himself on creatures, thereby transgressing the commandments. From that fall, he must again ascend. In three times three steps, in three ascents along three rungs each, he must manage to rise up out of that valley.

The first ascent is conversion; the second, putting love in order; the third, finally, the sanctification of the faculties. The three steps in the first ascent, or staircase – that of conversion – are sorrow, confession, and satisfaction. The three steps in the second staircase – that of the ordering of love – are fear of punishment, hope of reward, and enlivening and confirming of love, which must become steadfast. Then comes the third step upon which the primal fall, involving the deterioration of the faculties, must be undone, and thus everything be readied for arriving at the sanctification of those degenerate faculties.

This is the difficult part. But here God's help is also the strongest. Here, too, Zerbolt distinguishes three steps; the lowest, on which beginners stand; the middle step, which the somewhat advanced have already managed to reach; and the highest, to which the perfect with God's help have climbed.

Although the work of the third ascent is the most difficult, it may, in brief, be said to be the struggle against the capital sins, in a resolute and rigorous, but at the same time joyful, opposition to our wrong inclinations; and in the practice of the opposite virtues of moderation (against gluttony), of chastity (against impure inclinations), of poverty (against attachment to earthly things). These first three virtues are directed to the sanctification of the faculty of desire. There follow the virtue of forbearance (against temper), of love of neighbor (against envy), of love of God (against tepidity and sloth), of self-humiliation (against self-exaltation and self-complacency). These four virtues reform the faculty of striving. Finally, there is the virtue of humility (against the root of all evil, pride).

The longer this process lasts the more resolutely and harder it must be fought. Zerbolt traces virtue by virtue the way we can and must ascend from the most common to the most heroic and resolute exercises.

For the Modern Devotion, the practice of virtue is the main concern. Next to this – Zerbolt speaks of parallel to this – comes the ordering of love. For him, this is the second ascent, while the practice of virtue is the third. The one stair without the other, as he also declares, is unthinkable and also not to be climbed. Both must go hand in hand. When we speak of "methodical prayer," we think rather of this second ascent – about which a word in the next article.

II

Spiritual Ascents – II

The great teacher of the spiritual life, St. Teresa of Avila, tells us in her description of the interior life of prayer that, even if this life ascends to the loftiest mystical heights, the practice of virtue must precede, accompany, and crown prayer. Without the practice of virtue, a true life of prayer is unthinkable.

Did not Our Lord himself say that not those who cry, "Lord, Lord," are his chosen ones, but those who do the will of the Father in heaven?[8]

8 Mt 25, 11.

The Church has always warned against quietistic tendencies in the life of prayer, and against a concept of the spiritual life which emphasizes in too one-sided a manner inner communion with God without good works and the practice of virtue. Rising after a strong intellectual current led by the mysticism of Eckhart, the Modern Devotion in the 14th century strongly emphasized exterior good works and the systematic practice of every sort of virtue. At first very healthy, this school, in the course of the 15th and the beginning of the 16th century, deteriorated into an exaggerated glorification of good works, so that the Reformation, not without reason, stressed an interiorization of communion with God – for its part, sad to say, also too one-sided, but that is the way with the changing moods of the human spirit.

Be that as it may, in the first success of the Modern Devotion, in its first writers and spokesmen, there is no word about this one-sided glorification of good works; and if they strongly emphasize the practice of virtue, it is in every respect in a sound manner. The later hardening in no way reflects the spirit of the first writers, who exactly linked the interior with the exterior in wonderful harmony, and made the life of prayer again fruitful by characterizing it as pertaining to the whole person, who must try to place all his faculties at the service of God.

Quite in the spirit of nascent Modern Devotion, of which we have given the word to Gerard Zerbolt of Zutphen, one of its most authoritative spokesman, we have in our previous article sketched the manner in which Zerbolt, in his description of the "ascent" of the spirit to God in the most fervent life of prayer, gives a place to the practice of virtue. Now, a word about his description of the prayer accompanying it.

Here, too, there is method and system. Geert Grote already insisted on preparation for prayer, and strongly advised against simply letting prayer happen, trusting that good thoughts would follow, if one were but to sit down and pray. For this, since the fall from grace, we are too much under the influence of our sinful inclination, and our love for God is disorderly. Hence, the need always to take care to regulate and order our love. Not only must

love of wrong be suppressed and antipathy to the good be conquered; we must also try to remove all inconstancy from our love.
For that reason, three sentiments must also rule our prayer and
lead and regulate our ascent to God. In the first place, we must
not think that we can dispense with the fear of eternal punishment. The feeling of bitter repentance over sin, aroused and
strengthened by that fear, will help us to suppress and master our
cravings. Yet it would naturally be wrong to allow ourselves to be
exclusively led by that fear. Besides that, we must increasingly
strengthen our hope of heaven, and realize that this raises up our
spirit and makes us despise the world and its allurements, thus
elevating and purifying our cravings. Finally, we must strive continually to strengthen our love, to see the practice of this virtue as
something beautiful, so that we find our happiness in being
allowed and able to practice it, because this virtue directs our heart
to God and keeps it fastened there.

There are also three kinds of repentance, nobler and finer
according as one's motive is nobler and finer. It is good and profitable to be filled with repentance and to maintain it, because of
the punishment we deserve; it is finer, if we also cause it to arise
from a desire for heaven; but remorse is finest, if it is supported
in us by a sincere desire for fervent union with God.

To keep these feelings alive in us, Zerbolt points to a number
of subjects which we should make the object of meditation. Here
lies the pith of the matter. Although putting love in order is the
ideal, the Modern Devotion, very psychologically oriented, has
already fully understood that the will is led by the intellect, that
the faculties of desire and striving are directed along the path of
the faculty of the intellect.

First of all, Zerbolt indicates a few points which must serve as the
springboard of meditation, which each time must again be taken as
the subject of meditation, although here, too, a gradual ascent is
desirable. As already mentioned, he distinguishes three steps, and
these steps each have their own subjects, which then each come into
prominence; but that does not say that they should so constitute the
exclusive subject of meditation and contemplation that those of the

previous and higher steps must remain unconsidered. As we shall more fully explain in a following article about "spiritual descents," it is a matter of constant going up and going down. Now one thought dominates the life of prayer, then again another. It is not good to concentrate too exclusively on one point. In that way, the riches upon which the spirit can draw in meditation remain unappreciated and wasted, with great damage to the spiritual life, which in its time must tap into the various springs of living water.

First of all, the spirit must occupy itself with pondering former sins and still present faults. This is most needful, in order to remain standing on the solid ground of humility and to have a clear vision of one's relation to God. Where the spirit is still so weak that it constantly makes itself guilty of sin, it is in the nature of things that still stronger emphasis be placed on this weakness, in order that a person realize that he must bend all his efforts to oppose it. In order to strengthen oneself for this task, the omnipresence of God, the brevity of earthly existence, the eternal and unalterable judgement after death, and also the frightfulness of the punishment of hell must be repeatedly contemplated and deeply impressed on the spirit. If these points are so vividly and profoundly meditated upon that they become the predominating idea of a person's spirit, and have become a true guideline for daily conduct, then the spirit can ascend higher and attend to how far we are still separated from heaven, how ungrateful we actually are in comparison with the great goodness of God, while it is so wonderful to live in God's love and bear within us the consciousness that we belong to his elect. Finally, the spirit must try to delight in the union with God which it can share; to unite itself as intimately as possible with Christ, who came into this world precisely to unite us to God. In the close relationship with Christ and in the following of his life, step by step, action by action, the spirit must find the way to arrive at ever more intimate union.

While Zerbolt proposes these thoughts as the starting-point of our meditations, he specifies death, judgment, and hell as the actual subjects for the first step; for the second step he suggests heaven, the significance of grace, and the riches of God's gifts in nature and supernature – yes, even in the mystical life – given us in overflowing measure; while in the third step, we cannot pay enough attention to the life and Passion of Christ in all the forms in which they are revealed to us in the Old and New Testaments in type and actuality.

To arrive at this point, we must begin to read about all these matters and to listen to explanations of them. These thoughts do not arise spontaneously in us, we must take them in. But this is not enough. Meditation must impress the thoughts more deeply into our spirit and make them living and fruitful, so that in the end we are so filled with them that they are our object of meditation all day long, and we thus come to lead a life of prayer. As long as this is not the case, we must continue our exercises. Those exercises will occupy us all our life long.

III

Spiritual Descents

After having spoken about the "ladders" of the spiritual life and the "spiritual ascents," we must bestow a moment on a seemingly opposite exercise of the spiritual life; namely, the exercise also necessary to that life, the "descents." Zerbolt of Zutphen, whom we followed in his description of the "ascents," also emphasizes "descending in due course."

We have already said that the image of the "ladder" in mystical literature has its origin in the symbolical interpretation of the ladder of Jacob, which we know from Sacred Scripture. The patriarch Jacob saw in a dream a ladder, of which the top reached into heaven, and on that ladder he saw God's angels ascending to him, but also descending, only to ascend again.[9] This image is used in mystical literature to make clear to us that, in our ascent to God, we must not only think of the ascent of our soul to God and of the perfecting of ourselves through the practice of various exercises

---

[9] Gen 28, 12.

which raise us ever higher and make us fit to dwell in the spheres of heaven, but besides that be mindful of what, in accordance with the image of Jacob's ladder, are called "descents." In the above-mentioned work, Zerbolt devotes the last seven chapters to them.

He begins with warning us that we must not understand that descent in the sense of a temporary, weaker effort, of an interruption of the practice of virtue in the sense of a period of rest, because the bow should or could not remain bent. He means something entirely different, and points out that the angels on Jacob's ladder in no way show weakness or imperfection by descending, but on the contrary, only according to God's desire, do not immediately return to him, thus doing precisely what he asked of them. Their seeming aversion to God was designed to fulfill his holy will with regard to creatures. Ruusbroec has a beautiful expression for this: to leave God for God.[10]

Zerbolt sees this descending as two-fold, and points out that we must descend, now to ourselves, now to our neighbor, lest to our detriment we lose sight of ourselves and our neighbor, on the pretext of being occupied with God and of ascending to him.

This two-fold descending Zerbolt again divides into three steps each. The first step of the descent to ourselves is the return from higher to lower motives, in order to make them harmoniously exercise all their influence and thus arrive at strengthening and innerly consolidating them.

The second step consists in this that, although we may be as holy and perfect as can be, yet according to nature we remain human. Thus, we must also attend to our bodies, to outward things, to make sure these are in harmony with our higher attitudes, and are proper and controlled. Our exterior should correspond to our interior.

The third step, finally, is that we should not be afraid to allow our bodies to do any kind of work, and through manual labor to bridle our love of ease.

---

[10] This expression is not found in the corpus of Ruusbroec, but several spiritual authors or mystics are using it.

The first step of the descent to our neighbor is to recognize our betters and to subject ourselves to them in obedience. This is already a whole step down, a step which often costs a good deal of effort, but for that very reason must be taken.

The second step is the recognition of our peers and loving social dealings with them. This step may not seem to be as difficult as the first; yet it seems that often in the practice of the spiritual life it is somewhat lacking, and so this descent is also one of the greatest importance.

Finally, the third step, the right and proper descent to unimportant people, is no less significant for the spiritual life.

Another word about each of these steps.

With regard to the descent to ourselves, it may seem beautiful and grand to live in complete trust in God's unending goodness, in joyous anticipation of heaven, in ascending lovingly to God in the contemplation of his election of us, in exulting and rejoicing over our felicity – all this is truly beautiful and grand. It is regretful enough that we do not more often arouse in ourselves happy sentiments on this account. But, on the other hand, it is useful; yes, necessary, to return now and then to the earlier motives of our interior life: to meditation on the judgment of God, on death, on hell, and with these reflections to interrupt the grand consideration of our happiness and election. The interruption can gradually become shorter and less frequently necessary. We should not too quickly consider ourselves secure, and, for the sake of the security of our conversion to God, we should allow any motive to act upon us in their full strength. Otherwise, we lose what we have already gained. We remain weak human beings. We must never lose fear and caution, and we must often return to them. To be sure, our holiness should not become sanctimoniousness, and we should not allow virtue to consist in outward appearances, and yet we should be an example to others and by strong self-control show that we possess mastership over ourselves. Here, Zerbolt descends to rather minute particulars and seems to lay great store by our forming ourselves not only interiorly but also exteriorly; by our forcing ourselves to be what others expect of us, if we want to stand as servants of God in the world. In our words and answers, in our posture and gestures, in our clothing, we must be recognized as the servant of God who goes about in the world.

If, thirdly, Zerbolt insists on a certain bodily activity, this does not mean that he firstly wishes to point out that work does not need communion with God and thus also may not be interrupted. But he goes further and is of the opinion that taking upon oneself of any kind of bodily work, and not leaving it entirely over to others, as though it does not become us, is of the greatest value for making one who wishes to lead a spiritual life remember his place in human society. Besides, bodily work is good for keeping our body in check with regard to its desires and inclination to rest and idleness. He grants, however, that not all work is of equal value to the spiritual life, and that, therefore, as a support of the spiritual life one must make a distinction between various forms of bodily work, if there is a proper occasion for it. We know that in the circles of the Modern Devotion, the copying of books was especially sought after, not because this was less strenuous than many other forms of work – often the contrary – but because, on the one hand, the scribe, on the other, the one for whom he performed the work, was instilled with good and edifying thoughts.

For Zerbolt, the descent of the spiritual person also has, as we have said, three steps, and in this connection, he keeps in view the three-fold relation a person has to his neighbor: as his inferior, as his equal, and as his superior. It is a quite psychological approach on Zerbolt's part that he begins with the relation of the inferior to his superior. To be inferior has always been very difficult, although there is no disguising the fact that for many it also costs a great effort as superior to associate with inferiors in the proper manner.

In the practice of the spiritual life, too, one must know how to recognize one's superiors. Unfortunately, it happens only too often that one acts too wilfully, and allows prayer to take precedence over work which is ordered by powers set above us or by circumstances arranged by God. We should be able to rise instantly from the most exalted and beautiful communion with God, when someone like Martha in Mary's house announces to us that the Master is there and is calling us to other work. But Zerbolt places more emphasis, if possible, on the descent to the neighbor whom we regard as our equal. St. Paul would never have ascended to the third heaven, Zerbolt claims, had he not been everything to everyone.[11] He warns against a concept of the spiritual life which is selfish and fitted to our own ideas and tastes. We profess belief in the communion of saints, but then we must also conduct ourselves in the spirit of that communion, no matter how strongly we are attracted by solitude and doing what is pleasing to us. In the same spirit, he points out that one who knows himself to be superior to another should feel himself forced continually to use his influence for good, in order to raise up that inferior person and to be of benefit to him. He also considers that what was said to the brothers of Joseph applies to us; namely, that we will not see the countenance of the Lord our Savior, if we do not bring our little brother with us.[12] Certainly, the danger then exists, of which St. Paul speaks, that while preaching to others, we ourselves will be lost.[13] Therefore, Zerbolt says, one should not desire to be or to become superior, and if this is the case we should be doubly on our guard.

[11] 2 Cor 12, 2; 2 Cor 9, 22.
[12] Gen 42, 20..
[13] 1 Cor 9, 27..

Saint Lidwine of Schiedam[1]

I

These days we are following with great interest the happenings in Konnersreuth.[2] Not only Catholics but non-Catholics in great numbers go to the small and remote Bavarian village to see and speak to Teresia Neumann, to witness her visions of the Passion, to behold the signs of the wounds of the Passion of the Lord impressed on her body, and to obtain further information from those who have seen and heard the many wonders related about this simple farm girl: how she has been tried by illness after illness; takes upon herself the suffering of others; sees into the depths of the soul and unveils secrets of conscience; reveals hidden things; and what sounds even most unbelievable, for eight years has had no food nor drink and is fed alone on frequent Communion.

Bishops and prelates visit her and reverence her word, famous scholars come with scientific curiosity to see her at first hand and judge for themselves. They write books and articles about her and concern themselves with her in wide-ranging discussions; just as the uneducated, the simple country man and woman, who partly from curiosity, partly to be edified by that spectacle, go to Konnersreuth to see Teresia and speak to her. It is a daily coming and going of persons of every rank and file, of the most varied persuasions and

---

[1] From *De Gelderlander*, Feb. 11, 18,15, 1939.

[2] Titus was considerably interested in the stigmatist of Konnersreuth. See "Teresia van Konnersreuth en Lidwina van Schiedam," *Jaarboek van de St. Radboudstichting 1931*, Nijmegen, 1931, p. 52-56; "Teresia Neumann van Konnersreuth; waarde der verschijnselen," *Het Schild*, 13 (1931), 5-17, 49-58; "Wondteekenen en lijdensvioenen; van Konnersreuth naar Hohemark," *De Maasbode*, May 6, June 2, 23, July 7, 21 1935.

education. She has become the center of much discussion, the object of universal interest.

Thus, we are experiencing something that is occurring at a great distance. But distance in space is not only bridged by witnesses in this way; the same takes place with regard to what is distant from us in point of time. In this case, too, witnesses are in condition to make us experience what was a fact long ago, to bring vividly before our spirit what was reality in ages long past.

But if that is the case, we need not leave the boundaries of the fatherland in order to see in Konnersreuth an image of the suffering Savior, a visionary of the Lord's Passion, one who lives only on the Eucharist as the only nourishment afforded her.

Thus, on the soil of the fatherland we go in spirit to Schiedam, in order to see there five centuries ago another Teresia, a Saint Lidwine, like the seer and sufferer of Konnersreuth the object in her day of general discussion. She was also visited by persons of every rank and file, coming to her from far and near. Suffering, as an image in her body of the Lord's Passion, fell to her lot in an even severer and long-lasting degree. She saw into hidden things and revealed the secrets of the soul. She partook of neither food nor drink and knew no other nourishment than the sacred Host, not for six[3] but for nineteen years.

Why would we go to the trouble of hearing tell of Teresia Neumann and neglect to listen to the witnesses who still tell us about our native saint, whose life speaks even more clearly of the Passion of the Lord?

Both to a large degree have this in common: we may call both apostles of the Passion, both fulfill the very special vocation and mission of calling attention again to the Lord's Passion; not only that, but also of preaching love for that Passion, not with words but with deeds, with following close at hand, with warm participation, with reaction on the body, while that union with the suffering Savior is sustained by their exclusive nourishment with the body of the Lord, without their being able to participate in any

---

[3] Above Titus speaks of eight years.

other food or even drink. The well-known Franciscan, Father Brugman, who had such an apt way of saying things that we still say, "being able to talk like Brugman," to express the greatest eloquence – that Father Brugman once said so beautifully of Lidwine that meditation, contemplation of the Passion of the Lord and Holy Communion were the two arms with which she embraced her Beloved. We may say the same of Teresia Neumann, whose life is also taken up with experiencing the Lord's Passion and only draws strength and sustenance from receiving the Holy Eucharist. If Teresia Neumann seems in these times to deserve to be considered one sent by divine Providence to declare – where neither priests nor lay apostles are listened to – how God so loved the world that he delivered up for us his only-begotten Son, the divine Word, then the figure of Saint Lidwine is no less providential.

The name of Saint Lidwine is once more on the lips of many. Devotion to her lives again. Her official enrollment in the ranks of the Blessed of the Church has given new life to the veneration which lived on – though without formal ecclesiastical approval – among the people, specifically in Schiedam and the diocese of Haarlem, and also in all of The Netherlands and Belgium. Biographies appeared and were eagerly purchased. The Dominican, Father Meyer, translated the life of Lidwine written by Father Brugman and enriched its second edition with many interesting notes and appendices.[4] The Reverend Nuyen published a translation of the life of Saint Lidwine by Thomas a Kempis that also experienced a second printing.[5] In the same year that this second printing appeared, Joannes Mercator published a new translation of the same life.[6] In 1928, the Lazarist, Father Meuffels, added a fine adaptation of the various ancient lives in the form of a beautiful

---

[4] G.A.Meijer, *Het leven der Heilige Lidwina door Joannes Brugman*, Nijmegen, 1890.

[5] Thomas a Kempis, *Leven van de Maagd Lidwyde*, tr. by C. Nuyen, Amsterdam, 1923.

[6] Thomas van Kempen, *Het leven van de Heilige Lidwina van Schiedam*, tr. Joannes Mercator, Amersfoort, 1924.

biography suited to these times, by all means the best that we have at the moment and worth recommending in every respect.[7]

An interesting biography which has done much to make Saint Lidwine revered beyond the boundaries of our fatherland and to place her figure in a favorable light was written by the famous French author, Huysmans.[8] It presents a spirited picture of the patient sufferer in her love of God and fellow humans; a book which inspires love and reverence for her and has made her shine as a heroine before the eyes of many who do not read the average lives of saints. He is eloquent in his discussion of the meaning and great value of suffering, particularly where he contrasts sickness and want, penance and sacrifice, with what so many in the world do for their health, with the craving for possessions and pleasure in every form, with the flight from anything that resembles sacrifice.

In other places, his work is less successful, his presentation is not always historically correct, and in more than one place he is more the novelist who is developing a striking image – and almost too realistically – than the historian who carefully distinguishes his sources and in his sketch is aware that he is writing the life of a saint whose whole life was directed to the edification of her fellow humans. Thus, if Huysmans' book has its failings, certain it is that it has brought Lidwine to the whole world and has made her known and revered as a figure of suffering, which is how in any case she principally has meaning. His *Vie de Sainte Lydwine de Schiedam* has had more than thirty editions.

I say nothing of the many smaller biographies, the many translations and editions of her life in French, German, English, and Italian. It would take me too far afield to enlarge on this subject, but the fact that I can mention them shows that devotion to Saint Lidwine has taken on large proportions, and that she can be numbered among the popular saints of the Church. On the occasion of

[7] *De Heilige Lidwina van Schiedam*, 's-Hertogenbosch, 1928.

[8] J.-K. Huysmans, *Sainte Lydwine de Schiedam*, Paris, 1901 (etc.). See the review by J.Manders, S.C.J., *Sancta Liduina*, no. 8, May 15, 1932, pp. 132-135.

her centenary, a richly illustrated monthly appeared for a period of two years, in order to introduce her to the widest possible circles.[9]

But I may not confine myself to referring you to books and periodicals in which you can see and read about Lidwine; I may not even pass over the privilege of writing a single word to characterize and glorify her. I have just referred briefly to the old lives of the saint written by Father Brugman and Thomas a Kempis. An even older life is that by Joannes Gerlachsz, who was her relative and lived with her for years under the same roof. His life was developed and amplified by Father Brugman, and this account was again rewritten and revised in his own charming manner by Thomas a Kempis. The first writer was an eye and ear witness of what he wrote about, while both the others had their information at first hand and clearly attributed the greatest value to reproducing carefully what they had heard. We may say with the Bollandists that there are few saints' lives about whom the information is so reliably transmitted.[10] It is not possible in so short a space to provide a sketch in any way complete of so beautiful and rich a life. I must confine myself to a few random traits which are most prominent and characterize her most sharply. For Lidwine is a very special kind of saint.

She was a lovely, darling little girl in her youth, lively and playful, but at the same time pious and deeply religious. She was a true child of Mary, who loved to spend long hours before the statue of Our Lady of Schiedam and mirrored her own life on Mary's. But she also diligently helped her mother about the house and was a happy companion of her playmates in the city. Soon a young man asked for her hand; she was only fifteen years old, but at that age she had already decided that she would belong to no one but God and not allow her heart to be divided between earthly and heavenly love.

How dear the Lord was to her appears from the heroic prayer in which she offers up her charm and beauty, in order not to tempt any youth. She would rather be deformed and crippled;

---

[9] *Sancta Lidvina: gewyd aan de voorbereiding van het Ve eeuwfeest*, Schiedam, St. Liduina-Comité, 1931-1933.

[10] Jan Brugman, *Vita posterior, Acta Sanctorum*, Aprilis, II, 302-361.

then she would be loved by no one but God, who does not regard externals but only the internal. To be the object of God's love to the exclusion of every other lover was for her an ideal that she valued much more than the physical beauty and charm she had received from God.

This is the first sign of her inclination to suffering, in order through suffering to be the object of God's special love. I emphasize here her longing to be the *object* of God's special love. That is something unique and characteristic in Saint Lidwine's life. Other saints will excel as ardent lovers of the Lord, but in their case their main concern will be to awaken love for God in their hearts, to pour out sighs of love for God, to form thoughts which will cause their hearts to glow, to speak words that give expression to the feelings of the heart – in a word, actively to be the *subject* in the battle of love between God and his beloved. In Lidwine's case, love has a different character. To express it too sharply with too strong a contrast, she did not wish first of all to love but to be loved. She wanted to make herself worthy of the love of God and, conforming herself to the divine Redeemer, like him to be the object of the love of the heavenly Father. To be, not the active subject but the passive object: that is her ideal. This finds expression in this first revelation of her desire for suffering and in the course of her lifetime will often manifest itself again.

II

The remarkable and certainly very heroic prayer of Lidwine that God would remove her physical beauty and loveliness, in order that she would never again be desired by a young man but would be loved by him alone, must have been a sacrifice particularly pleasing to God. Soon, it was quickly and completely answered. God thereby marked her as his bride. From now on she would belong to God alone. God took away her beautiful features. He took away her health and bodily strength. For others an object of pity and horror, she was now exclusively the object of a love which extends beyond material forms and looks to the interior.

A fall on the ice, when in true Dutch fashion she was enjoying herself with her little friends – it was around the feast of Candlemas, the feast of the Presentation of Our Lord in the Temple[11] – was the beginning of thirty-eight years of illness. What sort of illness was it? The breaking of a rib at the fall was followed by a painful swelling, which in turn was the cause of fever, which made her suffer thirst, while the inflamed muscles and nerves caused her pain in all her members. Terrible headache and tooth pain, the fiercest pain imaginable, tortured her, so that she could find no rest in any position. She could not walk, or even remain at rest; hence she crawled about the house, until she was compelled through weariness to remain lying still.

It is true that she was heroic, but her trial was almost too much for her, and she prayed, as Christ had done in the Garden of Olives, that that chalice might be taken away from her. She still wanted to recover. But that was only in the first couple of years. Thereafter, she no longer prayed for healing; she had grown to love suffering and asked for even more. The continual contemplation of the Lord's Passion, which according to medieval devotion she divided into the seven Hours recited by priests and religious, brought her to that desire for conformity with the suffering Savior.

The featherbed was replaced by a straw tick, which was endured only a few years, after which Lidwine took her rest on bare boards. These reminded her best of the wood of the cross of the Lord. Eating became each day more difficult; already in the first years of her illness she could no longer partake of solid food, soon also no other liquids than water; finally, she could no longer manage even a few drops of water. All she could still swallow was the sacred host, and so for nineteen years Jesus' holy body became her only food.

This beneficent influence of the spiritual food of the holy body of the Lord on the condition of the human body into which it is received is by no means a unique instance in the history of the saints of the Church. The canonical hours for the feast of Saint Catherine of Sienna on April 30 relate how this heavenly banquet supported

---

[11] February 2.

her temporal life. And Saint Teresa in her beautiful works expatiates at length on how the living God, who comes to dwell in us in so special a manner, often in the profusion of his love, bestows new life on the body, which on the reception of Holy Communion is instantly freed of its ills. Such was the case with Saint Lidwine. She was one of those persons beloved of the Lord whom he wished to keep alive at first hand by uniting himself so intimately with her that the body underwent the beneficial influence of the strengthening of the soul. How intimate must that union have been!

We, too, sometimes forget that, when delighted by something delicious, food and drink, in the pleasure we spiritually taste we feel no bodily needs for a short while; but the pleasure must be very great indeed, if it is not soon disturbed by our need of food. After a short time, the body again claims its rights and makes itself felt. For Lidwine, all needs were satisfied by Holy Communion in such a way that she not only gave no thought to eating and drinking but was not even able to partake of them. The Lord's body, says Thomas a Kempis, was her medicine and comfort, the food that gave her strength, the rest that refreshed her.

Her great sorrow was that the clergy of the city did not understand her desire for the sacred body of the Lord and, considering her devotion exaggerated, seemed not inclined to bring her Holy Communion often. Sometimes she had to go to great pains to be able to receive Holy Communion. In the beginning of her illness, although she really could no longer walk, she dragged herself to church. With a crutch or kneeler, she managed to get to church at Easter at least to make her Easter duty. Later, there was no question of her being able to do this. She was confined to her bed of pain for good. Thereafter, the priest brought the body of Christ a second time; somewhat later, every two months and on big feasts. Particularly Reverend Andries, who apparently became pastor of Schiedam in 1407, was hard on Lidwine in this matter. She was then twenty-seven years old and ill for eight years. Already the condition had set in that she could nourish herself only with the sacred host and she thus more than ever needed this spiritual food. Especially at first, Master Andries showed himself very unsympathetic toward the mystical invalid. He openly declared that he did not believe in her. He also told Lidwine that he had little faith in those strange things, that he did not trust her, because in any case it was impossible to remain alive without eating and drinking. He did not stop at this. He went so far as to put Lidwine to a test which for her was very painful. It was on the feast of the Nativity of Mary,[12] one of the days when Lidwine was allowed to receive communion at home. When Lidwine asked for this, he immediately agreed to hear her confession and bring Holy Communion. In order to test her, he brought her an unconsecrated host. He thought that Lidwine, thinking she was receiving Holy Communion, would swallow and digest the host as a consecrated one. But it was impossible for her to do this. At the same time, Lidwine saw through the ruse of the priest. She spat out the host, or rather, she was compelled to spit it out; the least nourishment she took caused her to vomit. But the pastor insisted on pretending that he had given her Holy Communion. He became indignant because Lidwine spat out the sacred host so irreverently. But Lidwine said to him, "Sir, do you think I haven't any sense and do not know the difference between the body of the Lord and unconsecrated bread? I can digest the body of the Lord, but I cannot eat ordinary bread without having to vomit it out immediately." The pastor still did not admit defeat. He stood up angrily and did not give her one of the sacred consecrated hosts which he had with him. And he would not bring her Holy Communion any longer and even did not want other priests who distributed "the Lord" to stop off in the cottage of Lidwine. That was a sorry trial for Lidwine. Not only was it hard that the pastor of the parish took such an attitude towards her, would hear nothing of the grace of which she nevertheless was so intimately conscious, but it was even much harder for her to be thus deprived of what was her consolation above all else: partaking of the sacred body of the Lord.

If such occurances may have taken particular forms in Lidwine's life, they occur in the lives of all mystics. At certain times, it is as

[12] September 8.

though everything conspires to place the greatest obstacles in the way of union with Christ. How easy it would have been for one not schooled in suffering to break out in bitter lamentations, to rebel against that servant of the Church, to have reported him; in a word, to consider having every cause to speak of violated rights and to demand administration of the sacraments by a priest. In the matter of physical suffering, Lidwine showed patience, heroic patience in unutterable pain, but to remain patient under the lack of comprehension by the priest, the denial of Holy Communion, the suspicion that what was taking place in her came from the devil – this was something much greater and holier. She would not have become the leader and teacher in the school of patience, if she had not in this case given the most wonderful examples of patience.

But we see it again in so many other lives of saints; I will recall only St. Stanislaus Kostka who, when he was denied access to the table of the Lord in the house of a Protestant brother in Vienna, was privileged to receive Holy Viaticum from the hands of angels. Our Lord did not wish to be kept away from Lidwine. If the priest refused to carry him to the sick, our Lord would find his own way to come to her. Brugman tells us that Lidwine remained three months thus deprived of Holy Communion. It was a long time, but for Lidwine, who nevertheless communicated spiritually and according to her receptivity received great graces, it was a time of heroic practice of virtue, the best preparation to receive ever greater graces. During those three months of patience, she was interiorly made strong by God, strong enough to overcome new difficulties to come. That is how it is in the spiritual life. There is no virtue, says the great St. Teresa, except that which is tried by struggle. Now that Lidwine has been tried in this way, we have respect for her spiritual life that withstood even the heaviest trials. Now we see her grow in virtue and be prepared for new gifts. What humans denied her God himself would give her. He sent an angel to complete his work. An angel appeared at Lidwine's bedside and announced the first of her visions of the passion. She would not see Christ under the form of the sacrament; he himself would come to her in his own way.

III

In compensation for what she had been made to suffer by the pastor, an angel appeared to Lidwine on the Feast of Our Lady's Expectation, which falls on December 19, to gladden her with the news that she would be allowed to see the Redeemer crucified and dead. This sight was meant to help her through all manner of suffering. Instead of feeling herself unfortunate, she would long for even more suffering and vilification. At the same instant, she saw a processional cross at the foot of her bed. The Savior was affixed to this cross in the form of a child. She glimpsed it only briefly, but it filled her with joy and gratitude. When after awhile the cross lifted itself up and, gradually rising, seemed about to disappear from sight, she cried out, as once St. Peter did on the sea of Gennesareth, for a proof that she had not been misled by her senses: "Lord, if it is truly you, leave me a sign." Thereupon, the Child attached to the cross again descended but took the form of a sacred host. On this host, which was a bit larger than the ones usually given to lay persons but smaller than the one consecrated during Mass, the five wounds were discernible. From the wound in the side, blood had run together. A few witnesses saw the sacred host just as Lidwine had. At the request of Lidwine, her brother notified the pastor. Although the latter had already gone to bed – it was about nine o'clock in the evening – he got up and went to see the patient. Although he also plainly saw the host, he refused to believe in a heavenly intervention and called this also the work of the devil. Nevertheless, he succumbed to Lidwine's insistence, and gave it to her to consume. Quite remarkably, this time she did not need to vomit. The pastor was still not convinced, and the following morning brought the blessed sacrament to Lidwine's house, not only to give her Holy Communion but at the same time, as he openly declared, to safeguard her against the deceit of the devil, of which she was a victim. He besought the gathered crowd to pray with him for Lidwine's disenchantment.

It is sometimes thought and written that in the Middle Ages priests and religious immediately gave credence to all sorts of miracles. The attitude of Master Andries shows us that this was not so in Lidwine's case, and that she had to undergo severe testing. But the attitude of Pastor Andries also appeared to the people of Schiedam to be very unreasonable and unfair. They were highly offended by him and openly expressed their disapproval. The discontent ran so high that the matter was brought before the higher ecclesiastical authorities. In this way, the incident was submitted to a thorough investigation.

The auxiliary bishop, Matthias of Utrecht, undertook the investigation on behalf of Bishop Frederick of Blankenheim. Father Brugman sums up the results of this investigation in the words: the bishop praised God for the unutterable love he had shown for Lidwine by this miracle and decreed that the sheet above which the host had hung suspended should thenceforth be used only in the service of the altar. After this investigation and declaration of the bishop, the pastor finally changed his opinion. Thereafter, he brought Lidwine Holy Communion every two weeks. This he did until his death in 1413. His successor also regularly brought her Holy Communion. Hereby, Lidwine's severest suffering was over. For, although her physical suffering rather increased than grew less, she now had her regular consolation, and with all her pain and affliction there was the anticipation of again soon receiving Our Lord, which for her was a reason for resignation and patience, a happy thought that repelled all sensation of pain.

She is pre-eminently the Saint of the Eucharist and, particularly in our times of frequent Communion, an example. She lived in a time when there was no question of daily Communion, especially for someone living in the world. It was already a special privilege for her to receive Holy Communion every two weeks. But what strength she drew from it! It was not only her only food, but its strength revealed itself – more emphatically than in her body, which it miraculously kept alive – in the inexhaustible patience she showed precisely through the strength of this sacred food. There lies the secret of Lidwine's patience. We are used to see her as the patient sufferer and to put this virtue in the foreground in her case. We might ask ourselves whether we should not give more thought to the foundation on which she built up that patience in herself, on her life drawn from Jesus in his Blessed Sacrament, of which she is such a wonderful example. We look up to her as a model of patience in suffering, we are driven to follow her in this respect, even though only from afar. We will attain to this only by uniting ourselves, after her example, most intimately with God, our strength, who descends to us in Holy Communion.

Nourished only by him, she began more and more to resemble him, not only by her patience, humility, and meekness, her exceeding love for people, but also exteriorly, in that there was no longer any soundness in her flesh, no beauty in her features; her whole body was one wound from head to foot. At the occasional changing of the bedding, it was greatly feared that her body would fall apart, so severely was the connecting tissue affected by festering and suppuration. The most skilled physicians appeared at her bed and treated her with devoted care. They had to admit that they were confronted by enigmas. The cure of one complaint caused other new complaints to arise with even more severe suffering, so that after a few years she was known throughout the land as the patient without peer, into whose body, in the expression of Pope Benedict XIV, a whole legion of ills had moved.[13]

But even more than for her patient suffering, she became known for the gifts which God apparently attached to this heroic suffering. After she had sought for years through the contemplation of the sacred passion for the strength continually to purify herself from all stain and at the same time to acquire the virtues which become the bride of such a heavenly Bridegroom, the latter united himself ever more intimately with her and dwelt in her company and caused her to share in his presence with such profound intimacy that she fainted away and remained lying for hours in ecstasy, dead to the world but living with God, who not only granted her the contemplation of his life, passion, and death, but made her

---

[13] *De servorum Dei beatificatione et beatorum canonizatione,*. III, 30, 7:.*"Magnus... morborum exercitus corpus ejus invasit."* Cited by Hubert Meuffels, "Het naderende Jubilé, *Sancta Liduina,* no. 11 (Aug. 15, 1932), 192.

share in the carrying of the cross and in death with him on the cross, only thereafter to lead her back again to the joys of heaven and the sight of the angels and saints. Once she had regained consciousness, she spoke so beautifully about the passion of the Lord, told about God's angels and saints, that people vied with each other to hear her words, which were regarded as tidings from another world to which she was privileged to belong. Certainly, her own imagination played a part in all this, and the images correspond to her development and ideas, but this does not detract from the fact that it is difficult to explain them in a natural way. All sorts of wondrous communications establish and strengthen the impression that in those moments she was privileged to experience the presence of God and was illumined by him in a special way. She became the great Seer of the Passion, and her visions of the Passion, on the one hand, a beautiful reward for her life of sacrifice, were on the other hand again instruments in God's hand for giving her strength, courage, and love to accept new suffering, of which the visions were the harbinger, and to accept those sufferings with joy.

We have seen how, besides physical suffering, she had to undergo misunderstanding. The most painful was that on the part of the pastor of the parish, Master Andries, but others were also sometimes hard on her. We read this, among other things, about one of her sisters-in-law, who treated her with great unkindness. Also known is the incident in her life when four soldiers in the following of Philip the Good, Duke of Burgundy, on a visit to Schiedam – one of them is supposed to have been a physician – requested admittance to her presence and treated her in the rudest and coarsest manner, as if she were the greatest impostor.

Thus, no suffering was spared her. But all suffering was sweet to her because it made her like Jesus; she wanted to be like him in death. She wanted to die abandoned by all. She had been ill thirty-eight years. Her life seemed to be drawn out to make her suffer, until at last the measure of love was full, and God gave her to understand that the end was near. "The rosebush is in full bloom, no bud is still closed," she cried out after a long ecstasy in January of 1433. That was the sign that she was ripe for heaven. During her walks in the garden of heaven with her guardian angel, he already showed her a rosebush, an image of herself. It was already advanced in bloom, but only when all the buds were open, would this be the sign for her that she was ready for the garden of heaven. That was made clear to her in January of 1433, and joy filled her heart, in spite of the even more severe pain that followed this heavenly vision. It was Thursday of Easter week when the end finally came.[14] God arranged that all were away when he came to fetch her and transplant her in his garden.

As a particularly remarkable thing, Father Brugman tells us how death completely changed her features and restored her body, deformed and distorted by illness, to its lost beauty. It was the first sign of her glorification. Miracles which occurred at the invocation of her intercession confirmed it for the devout population. Although Lidwine had already been revered as a saint during her lifetime, now after her death she was regarded even more as the patron saint of the city. She was invoked in every need; at birth, children were already placed under her protection by being given her name; in a word, the pope could truly speak of a cult shown her from immemorial time, when he approved her cult in the Church on these grounds.[15]

---

[14] In 1433, Thursday of Easter week fell on April 16.

[15] Lidwine was canonized by Pope Leo XIII on March 14, 1890. See B. Kruitwagen, O.F.M., "Het proces der heiligverklaring van Sinte Liduina, *Sancta Liduina*, no. 4, Jan. 15, 1932, pp. 55-58; *ibid.*,no. 5, Feb. 15m 1932, pp. 71-73; *ibid.*, no. 7, Apr. 15, 1932, pp. 107110.

Father Brugman[1]

I

The well-known medieval Church historian, Prof. Dr. Willem Moll, not without reason states in his introduction to his two volumes on Joannes Brugman that of all the names that have come down to us from the history of the Church in the Middle Ages none is more generally known than that of Father Brugman. Nevertheless, he adds, this person, who is daily spoken of in all parts of our land by individuals of all stations and stages of culture, nevertheless to most people remains a complete stranger.[2]

It is the particular merit of Prof. Moll that he, a Protestant scholar, has again restored the credit of the Friar Minor Brugman; that, after acquainting himself with the truth about Brugman's life and extant writings, has revised the prejudices which by his own admission he held against this famous popular preacher and has wished to witness to the fact that, as he himself states, this religious deserves a worthy place among those who were a blessing to the Christian Church in these lands and thereby have also contributed largely to making The Netherlands the great influence they had on the fifteenth century, particularly in the area of the spiritual life.[3]

Where and when Brugman was born cannot be ascertained with complete certainty. Although Ubbo Emmius seems to insinuate

---

[1] From *De Gelderlander*, June 18, 25, 1938.

[2] W. Moll, *Johannes Brugman en het godsdienstig leven onzer vaderen in de vijftiende eeuw*, (2 v., Amsterdam, 1854), I, xxi.

[3] See: Frits van Oostrom, *Wereld in woorden*, Geschiedenis van de Nederlandse literatuur 1300-1400, 191-192.

that he considers Brugman a Frisian,[4] more credence is to be given to the many who identify his birthplace with that of Thomas a Kempis, the town of Kempen in the Rhineland, then still belonging to Gelderen and actually Dutch territory. This seems to have been confirmed forty years ago by the discovery of old murals in Kempen, in which Brugman occurs because he was there considered to be a citizen. From this, Brugman is generally said to have been born in Kempen. Some have concluded from the name, Brugman, that his father had been in charge of the bridge, and was thus the bridge-keeper, although this is only a conjecture. It is quite likely that here the proverb is true, that guessing is bound to be wrong.

As the year of his birth we might accept the end of the 14th or the beginning of the 15th century. In 1462, Brugman calls himself an elderly man; in 1470, "a poor old fellow"; and still in 1473, the year he died, "a worn out graybeard," bereft of strength through the years and powerless to sharpen a pen with "trembling hands."[5]

We also know very little about his education. It is to be excluded that he, like Thomas a Kempis and his older brother, who – especially the former – were contemporaries of Brugman, received his first formation in Deventer.

In a letter which as an old man he wrote to the Brothers of the Heer Florenshuis in Deventer, he expresses his sincere regret that he has not had the privilege of being educated in one of their schools. "About three things my soul is sad," he writes, "and about a fourth I cannot weep enough. The first is that I have offended my God and Father; the second, that I have not been reared according in the wholesome rules by which you rear young boys; the third, that in my youth I chose examples for my conduct bad and ungodly companions who had no inclination to religious life.

---

[4] Ubbo Emmius, *Rerum Frisicarum historia*, lib. XXIV, Lugduni Batavorum, apud Ludovicum Elzivirum, 1616, p. 374: "*Vivebat eo saeculo Groningae....*" This phrase may have led Titus to his suspicion.

[5] Moll, *Johannes Brugman*, I, 2.

Finally, the fourth is that, taken up into their midst, I rejected and unfavorably judged the way of life of the Observants and of yours, so adapted to the spiritual life. Oh, had I thought as a boy, when I was a boy, and stood under the discipline of your rod."[6]

In another place he says again, "University studies are most certainly something good, because thus knowledge is acquired, but one will seldom learn virtue there. I wished that the time I spent in Paris was spent in Deventer.""[7]

From this one may conclude that after his earlier studies he went to Paris for higher studies, after that he entered the Order of the Friars Minor. At first, he was on the side of the Conventuals, also known as *Gaudentes*, and had little sympathy for the movement of Stricter Observance then just beginning. Later, he was converted and came to a better insight.

From a sermon preached in Amsterdam in 1462, one may deduce that he had already spent his youth there and had led a rather dissolute life. From his description, one would conclude that this happened before he became a Friar Minor. When he asks himself rhetorically why he came to Amsterdam, he admits that he had been there previously for less noble motives. He speaks of carrying long knives and frequenting houses of ill repute, which seems to refer to the unedifying conduct of young students, who liked to fight and duel and for whom the whorehouses principally existed.

Besides in the sermon already mentioned, Father Brugman has also described his frivolous youth in two poems which with considerable certainty may be attributed to him. The first is the so-called "Soul Hunt" (*Zielejacht*), an image often used in those times. After having said in the first stanza that he has tried throughout his life to be a child of Mary, he sings:

> I have been led astray in this hunt,
> The world has lied to me.
> I greatly esteemed pleasure,
> I have been deluded.

---

[6] Letter of Nov. 6, 1470, cited by Moll, *Johannes Brugman*, I, 205-26.
[7] Reference not found.

I have loved riches and praise
And have chosen idleness.
In hunting I have been thus blinded,
I have lost the way....

I want to stand up—it is more than time—
And seek only him,
The Virgin's Son, who gladdens all things;
Jesus it is whom I love....[8]

This decision to convert is expressed even more strongly in a second poem that has found a wider diffusion and occurs in longer and shorter versions; yes, even in German under another's name. Nevertheless, it is ascribed to Brugman in various manuscripts and thus attributed to him by Prof. Moll. We shall return to these poems on another occasion.[9] In this second poem, known as "Eternity is so long," because of this constantly recurring refrain, Brugman sings:

Goodbye to loving the world,
Goodbye, it is already done;
I have a new use
To make of my senses.

I want to seek adventure,
To walk another path,
Even though it became painful to me.
Ah me, eternity is so long....[10]

II

The place and the year that Brugman joined the Friars Minor are not indicated with certainty. The year 1424 is proposed. Certain it is at least that he spent many years in St. Omer in northern France and there entered the Stricter Observance, which at the time, after

---

[8] Moll, *Johannes Brugman*, II, 212-213.
[9] Titus does not seem to have carried out this plan.
[10] Moll, *Johannes Brugman*, II, 210.

a period of relaxation, was introduced with great strength into the Order of St. Francis, led and inspired by saints such as John of Capistrano and Bernardine of Siena. It is also certain that Brugman was lector in theology at St. Omer. This title indicates that he was entrusted with teaching philosophy or theology and as a consequence was held in high esteem. Only to the best was the formation of the young entrusted. It is quite likely that when a request came from Gouda in 1439 for the introduction of the Stricter Observance there, Brugman was one of the six priests sent from St. Omer. However, this is not quite certain, though it is certain that the impetus for the reform of the convents in the Netherlands came from St. Omer. But if it was not in 1439, then it was soon thereafter that Brugman came to the northern Netherlands from St. Omer. If Wadding calls him one of the founders of the reform, he at least belongs to the workers of the first hour, and it cannot surprise us that, after the province of Cologne acquired its own vicar provincial in 1447, Brugman was called to that office in 1462. Evidently, he was one of the leading figures.[11]

This worked hand in hand with his reputation and fame as a preacher. While we see him active in the promotion of the reform of his Order in these lands, at the same time we see him travelling through town and country to bring the people to a better observance of the faith. He reached as far as Westphalen, where he preached in Münster and Bocholt. Friesland and Groningen were the special areas of his activity. In 1450, he had a large part in the reform of the Franciscan convent in Groningen, where he seems even to have lived four years.

In 1454, he became guardian of the convent in Sluis, but already the following year he is again in Friesland, where he must have spent a rather long time in the convent of Bolsward, which he did not immediately manage to reduce to the Stricter Observance. However, when I say that Brugman seems to have lived a few years in Groningen and Bolsward, this does not in any way

---

[11] Lucas Wadding, O.F.M., *Annales Minorum*, (6 v., Lyon, 1625-1654), t. XII, p. 305.

mean that he regularly stayed there. For one thing, this was contrary to the nature of his calling, which was rather directed to going at stated times from the convent in which he lived to the surrounding cities and towns, in order to preach and hear confessions. Franciscans worked in this manner throughout Groningen and Friesland, although they had only one convent in each of these provinces. Especially Brugman, the famous preacher, will have been journeying often. About this we still have a few details.

Ebbo Emmius relates about Groningenland: "In those days, a man appeared in the land of Groningen, a friar of the Franciscan Order, and scion of the house of Brugman, of an austere and blameless conduct, animated with a burning zeal for the instruction of the people. When he beheld the profound depravity which reigned in every level of society... as though seized by the Spirit of God, he scourged everyone with outspoken words and predicted to the people the wrath of God and coming punishments, foreign wars, and civil disputes; indeed, he predicted so accurately events which happened fifty years later that posterity considered him a prophet."[12]

About Friesland we have the testimony of the historian, Jancko Douwama, who writes in his chronicle: "And there also great peace and harmony came to the land through a holy friar of the Order of St. Francis, named Bruckman. This Bruckman traversed all of Friesland, preaching the word of God."[13] Gaasterland was the special theater of his activity, and he continues to be remembered there as the preacher of peace and harmony in the days of the *Schieringers* and *Vetkoopers*, who managed to bring these fiercely opposed parties to leave off their wrangling. He appeared as an ambassador of God.

In his work about Brugman, Prof. Moll relates yet another noteworthy fact. "When in 1463," he writes, "all of Gaasterland was ablaze with war, and the inhabitants prepared their ruin by

---

[12] *Rerum Frisicarum historia*, lib. XXIV, p. 374; cited by Moll *Johannes Brugman*, p. 165.

[13] Jancko Douwama, *Geschriften*, ed. Friesch Genootschap, Leeuwarden, 1849, pp. 62-63.

the bitterest factions, Brugman, at the time already an old man, betook himself there in haste. After the strife had already cost human lives, he preached various sermons, in which he adjured all to lay down their weapons and make peace. At one of these sermons, he had a child brought forward, whose father had been killed by his fellow citizens. He had already spoken at length about the virtue of forgiving wrongs, but he dared not place his trust in the power of his word over the current of strong feelings. He suddenly asked his listeners whether they dared continue to sin against the will of the God of peace, if a small child might give a sign by its example of how dear in the eye of God is the work of forgiveness and reconciliation. Hardly had he asked them the surprising question, when he spoke to the child already mentioned, 'My little child,' he said, 'if you love peace and will renounce vengeance, when you are grown up, raise your hand.' To the amazement of all, the child raised its hand, and historians relate with no less amazement that from that day on the war came to an end."[14]

Peter Thabor, of the convent of Thabor-bij-Tirns near Sneek, provides a last account. In his *Historie van Friesland*, he says, "In the year of our Lord 1456, there was a very great and hateful war in the Gheesten (Gaasterland). To that war, a Friar Minor named Brugman brought peace, and that peace endured. In other words, a child promised not to wreak vengeance for the death of her father."[15] In his *Friesche Historiën*, Book X, Schotanus repeats the account in detail and adds that the child was only a few months old.[16] Moll, from whom we borrow this, has yet another reference to a tragedy, *Ats Bonninga*, published by Hälmael in Leeuwarden in 1830.[17]

[14] Moll, *Johannes Brugman*, I,175, 193.

[15] Petrus van Thabor, *Historie van Friesland*, in *Archief voor vaderlandsche en inzonderheid Vriese geschiedenis, oudheid en taalkunde* ed. H.W.C.A. Visser and H. Amersfoordt, (3 pts in 1,Leeuwarden, 1824-1828), I, 21.

[16] C. Schotanus, De geschiedenissen, kerckelijk ende wereldlijck, van Friesland, oost en west, Franeker, 1685, cited by Moll, *Johannes Brugman*, I, 176, note 1.

[17] Moll, *Johannes Brugman*, I,176, note 1.

Jancko Douwama of Oldeboorne, mentioned above, relates a similar event. "It happened," he writes, "that Brugman was preaching with great fervor in Stavoren. Among the audience was a man who had stabbed a fellow citizen to death in an argument, but his heart was now pierced with remorse. He fell upon his knees before the woman whose husband he had murdered and asked forgiveness for love of God. The woman looked at him but, overcome with sadness, could utter not a word. God willed it thus. But behold! The woman had in her arms a young child, whom her husband had left behind. All its life it had not yet spoken a word. That child now said with perfect and modest speech in the hearing of all the bystanders, 'I gladly forgive you the death of my father for the will of God.' This miracle is depicted in a scene hanging in the northern side of the North Church (*Noerder Kercke*) in Stavoren."[18]

The church in question no longer exists, the painting has disappeared, but Douwama has caused the memory of it to be preserved as a noteworthy proof of how popular Brugman must have been, in that these stories not only lived on among the people, but were even materially expressed in paintings.

When we picture Brugman to ourselves as the restorer of peace in Frisian territory, we should not imagine that he accomplished this by his eloquence alone, that his activity was a spark of fire lasting a few hours during which he enthused the crowds. In Bolsward, we have proof of how thoroughly he went about the work of making peace; he did not merely manage to quell wrath briefly, but also knew how to remove the causes of differences. In Bolsward, Brugman in 1455 managed to have a broad revision of the municipal laws made, which the administration and citizens were henceforth obliged to follow, a so-called *Stadsboek*, which once composed, approved by Brugman, introduced, and, it seems, was taken as an model by Sneek and perhaps other towns by which to draw up their own *Stadsboeken*. In the city hall of Bolsward, a copy of this *Stadsboek* is still preserved and displayed, beautifully written on parchment with the opening words: "In the name of

[18] Douwama, *Geschriften*, p. 63.

the Father and of the Son and of the Holy Spirit, made upon advice and consent of the Reverend Father John Brugman, aldermen, and counsellors, and by consent of the Thirty-Two, and of the municipality of Bolsward in the year of the Lord 1455."[19] The well-known national archivist of Zwolle, formerly active for so many years in the National Archive of Leeuwarden and especially knowledgeable about the history of Frisia, Dr. M. Schoengen, who also wrote a monograph on the Friars Minor of Bolsward, tells how even today the first municipal law of Bolsward is quoted with distinction and praise by foreign universities, and so the knowledge, insight, and great service of Brugman are broadcast abroad.[20]

We consider a direct result of Brugman's activity in Friesland the founding of a second convent of Friars Minor there, actually in the capitol of the province, in Leeuwarden, in 1457. We can confidently call him its founder. The founding of the convent of Friars Minor in Leeuwarden is described in greater detail in the Franciscan house chronicle of around 1723, published in the *Archief van het aartsbisdom Utrecht*.[21] There the date 1457 is cited, while the Frisian *Papsturkunden* quote the year 1459.[22] The discrepancy, however is easily reconciled, because usually some time elapses between the founding and the papal confirmation. Likewise, the statement in the *Vrije Fries*, that speaks of a date around 1460, can easily be accepted.[23] This source mentions a certain Tjamme Wiarda as founder. Eekhoff gives the year 1472,[24] which perhaps refers to a more definite completion of the foundation, perhaps the blessing or consecration of the chapel. Eekhoff makes of the foundation a double convent. The convent of the Fathers was moved to

[19] Moll, *Johannes Brugman*, I, 170-173.
[20] M. Schoengen, *Monasticon Batavum*; rev. by P.C. Boeren, Amsterdam, 1941-1942, 3 v.
[21] Vol. II, p. 41.
[22] *Friesische Papsturkunden aus dem Vatikanischen Archive zu Rom*; hrsg. Heinrich Reimers, Leeuwarden, 1908, p. 53-54.
[23] Vol. XII, p. 166.
[24] V. Eekhoff, *Geschiedkundige Beschrijving van Leeuwarden*, (2 v., Leeuwarden, 1846-1848), I, 123.

the Tweebaksmarkt in 1498. Both before and after the move, the convent of the Friars Minor was called "Galilea." Eekhoff states that there were still Gaudenten in Leeuwarden in 1474.[25] This term no doubt refers to the Friars Minor, although by that time the name Gaudenten no longer made sense, because the Fathers in Leeuwarden no doubt belonged to the Observants. However, they once had had that name and will have retained it for some time and in some circles. That the convent in Leeuwarden soon became quite extensive can perhaps be deduced from the fact that a provincial chapter was held there in 1475 on July 15.

Although we may agree that Brugman was active especially in Groningen and Friesland during the years 1450-1465, it would be entirely incorrect to restrict his activity to these two provinces. We have ample information that he meanwhile worked in Overijssel, Gelderland, Limburg, North and South Holland, as far as Flanders, Brabant, and Westphalen, and in 1462 his well-known sermon in Amsterdam, of which we have already spoken, took place. Everywhere he was received with the greatest distinction, and invitations were sent to him in the most honorable terms. It would take us too far afield to enter into detail. He is known to have resigned his role of vicar provincial around 1464 and retired to the Observant convent in Nijmegen, there to spend his last years and die. There he still wrote his beautiful, moving letters, more about which in a subsequent article.[26]

---

[25] Ibid., I, 320.
[26] Cf. the articles in De Gelderlander, June 2, 9, 1938, not translated here.

God, a Light in Darkness[1]

I

In our medieval spiritual literature, an aspiratory prayer is known and rather widespread, in which God is praised as a light in darkness. This, however, is only the beginning of the praise, which proceeds in the same tone and praises God in yet many other respects. Besides this aspiratory prayer, however, we also have a further description and commentary on it, preserved in several manuscripts. The author of either the prayer or the commentary is unknown, but the search for the writings of Father Brugman has led us to a trail which may perhaps lead to the conclusion that this beautiful prayer was preserved for us by Father Brugman and that he is also the author of the commentary.

Brugman cites the prayer in the treatise he wrote as a stimulus to meditation on the Passion of Our Lord, *Tractatus valde incitativus exercitiorum Passionis Domini*. Written in Latin, it is preserved in the library of the Benedictine abbey in Einsiedeln, provenant from the library of the monastery of the Canons Regular of Gaesdonck. Although his treatise is written completely in Latin, Brugman reproduces the aspiratory prayer untranslated in Netherlandish, and adds that it was composed by a maiden, whose memory, he thinks, is held in benediction.[2] However, he does not identify her, but in another place he has another bit of information of the same source, about a pious maiden, who, he says, was wholly taken up in the Passion of Our Lord.[3] Quite unconsciously one relates these two sources and

[1] From *De Gelderlander*, Nov. 2, 9, 1940.
[2] *Tractatus*, fol. 172.
[3] *Ibid.*, fol. 164.

thinks at once of St. Luduina, who was an object of special veneration for Brugman, to the extent that he wrote three biographies of
her.[4] Yet, the aspiratory prayer appears in none of these three lives,
nor do his notes, so that we do not have sufficient evidence about
authorship. But, although we therefore cannot ascribe the prayer to
Liduina with a certain probability, it remains that it is handed down
to us by Brugman as the work of a pious maiden.

The aspiratory prayer in its entirety reads as follows:

> Jesus, Son of God, is a light in darkness, he is consolation in sadness,
> he is a master of the schools, he is a true friend of souls, he is a holy
> warrior in temptation, he is a balm in sickness, he is rest in labor,
> he is a spring in thirst, he is a glory on the altar, he is a mirror for
> the eye, he is a melody in the ears, he is a trumpet for calling, he is
> perfume to the smell, he is honey to the taste, he is jubilation in the
> heart, he is truth in the understanding, he is love in the desired one,
> he is joy in depression, he is a guide on the way, he is life in death,
> he is a sure refuge in our need.[5]

In the Staatsbibliothek in Berlin, there is a manuscript which contains the same aspiratory prayer in German.[6] The Netherlandish
version occurs in another manuscript of the same library;[7] this

---

[4] See.Titus Brandsma, O.Carm., "Schreef Pater Brugman wel drie Liduina-
levens?" *De Gelderlander*, June 21 and 28, 1941.

[5] Ihesus Godes zoon is een licht in der duysterheit, hi is een troost in der
droefheit, een meyster in der scolen, hi is een trou vrient der zielen, hi is een vroem
kemp in der bekoringhe, hi is een zalf in der crancheit, hi is een rust in den arbeit,
hi is een fonteyn in den dorst, hi is een glory in den altaer, hi is een spiegel in den
oghen, hi is een melodie in den oren, hi [is] een besoen in het roepen, hi is een
balzaem in 't ruken, hi is een honich in den smaeck, hi is een jubilieringhe in den
herten, hi is een waerheit in der verstantenisse, hi is een minne in der begheerten,
hi is een blijtscap in der verswaertheit, hi is een leitsman in der wegen, hi is een
leven in den doot, hi is een zeker toeverlaet in onser noet.

[6] Ms. Germ. Oct. 328, fol. 153.

[7] Ms. Germ. quarto. 1085, fol. 248. Titus Brandsma Instituut, Brandsma Collectie, Album 9-13. Willem de Vreese, *De handschriften van Jan van Ruusbroec's
werken*, Gent: Siffer, 1900-1902, p. 130-137; Monika Costard, *Spätmittelalterliche
Frauenfrömmigkeit am Niederrhein: Geschichte, Spiritualität und Handschriften der
Schwesternhäuser in Geldern und Sonsbeck*, Tübingen: Mohr Siebeck, 2011.

manuscript is provenant from the monastery Nazareth in Geldern. There are other Netherlandish copies in the Universiteitsbibliotheek in Amsterdam[8] and in the Koninklijke Bibliotheek in Den Haag.[9] In these manuscripts, the aspiratory prayer is followed by a paraphrase, or explanation, and it is worthy of note that in the Netherlandish version in Berlin, the paraphrase, characterized as "*een schoon devote collatie,*" (a beautiful, devout collation) immediately follows the sermon about "*een geesteliken wagen met vier raderen*" (a spiritual wagon with four wheels). The sermon, as well as the collation, is there listed as anonymous, but from other manuscripts we know the sermon to be Brugman's.

The Amsterdam manuscript is provenant from the monastery of "*de Susteren der 3der oerden toe Hoesden* (the Sisters of the Third Order in Hoesden); that of Den Haag, from "*dat besloten convent sinte ursulen te Delf*" (the cloistered monastery of the Ursulines in Delft). The copy in the manuscript of Den Haag is dated 1452, a date which certainly is contemporary, while the Amsterdam manuscript places the text in the first half of the 14th century. This is rather early for a Brugman manuscript: Brugman died in 1473, but recently to my surprise I discovered that Brugman's second life of St. Liduina, dated by the Bollandists before 1448, was already copied by a Carthusian of Trier in 1440. This copy is still preserved in the Stadtbibliothek in Trier. A photocopy of it, as well as of the aspiratory prayer and paraphrase in the abovementioned manuscripts, with the exception of the Amsterdam manuscript, are preserved in the Instituut voor de Geschiedenis der Nederlandsche Mystiek in the Catholic University of Nijmegen[10] and in the Carmelite convent in the same city.[11]

If the aspiratory prayer itself is noteworthy for the beautiful metaphors with which God, or specifically Christ, is praised, the

---

[8] Ms. 520, I.G.10 b, fol. 37v.

[9] Ms. 624, 132 F 17, fol. 182v.

[10] Titus Brandsma Instituut, Brandsma Collectie, Album 125-129.

[11] The convent was destroyed in World War II, but the photo is now in the library of the Carmelite Historical Institute in Boxmeer.

explanation amplifies the metaphors and expands them, so that from this point of view it also deserves attention, since its metaphors are perhaps also a means of identifying the author with greater certainty. Because these metaphors may be an incentive to others to find the author, we reproduce them here in their entirety.

First, we want to point out that a few small variants naturally occur in the individual manuscripts. The most striking are that in The Hague and the Netherlandish Berlin manuscripts, in place of "a good friend in the soul," God is called "a good word in the soul" while in both Berlin manuscripts, as well as that of The Hague, in place of "a glory on the altar" one reads "*een gelove*" (faith), and in the same connection the Netherlandish Berlin manuscript in place of "altar" has "*twijfel*" (doubt). However, the explanation, "a good word in the soul" is again rewritten as "a good friend," while faith in the Bl. Sacrament of the altar seems to find support in the figure of a mirror which is shattered in pieces, while a person is reflected in each piece, though he is but one person. This radiation can be understood as a glory of the Blessed Sacrament and thereon be applied to faith. A scribal error of "glory" for "gelove" is, of course, also possible, but the Einsiedeln manuscript has the word "glory" written very clearly.

> First of all, then, God is a light in darkness. If in beholding the things of the world, I dwell in darkness on account of the limited light of my understanding, then God is to me a lantern which enlightens my understanding and reveals how the devil as an enemy waylays me, how the world seduces me with its fraudulent beauty, how sick and weak I am, and finally how kind and merciful God is on our behalf.

> God is a consolation, or a consoler in sadness. In temptation, he strengthens me so that I am not misled. If I am dejected, he gives me courage and patience. If I am laden with care and in need, he forestalls my succumbing. When I have severe suffering to bear, he points to the merit I will earn by it; this is so great that no mortal can picture it, no mouth can utter it, nor ear hear it, nor heart conceive it.

God is a master of the schools. I am stupid and unknowing, but when I see the life of my master, Our Lord, from the moment he entered this world to the moment of departure, I hear such good words from his mouth that I must hold him to be a good master, especially when he lovingly instructs me from the cross, where with his blessed blood he wrote letters on the parchment of his virgin body.

He is a friend with good words for the soul. I feel that he comes into my heart like a father who desires to give his child imperishable riches; like a friend, or lover, who prepares a feast and a dwelling for his beloved; like a bridegroom who won his bride at the cost of much suffering and sacrifice of much that was dear to him, who now wishes to make her his forever. Therefore, I unlock my heart and soul to him, for Jesus is for the soul a word so full of sweetness that she can never understand it.

II

God is a warrior for me in temptation, because, when the devil assails me with temptation to pride, he makes me strong with his humility. When the world assails me with desire of money and goods, he makes me strong with his poverty. When the flesh assails me with its evil desires, he makes me strong with his sacred Passion. In this way, neither the devil, nor the world, nor the flesh can separate me from my Lord and my God.

In several manuscripts, a passage is inserted here about God as a recreation or pastime in our life. This aspiratory prayer is omitted by Brugman in the Einsiedeln manuscript. We present it here according to the other manuscripts:

God is a recreation or pastime in our life, because he is beautiful to behold. It is sweet to enjoy his presence, while his great mercy makes me glad to have him near me; his great beauty never wearies me of enjoying the sight of him.

God is a physician when I am ill. The most precious balm that was ever made was the balm my Lord and God made on the cross from his body and blood. Whatever pain I feel in my soul, as soon as I have anointed myself with this noble balm, I am cured.

God is rest from labor. When I have wearied myself with fasting and vigils, with prayer and exercises of contrition, then I hie me to my beloved Lord and lay myself in his arms, which he spread so wide for me on the cross. Then I press my unworthy lips on his, which he lovingly presented to me to be kissed, while he opened his side in order to let me rest therein. When I thus comfortably rest in the arms of my beloved Lord, I forget all the suffering that can possibly be my lot.

God is meat when I am hungry. When I am hungry, I hasten to my beloved Lord who is the very best food that can ever enter my soul. For he is that living bread of heaven that is sweet to see, sweet to taste, sweet to smell, sweet to know, sweet to love, sweetest, finally, to partake of.[12]

God is drink when I am thirsty. When I am thirsty, I hasten to that noble wine, of which my Lord and God on Good Friday for love of me opened a vat in seven taverns or festive halls in his sacred body: two in his sacred hands; two in his sacred feet; one in his side, opened with a spear; one in his back, scourged with rods; one in his sacred head, pierced by thorns. To whichever of these I go, I find noble wine in all of them, so abundant and so sweet that I drink so much of it, yea, more than my senses or faculties can understand or bear.

God is a staff on my way. For if I cannot travel some roads because they are too steep, or too inclined, or too long, or unpaved, then I take my beloved Lord as a staff. He levels steep roads with his humility; he fills in downward inclined roads with his generous riches; he shortens distant, lengthy roads with his sweet inspirations; he makes unpaved roads even and soft with his sacred Passion.

He is the light of faith on the altar. If doubt sometimes arises in me with regard to the faith, then I hasten to my beloved Lord and ask him whether he can really be present as God and man under the species of bread, and discover that it is possible for him, just as he can be born God and man from the body of a virgin. If I doubt whether he can be present in all places at the same time, then I take a mirror and break it into many pieces. I see myself at the same time in all those pieces, and yet I am only a single person.

---

[12] Not in the prayer cited above.

God is a mirror for the eye. The most beautiful mirror ever made is the divine face of the Lord. One who has looked at it once is able to behold all things therein. When I feel that I shall be able to see in that wonderful mirror all that my heart desires, then, truly, it is for me the severest pain that I am still held so far away from it.

God is honey in the mouth. If I but hear the sweet name of my beloved Lord Jesus which contains such sweetness, then there is no honey so sweet for my mouth as this sweet name of Jesus, my Savior.

God is a perfume to the smell. The most fragrant perfume ever to be poured out on earth was that spilled on Good Friday from the body of my beloved Lord, when his noble soul was parted from his body. He was a joy to the angels. He destroyed the might of the devil and freed the prisoners from Hell.

God is a melody to the ear. From the cross, he sang the sweetest song ever heard, when he uttered those seven words from the cross. The first was that he prayed for those who were crucifying him. He sang so loud that the stones were rent. The dead arose, the sun no longer allowed its rays to shine. And he was heard by the Father because he deserved it, because that sweet nightingale sang himself to death.

In the Berlin manuscript in German, the text ends; in the other manuscripts the elucidation of the aspiratory prayer continues. From the last lines, we see that the explanation somewhat alters the sequence of the sentences of the prayer. In the Brugman quotation, after "He is a mirror in the eyes," comes "he is a melody in the ears, he is a trumpet for calling, he is perfume to the smell, he is honey to the taste"; while the explanation, after "He is a mirror in the eyes," has: "He is honey in the mouth.... he is perfume to the smell, he is a melody in the ears." The sentence, "He is a trumpet for calling," is omitted. We opted for the sequence of the manuscripts. To continue:

God is jubilation in the heart. When my beloved Lord comes into my heart, he comes with such sweetness that, through the bliss which my soul enjoys in his presence, I am totally transformed; and through the great happiness he gives me, I no longer feel anything else than the will and life of my beloved Lord.

While "he is truth in the understanding" is omitted, the explanation continues:

> God is the object of love for my will. In him I find everything I would possibly love. I love him with his heavenly Father for his obedience, with his holy mother for his humility, with the patriarchs for his truth, with the angels for his wisdom, with the apostles for his patience, with the confessors for his justice, with the martyrs for his strength, with the virgins for his beauty, with the poor for his generosity, with the sinners for his mercy, with the just for his sweetness.
>
> God is joy in depression. His presence is a delight. When I consider that I may possess him as entirely as I want, that I may enjoy his presence, then he is the greatest joy my soul can ever imagine.
>
> God is life in death, because when I think of the life which is my beloved Lord himself, and that I may live forever, then I long for nothing other than the death I shall sometime have to die, and for nothing other than the life I may live forever with my beloved Lord.
>
> God is a refuge in every need. He is truly the one to whom I may fly in every need, and shall fly as well as from need, as by right, as from love"; or as the Middle Netherlandish so aptly formulates it: "*van node, van rechte, ende van mynnen*" (from need, by right, and from love).

Francis Vervoort, O.F.M.[1]

I

The Desert of the Lord

A few weeks ago we spoke about Sister Mary of Saint Joseph. Descended of the noble family of Roon, she entered the Carmel of 's-Hertogenbosch in 1629, but the same year, at the capture of the city by Frederick Henry,[2] took refuge in Cologne, where she was received in the Order of Carmel. Later she transferred again on the occasion of new foundations; first, to Düsseldorf; later to Münstereifel, where she died in the odor of sanctity on March 31, 1676.[3]

At the time, we wrote that we did not know where the body of the Reverend Sister was now to be found, after the suppression of the old monastery of Münstereifel.[4] We made mention of a request for further information sent to Münstereifel, to which there was no reply.[5] Meanwhile, we heard from the Reverend Deacon of Münstereifel that the former Carmelite monastery had later come into the hands of the Ursulines of St. Savior, who had brought the venerable relics with them to Roermond during the Kulturkamp. There they are still reverently preserved by the Ursulines in the

[1] From *De Gelderlander*, March 9, 16, 23, 1940.

[2] J.D.M Cornelissen, "Het beleg van 's-Hertogenbosch in 1629," *Mededelingen van het Nederlandsch Historisch Instituut te Rome*, 9 (1929), 111-148.

[3] "Een Carmelites uit het huis van Roon in het Rijnland in de 17de eeuw: Zr. Maria van Sint Jozef," *De Gelderlander*, Jan. 13, 20, 27, 1940.

[4] The Discalced nunnery of Münstereifel, founded in 1659, was suppressed by Napoleon in 1802; Ambrosius a S. Teresia, O.C.D., *Monasticon carmelitanum*, in *Analecta Ordinis Carmelitarum Discalceatorum*, 23 (1951), 363.

[5] "Een Carmelites," *De Gelderlander*, Jan. 27, 1940.

Zwartebroekstraat. The bones are contained in a shrine. And so we had looked too far away for what was close at hand.

In the sketch of the life of Sister Mary of St. Joseph, we referred to four small spiritual books which had formed the nourishment of her soul: *De Navolging van Christus* (The Imitation of Christ), *Het Bondelkijn van Mirre* (The Little Bundle of Myrrh), *De geestelijke Wijnpersse* (The Spiritual Winepress), and *De Woestijne des Heeren* (The Desert of the Lord). We promised to return later to this reading-matter. The weeks of Lent, now at hand, provide the occasion to take a closer look at the last named book, *The Desert of the Lord*.

The little book, first published in 1551, is one of the most widely circulated spiritual books in the 16th and 17th centuries.[6] For that reason alone it is worthy of our attention. In one century it was reprinted ten times.

Like the other two books just referred to with *The Imitation of Christ*, *The Desert of the Lord* is an ardent meditation on the Passion of the Lord. It is not a continuous account, but a rendition in great detail of the principal facts of the Passion, interspersed with expressions of ardent feelings and reflections.

Although the name of the author is not provided in any of the nine editions, nevertheless he is not unknown to us. It is the best-known work of the prolific Franciscan author, Francis Vervoort, who died in the convent of Mechelen on November 24, 1555. He is the author of about forty spiritual works, of which twenty were published and preserved for us in one or more editions. Vervoort is the most important representative of Franciscan spirituality in the 16th century, together with the less deserving Mathias Weynsen, author of among other works, *The Little Bundle of Myrrh*, which we noted among Sister Mary's books. In their writings, Vervoort and Weynsen are the worthy successors of the famous figures of the last half of the 15th century, Henry Herp, Dirk Coelde, and

---

[6] *Die woestijne des Heeren, leerende hoe een goet kersten mensche Christum, dlicht der waerheyt, sal navolghen in dese duyster woestijne des bedroefder werelts in allen duechden der volmaectheyt*, Antwerpen, Hans van Liesveldt, 1551.

John Brugman. In our parts, they are the faithful followers of St. Bonaventure and have contributed greatly to this mystical writer's retaining such great influence here. Against the more speculative school, still influenced by Eckhart and Tauler, Francis Vervoort, more than the other Franciscans mentioned above, is the man of the affective tendency. Especially in his description of and meditation on the Passion of the Lord, he is ever set on providing as graphic as possible a presentation and combining with it the most ardent effusions.

This is also a strong point with Brugman, but it seems to me that he is surpassed in this by Vervoort, I would not want to say, always to Brugman's disadvantage. In the case of Vervoort's descriptions, one cannot avoid the impression that, led by devotion and empathy, he allows too free a rein to his imagination, and that here a more intellectual meditation would have counseled a bit of restraint without doing damage. Pious exaggeration has its uses, but one must apply it with caution, because it easily weakens the the impression of the whole which it is trying to strengthen. This is the case, here and there, with Vervoort. Brugman, who certainly betrays a strong inclination to picturing reality and thus attempts to draw a vivid description, is more moderate in this respect, so that his realism is to be considered healthier, indeed, is more real.

To be sure, the passion of Christ was appalling, beyond all describing.[7] We can hardly form an idea of how cruelly people treated each other in the Roman punitive system; of how full of shadow, indeed, how black this side of Roman civilization is. The

---

[7] Bl. Titus himself had had experience in describing the Passion in his meditations on the Stations of the Cross by the Flemish expressionist painter, Albert Servaes: "De Kruisweg van Albert Servaes," *Opgang*, 1 (1921), 129-145. See also Hubertus Hechtermans, S.M.M., "Albertus Servaes en Titus Brandsma: zij gingen hun eigen kruisweg," *Middelares en Koningin*, 53 (1986), 286-272; Adrianus Staring, O.Carm., "Titus Brandsma (1881-1942) and the Mysticism of the Passion," *Carmelus*, 28 (1981), 213-225. Titus Brandsma & Albert Servaes, *Ecce Homo, Schouwen van de Weg van Liefde / Contemplating the Way of Love*, ed. Jos Huls, Leuven 2003.

reality of death by crucifixion and all it involved is atrocious enough without being made even more horrible through exaggerated description. In the description of the visions of Anna Catherina Emmerich, one has a rich source for imagining this stark and terrible reality.[8]

Devotion is not exclusively nourished by such realistic descriptions; not all who meditate need them to be roused to sympathy and love, to sorrow and penitence. There are those who are sooner moved by the humiliation offered to the Son of God, the indignity and ingratitude shown him than by other considerations. But the startling reality of the Passion is already to be found in the Gospels. Although they are relatively sparing in their information, they relate enough horrible details to cause one to be struck to the depths of the soul. Picturing to oneself the Passion in all its horror is by no means to be disapproved of. It is a source, given and indicated by God himself, of the most exquisite feelings, and we can imagine that, considering the rich variety of temperaments, some people feel themselves particularly attracted and receptive to the graphic representation of the Passion of Christ. And so it is again a richness for spiritual literature that such expression and delineation are not lacking. Meanwhile, here, too, the proper measure is to be maintained. Although we admit that some portrayals of the Sacred Passion by Father Francis Vervoort have a strong dramatic effect and we may rate their literary value quite high; in others, to my mind, he goes definitely too far and so is led too much by effect and feeling rather than by intellectual

---

[8] Bl. Titus took a keen, if cautious, interest in contemporary mystical phenomena, especially those of Konnersreuth, which excited great interest in the Catholic world at the time, and to which he dedicated several studies: "Teresia van Konnersreuth en Lidwina van Schiedam," *Jaarboek van de St. Radboudstichting*, Nijmegen, 1931, p. 52-56; "Teresia Neumann van Konnersreuth: waarde der verschijnselen," *Het Schild*, 13 (1931), 5-17, 49-58; "Wondteekenen en lijdensvisioenen: van Konnersreuth naar Hohemark," *De Maasbode*, May 6, June2 and 23, July 7 and 21, 1935. See also Bl. Titus' articles in the *Katholieke Enciclopedie* (Amsterdam, 1933-1938): "Neumann, Teresia, 1898-, XVIII, 494-495; "Wondteekenen (stigmata)," XXIV, 334-336.

reflection. Meanwhile, this should not prevent lovers of the Passion from making use of his gripping and fervently felt meditations, in order to nourish their devotion.

As an example of an emotional description which goes too far, I point to the description of the crowning with thorns. After describing the crown and the crowning, the meditation continues: "There they struck his sacred head with reeds so cruelly and mercilessly that the thorns pierced his temples on all sides into his sacred brain, so that the points of the thorns on both sides reached one another."[9]

Well-known and fervent is also the devotion to the shoulder wound, which Our Lord received in carrying his cross, through the chafing and pressing of the heavy beam of the cross on his already wounded shoulders. But here, too, Vervoort exaggerates in a well-meaning, but to my mind, not commendable manner. He writes:

> And one side of the cross, with the slipping and shaking of the cross, chafed loose a great piece of his blesssed shoulder which lay on his arm and grievously hung there, so that one could easily see the little bones of his neck exposed.[10]

Is not the crucifixion dreadful enough, without it being necessary to add the description that the limbs were stretched to meet the holes which were bored much too far forward, so that the body was extended much worse than on a wrack, and one might insert one's finger between the joints, and the veins and nerves were entirely torn apart?

After the right hand is nailed to the cross, the opening for the left hand is bored a quarter too far; that for the feet is a foot too low. A rope is first tied to the left arm, then to both feet, so that the bored holes can be used. To be sure, there is a relationship with reverential visions here, there is much that is beautiful and

[9] Prosper Verheyden, *Passsietooneelen uit Frans Vervoort's Die Woestijn des Heeren (1551)*, Antwerpen, De Sikkel, 1924,, p. 98.
[10] *Ibid.*, p. 118.

gripping, but I would like to know, do not such descriptions, which cannot be held free of exaggeration, rather injure than help one's impression?

Although we thus did not intend to overlook the shortcomings of Francis Vervoort's meditation on the Passion, this does not detract from the fact that on the whole the meditation is of no little value, not only for awakening devotion, but also for the art which it reflects and because of which it continues to inspire.

II

Although the description of the Passion in *The Desert of the Lord*, by Francis Vervoort, may here and there be somewhat exaggerated, and the author may thereby have given way too readily to the pious compassion which filled his heart and which he wished to awaken in others; on the other hand, it must be admitted that on the whole he manages to depict and envision the Sacred Passion, not only with great fervor but also with admirable descriptive powers.

This is all the more important because the generally brief scenes of the Passion are designed as a starting-point and fulcrum for the feelings of love and compassion they are to arouse. For this reason, the pictures had to be vivid, in order that spirit might find material in those images addressed to the senses for its reflection and effusions.

The Desert of the Lord is a method of meditation on the Passion, in order thus gradually to arrive at the most fervent love and always to keep the image of God before the eyes.

The title is suggested by what Sacred Scripture relates about the holy prophet Elijah, who, while fleeing from the wrath of Jezebel, lay down in the wilderness under a bush, but was awakened by an angel with the words, "Thou hast yet a long way to go: *Grandis tibi restat via*". By virtue of the food pointed out to him by the angel – a cake baked on hot stones – Elijah walked forty days and forty nights, until he came to the holy mountain of God, Horeb, where he received the privilege of beholding God's nearness.

In like manner, the spiritual food of meditation on the Lord's Passion – the cake baked on hot stones is an image of the suffering and dying Christ and through it of Holy Communion – must bring us in forty days, to the holy mount, in order there to behold God's glory.

Father Francis Vervoort is by no means satisfied with limiting himself to the account of the Passion; it performs no subordinate role but is always the starting-point for the ascent to God. So the little book is truly a lyric work, replete with the most profound meditations and reflections, under this aspect a model of meditations on the Passion, which, closely connected to the account of the Passion, cause it to conduce to fitting expressions of love and devotion.

The vivid picture is striking, but the reader is much more carried along by what the pictured scene of the Passion suggests in the way of feeling. This is indeed a powerful example of the interplay between sensory imagination and intellectual reflection, a fine example of the concerted action of the various human faculties, in order to achieve fruitful reflection on the Sacred Passion.

"Thou hast yet a long way to go." With these words each of the forty days begins anew. There is so much to learn in each Passion scene that it is a long way for one to go before one absorbs the lesson and puts it into practice. But each time the reader is enticed by the prospect of the reward for those who walk this way; by the benefit and blessing there is in mirroring himself each time in the suffering Jesus and with him to climb the mount where our eternal good is achieved.

Vervoort is no doubt thinking of his father, St. Francis, when he says that "some obtained such abundant relish and feelings of love that they became inebriated with the fruitfulness of the cross, and were often enraptured in spirit; yea, were visibly marked in their bodies with the wounds of Jesus, and during their lifetime received many graces and gifts, and within a short time arrived at the perfection of virtue" (Prologue).

Prosper Verheyden, who has dedicated a special study to Francis Vervoort and published an anthology from *The Desert of the*

Lord, acknowledges in his extensive introduction to the rather brief anthology, "Reflection on the Passion is thus a means to the ascent to God, to the mystical life."[11]

As a matter of fact, in the beginning of the little book, the title is explained as, "The Desert of the Lord, which teaches how a Christian shall daily exercise himself in the Passion and bitter suffering of the Blessed Jesus and to be his bridegroom above all else, according to the word of the Apostle, through mutual feeling and compassion for him who out of love desired to taste death on the cross for his bride."[12]

There follows: "The First Day's Journey into the Wilderness. This day's journey teaches you how life is proclaimed to us on the cross and how we are delivered from death. And how the life of man is nothing else than a day's journey unto death. And how we shall prepare ourselves for eternal life according to the word of the Apostle, 'For we have not here a lasting city, but we seek one that is to come.'"[13]

In the second "day's journey," the soul ponders the Incarnation of the Son of God; in the third, the institution of the Blessed Sacrament of the Altar; in the fourth, Jesus betakes himself with his apostles to the Garden of Olives, while the fifth interrupts the just begun account of the Passion with the reflection that in Jesus the oil of God's mercy is poured over us, and that his name is like oil poured out. The sixth "day's journey" then meditates on the prayer in the Garden of Olives; the seventh, the capture of Jesus and his consignment to Annas: the Strong One is bound, eternal Wisdom is mocked. Then the narrative is again interrupted, and in the eighth "day's journey," the thought is proposed that, though born blind, we gain sight by washing ourselves in the sacred blood of the Lord. The ninth and tenth again proceed from a given scene in the Passion: the ninth, from the mistreatment of Jesus in the

---

[11] *Passsietooneelen uit Frans Vervoort's Die Woestijn des Heeren (1551)*, Antwerpen, De Sikkel, 1924, p. 9.
[12] *Ibid.*
[13] Heb 13,14.

palace of Annas; the tenth, from Jesus' painful way through the
streets of Jerusalem; after which, the eleventh is then a reflection
on the inadequacy of our protestation of love and profession of
faith, when not accompanied by the practice of the virtues Jesus
teaches us. The twelfth tells of Jesus' examination and mistreatment by Caiphas; the thirteenth, of the dragging back and forth
of Jesus from Caiphas to Pilate, from Pilate to Herod, and from
the latter back to Pilate again. This is an image of Jesus' chase after
our souls. The fourteenth treats the following of Christ as pledge
of our happiness and eternal blessedness. The fifteenth "day's journey" leads us to Jesus at the pillar of the scourging: the noble grape
of Cyprus is pressed and gives us the noblest wine, which must
foster virginity in us. The sixteenth is a call to remember the love
of Christ. In the seventeenth, the crowning with thorns follows;
in the eighteenth, the "Ecce homo." In the nineteenth, Pilate
washes his hands of guilt: May we understand that we are guilty
and oppose our compassion to Pilate's indiference.

After the meditation in the twentieth journey on the way Jesus
carries his cross, there is again in the twenty-first a meditation
which is related to the sacred Passion, but not with a specific
scene, and instead shows that it is our duty to take up our cross
daily.

In the twenty-second journey, Jesus is stripped of his garments;
in the following ones, slaked with gall and vinegar, cast down on
the cross, and then first his hands, then his feet nailed to it. In the
twenty-seventh and twenty-eighth day's journey, the cross is raised
up before us, so that we might behold it and never lose sight of it.
In the twenty-ninth, we hear with the good murderer that we will
enjoy the fruit of his Passion together with Jesus in paradise. The
thirtieth tells us that it is out of love that God hangs there before
our eyes; the following one rouses us to love him in return.

In the thirty-second day's journey, we see Jesus on the cross, an
object of mockery and scorn; we are given solace and sweetness.

The thirty-third makes an example of Jesus' silence. The thirty-
fourth then ponders the touching manner of Jesus' death: Life dies
in order that we who are dead might live. The following day's

journey is dedicated to the thought that there on the cross our salvation was won. In the thirty-sixth, one of the most beautiful of all, Jesus' Sacred Heart is pierced and his body laid in Mary's lap. The thirty-seventh is again an intermediate meditation on how all depends on an edifying death, while the thirty-eighth meditates on Jesus' burial. The last but one presents the thought that Jesus only briefly withdraws himself from our sight, in order in the last day's journey to announce that he summons us to eternal life, to the union with him which we must make the only object of our existence.

Thus, meditation on the Passion is the ascent to God, the way through the wilderness to the Holy Mount, in order to learn to see God in everything that happens to us.

III

Sermon on the Resurrection of Christ

Father Vervoort concludes his *The Desert of the Lord* with its forty "day's journeys" with a *Sermon on the Resurrection of Christ*.

After we briefly considered during Lent this widely circulated meditation book on the Passion of Our Lord, which we may call the principal work of the mystic Franciscan, we intend also to dedicate the vigil of Easter to a brief consideration of this Easter sermon as a continuation of the previous articles.

The sermon begins with a beautiful meditation on the love of Mary Magdalen, who set out early to the Holy Sepulcher of the Lord, finding no rest and driven by her desire to show her Beloved every honor of which she was capable, with fragrant balm and perfumes.

It is an image of the love which should inspire us, of the desire which should consume us to be near Jesus and in the early morning hasten us to the place where Jesus' sacred body is buried.

Nothing could restrain Magdalen, neither the shame which Jesus had undergone and which must recoil on her who yet wished to show Jesus honor and love, nor the cruel might of sentries and soldiers who would surely deter her. Her love was rather increased by the effort to draw near to Jesus. She defied all obstacles.

The one difficulty she could not overcome was the heavy stone which made the tomb inaccessible to her, but it seemed that she had not anticipated the problem, and it was only when she drew near tomb that she asked herself, "Who shall roll us back the stone, that we may approach him?"[14] But this difficulty had already been removed by Jesus himself, who knew that Mary's love would bring her to him, in order that, when she entered the open tomb, she would see and hear that he was risen. An angel in the guise of a young man clothed in white came to meet her with the words that he well knew she was seeking Jesus, but that Jesus was risen, as he had foretold.

Thus, he whom she sought with all the fervor of her love was not there. When he was on the cross, she could still embrace his feet and moisten them with her tears. Having come here to anoint and embalm him, she found only that the tomb was empty. He is not here, the angel said. This word made a deeper impression than the glad tidings that he was risen. She sought and did not find him. She was entirely deprived of the object of her love. Where could she find him? The angel mentioned Galilee, where his disciples would see him again. Would the Lord then abandon her, and no longer allow her to see him? She envied the apostles and at the same time wept at her loneliness.

She had so ardently longed to see him again, and now he was withdrawn from her sight. She could not believe it, and the thought occurred to her that she had been misled, and that the body of her Jesus had been removed and perhaps laid in another place. When she had wept over her sins, she had obtained their forgiveness; when she had wept over Lazarus, she had been gladdened at his resurrection to life; now weeping over Jesus' departure and her abandonment, she deserved to have Jesus come to her in

---

[14] Cf. Mk, 16,3. The English Vulgate reads, "Who shall roll us back the stone from the door of the sepulchre?" In Mark, Mary Magdalen is accompanied by Mary, the mother of James, and Salome.

the form of a gardener. That is the way Jesus rewards the love and longing of those who seek him with their whole heart and cannot live without him.

Jesus asks her why she is weeping. Now her love finds full expression: "They have taken away my Lord, and I know not where they have laid him."[15] This is the frank acknowledgment that she seeks Jesus and cannot find him, and now her feeling of abandonment causes her to weep. We also would weep – should weep – if we do not know that Jesus is near, if he is hidden from our eyes. We should know no rest until we have found him for whom our heart longs. If Jesus' absence leaves us cold, if we feel no grief, do not weep when we do not possess him, where then is our love?

But how can Jesus ask Magdalen why she is crying; he who yet had said of her that much had been forgiven her, because she had loved much. Thus, he was aware of her great love. And that love – nothing but that love – was the cause of her tears, now that she did not find her Beloved. How can the beloved Jesus, who had sought out the Samaritan woman, who had told Mary Magdalen that she had chosen the better part which would not be taken from her, now that she lay at his feet, deprive her of the joy of seeing him again? Proverbs reads: "Who loves me, him shall I in my turn love, and who seek me early in the morning shall find me."[16]

She desires to find him; she desires to take him away with her and possess him. I will take him away, she tells the gardener.[17] If he is not buried here in your garden, if he has not been allowed to remain in the tomb his friends have given him, "I will take him away" and be rich in his possession. Had she been with him at his capture in the garden, at his mockery and condemnation to death on the cross, at his scourging and crowning with thorns, she would have uttered the same words and in fact would have tried to carry them out. She would have taken him away out of their midst.

---

[15] Jn 20, 13.

[16] Prov 8, 17. The English Vulgate reads, "I love them that love me; and they that in the morning early watch for me, shall find me."

[17] Cf. Jn 20, 15.

She would have defied death. Her love was stronger than death. Love makes strong the weak of the world. While the apostles remain away, she, a helpless woman, goes to the tomb surrounded by sentinels. She would not have denied the Lord, as Peter did; she would not have left her cloak in the hands of soldiers;[18] she would have testified to her love, as she did beneath the cross.

Such great love did not remain unrewarded. A single word is enough to change her sorrow into the greatest happiness and to fill with the sweetest satisfaction her lonely and abandoned heart. With the bride in the Song of Solomon she could sing that her soul was melted as wax, because the Beloved had spoken.[19] The single word, "Maria,"[20] which contained the assurance that he knew her and by pronouncing that name recalled to her memory every circumstance in which he had already revealed his love, now also unveiled to her the mystery of his resurrection and told her that he was alive – alive for her – and that he still loved her more than many others to whom he did not appear, to whose eyes he remained hidden.

And so, in the single word which Magdalen thereupon spoke, there lay a stream of emotions which must have risen in her heart at the startling revelation of the resurrection. Her single word, "Master," expressed most beautifully what first and foremost inspired her at this blessed moment, and should inspire us on this joyous feast of Easter, now that with Magdalen we see the risen Lord and hear him also address loving words to us.

But in Mary's word, beside joyous surprise, there is a ring of wonder that he had allowed her to seek and wait, that he could have so hidden himself from her. But he is the Master, he is the Lord, we do not understand his wisdom and his ways, but we

---

[18] Mk 14, 51-52. "And a certain young man followed him, having a linen cloth cast about his naked body; and they laid hold on him. But he, casting off the linen cloth, fled from them naked."

[19] Song 5, 6. Latin Vulgate: "Anima mea liquefacta est, ut locutus est." The English Vulgate: "My soul melted when he spoke." The Revised Standard Version: "My soul failed me when he spoke."

[20] Cf. Jn 20, 16.

submit to his judgment, we conform to his teachings. Mary again casts herself at his feet in order to embrace them, as she had once done in the house of the Pharisee, Simon, as she had again done at the foot of the cross, and now wished to do a third time, in order to anoint them again with the precious perfumes which she had brought with her. But now Jesus fended her off, because, according to St. John Chrysostom, he who had received her anointing on his mortal body now stood before her in his risen human nature, more as God than man; as victor over death, he no longer needed her anointing.[21]

She is called to a more exalted and noble work: "Go to my brothers to bring them the glad tidings that I am risen and ascend to the Father, my Father and your Father, my God and your God."[22] She is called to announce to the apostles the crowning of the work of redemption, and thus forms a beautiful contrast with the woman in the garden of paradise, who, in the words of St. Gregory,[23] brought guilt and punishment upon the world, while here in the garden, Mary Magdalen receives the mandate to announce that the guilty human race is acquitted of sin and is granted complete satisfaction for its guilt. From the garden, the glad tidings now go out with Mary over the whole world that death is conquered, that eternal happiness is again acquired, and that we are again adopted by God as his children.

"For this, we want to praise the Lord forever," thus Father Vervoort ends his book, "who has snatched us from eternal death. In this life, we seek him with all earnestness and ardent longing, as our Mary Magdalen has taught us.... seeking him with the balm of good works, so that with David we may in all truth say, "As a hunted hart thirsts for the waters of fountains, so, O Lord, my soul yearns for you. When will I come...."[24]

---

[21] Reference not found.

[22] Cf. Jn 20, 17.

[23] Reference not found.

[24] Ps 42, 2; 41, 1. English Vulgate: "As the hart panteth after the fountains of water, so my soul panteth after thee, O God.... 3.... When shall I come...."

The Spiritual Life of St. Peter Canisius[1]

The singer in the Psalms sees the inner greatness of the king's daughter as the basis of her glory.[2] Now that we are come together to praise him whom we may in a broad sense call a child of a king, so beloved was he of the great King and so in turn filled with love for him, we may take a moment to search out the profoundest reason for his fame.

One of Canisius' last eulogizers, looking for signs of holiness in that life so completely filled with external works, comes to the conclusion that the secret lies in his interior life.

However, this explanation does not completely satisfy me. For him, this is the answer to the question of how Canisius, besides all he achieved, found time and means to become a saint, a great saint.

I realize the danger that lies in such a busy life as Canisius led. I recall the words, full of fear, of St. Paul, that after having preached to others he might himself become a castaway,[3] but to avoid all misunderstanding, I would like at once to make a sharp distinction between considering Canisius' holiness in spite of his activity in the world and his holiness in and through his activity, in order to lay the emphasis on the latter viewpoint. We may look upon it as providential that in his day Canisius was destined to rise to a holy and mystically graced life, which revealed itself in the most extensive activity, but also that he is canonized and thus once again appears among us at this time, when a movement has arisen

---

[1] *A discourse held before the Senate of the Catholic University of Nijmegen at the unveiling of the statue of St. Peter Canisius, June 8, 1927.*

[2] "All the glory of the king's daughter is within." Ps. 44, 14 (the Douay Rheims English version of the Vulgate which Titus would have used).

[3] 1 Cor 9, 27.

to bring the mystical life into conflict with activity on behalf of the Lord. The same fallacy lies at the root of the idea that Canisius, and with him often the whole Society of Jesus, are the enemy of that glory of Catholic life called mysticism. When one recalls Canisius' edition of Tauler at the very time he casts himself before Blessed Peter Faber to become a Jesuit, one might see in his "conversion" an aversion to mysticism. Is it not, as if reading Ruusbroec, one came across Van Otterloo,[4] for whom mysticism is an important and influential phase in the development of a devout life, but nevertheless a standpoint that must be overcome? By all means give glory to Canisius, the man, but at the same time remember the words of God, that we can do nothing without him and everything, if he gives us strength.[5] If anyone, it is Canisius who is the man of divine Providence; for the Church, a light in dark times. In his appearance, we see the promise again fulfilled that Christ is with his Church to the end of time.[6] God is so clearly evident in the background of Canisius that we do not see him in his complete greatness, if we do not see him in his most intimate union with God. We must see him at the side of God.

He himself thought he saw the finger of God in his birth on the feast of the Appearance of St. Michael.[7] The image of this fighter for God's greater glory was dear to Canisius, representing a more exalted companion with whom, as the angel guardian of the German people, he wished to become the apostle of that nation. But he did not forget that this archangel was one of those whom another archangel told Tobit that they stand together before the face of God.[8] Compared to his interior activity, Canisius' exterior work, like that of the angel, was hardly to be called more than an appearance, beautiful though it was, behind which the contemplation of

---

[4] Antonie Adriaan van Otterloo, *Johannes Ruysbroek: een bijdrage tot de kennis van den ontwikkelingsgang der mystiek*, Amsterdam, 1874; 2nd ed., 1896.
[5] Jn 15, 5; Phil 4, 13.
[6] Mt 28, 20.
[7] *Werken van Petrus Canisius. Uitgegeven bij gelegenheid van zijn heiligverklaring*, Tilburg, 1925, p. 6.
[8] Tb 12,15.

God and union with his love were only hidden for one who did not see beyond to its profoundest depths.

More clearly, Canisius says himself that God's guidance was to be seen, his voice to be heard, when here [in Nijmegen] in the beautiful but scandalously neglected church of St. Stephen and later in that of St. Gereon in Cologne he prayed for light in his choice of a state of life.[9] When at the same time he was attracted to pious performances, to attending and imitating church ceremonies, then, he says, wise persons must see therein the wondrous guidance of Providence. He recognizes then the guidance of the guardian angel. He feels that he cannot preserve purity without God's special grace, but strengthened by divine inspiration, trusting in his dearly beloved mother Mary, at once his help and example, he does not hesitate, while still a boy, to take a vow of perpetual chastity.

Canisius considered his life's course to be signed by God, and even shortly before his death, he revealed that already in his youth a devout widow from Arnhem and also a pious young woman of Brabant foretold his later calling and activity to be in God's name. "I call God to witness," he added, "that I am not making anything up but simply giving witness to the truth."[10] But in particular he sees God's guidance in his departure for Cologne and his acceptance there by a group of friends who smoothed the way to his calling. First among them is the priest from Brabant, Nicholas van Esch, whom he calls another father.[11] From him he received his first spiritual formation. He not only went to confession to him but every day revealed to him the faults he had committed that day. His life was regulated in the smallest detail. Daily meditation, regular mortification, but especially constant examination of conscience with Van Esch's *Exercitia* prepared him then to later follow the *Exercises* of St. Ignatius. He applied himself diligently to the study of an introductory course in law, "Yet," he says, "I felt myself

---

[9] *Werken*, p. 9
[10] *Ibid.*, p. 21.
[11] See the chapter on Nicholas van Esch above.

more drawn to mystical theology and the study of the spiritual life."[12] "I did not yet know," he later wrote in an outpouring to God, "whither your Spirit wished to bear me, as to a safe harbor."[13] At the same time, he acknowledges that God gave him a favorable wind in the journey to the harbor, that in other words the training school in Cologne was regarded by him as the finest preparation for his later calling. "Often I felt myself drawn by my love for quiet and contemplation to the life of the Carthusians."[14] He is filled with admiration for this life, which he does not wish to see condemned, although not everyone is called to it. "Although we, who are all too dandified warriors"-so he refers to himself – "cannot or will not live that strict life, far be from us all envy or foolish criticism."[15] How beautifully then does he pour out his heart over his weakness, over the help he received from God, which finally led to the complete abandonment of himself into the hands of God!

By that surrender to God, that union with him, Canisius hoped to be admitted to the ranks of those who fear God, keep his commandments, and glorify and help glorify his name. Those whom God calls to the contemplative life may beseech the divine majesty on behalf of one who feels himself too weak to lead such a life and repeat the doxology, Holy, Holy, Holy.[16] Here we already find the deep consciousness of the communion of saints, in which God stamps one as a teacher, another as a prophet, but holds all united in one mystical society. Let us not become obsessed with a contrast which is basically a whole: to know, love, and serve God. Cologne, not Mainz, was Canisius' Damascus of divine enlightenment. Nicholas van Esch was his Ananias.[17] Van Esch also did not feel himself called to the Carthusian way of life, although he was their close friend and had a cell in their monastery, where he often shared their life.

[12] *Werken*, p. 22.
[13] *Ibid.*
[14] *Ibid.*
[15] *Ibid.*, p. 23.
[16] *Ibid.*, p. 31.
[17] Acts 9, 1-19.

The monks there were broad-minded enough to see both Van Esch and Canisius go their separate ways without feeling that the bonds of the closest friendship had been broken. How enthusiastically does Canisius in later letters describe his life in the Society without thinking of contrariety or experiencing the slightest lessening of respect for that focus of mystical life and of the dissemination of mystical works!

It was there, nevertheless, that Canisius was taught the doctrine of Tauler. There he began his edition of Tauler, of which a general of the Order will later say that it did not suit the spirit of the Society. Did Canisius go astray here after all, at least as regards the harmonious development of his spiritual life?

To be sure, Tauler was much loved by the Carthusians of Cologne. The monastery was the center of veneration of him. But the Protestant reformers also reverenced Tauler. In 1516, Luther issued the first, and in 1518 the second, complete edition of a manuscript to which he gave the name *Deutsche Theologie*.[18]

It belongs to the German mystical school in a somewhat vague sense of the term. In addition, the manuscript edited by Luther, or Luther's edition itself, lacks parts, which, though not extensive, regard man's own activity and are important for the proper understanding of the manuscript. Published by Luther himself and spread among his circle, it came to be- – in itself quite understandable – taken in a Protestant sense. The little book Luther made pass for the best condenser of the sermons of Tauler. It was not long before editions of Tauler appeared, revised in that spirit. What Canisius did with Tauler in his youth is quite in line with his later activity: to place the authentic Tauler over against an incorrectly edited one. And not only he but his whole environment felt the need for a trustworthy edition of Tauler. After Canisius had provided the German edition, there appeared, five years later, the Latin edition based on it by the Carthusian Surius, to which the prior, Gerard Kalckbrenner, upon the authority of Nicholas van Esch added an observation

---

[18] *Eyn Deutsch Theologia*, Wittenburg, apud Joannem Grünenberg, 1518.

on the desirability of a translation into Low German and the dialect of Brabant.[19] This, notwithstanding the fact that there already existed quite a few Low German translations in all sorts of dialects. In his research Prof. de Vooys discovered that there are many more than one would think.[20] Dolch describes ten translations still extant in The Netherlands and twenty-two abroad,[21] and recently Dr. de Man discovered another in the Universiteitsbibliotheek in Amsterdam.[22] Many of them are notably older than 1548, the year in which Kalckbrenner expressed his wish. They will not have been entirely unknown to him. This is an indication that for The Netherlands also there was need for a new, unadulterated translation, in which ambiguity would not give rise to abuse.

Especially noteworthy, incidently, is the fact that we have a letter of the same Prior Kalckbrenner, written shortly after Peter Canisius entered the Society of Jesus in Mainz. It is addressed to the prior of the Carthusians in Trier, whom he enthusiastically informs of the *Spiritual Exercises* of St. Ignatius,[23] as these are presented in Mainz by Bl. Peter Faber. He sees no contradiction; on the contrary, he describes them as a higher development in the practice of the spiritual life, a perfecting of the *exercitia*, so far followed; as something fine and fruitful, though by this he did not mean that the old forms should be neglected. Five years later, he

---

[19] Johannes Tauler, *Tam de tempore quam de sanctis conciones plane piissimae caeteraque... opera omnia*; nunc primum ex Germanico idiomate in Latinum transfusa sermonem a Laurentio Surio, cartusiano. Coloniae, Ioannes Quentel, 1548. Epistola nuncupatoria Gerardi ab Hamont [Kalckbrenner], pp. III-VIII.

[20] C.G.N. de Vooys, *Meister Eckhart en de Nederlandse mystiek*, 's-Gravenhage, 1904.

[21] Walter Dolch, Die Verbreitung oberländischer Mystikerwerke im Niederländischen auf Grund des Handschriften dargestellt, Weida i. Th., 1909.

[22] Dirk de Man, "Een onbekende middelnederlandsche vertaling van Johann Tauler's preeken," *Nederlandsche Archief voor Kerkgeschiedenis*, 20 (1927), 1-8.

[23] Exercitia spiritualia sancti Ignatii de Loyola et eorum directoria, in Monumenta Ignatiana, series secunda, Madrid, 1919. For Kalckbrenner's letter see Joseph Greven/Wilhelm Neuss, Die Kölner Kartause und die Anfänge der Katholischen Reform in Deutschland, Münster, 1935, p. 96.

was still urging the dissemination and translation of Tauler.[24] This letter of the prior shows with what a happy feeling the environment of Canisius at Cologne accepted the *Spiritual Exercises*, and to what extent Canisius was prepared for them. This is confirmed by his guide in those exercises, Bl. Peter Faber, of whom St. Ignatius said that no one had more deeply penetrated their spirit and knew how to share it with others.[25] The first of the exercises passed so quietly: Canisius had already traversed the way of purification. Also, Peter Faber ascribes this to that preparation. He calls it a usual phenomenon in the case of those who have long practised prayer.[26]

It is worthy of remark that Canisius' Tauler edition finally appeared a few days after he was admitted to the Society. After having made the *Spiritual Exercises*, he was admitted on May 8, 1543. The presentation of the book is dated June 3.[27] The book itself appeared a day later. It has been suggested that it would perhaps be preferable not to call the Tauler edition the first book published by the Jesuits, because this would be true only according to the letter, not according to the spirit. Canisius apparently thought otherwise, because what would have been simpler than to date the book, which in any case would have been ready before his entrance, from that time? It must have meant a good deal to him to sign it as a Jesuit. And Peter Faber must have been aware of it. Yet he did not express the wish or require Canisius to close his life before his entry with that edition, in order to make a new start in the Society. He must have expressly allowed the young novice to occupy himself intensely

---

[24] Piissimae tam de tempore quam de sanctis homiliae operaque eiusdem alia… interprete Laurentio Surio, Coloniae, ex officina haeredum Ioannis Quentel, 1553. Gerardus ab Hamont, Epistola nuncupatoria.

[25] Otto Brausberger, Het leven van den zaligen Petrus Canisius, Bussum, 1918, p. 12.

[26] Idem.

[27] Des erleuchten D. Johannis Tauleri, von eym waren Evangelischen leben, goetliche Predig. Leren, Epistolen, Cantilenen, Prophetien, Keulen, 1543. See also B. Kruitwagen, "De zalige Petrus Canisius en de mystiek van Johannes Tauler," Studiën, 95 (1921), 347-362. On Canisius' profession, see his own witness, Werken, p. 31.

with the works of Tauler, for it is not an indifferent matter for a young man of twenty-two to put the finishing touches on a work of 700 pages, see to the printing of it, and write an introduction. In the facts around Canisius' edition of Tauler we see an indication of great reverence for the works of Tauler on the part of the promotor of and authority on the *Spiritual Exercises*. Let it not be said, therefore, that the Society of Jesus had no use for medieval mysticism, but rather that they confined themselves to the need of giving the preference to the *Spiritual Exercises*, a preference which also a Kalckbrenner was inclined to allot. The Jesuits were opposed only to a one-sided idea and erroneous understanding of Tauler's work, to an exaggeration of its value compared to the *Spiritual Exercises*. This appears from the judgement pronounced in 1578 by a visitator of the Order on the spiritual trend followed by Father Alvarez, S.J., confessor and director of St. Teresa. Her method of prayer was of itself approved, but it might be taught and disseminated only if the *Exercises* were not underrated as a result.[28]

Meanwhile, it may not remain unnoticed that nevertheless the general of the Order, Father Everard Mercurian around 1578 forbade the reading in general of Tauler by members of the Society and even was unwilling that his works were available to all. Permission to use them was confined to the provincials. Tauler's writings were ranked among those of emphatically spiritual writers, which were indeed edifying but less fitted to the spirit of the institute.[29] A great many reasons have been adduced to explain this prohibition. I prefer the explanation the Spanish Cardinal de Quiroga wrote concerning his rather sweeping ban on spiritual books which had been imported, translated, or circulated, consciously or unconsciously in support of a trend which had only the appearance of true mysticism. "It should be borne in mind," he says among other

---

[28] Exact source not found, but see Cándido de Dalmases, "Santa Teresa y los Jesuitas; precisando fechas y datos," *Archivum Historicum Societatis Iesu*, 35 (1966), 347-378.

[29] Epistolae praepositorum generalium ad patres et fratres Societatis Iesu, Romae, 1615, pp. 228-229.

things, "that if books appear on this list by persons of high Christian ideas... this does not mean that they have strayed from the Holy Roman Church or from what she has always taught and still teaches... but it can mean among other things that they contain matters which learned and devout writers all in good faith and according to their intention have said in a good and Catholic sense, but in these evil times are seized upon by the enemies of the faith in order to distort them in favor of their reprehensible teaching."[30] The latter case is especially Tauler's. Not the Jesuits, but the *alumbrados* of Spain and the Lutherans of Germany brought it about that Tauler was pushed, had to be pushed, into the background, because according to the reformed mentality his teaching became the nearest occasion for fatal misunderstanding. Also, De Quiroga was speaking for an individual instance of danger. With Wilhelm Oehl, I think I may say that the ban on Tauler in the Society was a transitory happening, determined by the changing trends in the spiritual life.[31] It is of note that the revival of respect for Tauler's mysticism was most strongly promoted by the Spanish mystics, particularly St. Teresa and St. John of the Cross. Their lucid teaching caused Tauler again to be understood in the proper sense, removed ambiguity. However, the mysticism of Tauler was spread about in Spain especially through Surius' Latin translation, which like almost all later editions of Tauler was founded on the work of Canisius. Thus, Teresa completed what Canisius began.

Thus, too, Canisius was a pioneer in mystical theology. His daring attempt may not have been crowned with immediate success. He had to live a long time to see the seed he planted in the garden of the Church sprout forth as a beautiful flower, one of the most beautiful that the Church has produced. Yet one should not make it appear as if the Society smuggled away the Tauler edition of Canisius. For how is it then that in 1556 the strict Inquisitor, Melchor

[30] "Cardinal Gaspar Quiroga in his introduction to the Index of 1583," in H. Reusch, *Der Index der verbotenen Bücher*, Tübingen, 1886, I, 490-498.
[31] Wilhelm Oehl, *Tauler*, in Auswahl und hrsg. von W. Oehl, Kempten, 1919. Not available for consultation.

Cano, reproached the Company that they had settled themselves in the school of Tauler,[32] that, for instance, at Dillingen, the house in fact where the young Jesuits were formed and educated, a year before the decree of Father Mercurian, Tauler was publicly read in the refectory?[33] This points in an entirely different direction. A passing ban on a few mystical works points to the fact that the highly developed knowledge of God, deepened by continual contemplation, together with the love flowing forth therefrom, threatened to make the temptation too strong for some members of the Society to sit down with Mary at the feet of the Lord, while a proper understanding of love should have convinced them to leave God for God and at the voice of the Lord to become Martha. Canisius must have struggled all his life with that temptation. Had he not penetrated so deeply into the nature of mysticism, had he not in his great love surrendered himself into the hands of God as his servant, as his slave, we would be tempted to say, in order to express it as strongly as possible, that Canisius would never have become for us what he was.

In the mysticism of Tauler he sees, not the quiet of the Quietists, nor the worthlessness of our actions in the manner of Luther; for him, Tauler is a mystic who requires deeds, works in keeping with the will of God, performed under the eyes of the Master, who must always be present to us in our inmost heart, where he dwells and works, listens to us, and speaks to us. Mystical grace will only follow, if we place ourselves entirely in the hands of God, do — really do — what he asks of us. This was Canisius' understanding. This idea was ingrained even deeper in him by the *Spiritual Exercises* under the guidance of Peter Faber.

If at first he had felt weak against the temptation I mentioned, now he was clearly conscious of his vocation. "I can hardly describe," he writes to a friend, "what a powerful influence the *Spiritual Exercises* have had on my soul as well as on my body. I

---

[32] F. Caballero, *Melchor Cano*, Madrid, 1871, p. 500.

[33] Monumenta Historica Societatis Iesu, Litterae Quadrimestres, III, Madrid, 1896, p. 344.

felt how my soul became enlightened by rays of heavenly grace, how new energy flowed through it. It seemed to me as if the fullness of divine gifts also poured over my body, steeled my whole being, as if I had become a different, a new being."[34]
He would acquire an even greater master in the person of St. Ignatius himself. Late in 1547, Canisius, after having performed a good deal of work in Germany, was to participate in the Council of Trent at the request of Ignatius in Rome. He could not forego revealing his happiness to his beloved Carthusians in Cologne. "Every day," he writes, "I meditate on spiritual matters. I try ever to penetrate more deeply the spirit of our Order. In that, Master Ignatius, our superior, shows himself a guide of the richest experience."[35] "If I could only describe my happiness to you," he writes to another friend, "I can associate with so many outstanding confreres, with our reverend superior, Ignatius. Never have I made such progress as now."[36]
The result was that on being asked whether he was willing to go to Messina and fill any office whatsoever, he replied that he was ready for anything, willing to go anywhere in the world, be a teacher or a cook, a gardener or a porter. He was ready to leave in a moment.[37]
God called him to Germany, where he was to become professor and even rector of a University, or rather all things to all men, an apostle of Germany. In St. Peter's, God revealed this to him. As an escort he gave him St. Michael. "You opened to me," he gratefully addresses God, "your most sacred Heart and invited me to draw the waters of salvation from that source.... And I presumed to approach your sacred Heart and slake my thirst therein. Then you promised to clothe me with peace, love, and steadfastness."[38]

---

[34] *Beati Petri Canisii epistolae et acta I*, ed. Otto Braunsberger, Friburgi Brisgoviae, 1896, p. 77.
[35] Braunsberger, *Leven*, p. 25.
[36] Idem.
[37] *Canisii epistolae*, ed. Braunsberger, p. 263.
[38] *Werken*, p. 33-34.

That is, therefore, the clothing with which God clothed Canisius: love, which expresses itself in deeds, deeds, deeds, besides the peace of interiority, of self-conquest; rest in God on the one hand and on the other steadfastness not to be broken by any weariness nor discouraged by any opposition.

We shall not follow him on his long journey. When we regard his soul, we see in every movement of his life a stillness whereby he does indeed ask for work, always new work, but indifferent to which it may be, as long as God requires it. And God made use of him in keeping with his temperament. He accomplished God's work. During that whole life, the finger of God leads.

Canisius knows it, he is clearly aware of it, he often expresses it. He constantly prays and asks for prayer that he will preserve that union with God. He is so penetrated by this conviction that he always sees God at his side, speaks with him, disputes with him as his immediate principal. He is on familiar terms with God in the most trusting way. God is his companion wherever he goes. He can only work with God; he trusts him. In him, he can do all things. No, without an eye to his union with God, Canisius' life is an unsolvable puzzle, already from a purely psychological viewpoint, more so from a purely natural point of view, if we want to know its full worth and meaning.

Although we shall not follow the apostle of Germany along the winding path of his apostolate, we may not omit casting a glance at the years at the end of his life, when he seems to be separated from his life's work. For, strange as it may seem, the strength, the significance of Canisius stands out most wonderfully in those days of his weakness, in the years when he diminished in importance.

His last seventeen years he spent far from German territory in Swiss Fribourg. Oh, he performed incalculably much good there, he became a blessing to the city, a father beloved and revered, the city's fame and glory. But what was Fribourg compared to all of Austria and Germany which his wide heart embraced in measureless love.

Canisius' life has been conceived as a pyramid lacking the top, because Providence, obedience, old age, and bodily weakness had not permitted him to complete the works he had begun. But the top is not lacking. The top is clearly discernable to one who knows how to penetrate the mists of faith. There Canisius is found praying. He had always prayed much. He had prayed so much that the question has been asked how it was possible that anyone who prayed as much as Canisius did still found time for an active life.

But here in Fribourg he is taken up for hours and hours in prayer, a solid three hours in the morning and another three in the afternoon, more often longer, a great deal longer. Here Canisius prays as he had always wanted to pray but could not, might not. Here we see his love of prayer. That is something one doesn't begin to get in old age. Old age reveals how Canisius' whole life was supported by prayer. But here he also accepts from God's hand that he no longer permits him to work. He still considers himself the apostle of Germany by offering himself up entirely for its sake.

He understands that he can only be an apostle if he conforms himself ever more closely to his divine master, Christ. At the end of a retreat, which he made at seventy-three years of age, he ends his good resolutions, which he had committed to paper, resolving that he would require of himself a very particular zeal in the practice of virtue and also would continually look up at Christ. For more than one reason, these retreat resolutions of the aged Canisius are worthy of note. He resolves[39] not to be so forward in speech, to refrain from judging others, to regard others as his betters, to overcome his pride, gluttony – and he was so moderate – and spiritual sloth, to moderate the desire to study and concentrate more on keeping trusting company with God, to make progress in self-mortification and zeal for souls, not lightly to rebuke anyone, to close an eye to the faults of others, rather to see the beam in his own eye, often to meditate on pure love of neighbor, to exert himself to dispose his heart to devotion.

Canisius resolves to become ever more like Christ, whom he already so closely resembled. A few months before his death, he still wrote, "Only to Jesus, our savior and redeemer, will I direct

[39] *Werken*, p. 47.

my thoughts."[40] Could he resemble him more than when he saw himself in no state for anything, powerless, as he writes, to do anyone a service of love, unemployed even, as he says, in excessive humility, a barren branch of the vine to which he likens the Society; and when he accepts that powerlessness from the hand of God in order to resemble Christ who died on the cross? A barren branch! Never was he more fruitful. We may safely regard those last years as the most fruitful of his life. The heroism shown then and clearly placed before our eyes reveals to us what a hero he was in the days of his strength; show that, with the diminution of strength of body, the strength of the soul remains constant. In the prospect of his merits, God must have included in the fruits of his wondrous apostolate his prayers and offering of self at the end of his life. Without sacrifice no apostle. The greater the apostle the harder the sacrifice. To the great apostle of South America, St. Peter Claver it was revealed that his work had been blessed with such rich fruit due to the prayers and good works of a holy confrere in Spain, St. Rodríguez. We would not be speaking in the spirit of Canisius if we did not take into account the thousands in whose company he lived; but among the many, his own figure stands in the foremost ranks of those who have prayed and made sacrifices for Germany. We may not leave out of consideration the great and beautiful mystery of the communion of saints, but even more so the heroic sacrifice of Canisius, which brought him closest to God and was the foundation of the blessing God bestowed on that country. Without that sacrifice, without those last years, the figure of Canisius, mystically speaking, would be like a truncated column. Now it is complete.

To have ended his life in that way may seem sad to the world. It is another proof of Canisius' election, of mystical conformity with Jesus. May Canisius remain the well-understood glory of the Society, great above all through his interior life.

[40] *Ibid.*, p. 49.

Jan Pelgrim Pullen (1550-1608)[1]

I

A remarkable example of a holy priest, living at the time the Church in the Netherlands is considered to be in general decadence, Jan Pelgrim Pullen was born in the middle of the 16th century, in 1550, and died in 1608. His parents lived in Stralen, near Geldern, but he was born in Vlodrop, where his mother temporarily resided. Where he made his studies is not clear, probably in Cologne. He was ordained a priest while still quite young and soon was reputed a priest of particular holiness, from whose features purity and holiness shone, and who excelled in self-mastery and modesty. As a young priest, he came to live in Roermond, where he enjoyed the particular friendship of Bishop Lindanus.[2] In fact, he long resided in the house of the bishop, until the latter, around 1583, named him pastor or rector of the beguines of Roermond, among whom there were many women of great perfection; of particular note, a certain Gerardina van Biechden, or Beegden. He enjoyed the confidence of the bishop to the extent that the latter, during his journey to Rome from the end of 1584 to the end of 1585, practically left him in charge of the diocese. It would appear that, shortly after the bishop's return, Pelgrim settled in Cologne, in order to flee the bustle of the world and to live a life of greater prayer and contemplation in the circle of the Cologne Carthusians. Lindanus, how-

---

[1] From *De Gelderlander*, Sept. 17, 24; Oct. 1, 1938.
[2] Cf. Wilhelm Schmetz, Wilhelm van der Lindt (Wilhelmus Lindanus), erster Bischof von Roermond (1525-1588): ein Beitrag zur Kirchengeschichte des Niederrheins und der Niederlande im 16. Jahrhundert, Muenster in Westfalen, Aschendorff, 1926 (Reformationsgeschichtliche Studien und Texte, 49)

ever, could ill afford to lose him and strongly urged him to return
to Roermond. There he again resided with the bishop, who took
him for his spiritual director. When Lindanus was transferred to
Ghent in 1588, Pullen followed him. Lindanus soon died after
three months. Pelgrim Pullen, now freed again, returned to Roermond, but the crowd that attended his confessional drove him once
more to Cologne. When a few of his spiritual children settled there,
to avail themselves of his spiritual direction, and many others joined
them, he again fled the bustle of people and went to Lier, but there
did not find the atmosphere corresponding to his spiritual expecta-
tions. From Lier, he went to 's-Hertogenbosch and remained there
until his holy death, henceforth resigned to being for many the
greatly revered director in the spiritual life.

In spite of the most attractive offers, he took up residence with
the beguines. He lived in the simplest possible manner. He never
imposed himself as a director or master. All his letters begin with
the statement that he was writing at the request of another person.
He never allowed himself to become involved in an argument. If
the conversation threatened to lead to it, he immediately agreed
with his opponent or kept silent. His lodgings were designedly
poor, but he made a point of keeping them neat and tidy. He
spent hours in prayer, the reading of mystical works, and contemplation. During Mass especially, he hardly managed to suppress
the raptures his spirit experienced. Erycius Putaneus, Eerijck, or
Honorius van den Born tells us that then often his feet no longer
touched the ground.[3] In eating and drinking he was most moderate. Meat he never ate; fish, seldom. He was satisfied with some
greens as a side-dish. Mostly, he ate bread, sometimes so old it was
mouldy. He had only one cassock, made of the meanest material.
At night, he did not remove it; yet, for the sake of tidiness, he
made a point of duly changing his underwear. At night, he slept
on a few planks or in his chair.

---

[3] In his letter about Pullen, written to Josephus Geldolphus a Ryckel and
printed in Ryckel's *Vita S. Beggae*, Lovanii, 1631, p. 475. This phenomenon was
also testified to by others; see Ryckel, *Vita S. Beggae*, pp. 651-657.

He had a wonderful gift of fathoming the character of the persons who came to him with their difficulties. His spirit often seemed to be supernaturally enlightened, and his biographers explicitly credit him with the gift of prophecy, as well as with more than one miraculous cure. But, above all, the more spiritually knowledgeable persons wondered at the gift he had of speaking about the loftiest subjects in the most detached manner, as though he had them all clearly before his eyes. Those who most enjoyed his direction and teaching were, of course, the beguines. Among them was also Gerardina van Biechden, or Beegden, whom he had already directed earlier in Roermond. She had followed him to Ghent, and when he left there, at his advice, had come to 's-Hertogenbosch, because of the sound spiritual ambience to be found there. This sound spirit probably later attracted him also. It was at the request of the beguines, and also of several other persons, that he here probably wrote most of the little spiritual books, which make him known as a mystical writer of more than ordinary moment.

It is a pity that it is so difficult to find the writings of so competent a hand. Recently, a few of his works have been recovered, but of a greater number we know little more than the title or an indication of their contents. Father Reypens published a tentative bibliography of the works attributed to Pelgrim Pullen, based on current Belgian bibliographies, but especially on two manuscripts in the Koninklijke Bibliotheek in Brussels and another in the Universiteitsbibliotheek in Ghent.[4] Pullen's works number about thirty, of which seven are found in the three libraries just mentioned; the rest, of which the title and contents are known, have until now been searched for in vain. Where are they? Walter Driessens, better known as Valerius Andreas, writes, "He wrote many works, which have remained in the possession of devout persons

---

[4] "Pelgrim Pullen (1550-1608); een heilig mystiek leider en zijn onuitgegeven geschriften," *Ons Geestelijk Erf,* III (1929), 22-44, 125-143, 245-277. On the manuscripts (Brussels, Koninklijke Bibliotheek, ms. 2957 and ms. 4920-4921; Ghent, Bibliotheek der Rijksuniversiteit, ms. 1335), esp. 129-140.

living in 's-Hertogenbosch, and are held in high regard."[5] Perhaps, they will yet make their appearance in one or other hiding-place.[6] Certain it is, that some of them were not only preserved in Pullen's handwriting, but were copied more than once. Father Lucius Verschure pointed out to Father Reypens yet another manuscript in Warmond.[7]

To the works discovered and described by Fathers Reypens and Verschure I can add another, a manuscript preserved in the Carmelite convent in Boxmeer.[8] It has a rather long title: *Den toepat om tot goddelijke kennis te comen, waar in geleert wort hoe den mensch doer een geheel ontblooten, vernieten, ende ontsincken sijn selfs en alder dingen tot de hoochste kennis, beschouwinge en vereenige met Godt sal comen. Gemaakt door den Eerw. Heer Pelgrom.*[9]. In a subsequent article, I hope to examine more closely this entirely unknown work of Pelgrim Pullen.

One word more about Pullen's other works. His most frequently quoted and mentioned work is no doubt *Tsaemensprekinge met de cluysenersse tot Gent* (A Conversation with the Anchoress of

---

[5] Valerius Andreas, *Bibliotheca Belgica*, Lovanii, 1643, p. 718.

[6] Indeed several new manuscripts and works have been found since then. For a complete list of the (now 14) manuscripts see Peter J.A. Nissen, "Onbekende handschriften met werk van Pelgrim Pullen," in Elly Cockx-Indestege and Frans Hendrickx (eds.), *Miscellanea Neerlandica; opstellen voor dr. Jan Deschamps ter gelegenheid van zijn zeventigste verjaarday*, Leuven, 1987, I, 273-292. (Courtesy of Dr. Peter Nissen, professor of spirituality, Radboud University, Nijmegen.)

[7] Reypens mentioned it in the last footnote of his article in *Ons Geestelijk Erf*, 3 (1929), 277, note 65. Later, Father Lucidius Verschueren published a description of the manuscript, "Onbekende werken van Pelgrim Pullen," *Studia Catholica*, 20 (1944), 1-7 and 84-96, esp. 88-94.

[8] This manuscript got lost during the Second World War, probably because Titus Brandsma kept it at that time in his room in the Carmelite monastery at the Doddendaal in Nijmegen, which was set on fire by the Germans in September, 1944. See Nissen, "Onbekende handschriften met werk van Pelgrim Pullen", pp. 278-279. (Courtesy of Dr. Nissen.)

[9] The Path to a Knowledge of Divine Things, wherein a person is taught how to come to the highest knowledge, contemplation, and union with God through a complete stripping, annihilation, and succumbing of self and other things. Written by the Reverend Pelgrim.

Ghent), in which he introduces himself in spiritual dialogue with a famous Flemish anchoress of Ghent, Clasina van Nieuwlant.[10] The little work is important, not only because of its author, but more perhaps because of what it tells us about this anchoress.

His most important work seems to be that which Father Reypen places last on his list, perhaps because, as appears from frequent allusions to it, it must be one of his last works: *Drie boecxkens van het Voorwerp* (Three Books about the Object). It consists of 56 chapters divided into 3 books, comprising 576 pages.[11] As far as we know, it was followed by *Die navolghinge Christi* (The Imitation of Christ), in 19 chapters.[12] When we examine Pelgrim Pullen's works more closely, we are struck by the subjects mentioned in them in various ways: the divine Being, the Most Holy Trinity, the Son of God, the Mother of God, the life of Our Lord, the lives of the Apostles, Holy Church, the steps of the spiritual life, the superessential life, being itself, life in heaven, a spiritual mirror, etc.

The recurring drift is that a person can and must lose himself entirely in God, and finds his highest and only happiness in this ascent to God. As far as we know, all his works are similarly filled with the nullity of human nature compared to God, and at the same time with the delight of ascending to and fading into God. The spirit is most powerfully drawn to God, and by the writer is led to the most exalted and intimate union with him. Emphasis is particularly laid on the great love of God, who desires to pour an ever growing love into the receptive soul. This election by God is reason for the greatest happiness. For this reason, a person must abandon all things, hold all things of little worth, including himself, and must detach and disengage himself from everything. All this must be done in and through Christ, who must live in us. At

---

[10] Cf. Paul Mommaers, *Claesinne van Nieuwlant, samenspraak*, Nijmegen, B. Gottmer, 1985. Conversation (extract), in: *Late Medieval Mysticism of The Low Countries*, ed. R. van Nieuwenhove, R. Faesen & H. Rolfson, Paulist Press New York * Mahwah 2008, 165-175.

[11] Brussel, Koninklijke Bibliotheek, Ms. 2421.

[12] Gent, Universiteitsbibliotheek, Ms. 1335.

this time, when the theme of experience of Christ flourished, Pullen is one who completely absorbed its spirit. Reypens characterizes his mysticism as one of divinization, but divinization in and through Christ.[13]

II

As stated in the previous article, the Carmelite convent in Boxmeer possesses a manuscript containing a hitherto unknown work of Pelgrim Pullen, titled: *Den toepat om tot de goddelijcke kennis to comen.* The subtitle, or expansion of the title, reads: *waarin geleert wordt hoe den mensch door een geheel ontblooten, vernieten, ende ontsincken sijnsselfs en alder dingen tot de hoochste kennis, beschouwingen, en vereeninge met God sal comen.*

This subtitle makes it at once clear that Pullen, as a condition for arriving at the knowledge of God, postulates such a detachment of self and all creatures as requires the use of terms like "stripping," "annihilation," "succumbing of self." This detachment, according to him, is demanded by the very nature of the divine Being, who is not knowable through any image or description. Every relation in which we find God must lead us to God himself, if we are to arrive at a concept at all. Over against God, we are so insignificant and negligible that we are as "nothing" compared to his eternal Being. We must eliminate everything that constitutes us, in order finally to see as our highest and only glory that we come forth from God, and, as emanating from his hands, bound to him. This bond with the divinity we must see in ourselves by overlooking everything else that is in us. That relation to God we must lay bare, which is equivalent to what Pullen calls a "stripping" of ourselves, an "annihilation" of ourselves, and which indeed is a "succumbing" of self. Thereby we draw near to the God who dwells in us, not through words, because words no longer make any sense. What God is cannot be expressed in words. There all is silence.

---

[13] Reypens, "Pelgrum Pullen (1550-1608), 264-268, esp. 264.

And so Pullen continues on, more closely describing that "nakedness" and "silence," as the first and necessary condition for coming to God; that is, to the only knowledge of God which turns into a contemplation of his Being and a conscious realization of being one with him from whose hand we constantly proceed as long as we live. In this way, Pullen declares, through annihilation the sublimity of our nature is saved and preserved; and the lowest place we occupy is also for us the highest, the closest to God.

We must surrender ourselves wholly to God. His light will penetrate us. The denial of our spirit is included in the denial of our nature. No worldly wisdom, no ingenuity or resourcefulness of fancy are of any assistance; only a complete ascent into God, who must be our all, besides whom nothing has any meaning. From active interiority – that is, from our effort to enter into ever profounder depths in ourselves – we arrive at a condition of quiet, of abandoning ourselves to God, which passes into passive interiority, in which God enthralls us and makes demands on us, and we, on our part, by his grace remain wholly oriented to him. We must come to understand how poor our spirit is, if it has not found those riches, and that this poverty consequently makes us rich. Then we understand how the saints have counted everything here on earth as nothing, have stripped and denied themselves everything which according to nature has any value and is pleasing, in order thereby better to understand and enjoy the riches God bestows. Poverty and misunderstanding, suffering in body and spirit the saints have embraced and greeted with joy as means of arriving at the full appreciation of God who lives in us.

Only along this way of complete detachment and "stripping" can we arrive at the fulfillment of God's command to love him with all our heart and all our faculties. Pullen also calls this a command for all Christians who truly wish to find and enjoy God. If this way were followed, wonders would occur in the world as well as in the monasteries, because wonderfully would God work in souls who sought him along this way. God takes such souls up into himself and makes all their actions divine, led by God, made living and fruitful.

However, it is not enough to enter upon this way or to arrive at its goal. It is of supreme importance not to leave the way any more and to continue to follow it. A person may, in a favorable moment, be caught in God's light and led by his grace, perhaps experience the delight of this enjoyment of God. It would be a pity, if he did not persevere in that way. In order to guarantee that this way, once entered upon, will not be later abandoned, one must enter the way with no other goal in sight than God, and with the sole desire of serving him, fulfilling his will, in utter trust that the way leads to God.

We no longer ask why God disposes of us in this or that manner; we find all his decisions in our regard acceptable. We attach ourselves to nothing. God is our all. When we seek an answer to the fact that so few persons live united to God, the answer lies in another fact that so few persons count for nothing all that they are and all that they do and could do compared to what God can and will achieve in them. "It will come to nothing," Pullen states, "it will all come to nothing, what you have, what you are, and what you do, because it is all nothing."[14]

As long as the apostles were not in a state of rapture, Christ could not reveal himself to them in his Being, but he sent the Holy Spirit to prepare them for it and to enrapture them. United now with God, they were changed into other persons and became strong, they who previously were wont to give witness of the weakest kind.

It is God's nature to share himself. But we kill the One who lives in us and desires to give himself to us. We live in a state of diffuseness of spirit, go forth from ourselves, and lose sight of him who dwells within us.

That the apostles saw so clearly in the divine light was due to no other reason than that by God's grace they were aware of living interiorly with God, detached from all things, free of all desire of

---

[14] Probably a quotation from Pullen's Dri boecxkens vanden voerworp (ms. Brussels, 2957), cited after Reypens, "Pelgrum Pullen (1550-1608)," 247. (Courtesy of Dr. Nissen.)

personal satisfaction, without ulterior motives or other object than to live and work for and with God. For Pullen, on that holy Pentecost they were so pure and undefiled of motive and intention as they were in the sight of God, in their eternal contemplation of their emanation from him. God was their strength, he led them, and was unwilling that they did anything other than what he had in store for them. St. Paul expressed it in his question, "Lord, what do you want me to do?" As soon as he had spoken that word in complete abandonment to God, the Spirit of God overshadowed him and he became enraptured.

After Pullen has described this ascent to God, this succumbing in God, and has pointed it out as the way of arriving at the knowledge and enjoyment of God, he comes – inevitably – to the reflection that man has hitherto not sufficiently understood this exalted purpose of his nature, has regarded himself too highly; in a word, is a sinner who needs conversion and not only must do penance but through a life of austerity and penitence must take care not to be further diverted from this single way to God and to his greatest happiness already here on earth. One who ponders this well will regard himself as the greatest sinner in the world, will do penance for his stupidity and shortsightedness, will pray God for compassion and mercy, and will submit to all that God will send, in order to bring his body, his nature under control. He will not rest until the rebelliousness in his nature is subdued and an end is put to all there is in him of wrong inclinations and passions. He will courageously follow Christ on the narrow way of austerity, to follow Christ unto the cross with all its horror of misunderstanding and reviling. He will be ready to be misunderstood by the world, to be a stumbling block to the world, to be accounted a fool.

Pullen goes so far in this matter as to present to the true lover of God the prospect of being mocked by the world, that is, by his environment. He uses here the word, Mardi Gras, of which the lover of God will become the sport. See, then the true lover and seeker of God must keep himself wholly directed to God and from the union with him draw the strength to permit all this, even to bear it gladly, and to maintain his peace of mind.

In a final article, I hope to sum up how Pullen further describes this ascent unto God, this "path to the attainment of the most exalted knowledge of God."

III

After Pullen has emphasized as strongly as possible that we must detach ourselves from all things, in order to be able to adhere to God, he calls attention to the fact that we must nevertheless again seek God in creatures, and that God himself each time again brings us in contact with them. Pullen teaches us how we are to do that without danger of again being fascinated by creatures and diverted from God. He notes that in everything that is of service to us, in everything we must use and own, we must not see only that is a gift of God, placed at our disposition by God's goodness. That is too superficial a view. We must rather reflect that everything is in its origin divine, that in the depths of its being it emanates from God, and that thus we should not regard it merely as given us by God in a physical sense, given in the way we give each other something, but that we should much rather reflect that God has created it for us, and that what is being offered us is entirely divine in origin. Then our nature will not think about its satisfaction, but will in the first place think of God, whose ideas are being served. Thus become accustomed to see God primarily in all things, we will feel ourselves attracted to actions which are more calculated to lead our thoughts to God; we will gladly attend Mass, receive the Sacrament of the altar, read Sacred Scripture, ourselves preach the word of God, or hear it preached by others. In all this, we must also unite ourselves more intimately with God and seek nothing else than God alone. Even if we were thereby to be granted visions or revelations, they should have little significance for us compared to God himself, who therein comes to meet us. He is not to be understood by any images or words, and we should therefore not seek to regard visions as most important. It will often happen, Pullen says, that in attending Mass, in receiving Holy Communion, and so on, you will be filled with sweet satisfaction. You will then be inclined to regard this as something wonderful and to set great store by it; so much so, that when you lose it, you think you have lost something great. And yet, your happiness and election do not consist therein. If you happen to be granted special enlightenment, and the Church's mysterious teaching is revealed and made clear to you, be on your guard, says Pullen, and try more than ever to regard yourself as small and insignificant, quite as nothing submerged in the divine infinity, to be united with whom is the highest good.

Those who have a clear understanding of this "path to God" seek only God, without seeking themselves in anything or yielding to their own satisfaction, even in intellectual knowledge or contemplation. These persons, Pullen declares, ascend higher in God in one day, nay, in one hour, yea, in one moment. They sink deeper in God's being than others who regard sweet satisfaction as the highest good and do not recognize the true nature of devotion.

One who loses himself wholly in God, is wholly free of self, will be the first to receive the full lustre of divine light and in that light remain so captivated and bound to God that he will leave him no more. Bound in this way to God, he will be able to work with effect, a thoroughly willing tool in God's hand. God will abide in him and in his work and fructify it for time and eternity.

If a person is not truly turned to God in his religion and devotion, if he does not simply and only seek him, then God is not living in him and in his work, and it will also not bear the fruit of which it is able, if it proceeded wholly from God. If such a one daily attends church, his service is not alive. Even if one has plumbed the meaning of Sacred Scripture and is learned in elucidating the mysteries of the faith, but is not inwardly turned to God and is not free of self, then he has not taken in the true meaning of Sacred Scripture and of the mysteries of the faith, because the true meaning God, who gives himself to us, who speaks to us in order to reveal himself to us in his deepest being – not in words and images, but in the stillness of the quiet renunciation of all gratification. Not the letter but the spirit vivifies. The letter of Sacred Scripture and of the greatest human science cannot make us understand what is incomprehensible, unless we thereby learn that God has thus precisely wished to tell us how infinite and incomprehensible his Being is, and through this concept of incomprehensibility in humble acknowledgment of our limitation and of all revelation, as blind we see in blinding light. A little less knowledge and a little more of that light which makes us recognize that we are blind could be useful to us.

For Pullen, the explanation of the fact that the Fathers of the Church occasionally are wanting in knowledge lies in their sanctity. He acknowledges that they cannot be said to be free of error in the explanation of Sacred Scripture and the mysteries of the faith, but what harm is there in that, he asks. We mustn't take it too seriously. Much more important is the fact that they sought and managed to be united to God, and that they showed us the way to him. They understood the real and the essence and that is the most important matter. That they here and there went astray is an indication that they probably looked for strength in earthly knowledge and thus understandably failed. To the degree that they were more intimately united to God, so much the more abundantly God gave them his light and they were more safeguarded from error to which their knowledge made them susceptible. From their relatively few errors, we may take warning, also to unite ourselves wholly to God in the exercise of the holiest and most exalted science, and to protect ourselves from all error. But on the other hand, we must understand that it is much worse to lose sight of God even to the least degree than to be guilty of some error in science. It is really regrettable that so few persons fully understand the value of this "path" to God and lose themselves in earthly affairs.

Pullen points out that in every soul lies a hidden faculty which enables a person to see all things as coming forth from God and referring back to him. Would we were able to enter deeply enough into our being to discover this faculty and render it operative! But this involves our entering entirely into God and losing ourselves in him. Then God can reveal his Son in us and make him live there. This is his pleasure and joy. But then we must surrender entirely to God in all simplicity and in awareness of our helplessness, and make ourselves wholly receptive to his light without priding ourselves on what we ourselves do or could do. When we come to this degree of interior life, God gathers us up into himself and reveals himself in us and in our works.

Here Pullen refers to a book or treatise he previously wrote, *Het boeck vant overweselijck leven* (The Book of the Superessential Life), in which he treats this theme more fully. He then counsels a person who aspires to this union with God not to allow himself to be diverted from this way to God. He must strive always to remain under the rays of that divine light. He must always understand that no light of human science conveys him more surely to his goal than this divine light, which comes from God himself and unites him as intimately as possible with God. Therefore, that person must keep far from himself everything which can disturb or interrupt that union with God and try to persevere in that quiet and indescribable union with God. He must count for nothing all other knowledge, as long as he possesses this union with God. He must not even consider the lack of human knowledge a loss, because that higher knowledge of God, which cannot be expressed in images or words, so far exceeds it as to be counted for nothing.

It is to be regretted that so many people feed their spirit with swill for pigs, are entirely taken up with externals, and so remain deprived of the knowledge of the highest truth. They are like an ass that is draped with bells and attracts attention because of its harness; it remains an ass. But man knows that his glory lies in his inner union with God, and if he lends himself to it and does not presume on his own powers, God lives and works in him to his welfare and that of others.

Maria Petyt[1]

I

Among the flowers cultivated in our spiritual soil, a special place is held by an anchoress attached to the Carmelite church in Mechelen, transplanted to the heavenly garden, on November 1, 1677 – the Venerable Maria a Sancta Teresa, known in the world as Maria Petyt.

In recent years, attention has again been drawn to her. She has become the subject of study by the Discalced Carmelite, Father Jérôme de la Mère de Dieu, known, especially in Belgium, in connection with the controversy over Servaes.[2] and in an equally excellent manner, by the layman, Louis van de Bossche, among other places in *La vie spirituelle*.[3]

Maria appears under two aspects, in both of them as a model and worthy representative of the Carmelite Order in its twofold

---

[1] From *De Gelderlander*, Aug. 12, 19, 26, 1939.

[2] The reference is to the controversy which arose over the Stations of the Cross, executed in 1915 by Albert Servaes (1883-1966), Belgian espressionist painter, for the Discalced Carmelite church in Luythagen (Antwerpen). Titus himself was involved in the debate and wrote a meditation on the Stations, "De Kruisweg van Albert Servaes," *Opgang*, 1 (1921), 129-145. Titus Brandsma & Albert Servaes, *Ecce Homo, Schouwen van de Weg van Liefde / Contemplating the Way of Love*, ed. Jos Huls, Leuven 2003.

[3] Published separately as *Vie mariale; Maria a Sancta Teresia 1623-1677*. Fragments traduits du flamand par Louis van den Bossche, Paris, Desclée de Brouwer, 1928. See: Albert Deblaere, *De Mystieke Schrijfster Maria Petyt (1623-1677)*, PhD dissertation, Gent 1962; Maria Petyt, écrivain et mystique flamande (1623-1677), in: *Carmelus* 26 3-76. Karel Porteman & Mieke B. Smits-Veldt, *Een nieuw vaderland voor de muzen*. Geschiedenis van de Nederlandse literatuur 1560-1700, 829-8832.

character: in her dwelling with God in prayer in the most intimate way, arriving in the highest mystical spheres; and on the other hand, in her highly original devotion to Mary.

It is difficult to say which of these characteristics appears the clearest in Maria's life. They presume each other and flow over into each other. Her spiritual life is not understood if a particular place is not assigned to her devotion to Our Lady; and again, unless one sees the connection between her love of Mary and her marvelous interior prayer life. Thus, she is a person who was a worthy representative of the school of Carmel in her time and also in ours and deserves to be known in a wider circle than she actually is. She is a true child of Flanders, a flower of the land of Flanders.

Born on New Year's eve in 1623 at Hasebroeck (Hazebroek), she lived for almost fifty-five years. She grew up in very devout surroundings, where she felt herself entirely at home. At the age of five, she already revealed her desire to belong to our dear Lord and to enter the convent, where she thought she would be able to pray even more than she already did. At ten years of age, she received her first Communion and already made a vow of chastity, though for her it meant little more than that she chose no other bridegroom than Jesus. Just as St. Teresa as a child ran away from her parents' home in search of martyrdom in Africa among the Moors, so Maria fled the home of her parents to live on herbs in a remote place, alone with Jesus. Placed in boarding school in St. Omer to learn French, she not only showed herself thankful to her teacher, but allowed herself to be led by the Sisters in various practices of devotion; she became so attached to meditation that she often remained for two hours plunged and rapt up in it.

But periods of relaxation occurred in her youthful piety. It is well to point this out. As a child of perhaps six or seven years of age, she contracted smallpox and lost her former attractive beauty. One would have thought that this would bring her closer to God, but this did not happen in her case. Pampering during her sickness also weakened her devotion and fed in her an inclination for play and amusement, until a pious servant brought her back to her original devotion.

Shortly after she had returned from boarding school, the plague broke out in Hasebroeck, and in order to escape contagion she ended up with her uncle in Poperingen, a man of the world. Here she was again tempted by the desire for pleasure, for play and dancing, for attending the theater, for reading novels. Even a serious sickness seemed unable to bring her back to her former life of prayer and penance. It hurt her most that she had lost her beauty through the pox. No amount of finery could change that. Finally, in order to have her beauty restored by God, she went on pilgrimage to a shrine of Our Lady. The outcome was miraculous, but in an entirely different way than she intended. The fatuity of her wish at once became crystal clear to her, and she lost all interest in earthly beauty and in the world. Nevertheless, she still resisted the urge to become a religious and at first even refused to accept a book in which the holy lives of a number of religious were recounted for fear that her inclination to the convent might be strengthened, but in the end she accepted the book and decided to follow the saints' example. She again acquired a love of prayer and meditation and, in order to nourish that love, constantly carried about with her a picture of the Holy Face crowned with thorns, which she continually kept in view. She joined the Regular Canonesses of St. Augustine in Ghent, but she had hardly entered the convent when her vocation was again threatened: with the other Sisters she was obliged to take refuge for a time in Meenen due to imminent danger of war. Here her fervor again weakened, to become, however, once more fervent. Upon returning to the monastery, she was dismissed after a few months because of weak sight. She asked to be allowed to remain as a lay sister but was advised otherwise. After that, she entered the Little Beguinage. Here, enlightened by God's grace, she led a life of contemplation and mortification. Her father managed to have her accepted by the Poor Clares in Yperen, but her confessor told her that she would do better to continue her life of contemplation in the world and to give up the idea of entering convent. The monastery which had sent her away, hearing what a holy life she led and what wonderful progress she had made in virtue, decided to recall the decision previously made and invited her to return. This invitation she also rejected, to go live with another devout woman near the chapel of St. Anne in Bottelaer outside Ghent and there, under direction of a devout priest, to lead a life, separated from the world, wholly devoted to prayer. The two lived as anchorites. After a year, she placed herself under the guidance of the Carmelite Fathers and joined the Third Order of Carmel.

After she had first had another priest as a spiritual director for four years, she had the good fortune to receive as her director the later famous Father Michael of Saint Augustine Ballaert, then professor of Philosophy in the convent of Ghent. His excellent spiritual writings are still held in regard, and his Latin *Introduction to the Spiritual Life* has been reprinted in the beginning of this century by Father Gabriel Wessels, O.Carm.[4] Under Father Michael's guidance she made another year of probation in order to practice the presence of Christ, a practice so well described by her director in his works.

For the rest of her life, Maria remained Michael's spiritual daughter. Although in his capacity of provincial of the Belgian province, elected three times, and of prior in several convents, Father Michael could not always be Maria's immediate director, she always remained under his direction at a distance and a true reflection of the spirit which radiates from his works. She lived in a holy spiritual communion with him, but he took care that as much as possible she always found a priest who shared his own exalted ideals. Besides, he approved her revealing the state of her conscience to him three or four times a year, and then gave her his corresponding wise and careful counsel. All excess or sensuality was foreign to the conduct of both. In fact, so interior and wholly united to God was their conduct that to those who knew them the thought never occurred.

After she had lived many years in her anchorhold attached to the Carmelite convent in Ghent and was highly revered for her prayerful life, she left that city to begin an even stricter life in

---

[4] Introductio ad vitam internam et fruitiva praxis vitae mysticae. Nova editio curante P. Gabriele Wessels, Romae, 1926.

another anchorhold attached to the Carmelite convent of Mechelen. With a beguine who felt called to a life of the strictest seclusion and mortification, she allowed herself to be enclosed in an anchorhold built onto the Carmelite church in Mechelen, in order, after the manner of earlier immured or walled up solitaries – like another Bertken of Utrecht, attached to the Buurkerk – she might strive after and live an ideal of segregation from the world. In October of 1657, she entered the anchorhold with the beguin already mentioned. There, for another twenty years she lived her holy and mystical life, to enter, on All Saints' day of 1677, into everlasting union with God. She was buried in the Lady Chapel of the Carmelite church inside the Communion rail in front of the statue of St. Mary Magdalen dei Pazzi. Her grave became a revered place and her memory still endures.

II

After having briefly described the life of this devout anchoress of the Carmelite church in Mechelen, we wish now to examine briefly her fervent spiritual life. We have it from the detailed notes[5] of her spiritual Father, who was her constant though intermittent counselor, Father Michael of St. Augustine, in the history of the Belgian-Dutch province definitely the master in the description of the spiritual life.

We have already referred to the gradual development, the ascent of this mystical soul, interrupted, especially in the beginning, by relapses. They were not serious lapses, but they slowed progress, threatened to make her stray, but each time God brought her back, and she set out again with renewed fervor.

[5] *Het Leven vande Weerdighe Moeder Maria a Sta Teresia, (alias) Petyt*, I-IV, Ghendt 1683. The First part is her Life written by Maria Petyt herself: Maria Petyt, *Het Leven van Maria Petyt (1623-1677) haar autobiografie*, ed. J.R.A. Mer-lier, Klassiek Letterkundig Pantheon, Zutphen 1976; *Deinend op Gods tij*, Het autobiografisch verhaal van een grote Vlaamse mystica, voorwoord Koen De Meester o.c.d., inleiding Hein Blommestijn o.carm., Carmelitana Gent 2010. This autobiography will be published in 2014 in the collection *Fiery Arrow*.

It is worth mentioning that it was especially by the severest mortification that she tried to conquer and dominate that not easily overcome craving for pleasure and ease.

In her case we can truly speak of the "mortified" life, as she begins her spiritual life. Not only did she deem necessary strict fasting and abstinence from all that might flatter the taste – practices approved by her spiritual guide; not only did she do severe penance for her otherwise insignificant faults by means of scourging and hairshirts; as much as possible she denied her body every comfort, in order to subject it wholly to her will and to suppress all attraction to earthly things, or at least so to weaken it that they no longer formed an obstacle to her ascent to God and the most intimate communion with him. The poorest things were dearest to her. Cold or heat were no occasion for changing anything in her way of life or clothing.

A second feature in her spiritual life which may be called noteworthy is her steadfast and absolute obedience to her spiritual director. This was to her advantage, especially after she had received as a guide in the spiritual life one so experienced as Father Michael of St. Augustine. That docility and submission to the judgment of a wise and sensible confessor protected her from harmful exaggeration and made her receptive to the graces which God wished to bestow on her. She admired that obedience in the great St. Teresa of Avila, according to whose example she tried to erect "the castle of her soul," but she converted that admiration into a steadfast fidelity. She called herself Sister Mary of St. Teresa in order to express this imitation in her name as well.

Thirdly, special mention should be made of the fact that she regarded her spiritual life as a continual exercise in acquiring the life and virtues of Jesus. Her reflections had these as their object, but with the explicit purpose of expressing them in herself and thus being alike to Christ, living his life. She did not stop at *The Following of Christ*, the favorite of the Modern Devotion of the 14th and 15th century, but deepened its doctrine more profoundly than usually taught in the school of the Modern Devotion, to an intimate "life in Christ." In the Netherlands, the school of Oisterwijk, led by Nicholas van Esch, and described especially in the *Evangelische Peerle* of the 16th century, sketches its attractive degrees; but it is particularly Cardinal de Bérulle, under the influence of the Oisterwijk school on the one hand and on the other of Mary of Jesus and her Carmelite sisters in Paris, who provides such a fascinating description. Thus, we encounter this mystical trend, so intimately related to Carmel, in Father Michael of St. Augustine, who may be called a true apostle of "life in Christ." He extended it in a brilliant manner by interweaving it with "life in Mary."

For this reason, Maria's first concern was the continual practice of the consciousness of the presence of God in herself, of God's indwelling and constant action of grace. In order to persevere in this practice and nourish it in her, she was relentless in the practice of meditation. On this account, she prescribed for herself many hours for its practice. Whether she felt like it or not, whether she felt her spirit receptive or cold and unfeeling, she forced herself during these hours to direct her spirit to God's presence and indwelling, in order to draw the strength from this practice to live in God's presence for the rest of the day. Her life was the heroic fulfillment of the principal precept of the Carmelite rule: day and night to meditate on the will of God and watch in prayer in the appointed cell, unless other legitimate duties are to be performed. The coldness and insensitivity, which sometimes overcame her, were at first difficult for her to bear, but they strengthened her humility and attachment to self. She gradually conformed herself completely to what God willed and ordained.

This endowed her with a remarkable equanimity and peace, even on the occasions of the fiercest defamation and insinuation, to which by its very nature her life was occasionally exposed. Likewise, in the trials which God sent her in her interior life she managed, though only gradually, to preserve her equanimity. For four or five years God left her soul in the night of spiritual darkness, penetrated only a pair of times by a slight ray of light. But in the strength of her proven faith she persevered and made no change in her practices and devotions, in spite of dryness and insensitivity. If at first she soared like an eagle and seemed enraptured at the thought of God's might, wisdom, and love, she also, her biographer asserts, had to crawl over the ground like a worm and was unable to obtain from her meditation any satisfaction or enjoyment of God. But instead of shortening her prayer, she devoted more time to it and humbled herself before God for her weakness and imperfection.

She overcame all that physical and spiritual suffering by a thought with which she had been inspired: "Beware of abandoning the cross and seeking comfort. When nature threatens to weaken under the severity of the pain, cast your eyes on Christ, crucified and abandoned." That contemplation of Jesus on the cross, that continual union with him, was finally rewarded by God with an ardent love of suffering, a desire to suffer for souls and pray for them as a living sacrifice. She felt moved to prayer and was certain of being heard. More than once she received remarkable assurance of the manner in which God had heard her prayer. She lived in the most intimate communion with God and it seemed that God in turn spoke to her and revealed many things to her.

We may say of her that she lived entirely in God. She was vividly aware that her soul should be a dwelling of the Holy Spirit and that she had to be pure of heart in order to receive him. From her communion with God she understood that that communion made her pure, and that worldly things no longer had a hold on her, no longer moved her spirit. Finally, she no longer needed creatures to rise from them to God and to be immediately and continually united to him. God and God alone more and more became the object of her contemplation and love. If at first she still loved some creature as a gift of God, she later perceived that goodness of God directly and no longer needed images to rise from them to that concept, or to arouse her spirit.

So she became a heroine of the cross, courageous and joyful, who suffered much, while she maintained a state of virtuously undisturbed quiet. In a vision, she saw the cross placed in her arms, so that she might embrace it and not only continue to carry it but also to be fixed to it with Christ and to die on it with him. She had a particular devotion to the wounds of the Lord, especially that in his side, which to her seemed a wide, radiant opening in which her soul needed to hide itself in order to be wholly rapt in Christ and be one with him. It often seemed to her that Jesus took her up into himself, embraced her, stood at her side. She lived in continual union with him.

If she shared in Jesus' suffering in this way, sometimes Jesus also let her share in his glory, and she seemed to be with the apostles on Mt. Tabor. She enjoyed the experience but without thereby losing her love of suffering. If only Jesus were with her, it was a matter of indifference to her whether he brought happiness or suffering. "It is all one with me," she wrote to her confessor, "how my beloved embraces me and crowns me with roses or thorns." He in turn writes that it was as if in her life in and with Jesus the life of Jesus was again proclaimed. Her deeds, thoughts, sighs, and words were redolent only of Jesus.

III

A Mary-form Life

A fourth aspect under which we must consider her spiritual life, because it occupies a special place in the forms of spiritual life, is her life in and for Mary, her *Marielijck*, or Mary-form life. In this, she is no doubt the dutiful disciple of Father Michael of St. Augustine, who in the appendix to the fourth book of his *Introduction to the Spiritual Life* dedicates a most profound treatment of the subject.

In this Mary-form life, she gave expression to and developed in word and deed one of the most important elements of life according to the school of Carmel, so that in this respect she merits a special place in the history of the spiritual life in the Netherlands. It imparts a special mark to her mysticism.

She was a true child of Mary, who wore the garment of Carmel, the holy scapular, with a feeling of a vocation to the most intimate devotion to Mary. In one of her many visions, she saw herself accepted by Mary as her child, and this was a continual source of happiness for her. She was completely one with her mother. She has a place in Mary's motherly heart and loves to hide in it. That heart of Mary, which belongs so completely to God in his holy Trinity, so completely to Jesus, is for her the way to union with God and with Jesus. When she presents herself as a sacrifice to God, when she dedicates herself to God, she does so with the thought that she is hidden in the heart of Mary.

This Mary-form life by its very nature obliges her to lofty perfection and was for her a continual incentive to the practice of that conformity with the purest of all creatures, most intimately united to God, detached from all earthly and transient things. And her union with Mary was of the sort that when she occasionally acted or thought less perfectly, Mary would make her aware of it and gave her to understand that in that way she was not living in a Mary-form way, that she should quickly better herself and detach herself more from earthly things, in order to be her child and continue to hold a special place in her heart. Thus, it was one of the most powerful means for enabling her to attain sanctity.

An absolute condition for this Mary-form life was a continual practice of solitude and silence. She regarded a very important element of Carmelite mysticism to live as strictly as possible – at least spiritually – in solitude and detachment from the world and thereby to strive after a profound interiority and retirement by continually practicing silence and at stated times to abstain from all speech, the occasion for distraction. She liked to take as her model St. Mary Magdalen in Bethany, listening to what Jesus said to her, and placed herself under her protection to enable her to do as she did. She remembered how the Church, on the feast of Our Lady's Assumption, applied to Our Lady Jesus' words of approval, to the effect that Mary Magdalen had chosen the better part,[6] and desired that those words would apply to her as a child of Mary, as one with her mother.

It gave Maria much joy and satisfaction, when contemplating Mary as Queen of heaven, that she saw herself called to that glory

---

[6] Lk, 10, 38-42

together with her; saw herself raised to the dignity of queen together with Mary, sharing in her lustre and glory. This confirmed her concept of life as an ascent to heaven. She liked to join the idea that Mary was leading her into heaven with the idea that Mary was leading her to the Communion rail and there gave her not only a foretaste of heaven but at the same time a new guarantee of it. Then she again celebrated the union with Jesus, knew herself to be his bride, saw herself united through Jesus with the entire Holy Trinity, in order to realize herself again one with Mary through the Father, the Son, and the Holy Spirit.

In this, she found firm support in the knowledge that her spiritual director, heart and soul a Carmelite, and the whole Carmelite Order, to which she was bound as a tertiary, wanted her to be united to Mary as intimately as possible, lest otherwise she not be a worthy member of the Order and a docile pupil of her director. She is to be numbered among the most intimate devotees of Mary whom the Order had known and still had at that moment.

Although her union with Mary was very spiritual and for the most part originated beyond sensible concepts, she nevertheless continually nourished her spirit with ideas presented by the senses; she pictured herself as a child lying in Mary's lap, indulged herself at her breast, embraced her and took delight in her embrace. She sees Mary at her side during prayer, coming to her with her divine Child to be embraced and loved. She sees Mary with the friars in choir, as they sing the "Salve, regina" seven times daily,[7] and gladly shares in the blessings the veneration of Mary pours over the Carmelite Order and so also over her. She has a very special devotion to the hymn, "Ave Maria stella,"[8] and, in the spirit of the Order which traditionally represents Mary with a star on her shoulder, she liked to honor Mary as the guide to the haven of heaven. There, the "Flos Carmeli," the hymn of the Order to the "Flower

[7] In the Carmelite Rite, the "Salve Regina" was sung or recited after every canonical hour.

[8] In the Carmelite Rite, the "Ave Stella Matutina" was sung or recited after Vespers or Complin.

of Carmel," bestowed on her by St. Simon Stock, reaches its final climax, as the saint honors Mary as the "Star of the Sea," the guiding polestar.

All these practices of devotion to Our Lady introduced Maria to the actual Mary-form life, which she describes as a higher degree of perfection than the usual union with God as our greatest good. She sees it as a strengthening of our life with God, because, living with Mary, we can at the same time live in a better and more intimate union with God. We must rest in Mary, she tells us, entrust ourselves wholly to her, rejoice in that union, that oneness with Mary. We must be wholly taken up in Mary, wholly melted into her, motivated by no other thought than that we thus live united to God as intimately as possible. Precisely because Mary is wholly one with and like to God, we must be mirrored in Mary, not only as our model, but we must make ourselves one with her, in order to share wholly in her intercourse and union with God. In eating and drinking, in work and rest, in all things we should imagine ourselves living and working with Mary. It bathes the soul in a new light and causes us more securely to find and keep union with God.

God wills it so. He has appointed Mary to be our mediatrix and wishes that we do not reject her intercession; on the contrary, that we make it as fruitful as possible for our spiritual life. A deep and tender reverence for Mary is for one who has the proper understanding of it no alienation from or neglect of God but is the way to an ever more intimate union, because we receive the needed grace from Mary and with her assistance make the best use of it. Therefore, everything we do must be sealed with Mary's name and so become pleasing to God. The more intimately she unites herself with Mary and is, as it were, turned into her, the more she will share in Mary's grace through the communion of saints and be overwhelmed by God with his gifts. Her transformation into Mary is for her the key to God's treasure. These blessings will become ours as children of Mary, not only because Mary will obtain them for us, but also because God regards with complacency that conformity with his holy mother.

Because Mary's union with God was so thoroughly spiritual and intimate, this Mary-form life will not be primarily led and dominated by ideas arising from the senses, but will strive to be as spiritual as Mary's union with God and will be a collaboration of the same spiritual faculties of thought and love, of intellect and will. This spiritual concept of the Mary-form life, which meanwhile does not exclude the cooperation of images of the senses, will remove the objections which in Maria Petyt's time some spiritual persons made to her idea of the spiritual life; namely, that through being Mary-form the spiritual life could be too greatly dominated by images of the senses or the imagination. With her this was out of the question. But it would also be an exaggeration to exclude the imagination too radically from this Mary-form life, where it precisely is a great help for rising to the level of the intellect.

Maria's Mary-form life, usually described with the double terms "performing all our actions in and for Mary," is yet more fully described by the four terms, "performing all our actions in, for, through, and with Mary." Mary must be the life of the soul, union with her the great driving force and inspiration. The attitude of child to its mother of whom it is proud, whom it trusts, with whom it discusses everything, with whom it does everything, out of love for whom it is ready for everything – that is the way we should be children of Mary and make her virtues our own.

PRINTED ON PERMANENT PAPER • IMPRIME SUR PAPIER PERMANENT • GEDRUKT OP DUURZAAM PAPIER - ISO 9706

N.V. PEETERS S.A., WAROTSTRAAT 50, B-3020 HERENT